T0302309

INFLATION TARGETING AND CENTRAL BANKS

Over the last three decades, inflation targeting (IT) has become the most popular monetary policy framework among larger economies. At the same time, its constituting features leave room for different interpretations, translating into various central banks' institutional set-ups. Against this backdrop, this book investigates the importance of institutional arrangements for policy outcomes. In particular, the book answers the question of whether there are significant differences in IT central banks' institutional set-ups, and—if yes—whether they influence the ability of monetary authorities to meet their policy goals.

The book examines around 70 aspects related to independence, accountability and transparency of 42 IT central banks over the last 30 years. Based on the analysis, it can be concluded that the quality of the institutional set-ups materially affects monetary policy effectiveness. In fact, a visible improvement of institutional arrangements resulting from pursuing an inflation targeting strategy can be treated as its lasting contribution to central banking. Thus, despite the recent critique of the framework, its prospects continue to be rather favourable.

Overall, for the advocates of inflation targeting, the findings of the book can be seen as identifying the sources of IT strengths, while for IT opponents, they may be viewed as indicating which elements of IT institutional set-ups should be kept even if the need to replace this strategy with another regime will, indeed, result in a change. Given the role monetary policy plays within the economy, such knowledge may have significant implications. Therefore, the book will be relevant for different audiences, including scholars and researchers of monetary economics and monetary policy, and will be essential reading for central banks already pursuing an IT strategy or those preparing to adopt one.

Joanna Niedźwiedzińska is an economist who has worked in central banks for over 15 years. She started her career at the National Bank of Poland, but worked also a few years at the European Central Bank. She is now the head of the Division of Monetary Policy Strategy in the Department of Economic Analysis at the National Bank of Poland. As well as dealing with issues related to monetary policy strategy, she focuses on the central bank's communication of monetary policy decisions.

BANKING, MONEY AND INTERNATIONAL FINANCE

18. THE ECONOMICS OF FINANCIAL COOPERATIVES
Income Distribution, Political Economy and Regulation
Amr Khafagy

19. FINANCIAL INTEGRATION IN THE EUROPEAN MONETARY UNION
Sławomir Ireneusz Bukowski

20. BANKING IN CHINA 1890S-1940S
Business in the French Concessions
Hubert Bonin

21. MANAGEMENT OF FOREIGN EXCHANGE RISK
Evidence from Developing Economies
Y. C. Lum and Sardar M. N. Islam

22. BANKING AND EFFECTIVE CAPITAL REGULATION IN PRACTICE
A Leadership Perspective
Sophia Velez

23. INNOVATION IN FINANCIAL SERVICES
Balancing Public and Private Interests
Edited by Jan Monkiewicz and Lech Gąsiorkiewicz

24. CARBON RISK AND GREEN FINANCE
Aaron Ezroj

25. INFLATION TARGETING AND CENTRAL BANKS
Institutional Set-ups and Monetary Policy Effectiveness
Joanna Niedźwiedzińska

For more information about this series, please visit: www.routledge.com/series/BMIF

INFLATION TARGETING AND CENTRAL BANKS

Institutional Set-ups and Monetary Policy Effectiveness

Joanna Niedźwiedzińska

LONDON AND NEW YORK

First published 2022
by Routledge
2 Park Square, Milton Park, Abingdon, Oxon OX14 4RN

and by Routledge
605 Third Avenue, New York, NY 10158

Routledge is an imprint of the Taylor & Francis Group, an informa business

© 2022 Joanna Niedźwiedzińska

British Library Cataloguing-in-Publication Data
A catalogue record for this book is available from the British Library

Library of Congress Cataloging-in-Publication Data

Names: Niedźwiedzińska, Joanna, author.

Title: Inflation targeting and central banks : institutional set-ups and

monetary policy effectiveness / Joanna Niedźwiedzińska.

Description: Abingdon, Oxon ; New York, NY : Routledge, 2022. | Series:

Banking, money and international finance | Includes bibliographical

references and index.

Identifiers: LCCN 2021006552 (print) | LCCN 2021006553 (ebook)

Subjects: LCSH: Monetary policy. | Banks and banking. | Inflation (Finance)

| International finance.

Classification: LCC HG230.3 .N54 2022 (print) | LCC HG230.3 (ebook) | DDC

339.5/3--dc23

LC record available at https://lccn.loc.gov/2021006552

LC ebook record available at https://lccn.loc.gov/2021006553

ISBN: 978-1-032-03827-8 (hbk)
ISBN: 978-1-032-03826-1 (pbk)
ISBN: 978-1-003-18924-4 (ebk)

Typeset in Sabon
by Deanta Global Publishing Services, Chennai, India

CONTENTS

List of charts   viii
List of tables   xvi
Acknowledgements   xviii

Introduction   1

Initial remarks on inflation targeting 1
Motivation behind the study 2
Existing literature 4
Identified gaps in existing literature 5
Research hypothesis and the related analytical steps 6
Country coverage 7
Structure of the study 8
Research approach 9
Notes 10
References 12

1 **Indicating the origins, essential features, and prospects of an
   inflation targeting framework**   15

1.1 Introductory remarks 15
*1.2 Evolution of monetary economics as a basis for
    developing monetary policy strategies 15*
*1.3 Defining the concept of a monetary policy strategy and its
    institutional set-ups 28*
*1.4 Most common monetary policy strategies used by central
    banks 34*
*1.5 Institutional roots of an inflation targeting framework
    and arguments behind them 44*
*1.6 Challenges related to an inflation targeting framework
    posed by the recent crises 57*

CONTENTS

1.7 Possible directions of changes to an inflation targeting
    framework 62
1.8 Concluding remarks 67
Notes 68
References 75
Appendix 1: Monetary policy frameworks used worldwide 92

2 Describing differences in implementing key elements of an
  inflation targeting strategy   102

2.1 Introductory remarks 102
2.2 Collecting information on institutional set-ups of inflation
    targeting central banks 103
2.3 Acknowledging price stability as the primary goal of
    monetary policy 104
2.4 Public announcement of a numerical target for
    inflation 119
2.5 Formulating monetary policy on the basis of a broad set
    of information 135
2.6 Applying high accountability and transparency
    standards 149
2.7 Accounting for financial stability considerations and
    unconventional measures 155
2.8 Concluding remarks 167
Notes 168
Bibliography 176
Appendix 2: Inflation targets used by inflation targeting
    central banks   182

3 Constructing indices comparing institutional set-ups of
  inflation targeting central banks   185

3.1 Introductory remarks 185
3.2 Arguments behind the importance of central banks'
    institutional set-ups 186
3.3 Selected literature on indices comparing central banks'
    institutional set-up 191
3.4 Constructing indices assessing institutional set-ups of
    inflation targeting central banks 195
3.5 Comparing inflation targeting central banks' institutional
    set-ups 211
3.6 Constructing an index on approach to financial stability
    and on policy instruments 227

3.7 Concluding remarks 232
Notes 233
References 234
*Appendix 3: Indices of institutional set-ups in inflation
targeting central banks 237*

**4 Analysing the implications of differences in institutional set-
ups of inflation targeting central banks**   **249**

4.1 Introductory remarks 249
*4.2 Selected literature on links between central banks'
institutional set-ups and policy outcomes 250*
*4.3 Stylised facts on links between central banks' institutional
set-ups and policy outcomes 255*
*4.4 Data and empirical methodology used to analyse policy
outcomes 263*
*4.5 Models used to analyse policy outcomes and robustness
checks 267*
*4.6 Overall assessment of the results and policy
conclusions 294*
4.7 Concluding remarks 296
Notes 297
References 300
*Appendix 4: Data sources and additional estimation
results 304*

Conclusions   **331**

Final remarks on inflation targeting 331
Comparison with existing literature 333
Evaluating the research hypothesis 335
Conveying the main messages 337
Areas for further research 337
*Supplement: Indices of central banks' institutional set-ups in
inflation targeting economies 339*

Index   359

CHARTS

1.1	Changes in monetary policy strategies used by the 59 largest economies.	41
1.2	Monetary policy strategies used by 190 countries worldwide in 2017 (simple counting).	42
1.3	Monetary policy strategies used by 190 countries worldwide in 2017 (GDP-weighted counting).	42
1.4	Number of IT advanced and emerging market economies.	43
1.5	Share of inflation targeting economies in global GDP.	43
1.6	Inflation targeters and quasi-inflation targeters.	44
2.1	Objectives of central banks in IT economies.	105
2.2	Share of IT advanced and emerging market economies with different objectives.	105
2.3	Objectives of central banks in IT advanced economies.	106
2.4	Objectives of central banks in IT emerging market economies.	106
2.5	*De jure* classification of exchange rate regimes used by central banks in IT economies.	107
2.6	*De facto* classification of exchange rate regimes used by central banks in IT economies.	107
2.7	Authority responsible for setting an inflation target in IT economies.	111
2.8	Share of IT economies with different authorities responsible for setting an inflation target.	111
2.9	Involvement of government in central banks' decision-making in IT advanced economies.	112
2.10	Involvement of government in central banks' decision-making in IT emerging market economies.	112
2.11	Term of office of decision-making bodies in IT advanced and emerging market economies.	114
2.12	Dispersion in governors' terms of office in IT advanced and emerging market economies.	114
2.13	Possibility of reappointment of governors in IT economies.	115

2.14	Possibility of reappointment of members of decision-making bodies in IT economies.	115
2.15	Share of IT economies with explicit rules on the appointment and dismissal of policymakers.	117
2.16	Share of IT economies with different rules on monetary financing.	118
2.17	Share of IT economies with central bank independence guaranteed in legal act.	120
2.18	Number of reformulations of inflation targets in IT economies until 2018.	121
2.19	Initial motivation for announcing inflation targets in IT economies.	122
2.20	Number of reformulations of inflation targets until 2018 in IT economies.	122
2.21	Share of IT economies introducing any changes to inflation targets.	123
2.22	Different kinds of reformulations of inflation targets introduced in IT economies.	123
2.23	Type of inflation targets used by IT advanced economies.	125
2.24	Type of inflation targets used by IT emerging market economies.	125
2.25	Width of tolerance bands used by IT economies.	126
2.26	Countries with tolerance bands of ±1 pp. among IT economies.	126
2.27	Targeted inflation measures in IT advanced economies.	128
2.28	Targeted inflation measures in IT emerging market economies.	128
2.29	Time horizon of inflation targets in IT advanced economies.	131
2.30	Time horizon of inflation targets in IT emerging market economies.	131
2.31	Initial target level and date of IT adoption in advanced and emerging market economies.	133
2.32	Changes in target levels in IT advanced and emerging market economies.	133
2.33	Changes to inflation target levels in IT advanced economies.	134
2.34	Changes to inflation target levels in IT emerging market economies.	134
2.35	Dispersion in inflation target levels in IT advanced economies.	135
2.36	Dispersion in inflation target levels in IT emerging market economies.	135
2.37	Share of IT economies with different frequency of publishing projections per year.	136
2.38	Changes to the number of projections published per year in IT economies.	136
2.39	Share of IT economies with different forecast horizons.	137

2.40   Changes to the forecast horizon in IT advanced and
        emerging market economies.   137
2.41   Share of IT economies with different forecast variables.   138
2.42   Share of IT economies with different forms of presenting
        forecasts.   138
2.43   Share of IT economies with different ownership of forecasts. 141
2.44   Involvement of staff in decision-making processes in IT
        economies.   141
2.45   Composition of decision-making bodies in IT advanced
        and emerging market economies.   142
2.46   Share of IT advanced economies with different
        composition of decision-making bodies.   143
2.47   Share of IT emerging market economies with different
        composition of decision-making bodies.   143
2.48   Frequency of meetings per year in IT advanced and
        emerging market economies.   144
2.49   Changes to the meeting schedules in IT advanced economies. 145
2.50   Changes to the meeting schedules in IT emerging market
        economies.   145
2.51   Decision-making processes in IT economies.   146
2.52   Share of IT economies with different approaches to
        publishing voting records.   148
2.53   Disclosing information on voting records in IT economies.   149
2.54   Share of IT economies with different timing of publishing
        voting records.   149
2.55   Share of IT economies publishing different documents on
        monetary policy.   152
2.56   Share of IT economies using different ways of
        communicating monetary policy decisions.   152
2.57   Share of IT economies with forward-looking elements
        included in press releases.   153
2.58   Share of IT economies publishing minutes with different
        approaches to revealing disagreements.   153
2.59   Share of IT economies with different frequency per year of
        parliamentary hearings.   154
2.60   Share of IT economies with different frequency per year of
        submitting reports to parliament.   154
2.61   Share of IT economies with different authorities
        responsible for financial stability.   157
2.62   Share of IT central banks publishing reports on financial stability. 157
2.63   Number of IT central banks starting to regularly publish
        reports on financial stability in a given year.   159
2.64   Share of IT central banks with different frequency of
        publishing reports on financial stability.   159

2.65   Share of IT economies with interest rate and FX
        interventions as main policy instruments.   161
2.66   Share of IT economies using unconventional monetary
        policy instruments.   161
2.67   Number of unconventional measures used in a given IT
        economy.   166
2.68   Inflation targets since IT adoption.   182
3.1   Sources of information used to construct the proposed
        individual indices.   210
3.2   Sources of information used to construct Fully_fledged_IT index. 210
3.3   Topics included in the proposed individual indices.   211
3.4   Topics included in Fully_fledged_IT index.   211
3.5   Evolution of Fully_fledged_IT index in IT advanced and
        emerging market economies.   212
3.6   Changes of Mature_IT index in IT advanced economies.   213
3.7   Changes of Mature_IT index in IT emerging market economies. 213
3.8   Levels of Independent_IT index in IT advanced economies.   214
3.9   Levels of Independent_IT index in IT emerging market
        economies.   215
3.10   Changes of Informed_IT index in IT advanced economies.   216
3.11   Changes of Informed_IT index in IT emerging market
        economies.   216
3.12   Changes of Explicatory_IT index in IT advanced economies.   217
3.13   Changes of Explicatory_IT index in IT emerging market
        economies.   217
3.14   Changes of Transparent_IT index in IT advanced economies.   218
3.15   Changes of Transparent_IT index in IT emerging market
        economies.   218
3.16   Changes of Accountable_IT index in IT advanced economies.   219
3.17   Changes of Accountable_IT index in IT emerging market
        economies.   219
3.18   Changes of Fully_fledged_IT index in IT advanced economies. 220
3.19   Changes of Fully_fledged_IT index in IT emerging market
        economies.   220
3.20   Sources of changes to Fully_fledged_IT index in IT
        advanced economies.   221
3.21   Sources of changes to Fully_fledged_IT index in IT
        emerging market economies.   221
3.22   Sources of overall changes to Fully_fledged_IT index in IT
        advanced economies.   222
3.23   Sources of overall changes to Fully_fledged_IT index in IT
        emerging market economies.   222
3.24   Question on assigning the responsibility for financial
        stability to the central bank in IT economies.   229

3.25 Question on publishing reports on financial stability by a given IT central bank. 230

3.26 Question on the frequency of publishing reports on financial stability by a given IT central bank. 230

3.27 Question on the main policy instruments in a given IT economy. 231

3.28 Evolution of Mature_IT index in IT advanced and emerging market economies. 237

3.29 Levels of Independent_IT index at the time of an IT adoption by a given economy. 237

3.30 Evolution of Informed_IT index in IT advanced and emerging market economies. 237

3.31 Evolution of Explicatory_IT index in IT advanced and emerging market economies. 237

3.32 Evolution of Transparent_IT index in IT advanced and emerging market economies. 237

3.33 Evolution of Accountable_IT index in IT advanced and emerging market economies. 237

3.34 Average Mature_IT index in IT advanced and emerging market economies—all economies. 238

3.35 Average Mature_IT index in "old" IT advanced and emerging market economies. 238

3.36 Average Mature_IT index in "middle-aged" IT advanced and emerging market economies. 238

3.37 Average Mature_IT index in "new" IT advanced and emerging market economies. 238

3.38 Average Independent_IT index in IT advanced and emerging market economies—all economies. 238

3.39 Average Independent_IT index in "old" IT advanced and emerging market economies. 238

3.40 Average Independent_IT index in "middle-aged" IT advanced and emerging market economies. 239

3.41 Average Independent_IT index in "new" IT advanced and emerging market economies. 239

3.42 Average Informed_IT index in IT advanced and emerging market economies—all economies. 239

3.43 Average Informed_IT index in "old" IT advanced and emerging market economies. 239

3.44 Average Informed_IT index in "middle-aged" IT advanced and emerging market economies. 239

3.45 Average Informed_IT index in "new" IT advanced and emerging market economies. 239

3.46 Average Explicatory_IT index in IT advanced and emerging market economies—all economies. 240

3.47 Average Explicatory_IT index in "old" IT advanced and emerging market economies. 240

3.48 Average Explicatory_IT index in "middle-aged" IT advanced and emerging market economies. 240

3.49 Average Explicatory_IT index in "new" IT advanced and emerging market economies. 240

3.50 Average Transparent_IT index in IT advanced and emerging market economies—all economies. 240

3.51 Average Transparent_IT index in "old" IT advanced and emerging market economies. 240

3.52 Average Transparent_IT index in "middle-aged" IT advanced and emerging market economies. 241

3.53 Average Transparent_IT index in "new" IT advanced and emerging market economies. 241

3.54 Average Accountable_IT index in IT advanced and emerging market economies—all economies. 241

3.55 Average Accountable_IT index in "old" IT advanced and emerging market economies. 241

3.56 Average Accountable_IT index in "middle-aged" IT advanced and emerging market economies. 241

3.57 Average Accountable_IT index in "new" IT advanced and emerging market economies. 241

3.58 Average Fully_fledged_IT index in IT advanced and emerging market economies—all economies. 242

3.59 Average Fully_fledged_IT index in "old" IT advanced and emerging market economies. 242

3.60 Average Fully_fledged_IT index in "middle-aged" IT advanced and emerging market economies. 242

3.61 Average Fully_fledged_IT index in "new" IT advanced and emerging market economies. 242

3.62 Averages of Mature_IT index in IT advanced economies within "age" groups. 242

3.63 Averages of Mature_IT index in IT emerging market economies within "age" groups. 242

3.64 Averages of Independent_IT index in IT advanced economies within "age" groups. 243

3.65 Averages of Independent_IT index in IT emerging market economies within "age" groups. 243

3.66 Averages of Informed_IT index in IT advanced economies within "age" groups. 243

3.67 Averages of Informed_IT index in IT emerging market economies within "age" groups. 243

3.68 Averages of Explicatory_IT index in IT advanced economies within "age" groups. 243

3.69   Averages of Explicatory_IT index in IT emerging market
       economies within "age" groups.   243
3.70   Averages of Transparent_IT index in IT advanced
       economies within "age" groups.   244
3.71   Averages of Transparent_IT index in IT emerging market
       economies within "age" groups.   244
3.72   Averages of Accountable_IT index in IT advanced
       economies within "age" groups.   244
3.73   Averages of Accountable_IT index in IT emerging market
       economies within "age" groups.   244
3.74   Averages of Fully_fledged_IT index in IT advanced
       economies within "age" groups.   244
3.75   Averages of Fully_fledged_IT index in IT emerging market
       economies within "age" groups.   244
3.76   Average Stretched_IT index in IT advanced and emerging
       market economies.   245
3.77   Averages of Stretched_IT index in IT advanced economies
       within "age" groups.   245
3.78   Averages of Stretched_IT index in IT emerging market
       economies within "age" groups.   245
3.79   Indices of institutional set-ups in IT central banks since IT
       adoption.   246
4.1   Distribution of three-year averages of inflation levels—IT
       advanced economies.   268
4.2   Distribution of three-year averages of inflation levels—IT
       emerging market economies.   268
4.3   Distribution of three-year averages of inflation deviation
       from target—IT advanced economies.   270
4.4   Distribution of three-year averages of inflation deviation
       from target—IT emerging market economies.   270
4.5   Distribution of three-year averages of GDP growth—IT
       advanced economies.   280
4.6   Distribution of three-year averages of GDP growth—IT
       emerging market economies.   280
4.7   Distribution of three-year averages of output gap
       estimates—IT advanced economies.   282
4.8   Distribution of three-year averages of output gap
       estimates—IT emerging market economies.   282
4.9   Fully_fledged_IT index and inflation—IT advanced
       economies (2017).   310
4.10   Fully_fledged_IT index and inflation—IT emerging market
       economies (2017).   310
4.11   Fully_fledged_IT index and inflation variance—IT
       advanced economies (2017).   310

4.12 Fully_fledged_IT index and inflation variance—IT emerging market economies (2017). 310

4.13 Fully_fledged_IT index and inflation deviation from target—IT advanced economies (2017). 310

4.14 Fully_fledged_IT index and inflation deviation from target—IT emerging market economies (2017). 310

4.15 Fully_fledged_IT index and GDP growth—IT advanced economies (2017). 311

4.16 Fully_fledged_IT index and GDP growth—IT emerging market economies (2017). 311

4.17 Fully_fledged_IT index and GDP growth variance—IT advanced economies (2017). 311

4.18 Fully_fledged_IT index and GDP growth variance—IT emerging market economies (2017). 311

4.19 Fully_fledged_IT index and output gap—IT advanced economies (2017). 311

4.20 Fully_fledged_IT index and output gap—IT emerging market economies (2017). 311

4.21 Fully_fledged_IT index and inflation—IT advanced economies (full sample). 312

4.22 Fully_fledged_IT index and inflation—IT emerging market economies (full sample). 312

4.23 Fully_fledged_IT index and inflation variance—IT advanced economies (full sample). 312

4.24 Fully_fledged_IT index and inflation variance—IT emerging market economies (full sample). 312

4.25 Fully_fledged_IT index and inflation deviation from target—IT advanced economies (full sample). 312

4.26 Fully_fledged_IT index and inflation deviation from target—IT emerging market economies (full sample). 312

4.27 Fully_fledged_IT index and GDP growth—IT advanced economies (full sample). 313

4.28 Fully_fledged_IT index and GDP growth—IT emerging market economies (full sample). 313

4.29 Fully_fledged_IT index and GDP growth variance—IT advanced economies (full sample). 313

4.30 Fully_fledged_IT index and GDP growth variance—IT emerging market economies (full sample). 313

4.31 Fully_fledged_IT index and output gap—IT advanced economies (full sample). 313

4.32 Fully_fledged_IT index and output gap—IT emerging market economies (full sample). 313

TABLES

1.1 Main characteristics of exchange rate targeting, monetary targeting, and inflation targeting 37

1.2 Optimal level of inflation implied by alternative classes of models 50

1.3 Classification of monetary policy measures 59

1.4 Monetary policy frameworks used in the world in 2017 93

2.1 Exchange rate regimes (*de facto* classification) used by IT central banks 108

2.2 IT economies where the government has the right to influence monetary policy decisions 113

2.3 Possibility of reappointment of governors and their term of office in IT economies 116

2.4 Countries with explicit prohibition on monetary financing in IT advanced and emerging market economies 118

2.5 Formally independent central banks in IT advanced and emerging market economies 120

2.6 Different widths of tolerance bands used in IT economies 127

2.7 Different measures of targeted inflation in IT economies 130

2.8 Forecast variables other than inflation and GDP in IT economies 140

2.9 IT economies with different approaches to decision-making 146

2.10 Changes to decision-making processes in IT advanced and emerging market economies 148

2.11 Publishing voting records in IT advanced and emerging market economies 150

2.12 Publishing open letters in IT advanced and emerging market economies 156

2.13 Unconventional monetary policy measures in IT advanced economies 162

2.14 Unconventional monetary policy measures in IT emerging market economies 165

TABLES

3.1   Construction of Mature_IT index   199
3.2   Construction of Independent_IT index   200
3.3   Construction of Informed_IT index   202
3.4   Construction of Explicatory_IT index   204
3.5   Construction of Transparent_IT index   206
3.6   Construction of Accountable_IT index   208
3.7   Construction of Fully_fledged_IT index   209
3.8   Convergence of indices in IT advanced and emerging
      market economies   226
3.9   Construction of Stretched_IT index   228
4.1   Correlations between the proposed indices and
      macroeconomic variables in selected years   257
4.2   Correlations between the proposed indices and
      macroeconomic variables over the full sample   262
4.3   Estimation results of models related to inflation levels   271
4.4   Estimation results of models related to inflation volatility   273
4.5   Estimation results of models related to inflation deviations
      from the target   275
4.6   Estimation results of models related to inflation deviations
      from the target controlling for the sign of deviation   277
4.7   Estimation results of models related to GDP growth   283
4.8   Estimation results of models related to GDP growth volatility   285
4.9   Estimation results of models related to output gap   287
4.10 Estimation results of models related to output gap
      controlling for the sign of the output gap   289
4.11 Overview of the estimation results   292
4.12 List of variables with sources   305
4.13 List of variables with country and time coverage   306
4.14 Unit root test for variables   308
4.15 Robustness check of models related to inflation levels   314
4.16 Robustness check of models related to inflation volatility   317
4.17 Robustness check of models related to inflation deviations
      from the target   319
4.18 Robustness check of models related to GDP growth   323
4.19 Robustness check of models related to GDP growth volatility   326
4.20 Robustness check of models related to output gap   328
S1   Indices of central banks' institutional set-ups in the analysed
      inflation targeting economies   339

ACKNOWLEDGEMENTS

I would like to start by thanking my supervisor Professor Zbigniew Polański and the auxiliary supervisor Doctor Tomasz Chmielewski, from the Warsaw School of Economics, for their guidance and advice in shaping my PhD thesis that—after some adjustments—transformed into the book. Without their expertise that proved extremely helpful in formulating the research questions and choosing the methodology to look for the answers, this book would not have looked the same.

I am also grateful to Professor Marek Dąbrowski, from the Cracow University of Economics, and Professor Dariusz Filar, from the University of Gdansk, who provided invaluable reviews of my PhD thesis, indicating some shortfalls and weaker points to which more attention should be paid. I tried to address all their comments. In addition, I very much appreciate their kind words in assessing my work and suggesting to publish it.

My very special gratitude goes to my colleagues from the National Bank of Poland—in particular to Magda Ciżkowicz-Pękała, Witold Grostal, and Piotr Żuk—with whom I worked on many projects that deepened my understanding of central banking and allowed me to arrive at the idea behind the book. They also provided me with many ideas that I considered while preparing my PhD thesis.

I am also deeply indebted to Kristina Abbotts, Senior Editor in the Routledge Taylor & Francis Group, who—from our very first exchange of e-mails—was fully dedicated to the project. She not only shared her enthusiasm with me, but she was also able to convince others that the study was worth considering. Needless to say, she ran the publishing process very smoothly and it was a pure pleasure to work with her.

Last, but by no means least, I would like to thank my family, especially my parents, for their patience and support when they were needed to stay focused on the work. My parents were always ready to distract me when I needed a little rest, and to encourage me when I needed additional motivation—amazingly distinguishing between the right contingencies. Thank you a lot!

INTRODUCTION

Initial remarks on inflation targeting

In 1989, the Reserve Bank of New Zealand introduced a strategy[1] that later became known as inflation targeting (IT) and turned out to be very popular. Alan Bollard, the Governor of the Reserve Bank of New Zealand, quite rightly assessed that "inflation targeting is one of New Zealand's successful exports" (Bollard, 2008).

In the early 1990s, inflation targeting spread to other advanced economies[2] (Canada, Israel, the United Kingdom). Shortly thereafter it was also adopted by some emerging market economies[3] in South-East Asia and Latin America (Korea, Brazil, Chile, Colombia), as well as transition countries in Central and Eastern Europe (the Czech Republic, Poland). By the early 2000s, the number of advanced and emerging market economies with an IT strategy was equal and nowadays there are more emerging market economy inflation targeters than advanced economy inflation targeters.

Given the fact that, at the beginning, IT had no deep theoretical foundations, it is difficult to formulate its precise definition. However, based on analysing the experiences of inflation targeters, a consensus view is that—apart from acknowledging price stability as the primary goal of monetary policy and publicly announcing a numerical target for inflation—what should be treated as essential for an IT regime is formulating monetary policy on the basis of a very broad set of information, preferably including forecasts,[4] as well as applying high accountability[5] and transparency[6] standards to central banks' policies, which can be seen as supplementing the considerable independence granted to monetary authorities (Mishkin, 2001, p. 9; Svensson, 2008, p. 319).

The classification of central banks[7] as inflation targeters has typically been conducted by looking at their declarations. Only in the case of the euro area, Switzerland, and the United States—although they do not describe their frameworks as IT—these economies are often treated as inflation targeters based on the comparison of their monetary policy regimes with key IT characteristics.[8] This is also the approach adopted in this study. Thus, based on information from central banks' websites, cross-checked with an overview of monetary policy frameworks published by the International Monetary Fund (IMF, 2018), in 2018, an IT strategy was implemented by 14 advanced economies and 28 emerging market economies.[9] These numbers make inflation targeting one of the most commonly applied monetary policy regimes worldwide, meaning also that it has been employed by a relatively heterogeneous group of economies.

At the same time, the global financial crisis of 2008 and the European sovereign crisis of 2011 resulted in a critique of an IT framework. The reason was that focusing on maintaining price stability—which is one of the crucial aspects of inflation targeting—proved to be insufficient to deliver overall macroeconomic stability, including financial stability. Moreover, using short-term interest rates—which over the years became the main policy instrument of inflation targeters—in many economies fell short of providing an adequate policy stimulus needed at the time of severe downturn. Recognising these problems led to serious discussions on what the role of financial stability considerations in monetary policy, and the scope of employing unconventional[10] monetary policy measures,[11] should be (Bean et al., 2010; Svensson, 2010; Borio, 2011; Bayoumi et al., 2014; Cukierman, 2019). More generally, some economists doubt whether IT that was proposed as a way of combating too high inflation is equally suitable for combating excessively low price growth (Goodhart, 2018).

Looking at the current state of the debates, it is not easy to foresee their outcomes. At the same time, Frankel (2012) announced the death of inflation targeting prematurely, as the support for that strategy is still rather strong (Walsh, 2019). Not only, until now, virtually no retreat from IT has been observed, but several countries—mainly emerging market economies—are taking preparatory steps to become inflation targeters. And even if, at some stage, an alternative monetary policy framework is proposed, many institutional arrangements developed within an inflation targeting regime will most likely remain in place. Such a view has been, in a way, confirmed by the announcement of an average inflation targeting strategy by the US Federal Reserve in August 2020, whose novelty compared to hitherto pursued IT should not be overstated.

Inflation targeting has visibly enhanced monetary policy institutional set-ups which can be treated as its lasting contribution to central banking. For that reason, investigating key IT elements and reviewing their implementation across countries, as well as their evolution over time, seem valuable. The analysis of central banks' institutional arrangements and their implications has therefore been chosen as the topic of this study.[12]

Motivation behind the study

New Zealand[13] was the first country to use a publicly announced level of targeted inflation in an attempt to permanently lower elevated price growth in the late 1980s. Initially, inflation targeting was proposed as a pragmatic solution to the country's problem of persistently heightened inflation.[14] However, since the framework proved very successful in delivering price stability, it evolved into a fully fledged monetary policy strategy. It is worth stressing that IT turned out to be characterised by a high degree of flexibility, since the central banks that followed it recognised, at a very early stage, the need to pay attention not only to inflation deviations from the target, but also to output developments (King, 1997; Svensson, 2009). As a result, over the last 30 years, IT has become the most widespread framework among big and medium-sized countries.

The crucial elements of inflation targeting indicated above, i.e. emphasising price stability objectives, including comprehensive data analysis in conducting monetary policy, and setting high accountability and transparency requirements that accompany significant central banks' independence, are, however, formulated in rather general terms, and while in certain aspects some common practices have been established, it is hard to speak of a homogeneous approach to the strategy, or of its "standard" or "model" version, especially in some areas.[15] Differences can be seen, in particular, in the way inflation targets are set, the degree of independence[16] granted to central banks, the rules governing the composition of decision-making bodies,[17] and the organisation of decision-making processes, as well as in the extent of transparency with respect to the conducted monetary policy and its future course. All these aspects, and many others that have not been noted here, are parts of institutional arrangements that influence how monetary policy is pursued, and, in particular, how firmly inflation expectations are anchored.

In the study, institutional set-ups are understood as all the rules related to monetary authorities' independence, accountability, and transparency (in its various dimensions), which are the areas that complement the notion of inflation targeting. At the same time, these elements can also be seen as reflecting how seriously a given central bank is treating the strategy. The analysis presented below is aimed at answering the key questions that arise in this context, namely, whether there are major differences between IT central banks' institutional arrangements, and—if this is the case—whether these differences have a significant impact on the ability of monetary policy to meet its goals, assessed by looking at both inflation and output developments.

In order to address these issues, it is useful to review the extent to which the crucial features of an IT regime are homogeneously applied by IT central banks, and, in particular, whether any major differences in terms of central banks' institutional set-ups can be found between advanced economy inflation targeters and emerging market economy inflation targeters. Also of crucial importance is how IT central banks' institutional arrangements have evolved over time. Moreover, considering the recent critique of inflation targeting, it is interesting to see whether the global and European crises influenced the way an IT strategy has been understood and implemented. All these aspects will help to verify if IT central banks' institutional set-ups are affecting the ability of monetary policy to deliver its objectives.

The questions indicated above, i.e. whether IT central banks' institutional arrangements differ much between countries, and whether these differences impact monetary policy outcomes, may be of importance, especially for central banks—both those already pursuing an IT strategy, as well as those only preparing for its adoption.[18] The findings should help to understand which institutional set-ups are supportive of monetary policy effectiveness and which may hamper delivering the intended goals. Given the role that monetary policy plays within the economy, such knowledge may have significant implications.

Existing literature

Many of the indicated topics have been discussed in the literature. In particular, issues related to the evolution of institutional aspects of monetary policy were analysed by Bade and Parkin (1988), Grilli et al. (1991), Cukierman et al. (1992), Alesina and Summers (1993), and Fry et al. (2000). The scope of those studies varied, since the authors focused only on selected areas that they identified as potentially important for central banking. Moreover, different groups of countries were reviewed and over different time frames, with more emphasis placed on advanced economies, and a focus on periods before IT became widespread. However, taken together, developments concerning all of the elements listed above were investigated, namely, monetary authorities' independence, accountability, and transparency.

The general conclusion was that the degree of central banks' independence from governments[19] noticeably increased starting in the 1970s and 1980s, which was accompanied by the rising importance of communication in explaining monetary policy decisions that was especially visible in the 1990s and 2000s. These processes took place in parallel with the growing popularity of an IT framework and influenced the institutional arrangements of many central banks, but above all, those adopting an inflation targeting regime.

An important area of research has tried to empirically check whether differences in central banks' institutional set-ups translated into differences in terms of central banks' credibility,[20] and thus central banks' effectiveness in delivering monetary policy objectives.[21] The work of Alesina and Summers (1993) should again be mentioned, since it was one of the influential studies in that respect. Their findings—showing that independence was associated with lower and less volatile inflation without having much effect on real variables—supported the claim that monetary authorities should be granted a high degree of autonomy.[22] The consequences of central banks' independence for macroeconomic developments were also analysed by, for example, Posen (1993), Campillo and Miron (1996), Eijffinger and de Haan (1996), and Crowe and Meade (2008). However, while standard indices measuring independence were negatively correlated with inflation in advanced economies, this was not necessarily the case for emerging market economies. Likewise, the findings from research investigating the impact of central banks' growing accountability and transparency on monetary policy outcomes were often mixed. These topics were analysed by, among others, Cecchetti and Krause (2002), Sterne et al. (2002), Demertzis and Hughes Hallett (2007), Carpenter (2004), and Crowe and Meade (2008). Some of those studies showed that increasing democratic control and enhancing communication policies led to reduced inflation, while other papers, though not confirming such a relationship, suggested a downward impact on inflation volatility. Therefore, it would be interesting to again conduct an empirical examination of these issues, based on the already relatively ample experiences of inflation targeting economies.

Identified gaps in existing literature

The main contributions of this study to the existing literature include a detailed review of central banks' IT institutional arrangements and their evolution over time, a comprehensive comparison of various dimensions of monetary authorities' institutional set-ups, as well as empirical verification of whether the identified differences matter for maintaining price stability and stabilising output.

What distinguishes the approach applied in this work is that only economies following the same monetary policy strategy are analysed, namely, inflation targeters. It is important to note that implementing an IT framework requires monetary authorities to meet some prerequisites that encompass, in particular, setting high accountability and transparency standards. Whereas inflation targeters are not fully homogeneous, the emphasis they place on democratic control and communication makes them, in a way, special among other central banks. Thus, monetary authorities pursuing inflation targeting have a lot in common, and therefore—especially given the fact that the study focuses on the role of institutional arrangements— any comparison of their effectiveness in meeting monetary policy objectives seems more justified than assessing policy outcomes delivered under various policy regimes. At the same time, over the last 30 years, the group of inflation targeters has become big enough and the period of using this strategy has been long enough to allow for drawing conclusions based on a relatively broad data set, which should strengthen the results.

While analysing an inflation targeting framework, previous reviews of IT central banks' institutional set-ups should be recalled. Since the strategy emerged as an answer to specific problems faced by some economies in the 1990s, it has been evolving over time to address new challenges that policymakers have been confronted with over the last decades. Therefore, during that period, a number of papers have compared various aspects of the regime as put into practice by IT monetary authorities. Examples include Debelle (1997), Mishkin (2001), Heenan et al. (2006), Roger (2010), Hammond (2012), Naudon and Pérez (2017), and Grostal and Niedźwiedzińska (2019).[23] Some of these studies helped to build a general understanding of what constitutes the crucial elements of inflation targeting and promoted certain practices among central banks. However, the previous reviews focused on selected IT countries, mostly advanced economies, and presented the state of institutional arrangements at a given point in time. In order to fill the identified gap, this work analyses the three decades of inflation targeting as pursued by a large group of central banks. Thus, in contrast to other research, the study encompasses 42 central banks pursuing an IT strategy and indicates similarities and differences between advanced and emerging market economy inflation targeters. In addition to discussing in detail the key institutional features of the strategy as currently practised by the analysed monetary authorities, in many instances the study also describes changes introduced in the past 30 years to central banks' set-ups.

Research hypothesis and the related analytical steps

The analysis is focused on verifying the following research hypothesis: the quality of the institutional set-ups of monetary authorities pursuing an inflation targeting regime affects monetary policy effectiveness, understood, predominantly, as delivering low and stable inflation or meeting the inflation target, as well as stabilising output growth. Put differently, the study should enable to check whether there are significant differences in institutional arrangements governing IT central banks, and whether these differences have an impact on monetary policy outcomes, assessed by looking at both inflation and output developments.

Several steps will be undertaken in order to draw final conclusions.

First, the key elements of an IT regime will be reviewed, by looking at how they are implemented, translating into different central banks' institutional set-ups. Identifying the differences is essential for analysing their implications. As already noted, the crucial features of IT include treating price stability as the primary objective of monetary policy, defining a numerical value for targeted inflation, incorporating a broad set of information—and possibly also projections—in monetary policy decisions, as well as setting high accountability and transparency standards as complements to central banks' significant independence.

Second, central banks' institutional set-ups will be assessed, based on arguments raised in the literature favouring certain solutions over others, or—in the absence of a broader discussion of some issues—based on the dominant practice suggesting the arrangements preferred by decision-makers for pragmatic reasons. In this respect, the comparison of institutional set-ups used by IT advanced economies and those used by IT emerging market economies will be of particular interest. Evaluating the quality of the institutional arrangements is necessary to check its consequences for monetary policy effectiveness.

Third, it will be investigated whether IT central banks institutional set-ups have been improving over time. Improvement is understood as replacing the existing arrangements with those favoured in the literature or preferred by decision-makers, as noted above. This will allow for detecting any tendencies possibly supporting the claim that pursuing an IT regime enhances the institutional arrangements governing central banks.

Additionally, given the fact that the recent global and European crises have influenced IT central banks' approach to financial stability issues and broadened the use of monetary policy instruments by including non-standard measures, these aspects will be analysed as well. The indicated elements may help to assess the significance of the ongoing changes for the essence of inflation targeting. Although it is not directly linked to the main research hypothesis, it can be seen as a more forward-looking perspective to evaluating an IT framework.

Country coverage

The analysis includes the following economies: Albania, Argentina, Armenia, Australia, Brazil, Canada, Chile, Colombia, the Czech Republic, the Dominican Republic, the euro area,[24] Georgia, Ghana, Guatemala, Hungary, Iceland, India, Indonesia, Israel, Japan, Kazakhstan, Korea, Mexico, Moldova, New Zealand, Norway, Paraguay, Peru, the Philippines, Poland, Romania, Russia, Serbia, South Africa, Sweden, Switzerland, Thailand, Turkey, Uganda, Ukraine, the United Kingdom, and the United States.

Out of that list, as already noted, the euro area, Switzerland, and the United States do not describe their strategies as IT,[25] even though they follow monetary policy frameworks that share virtually all the key features of inflation targeting. Since their monetary policy regimes are indistinguishable from IT, they have been included in the review.

Importantly, until very recently, none of the countries that had adopted an inflation targeting regime had ever abandoned it.[26] Nowadays, the only exception is Argentina, which announced launching an IT strategy in 2016, but by late 2018 had to suspend it, and turned to monetary base targeting. Counting the Central Bank of Argentina until 2018 as a fully fledged inflation targeter had been rather problematic anyway, not least due to the fact that the bank had not been publishing inflation forecasts, which is an important feature of implementing an IT strategy.[27]

Another noticeable case is Iceland, which after the financial crisis of 2008 focused its monetary policy on stabilising the exchange rate. Interestingly, Iceland did not officially change its monetary policy framework at that time, and thus has been continuously counted as an inflation targeter.[28]

At the same time, reviews of monetary policy frameworks recently conducted in New Zealand and the United States have resulted in only some modifications to IT, and should not be treated as major changes to the regime.

Structure of the study

Chapter 1 covers both the origins and the prospects of inflation targeting, and thus its structure is less homogeneous than the following chapters that deal with much more narrowly specified issues. Chapter 1 begins with a brief discussion of the evolution of monetary economics as a starting point for the analysis. This will be helpful in understanding the role that monetary policy plays within an economy and the rationale behind considering price stability as the right goal for monetary authorities, irrespective of the monetary strategy used by a given central bank. Against this background, the concept of a monetary policy strategy and its institutional set-ups is introduced, followed by an overview of the most typical monetary policy frameworks. The key elements of an IT regime are also presented, including an indication of the main central banks' approaches to interpreting them. Reasons behind the still fairly strong support for an IT framework are noted alongside critical points raised against this strategy. An analysis of the consequences of the recent crises for understanding and implementing an inflation targeting framework, as well as the likely directions for the future evolution of an IT framework conclude Chapter 1.

Chapter 2 presents a survey of various aspects related to the institutional set-ups of IT central banks. Forty-two economies which can be classified as inflation targeters are reviewed. Since some elements of the strategy have been modified over time, changes to the analysed institutional arrangements are also covered. The whole period of pursuing an IT regime by a given monetary authority is considered. Taking into account the fact that different countries were adopting inflation targeting in different years, this means that the time frame will not be the same for all of the reviewed economies. With respect to the impact of the recent crises on an IT regime, the role of central banks in safeguarding financial stability, and the scope of employing unconventional monetary policy measures are also discussed.

In Chapter 3, building on the survey, a number of indices are proposed that will allow for a synthetic assessment of several dimensions related to the conduct of monetary policy. These indices will be helpful in comparing the institutional set-ups of the analysed IT economies, i.e. in identifying the main differences and similarities between inflation targeters. They will also be used to see if any tendencies can be observed in the way institutional arrangements have been shaped over the years. The indices cover a wide range of aspects linked to the independence, accountability, and transparency of IT central banks. The rules and practices related to central banks' policies are assessed taking into account solutions that can be seen as recommended in the light of the existing literature or recognised practice. This translates into a better (higher scores) or worse (lower scores) evaluation of the central banks' set-ups reflected in the value of the indices. As a result, it is possible to rank inflation targeters according to the proposed indices. Considering the consequences of the recent crises for an inflation targeting framework, an additional index is constructed to capture aspects related to financial stability and non-standard measures. The index will allow for comparing approaches adopted by IT central banks with regard to the two issues.

In Chapter 4, the proposed indices are used to see whether the identified differences in the institutional set-ups of IT central banks have an impact on monetary policy effectiveness. Monetary policy effectiveness is assessed by looking at both inflation and output developments, in order to acknowledge the fact that inflation targeters follow a flexible approach to the strategy. This means that the aim of any analysed central bank is to safeguard price stability, while limiting output fluctuations. For these reasons, as already mentioned, policy effectiveness is understood, primarily, as providing low and stable inflation or meeting the inflation target, taking into account the impact on gross domestic product (GDP) growth, its variance, and output gap estimates (Brzoza-Brzezina, 2011, p. 7). Finally, in order to answer the main research question, the conclusions stemming from the empirical analysis are discussed.

Research approach

The analysis builds on various research approaches. Reviews of the available literature are used to check which elements of an inflation targeting framework have been found to be most important, as well as to investigate the existing evidence of the significance of central banks' institutional set-ups for the effectiveness of monetary policy. A detailed survey of institutional arrangements applied by IT monetary authorities, including their evolution over time and comparison across countries, is carried out with the help of descriptive and comparative analyses. The assessment of the impact of the identified differences in institutional arrangements on monetary policy effectiveness is conducted using quantitative methods.

In order to construct indices comparing the institutional set-ups of IT monetary authorities, solutions applied over the period of pursuing an inflation targeting regime by a given central bank are investigated. While no database is available that would cover the issues of interest—even for a sub-group of the analysed countries or a sub-period of the reviewed history—the information necessary to build the indices is publicly accessible. However, to collect it, it is necessary to visit each central bank's website separately and look at various publications—at times archived.[29] Considering the scope of the analysed institutional arrangements, the number of reviewed IT central banks, and the period covered by the study, this results in creating a very rich and unique data set. Taking into account all of the listed dimensions, this gives around 45,000 pieces of information to be collected and coded.[30]

The econometric techniques employed in the study are empirical models of panel regressions. Each country is taken into account starting with the year of its IT adoption, which varies between different inflation targeters, until 2018, resulting in unbalanced panels. The sample includes economies that have been pursuing an IT strategy for at least 5 years covered by the analysis, i.e. until 2018. This means that the sample comprises 37 economies.[31]

The main variables used in the empirical analysis include inflation, GDP growth, volatility of inflation and GDP growth, oil prices, global inflation, exchange rates, terms of trade, trade openness, measures of financial depth, GDP *per capita*, as well as the proposed indices reviewing central banks' institutional set-ups. Data are collected, predominantly, from the International Monetary Fund (IMF), the Organisation for Economic Co-operation and Development (OECD), the Bank for International Settlements (BIS), and the analysed IT central banks.

The data investigated in the study cover the period until 2018. At times, when important developments occurred by late 2020, they are mentioned (mainly in the endnotes), but do not enter the database. Unless otherwise indicated, all charts showing the current state of a given phenomenon refer to 2018, whereas all charts showing an evolution of a given phenomenon cover the period starting in 1990 and ending in 2018.

Notes

1 When referring to the key principles of monetary policy, the terms "strategy", "framework", and "regime" are used interchangeably.
2 The terms "advanced" economies and "industrial" or "developed" economies are used interchangeably.
3 The terms "emerging market" economies and "developing" economies are used interchangeably.
4 The terms "forecasts" and "projections" are used interchangeably, whereas the literature sometimes distinguishes that forecasts are based on endogenous interest rate paths, while projections are based on external assumptions regarding interest rate paths (e.g. market-implied or constant interest rates).
5 The terms "accountability" and "democratic control" are used interchangeably.
6 The terms "transparency", "communication", and "openness" are used interchangeably.

7 The terms "monetary authority" and "central bank" are used interchangeably.
8 Although sometimes the euro area, Switzerland, and the United States are called quasi-inflation targeters. In what follows, quasi-inflation targeters are treated as inflation targeters and thus are not distinguished in the analysed group of economies. Likewise, a quasi-IT strategy is treated as inflation targeting. Interestingly, in August 2020, when the US Fed was announcing changes to its monetary policy strategy, the board members openly admitted that since 2012 the Federal Reserve had been following an IT regime.
9 This number does not include Uruguay, although it has been classified as following an inflation targeting framework by the IMF (2018). The reason is that the Central Bank of Uruguay describes its strategy as an inflation target scheme based on monetary aggregates.
10 When referring to monetary policy instruments, the terms "unconventional", "non-standard", and "unorthodox" are used interchangeably.
11 When referring to operational aspects of monetary policy, the terms "measures", "instruments", and "tools" are used interchangeably.
12 When referring to institutional aspects of conducting monetary policy, the terms "arrangements", "rules", and "set-ups" are used interchangeably.
13 When describing developments related to policies of central banks, for the purpose of simplicity, instead of writing about the given central bank, often only the name of a country is used. Thus, names of countries are treated as synonyms of their respective monetary authorities.
14 At that time, inflation in New Zealand exceeded 10%.
15 This is also the reason to call IT "an" inflation targeting regime, rather than "the" inflation targeting regime.
16 The terms "independence" and "autonomy" are used interchangeably.
17 The terms "policymakers", "central banks' officials", and "members of decision-making bodies" of central banks are used interchangeably. In turn, the term "committee" is used to indicate a "collegial decision-making body" of a central bank and these terms are used interchangeably as well.
18 The latter group includes, among others, Egypt, Jamaica, Mozambique, and Tunisia.
19 The terms "government" and "political authority" are used interchangeably.
20 The terms "credibility" and "reputation" are used interchangeably.
21 When referring to the final goal of monetary policy, the terms "objectives", "goals", "aims", and "targets" are used interchangeably.
22 This result was even interpreted as a "free lunch", suggesting that granting central banks more autonomy would allow for maintaining price stability without losses in real output that otherwise would be necessary for lowering inflation (Walsh, 2008, p. 730).
23 Some studies analysed the experiences of a relatively limited number of economies, but could be treated as a source of valuable knowledge about inflation targeting at the time when the new framework was only gradually gaining popularity. One example of a review covering advanced economies is Mishkin and Posen (1997), while Drop and Wojtyna (2001) is an example relating predominantly to emerging market economies.
24 The euro area is counted as one economy.
25 As already indicated, until August 2020, the US Fed was unwilling to officially call its strategy an IT regime, though Bernanke (2019, p. 5) implicitly called the Federal Reserve's monetary policy strategy inflation targeting, and similarly, Yellen (2014, pp. 31–32) described the Fed's strategy as entirely consistent with flexible inflation targeting.
26 Although some European countries that had pursued an IT strategy in the past (Finland since 1993, Spain since 1995, the Slovak Republic since 2005) subse-

quently joined the euro area. As this was a decision driven by a process of economic and political integration, these cases should not be treated as abandoning inflation targeting because of its inadequacy. Moreover, as already indicated, the euro area is following a strategy very similar to IT and has been counted as an inflation targeter.

27 It seems that Argentina wanted to gain some credibility by adopting an inflation targeting framework, before it was well prepared to do so. However, since only in late 2018 the Central Bank of Argentina declared abandoning an IT approach, Argentina has been taken into account in the review, but not in the empirical analysis.

28 In 2010, when describing Iceland's experiences with combating the financial crisis of 2008, the Central Bank of Iceland implicitly admitted that, in the wake of the crisis, it departed temporarily from inflation targeting (CBI, 2010, p. 7). However, when explicitly analysing the changes introduced after the crisis to its monetary policy framework, the bank did not indicate that (CBI, 2017, p. 10).

29 While most central banks do allow for quite easy access to documents published even several years ago, historical information dating further back is generally more difficult to find.

30 This means that—with 42 inflation targeters—updating the proposed indices by one additional year requires collecting and coding almost 3000 pieces of information.

31 Thus, the economies that are not included in the empirical analysis include Argentina, India, Kazakhstan, Russia, and Ukraine.

References

Alesina, A., Summers, L. (1993), "Central Bank Independence and Macroeconomic Performance: Some Comparative Evidence", *Journal of Money, Credit, and Banking*, 25(2), pp. 151–162. https://doi.org/10.2307/2077833

Bade, R., Parkin, M. (1988), *Central Bank Laws and Monetary Policy*, Department of Economics, University of Western Ontario, Canada.

Bayoumi, T., Dell'Ariccia, G., Habermeier, K., Mancini-Griffoli, T., Valencia, F. (2014), "Monetary Policy in the New Normal", *IMF Staff Discussion Note*. http://doi.org/10.5089/9781475561784.006

Bean, C., Paustian, M., Penalver, A., Taylor, T. (2010), "Monetary Policy After the Fall", *Proceedings From Economic Policy Symposium—Jackson Hole*, Federal Reserve Bank of Kansas City, pp. 267–328. www.kansascityfed.org/publicat/sympos/2010/Bean_final.pdf

Bernanke, B. S. (2019), "Monetary Policy in a New Era", in: O. Blanchard, L. H. Summer (eds.), *Evolution or Revolution? Rethinking Macroeconomic Policy after the Great Recession*, MIT Press, pp. 3–48.

Bollard, A. (2008), "Flexibility and the Limits to Inflation Targeting", *Speech at a Private Function*, Auckland, Reserve Bank of New Zealand, 30 July. www.rbnz.govt.nz/research-and-publications/speeches/2008/speech2008-07-30

Borio, C. (2011), "Rediscovering the Macroeconomic Roots of Financial Stability Policy: Journey, Challenges and a Way Forward", *BIS Working Paper, No 354*. www.bis.org/publ/work354.pdf

Brzoza-Brzezina, M. (2011), *Polska polityka pieniężna. Badania teoretyczne i empiryczne*, C.H. Beck.

Campillo, M., Miron, J. (1996), "Why Does Inflation Differ Across Countries?", *NBER Working Paper, No. 5540*, pp. 1–38. http://doi.org/10.3386/w5540

Carpenter, S. B. (2004), "Transparency and Monetary Policy: What Does the Academic Literature Tell Policymakers?", *FEDS Discussion Paper, No. 35*, pp. 1–18. http://doi.org/10.2139/ssrn.594842

CBI (2010), "Monetary Policy in Iceland after Capital Controls", *Special Publication, No. 11*, Vol. 4.

CBI (2017), "Monetary Policy Based on Inflation Targeting: Iceland's Experience Since 2001 and Post-Crisis Changes", *Special Publication, No. 11*.

Cecchetti, S. G., Krause, S. (2002), "Central Bank Structure, Policy Efficiency, and Macroeconomic Performance: Exploring Empirical Relationships", *The Federal Reserve Bank of St. Louis Review*, 84(4), pp. 47–60. http://doi.org/10.20955/r.84.47-60

Crowe, Ch., Meade, E. (2008), "Central Bank Independence and Transparency: Evolution and Effectiveness", *IMF Working Paper, No. 119*, pp. 1–28. https://doi.org/10.5089/9781451869798.001

Cukierman, A. (2019), "The Impact of the Global Financial Crisis on Central Banking", in: G. G. Mayes, P. Siklos, J.-E. Sturm (eds.), *The Oxford Handbook of the Economics of Central Banking*, Oxford University Press, pp. 171–192.

Cukierman, A., Webb, S. B., Neyapti, B. (1992), "Measuring the Independence of Central Banks and Its Effect on Policy Outcomes", *The World Bank Economic Review*, 6(3), pp. 353–398. https://doi.org/10.1093/wber/6.3.353

Debelle, G. (1997), "Inflation Targeting in Practice", *IMF Working Paper, No. 35*, pp. 1–34. https://doi.org/10.5089/9781451845310.001

Demertzis, M., Hughes Hallett, A. (2007), "Central Bank Transparency in Theory and Practice", *Journal of Macroeconomics*, 29(4), pp. 760–789. http://doi.org/10.1016/j.jmacro.2005.06.002

Drop, J., Wojtyna, A. (2001), "Strategia Bezpośredniego Celu Inflacyjnego: Przesłanki Teoretyczne i Doświadczenia Wybranych Krajów", *Materiały i Studia NBP, No. 118*.

Eijffinger, S., de Haan, J. (1996), "The Political Economy of Central-Bank Independence", *Special Papers in International Economics*, 19, pp. 1–92

Frankel, J. (2012), "The Death of Inflation Targeting", *Commentary of 16 May 2012*. www.project-syndicate.org/commentary/the-death-of-inflation targeting

Fry, M., Julius, D., Mahadeva, L., Roger, S., Sterne, G. (2000), "Key Issues in the Choice of Monetary Policy Framework", in: L. Mahadeva, G. Sterne (eds.), *Monetary Policy Frameworks in a Global Context*, Routledge Press, pp. 1–216.

Goodhart, Ch. (2018), "The Changing Fortunes of Central Banking", in: Ph. Hartmann, H. Huang, D. Schoenmaker (eds.), *The Changing Fortunes of Central Banking*, Cambridge University Press, pp. 376–389.

Grilli, V., Masciandaro, D., Tabellini, G., Malinvaud, E., Pagano, M. (1991), "Political and Monetary Institutions and Public Financial Policies in the Industrial Countries", *Economic Policy*, 6(13), pp. 342–392. https://doi.org/10.2307/1344630

Grostal, W., Niedźwiedzińska, J. (2019), "Inflation Targeting as a Monetary Policy Framework", in: J. Niedźwiedzińska (ed.), *Three Decades of Inflation Targeting, NBP Working Paper, No. 314*, pp. 13–41.

Hammond, G. (2012), *State of the Art of Inflation Targeting*, Centre for Central Banking Studies, Bank of England. www.bankofengland.co.uk/ccbs/state-of-the-art-of-inflation-targeting

Heenan, G., Peter, M., Roger, S. (2006), "Implementing Inflation Targeting: Institutional Arrangements, Target Design, and Communications", *IMF Working Paper, No. 278*, pp. 1–57. https://doi.org/10.5089/9781451865387.001

IMF (2018), "Annual Report on Exchange Arrangements and Exchange Restrictions 2017", April. www.imf.org/en/Publications/Annual-Report-on-Exchange-Arrangements-and-Exchange-Restrictions/Issues/2018/08/10/Annual-Report-on-Exchange-Arrangements-and-Exchange-Restrictions-2017-44930

King, M. A. (1997), "Changes in UK Monetary Policy: Rules and Discretion in Practice", *Journal of Monetary Economics*, 39(1), pp. 81–97. https://doi.org/10.1016/s0304-3932(97)00009-3

Mishkin, F. S. (2001), "From Monetary Targeting to Inflation Targeting: Lessons from the Industrialized Countries", *Policy Research Working Paper, No. 2684*, World Bank. https://doi.org/10.1596/1813-9450-2684

Mishkin, F. S., Posen, A. S. (1997), "Inflation Targeting: Lessons from Four Countries", *NBER Working Paper, No. 6126*, pp.1–133. www.nber.org/papers/w6126

Naudon, A., Pérez, A. (2017), "An Overview of Inflation-Targeting Frameworks: Institutional Arrangements, Decision-Making & the Communication of Monetary Policy", *Banco Central de Chile Working Papers, No. 811*. www.bcentral.cl/es/web/central-bank-of-chile/-/an-overview-of-inflation-targeting-frameworks-institutional-arrangements-decision-making-the-communication-of-monetary-policy

Posen, A. S. (1993), "Why Central Bank Independence Does Not Cause Low Inflation: There Is No Institutional Fix for Politics", in: R. O'Brien (ed.) *Finance and the International Economy*, Oxford University Press, pp. 40–65.

Roger, S. (2010), "Inflation Targeting Turns 20", *Finance and Development*, 47(1), pp. 46–49.

Sterne, G., Stasavage, D., Chortareas, G. (2002), "Does It Pay to Be Transparent? International Evidence From Central Bank Forecasts", *The Federal Reserve Bank of St. Louis Review*, 84(4), pp. 99–118. http://doi.org/10.20955/r.84.99-118

Svensson, L. E. O. (2008), "Inflation Targeting", in: S. N. Durlauf, L. E. Blume (eds.), *The New Palgrave Dictionary of Economics*, 2nd Edition, Vol. 4, Palgrave Macmillan, pp. 319–321.

Svensson, L. E. O. (2009), "Flexible Inflation Targeting—Lessons from the Financial Crisis", *Speech at a Seminar: Towards a New Framework for Monetary Policy?, Lessons from the Crisis*, Netherlands Bank, Amsterdam, 21 September. www.bis.org/review/r090923d.pdf

Svensson, L. E. O. (2010), "Where Do Central Banks Go From Here?", *Panel Discussion, Norges Bank Symposium on "What Is a Useful Central Bank?"*, 18 November.

Walsh, C. E. (2008), "Central Bank Independence", in: S. N. Durlauf, L. E. Blume (eds.) *The New Palgrave Dictionary of Economics*, 2nd Edition, Vol. 1, Palgrave Macmillan, pp. 728–731.

Walsh, C. E. (2019), "Alternatives to Inflation Targeting in Low Interest Rate Environments", *IMES Discussion Paper, No. 2019-E-13*, pp. 1–30.

Yellen, J. L. (2014), "Many Targets, Many Instruments: Where Do We Stand?", in: G. Akerlof, O. Blanchard, D. Romer, J. Stiglitz (eds.), *What Have We Learnt? Macroeconomic Policy after the Crisis*, MIT Press, pp. 31–36.

1

INDICATING THE ORIGINS, ESSENTIAL FEATURES, AND PROSPECTS OF AN INFLATION TARGETING FRAMEWORK

1.1 Introductory remarks

The analysis presented in Chapter 1 encompasses several steps. First, in order to see why price stability became, by far, the basic objective for central banks—which is a crucial aspect not only of an inflation targeting (IT) framework, but also of other strategies—it is helpful to start by outlining the main ideas developed within monetary economics over the past decades. The conclusions that followed from the review of these ideas, to a great extent, influenced the construction of the currently used monetary policy regimes. However, before describing the most common monetary frameworks, the general concept of a monetary policy strategy is introduced. The key role of nominal anchors and institutional set-ups is also briefly analysed as closely related notions. Against this background, an overview of the most typical monetary policy frameworks is presented, together with historical changes in support of the various regimes. This part shows, in particular, how an IT framework has gained popularity over the last 30 years, spreading to many different countries. To understand the reasons behind this phenomenon, the key elements of inflation targeting are considered, by indicating the broad principles that should be treated as IT constituting features, as well as areas where monetary authorities may adjust the framework to their own needs within a range of possible institutional set-ups.

General remarks on the main strengths of inflation targeting, together with its more recent critique, conclude Chapter 1. In particular, lessons for the strategy learnt from the recent crises are investigated. These parts are combined with discussing some ongoing debates on the already applied changes to an IT regime and its possible further evolution.

1.2 Evolution of monetary economics as a basis for developing monetary policy strategies

Before defining the concept of a monetary policy strategy, it is useful to look at the evolution of thinking about monetary policy itself. A broader context is also helpful for understanding the reasons behind the various nominal anchors currently used by central banks that constitute a basis for different types of monetary policy strategies.

At the same time, a comprehensive description of economic theories is not necessary for the purpose of the analysis, so only certain of their elements are recalled. The review is rather brief and underlines the key conclusions stemming from the indicated doctrines, which—unavoidably—does not do justice to many significant caveats and subtleties. The selection of topics follows from assessing their relevance in shaping the way monetary policy has been conducted, whereas the distinction between schools of economic thought is based on Snowdon, Vane, and Wynarczyk (1998).

The review is not comprehensive in terms of covering the whole history of monetary economics, which is a conscious decision motivated by several factors. While already classical economists analysed the relationship between money, prices, and real activity, with many of their ideas having been incorporated into more recently developed models (Steuart, 1767; Hume, 1752), for understanding the current approaches to monetary policy, it seems enough to start with less distant considerations.[1] Moreover, earlier contributions—despite recognising some role of money in periods of short-term imbalances—rather than seeing the need for monetary policy adjustments, emphasised the importance of market forces in restoring a long-run steady state (Hume, 1752; Ricardo, 1951), making them less relevant for modern central banking. This omission is, however, not aimed at disregarding that the origins of the quantity theory of money (expressed already by Martin de Azpilueta Navarro in 1556, and Jean Bodin in 1568—cited after Dimand, 2008, p. 699; extended later by Hume, 1752; Mill, 1848; Fisher, 1911)[2] and of the natural interest rate (formulated by Wicksell, 1898)[3] date back to economists developing their ideas centuries ago.

1.2.1 Keynesianism

It should not be too surprising to begin with ideas proposed by Keynes (1936), who saw the need to use economic policies—though much more fiscal policy compared to monetary policy—for restoring balance in the economy. The main claim of Keynesianism was that in an economy hit by a negative demand shock, the adjustments necessary to bring back full employment were by no means automatic (Wojtyna, 2000, p. 68), which, in the Keynesians' view, became painfully apparent during the Great Depression of the 1930s. Thus, to combat recessions, instead of relying on wage and price deflation, the government and monetary authorities should increase aggregate demand.

From the monetary policy point of view, the key reasoning was that the rising money supply should reduce interest rates, increasing investment and decreasing unemployment, even though this was conditional on a number of

assumptions.[4] However, Keynes believed that declines in the expected marginal productivity of capital during recessions would significantly mute the
response of investment to any reduction in interest rates. In Keynes's opinion, given the limits on acceptable interest rate changes, this made monetary
policy not capable on its own of stimulating the economy (Keynes, 1936,
p. 164, reprinted in 1947). Moreover, Keynes argued that if interest rates
become too low, the demand for money, i.e. liquidity preference, may turn
out to be virtually absolute, resulting in a liquidity trap, where monetary
authorities lose any effective control over interest rates.

At the same time, although cases when the scope for monetary policy
was potentially limited were clearly spelled out, this was not necessarily
equivalent to saying that monetary policy was impotent, as claimed by more
orthodox Keynesians. Overall, economists building on the main ideas of
Keynesianism treated inflation mainly as a cost-push phenomenon, and due
to links between money, interest rates, and income, claimed that in both the
short and the long term money is not neutral.

A formal representation of the Keynesian macroeconomic theory was
proposed by Hicks (1937), and extended by Hansen (1953), as a mathematical IS–LM model.[5] The model produced a Keynesian unemployment
equilibrium only after introducing a number of imperfections to the system,
including rigid prices and wages, interest-inelastic investment demand, or
income-inelastic money demand (Snowdon et al., 1998, pp. 110–111). The
result became known as a neoclassical synthesis that merged the Keynesian
and neoclassical theories.

1.2.2 Neoclassical synthesis

Samuelson (1955)[6] saw the neoclassical synthesis as a combination of the
short-term Keynesian approach and the long-run neoclassical solution. The
short-term part was describing output and unemployment fluctuations as a
consequence of changes in the aggregate demand, amidst rigid prices and
wages, whereas the long-term component was explaining long-term levels
of output and prices by the interactions of demand and supply, leading to a
general equilibrium (Blanchard, 2008, pp. 896–899).

An important extension of the Keynesian approach was offered by
the famous Phillips curve (Phillips, 1958) that, after the interpretation of
Samuelson and Solow (1960), enabled to account for inflation. The original
formulation showed an empirical inverse relationship between the unemployment rate and nominal wage growth. Samuelson and Solow (1960) noted
that with mark-up pricing, and assuming constant productivity growth,
there is a stable relationship between inflation and wage growth. After taking it into account when analysing the Phillips curve, they claimed that there
would be a trade-off—although in the short term—between unemployment
and inflation. Rising aggregate demand would increase employment and

decrease unemployment, but, at the same time, boost inflation (a decline in demand would have the opposite effect). The resulting policy conclusions seemed to be straightforward, since one simply had to choose between different combinations of employment and inflation, for example, accepting somewhat higher inflation in order to see lower unemployment. In such a framework, higher inflation could be treated as the cost of enjoying lower unemployment.

The neoclassical synthesis was highly influential in theoretical, applied, and policy work, and, to a great extent, dominated macroeconomic thinking for many years in the post-war period. Its prescriptions were compelling, with economic policies given a clear sense of direction when aiming at limiting business cycle fluctuations.[7] However, the Keynesian macroeconomics, together with its neoclassical reinterpretation, came under serious critique, when they failed to explain the stagflation[8] processes of the late 1960s and the early 1970s and the consequences of the oil price shocks of the 1970s and 1980s. This was the time when monetarists took the floor.

1.2.3 Monetarism

Monetarism, associated mainly with Friedman (1956), focused on analysing the macroeconomic effects of changing the money supply, and argued that an excessive expansion of money would inevitably lead to higher inflation. Monetarists referred to the quantity theory of money, and believed that fluctuations in economic activity were caused predominantly by the changes in the money supply (Belka, 1986, pp. 96–147; Cagan, 2008, pp. 677–683).

Given the assumption of relatively stable money demand, the reasoning was that changes in the money supply, resulting from monetary policy decisions, were the dominant factor behind developments in nominal incomes and prices. In particular, in the case of a rising money supply, if before the increase the public was already holding money balances to suit its needs, this would create money balance surpluses that would be spent, boosting aggregate demand and translating into higher nominal wages and prices (a decline in the money supply would have the opposite effect). However, changes in the money supply affected nominal incomes with long and variable transmission lags, implying that discretionary monetary policy may exert a destabilising, rather than a stabilising, impact on the economy.

In the monetarists' view, economic instability, including the Great Depression of the 1930s, should be blamed on volatile and unpredictable monetary policy that paid too little attention to money and, in particular, allowed for a massive contraction of the US money supply in the early 1930s (Friedman and Schwartz, 1963, pp. 299–419). To mitigate those unintended effects, monetarists strongly argued for conducting economic policies based on rules, rather than on discretionary choices, and explicitly advocated for making price stability the main goal of monetary policy (Taylor, 2011,

p. 29).[9] At the same time, active demand management via fiscal policy was, in their opinion, likely to be harmful, which followed from the link they saw between fiscal stimulus not only boosting consumption, but also leading to higher interest rates dragging investment.

Moreover, although expectations were indicated as a significant factor affecting economic choices already by Keynes (1936/1947), Friedman emphasised again their role, arguing that people would learn from past experiences, and thus cannot be constantly surprised by higher inflation without demanding higher wages (Friedman, 1968). Assigning an important meaning to the formation of expectations gave rise to the idea of using nominal anchors in monetary policy, i.e. announcing some narrow targets for a given nominal variable, such as money supply growth, inflation rate, or exchange rate (Mishkin, 1999, pp. 1–2; 2007, pp. 12–13). A clear benefit of providing a nominal anchor was that it could be used to reduce uncertainty about the future price level (Mishkin, 2006, p. 5).

Apart from assuming adaptive expectations, another important contribution of monetarists was to note that, unless people were acting entirely and continuously under money illusion, what counted were real, and not nominal, wages—making real variables more important than nominal variables. Those elements were critical in questioning the trade-off between unemployment and inflation, which could only be a short-run phenomenon related to unanticipated inflation. Therefore, an important distinction between a short-run Phillips curve and a long-run Phillips curve was introduced. The short-run Phillips curve was downward sloping, but shifted upward each time inflation expectations rose, whereas the long-run Phillips curve was vertical and showed that regardless of the inflation rate, unemployment always returned to its natural level. The critique of the Phillips curve and defining the natural rate of unemployment, that later evolved into a non-accelerating inflation rate of unemployment (NAIRU), were presented almost simultaneously by Friedman (1968) and Phelps (1967).

High inflation in the 1970s also led to a more vocal recognition of its costs, not least, as it increased uncertainty about relative prices and about future prices, reducing the efficiency of economic decisions. By interacting with the tax system, inflation also introduced additional distortions to the economy. Such observations supported the view that stable prices may, in turn, positively affect resource allocation, possibly leading to higher economic activity (Mishkin, 2006, p. 4).

Monetarists' arguments were instrumental in ending the prevalence of Keynesian macroeconomics and in arguing for a rule-based monetary policy focused on maintaining price stability. As a result, a number of countries started to conduct their monetary policy by targeting monetary aggregates.[10] Monetarists also paved the way for the new classical school that emerged in the 1980s.

1.2.4 New classical school

The natural unemployment rate hypothesis proposed by Friedman (1968) and Phelps (1967) was further formalised by prominent representatives of the new classicals (Sargent et al., 1973; Lucas and Sargent, 1978), who also took a leading role in advocating for including microfoundations and rational expectations into macroeconomics.

Whereas those two concepts, i.e. emphasising the importance of micro-economic foundations and incorporating rational expectations into macro-models, can be seen as the lasting contributions of the new classical economists to economic modelling (Taylor, 2011, pp. 58–60; Woodford, 2003, pp. 10–11), these ideas were not uncontroversial and some of other assumptions and conclusions of the new classicals were even more difficult to accept. In particular, the market was to clear at all times, which meant that, at any time, the economy was to have a unique equilibrium at full employment that was achieved via price and wage adjustments.

The new classicals argued that only unanticipated inflation could lower unemployment, and that the effect would be temporary.[11] That reasoning, combined with the rational expectation hypothesis eliminating the possibility of systematic mistakes, led to the conclusion that policies focused on changing aggregate demand would not have real effects, unless they were unpredictable, meaning erratic, which—by definition—would be destabilising for the economy.

Returning to less controversial ideas, a strong argument in favour of providing microfoundations to the models used for drawing policy conclusions was provided by Lucas (1976). Lucas argued that the correlations between aggregate variables tended to change whenever macroeconomic policy designed to take advantage of them was employed. In turn, assuming that the underlying microeconomic structure of the economy was broadly unaffected by policy shifts, microfounded models should be more appropriate for assessing the probable impact of policies. The famous Lucas critique largely invalidated policy advice derived from large-scale macroeconometric models, since the parameters of those models could not be considered "structural", in a sense of being policy-invariant (Mishkin, 1995, pp. 1–2).

Another important contribution of the new classical school to monetary economics was related to the rational expectation hypothesis, which is commonly associated with the work of Muth (1961), that was further developed, for example, by Lucas (1972) and Sargent and Wallace (1976). In its strong version, the rational expectation hypothesis assumed that economic agents described by a given model know the model, its parameters, and the nature of stochastic processes, and, on average, form their predictions consistently with the model (Sargent, 2008, pp. 877–882). Agents' expectations may, in some cases, be wrong, but over time should be correct, meaning that they should not be systematically biased, and should include only random errors.

20

While rational expectations were used to support the highly disputable conclusion about policy ineffectiveness (Sargent and Wallace, 1975), they have been widely adopted as a useful modelling technique, even outside the new classical macroeconomics, despite rather weak empirical evidence of their validity (Snowdon et al., 1998, p. 346).

The rational expectation hypothesis was also used in the analysis of Kydland and Prescott (1977) on dynamic inconsistency. The authors showed that economic preferences may change over time in such a way that they become inconsistent, resulting in policy being optimal at a given point in time, not being optimal at another point in time. Regarding monetary policy—as noticed and described by Barro and Gordon (1983)—the reasoning would start with a central bank announcing in advance the level of targeted inflation in the future, which economic agents would include in their expectations. Later, taking into account that unanticipated inflation may in the short term lead to higher output and lower unemployment, the central bank would be tempted to produce an inflationary surprise, despite its previous announcements. If agents learn that, and assuming that they act under rational expectations they cannot be constantly surprised, the outcome would simply be higher inflation and no gains in output, because inflation expectations would start to incorporate the expected subsequent monetary expansion. Thus, discretionary policy would bring suboptimal results, which was a very strong point for eliminating discretion in designing monetary policy.

Overall, the new classical school significantly changed the technical approach to modern macroeconomics, i.e. to economic modelling.[12] At the same time, its assumptions on a continuous market clearing and policy ineffectiveness were highly problematic, not least in explaining business cycle fluctuations. This is where the real business cycle school entered in the 1980s. Some authors have treated it as an extension of the new classical school (Fischer, 2008, pp. 17–22), while for others, it has already formed a separate economic theory (Snowdon et al., 1998, pp. 248–300).

1.2.5 Real business cycle school

Kydland and Prescott (1982), as the new classical economists of the real business cycle school, argued that business cycle fluctuations were caused by changes in productivity. In other words, this meant that cyclical upswings and downswings in output and employment resulted from permanent real, i.e. supply, shocks.

The general idea was that the economy experienced real shocks, with technological changes, including innovations, thought to be the most typical shocks that directly impacted capital or labour effectiveness. This, in turn, affected consumption–investment decisions and work–leisure tradeoffs, eventually translating into shifts in output. Since changes in technology were likely to come in waves, causing a series of positive and negative productivity shocks,[13] the resulting output fluctuations might be characterised by some persistence, which is typical for business cycles.[14]

The key element of the real business cycle theory was its assumption that business cycles were an equilibrium real phenomenon, resulting from the optimal responses of economic agents to exogenous shocks, given the structure of the economy. Under such an approach, the level of output necessarily maximised expected utility, with no room for fiscal or monetary stabilising policies. According to the real business cycle school, macroeconomic policies should rather focus on long-run structural factors.

One of the problematic issues related to the real business cycle theory was the treatment of money. Kydland and Prescott (1982) used only real variables in their analysis, but given a clear positive correlation between money and output, with money being a leading indicator (Sims, 1972), some extensions of the real business cycle models were proposed. King and Plosser (1984) incorporated money as a product of the banking sector that was expanding when the real activity was expanding to facilitate the growing number of transactions (when the real activity was declining, the opposite effect was to be observed), claiming that money was endogenous. Other attempts undertaken to account for the co-movement of money and output included introducing cash-in-advance constraint (Clower, 1967), or a money-in-the-utility-function concept (Sidrauski, 1967), but they were not allowing monetary shocks to significantly affect output.

The notions of policy ineffectiveness and the neutrality of money stood in sharp contrast with recessions observed in the early 1980s that resulted from disinflationary policies pursued in the United Kingdom and the United States. Those events, combined with high unemployment persisting in Europe in the 1980s and 1990s, gave grounds for developing the new Keynesian macroeconomics that, in comparison to the real business cycle school, put much more emphasis on the nominal side of the economy.

1.2.6 New Keynesian economics

The new Keynesian economics was to provide microfoundations to the Keynesian models and, in this way, address the main critique raised against Keynesianism by the new classical economists. Its constituting element was to allow for a number of market failures, such as imperfect competition, price stickiness, or wage rigidity, while assuming the rational expectation hypothesis.

Similarly to the previous Keynesian macroeconomic theories, the new Keynesian economics distinguished between a short-term and a long-term perspective, claiming that in the long run all prices should be regarded as perfectly flexible and the economy should be reaching an equilibrium— a notion to which the new classical school also subscribes. However, the macroeconomists' views on the short run diverged significantly.[15] The original contribution of the new Keynesian economics was to incorporate the rational expectation hypothesis into the framework, but, at the same time, to provide an explanation—based on microfoundations—for the presence of nominal rigidities in the short run. Thus, the assumption of perfect competition with price-taking agents was replaced with the assumption of imperfect competition with price-setting agents (Dixon, 2008, pp. 40–44).

The new idea of price-setting agents was developed within various models, including the approach based on menu costs (Sheshinski and Weiss, 1977; Mankiw, 1985; Akerlof and Yellen, 1985), the Calvo staggered pricing model (Calvo, 1983), and the Taylor contracts (Taylor, 1979).[16] Menu cost models pointed to the costs of changing prices, which may be thought of as the cost of deciding on the price change and its implementation. The presence of these costs implied that firms were not willing to change prices unless the benefit of such a move was not small, leading to an inertia in nominal price setting. While the menu cost approach initially focused on prices, it was extended to wages by Blanchard and Kiyotaki (1985). In turn, the Calvo pricing model assumed that in each period any given firm faced a constant probability of resetting its price with the probability being independent of the time that had elapsed since the previous price change. Such a price-setting process resulted in uncertainty about how long the price would remain in place and meant that the response of prices to shocks was spread over time. As a consequence, after any finite time, some proportion of prices would remain unchanged, which distinguished Calvo pricing from Taylor contracts, where a fixed length for contracts was assumed, and thus, after a specified period all prices were replaced.

The conclusion that was drawn from the new Keynesian economics indicated that the economy may fail to maintain full employment. Therefore, there may be a need for employing macroeconomic policies to stabilise output fluctuations, which would provide a more superior outcome than a *laissez faire* approach. This spoke in favour of a more active use of monetary policy to address developments in the real economy.

1.2.7 New neoclassical synthesis

In the 1990s, the new Keynesian approach was combined with the ideas stemming from the real business cycle school to form a new neoclassical synthesis. Some authors have been treating it as a separate school, while others have been analysing it as an extension of the new Keynesian economics (Kokoszczyński, 2004, pp. 44–45). The key features of the new neoclassical synthesis included the assumption of the long-run neutrality of money and acknowledging short-run nominal rigidities and imperfect competition.[17] Its models were fully dynamic and microfounded (Dixon, 2008, p. 40).

One of the building blocks of the new models was the new Keynesian Phillips curve, originally proposed by Roberts (1995). It could be derived from Calvo or Taylor models of pricing and explained inflation with the help of a current output gap and expected inflation in the next period. The modified version of the curve reflected the fact that the price setting process was believed to be forward looking, meaning that it was not only influenced by current inflation and current output, but also by the expectations of future inflation. Empirically, however, lagged inflation was also found relevant in the equation, resulting in a specification known as the hybrid Phillips curve (Galí and Gertler, 1999).[18]

Another crucial element of the new neoclassical synthesis was the Taylor rule, used to describe how nominal interest rates were set by central banks in response to changes in inflation, output, and other macroeconomic conditions (Taylor, 1993).[19] The original equation explained a short-term nominal interest rate with the divergence of actual inflation from the targeted level and the divergence of actual output from the potential output, as well as the assumed equilibrium real interest rate. Taylor stressed that the rule would stabilise inflation under certain conditions. The property implying that nominal interest rates should be raised by more than one percentage point for each one percentage point increase in inflation, resulting in higher real interest rates, is often called the Taylor principle (Woodford, 2001).[20]

The new Keynesian Phillips curve and the Taylor rule were used as parts of the new Keynesian dynamic stochastic general equilibrium (DSGE) models, built to analyse monetary policy.[21] Such a formulation, complemented with a dynamic IS curve, was proposed as a simple three-equation new Keynesian model that could be found, for example, in Clarida et al. (1999).

More generally, DSGE models have three parts based on microfoundations that are interrelated: a supply block describing the optimal behaviour of firms, a demand block describing the optimal behaviour of households, and a monetary policy equation (Galí, 2008).[22] The construction of the models followed from viewing the monetary policy reaction function as an element closing the model, and allowed for a complete description of relationships between the key variables: inflation, output, and nominal interest rates.

Within such a system, monetary policy was thought to play a stabilising role, and interest rates were the only instrument used (Woodford, 2003, pp. 24–37). This was a significant change, since traditionally the analysis of output response to monetary policy shocks related to output shifts driven by stochastic shocks to the money supply.[23] Recognising that monetary policy should be seen as reacting systematically with interest rates to the state of the economy was, in that respect, a valuable contribution of the new neoclassical synthesis. To a great extent, it was possible owing to research examining how various endogenous monetary policy rules performed within DSGE models (Christiano et al., 2018).[24]

The main claim of the new approach was to allow monetary policy to affect output in the short run, but to treat money as neutral in the long run, with no long-run trade-offs between inflation and output. At the same time, using expansive monetary policy to achieve short-run gains in output was not considered advisable, as it would simply result in higher inflation expectations. Instead, monetary policy should be used as a stabilisation tool when the economy was hit by a major shock, to try to offset its macroeconomic effects. This was especially true in the case of demand shocks when the direction of output and inflation changes were the same.

In general, with rational expectations assumed to be valid and inflation viewed as having negative welfare effects, it was advised that central banks maintain credibility through rule-based policy. This corroborated the intuitions behind inflation targeting, which entered central banking in the 1990s and gained more and more supporters. More or less concurrently, the Great Moderation followed.[25]

1.2.8 Crisis-related considerations

The Great Moderation indisputably ended with the outbreak of the global financial crisis of 2008, which—with respect to monetary economics—resulted in increased interest in several topics that, previously, were not at the centre of mainstream discussions. Among the most vital considerations from the central banks' point of view were secular stagnation and flattening the Phillips curve. These two issues, which deal with the concept of the natural interest rate and the trade-off between inflation and output, touched upon ideas that are essential for the effectiveness of monetary policy.

The term secular stagnation, which describes a state of negligible or zero economic growth, and—as a consequence—of a very low natural interest rate, can be attributed to Hansen (1939), who used it to analyse the long-term outlook for the United States in the late 1930s. Given the subsequent dominance of the Keynesian approach to macroeconomic policies resulting in an economic upswing, followed by the widespread views of the new classical macroeconomists denying the possibility of even short-term demand shortages, making a theoretical case for secular stagnation was, at that time, difficult (Backhouse and Boianovsky, 2016).

The muted response of aggregate demand to interest rate cuts after the outbreak of the global financial crisis, combined with weaker than expected inflation pressures in the main economies in the recovery phase, led the discussions on secular stagnation to resurface. Summers (2014) argued that the Wicksellian natural rate of interest could have fallen even to a negative territory,[26] thus—due to the limit on how low nominal interest rates can be (the so-called zero lower bound—ZLB),[27] and given persistently low inflation—the real rates may turn out to be permanently too high to permit the balancing of saving and investment at full employment.

And, indeed, looking at long-term real interest rates as a simple proxy for the natural rate of interest, these have been gradually declining since the Great Moderation period (IMF, 2014, p. 106; Blanchard and Summers, 2019, p. xxiii). While there are also less alarming voices, seeing no imminent risk of secular stagnation (Eichengreen, 2014), for monetary policy, the possibility of the natural interest rate declining to very low levels means that hitting the ZLB becomes more likely (Krugmann, 2014; Blanchard et al., 2014b).[28]

Regarding the Phillips curve, the renewed inquiries about the strength of the relationship between unemployment and inflation have been the result of two observations. First, a "missing disinflation" episode was recorded in 2009–2011, i.e. rather resilient price dynamics at the time of a severe economic downturn following the outbreak of the global financial crisis (Friedrich, 2016). Later, a "missing inflation" puzzle was noted, especially in the euro area after 2012, i.e. subdued price pressures at a time of already robust recovery fuelled by strongly expansionary monetary policy (Constâncio, 2015).

Several studies showed that the slope of the Phillips curve, indeed, decreased over the previous decades (Blanchard et al., 2015; Galí, 2015; Szafranek, 2017). A firmer anchoring of inflation expectations due to more credible monetary policy could partly explain that phenomenon (Bernanke, 2010; IMF, 2013, p. 94), being a positive development.[29] In turn, the flattening understood as the weaker responsiveness of prices to movements in activity for any given level of expected inflation has not been a reassuring finding,[30] since it meant that controlling inflation became more difficult.[31] In particular, again, in the case of excessively low price growth, when strong monetary stimulus is needed, the low sensitivity of inflation to shifts in demand may result in monetary authorities hitting the ZLB more often. This should translate into more pronounced reactions from central banks to changing economic conditions.

Thus, both secular stagnation and the flattening of the Phillips curve would imply a higher risk of confronting the ZLB. The significance of that threat hugely depends on whether the indicated problems prove to be temporary or permanent. Judging by the current discussions that, to a significant extent, are dominated by analysing ways to cope with the ZLB, central banks—especially in advanced economies—treat these topics very seriously.

Currently, another widely debated topic—discussed in more detail later—is how to define the role of financial stability in monetary policy considerations. Contrary to what was quite a widespread belief before the crises, maintaining price and output stability turned out to be an insufficient condition to promote financial stability (Mishkin, 2011, p. 29; Wojtyna, 2013, pp. 167–170). In fact, the Great Moderation period could have even encouraged more hazardous behaviour, what became known as a risk-taking channel of monetary policy. The arguments for such a view include arguing that a low interest rate environment fosters search-for-yield activities, leading to an overly optimistic valuation of incomes and cash flows, and favours the expansion of banks' balance sheets (through leverage and collateralised borrowing). As a result, the risk-taking channel might have contributed to the creation of excessive credit (Rajan, 2006; Borio and Zhu, 2008; Boivin et al., 2010).

The main lesson drawn from the crises has been that credit-driven booms should be counteracted. However, this is not necessarily the same as saying that monetary policy on its own should counteract them (Mishkin, 2011, pp. 39–41; Stracca, 2018, pp. 87–88). The key arguments against extending the goals of monetary policy are related to a possible trade-off between maintaining price and output stability and pursuing financial stability, which may weaken central banks' credibility. At the same time, monetary authorities are, in many respects, well suited to safeguarding macroeconomic stability in a broader sense, especially since they typically enjoy a high degree of independence. The resulting proposal that has been offered in the literature consists of strengthening financial supervision and developing macroprudential policies with, at least, the leading role in these two areas assigned to the central bank (Borio, 2011a, p. 12; Mishkin, 2011, p. 47; Sławiński, 2011, pp. 64–65).

1.2.9 Policy recommendations stemming from monetary economics

After the short overview of the evolution of monetary economics, it is useful to summarise the main policy recommendations stemming from the described theories. The most general point would probably be that the final goal of economic policies, at least since Keynesianism, has been seen in sustainably stabilising the economy at a possibly high level of employment. However, there have been differing opinions as to what that notion precisely meant, with some economists not seeing much scope for an effective support of self-regulating market forces.

In the context of monetary policy, the key conclusions that could be drawn from monetary economics have been that there was no long-run trade-off between output and inflation, and that inflation was costly. Most theories have also recognised the consequences of expectations responding to monetary policy decisions and emphasised that this was critical for the emergence of the time-inconsistency problem faced by central banks. They, in turn, have spoken in favour of conducting monetary policy in line with rules or using strong nominal anchors (Mishkin, 2006, p. 1).[32]

Considering the above observations and the recent debates, nowadays the mainstream view seems to see room for using monetary policy to offset shocks hitting an economy, taking into account both their real and nominal effects, and associating significant cost to high and to excessively low inflation. In a more traditional approach, this would simply mean that monetary policy should focus on providing price stability, at best in such a way as to mitigate output fluctuations (Clarida et al., 1999). By doing this, it will add to the overall stability of the economy. Since maintaining price stability proved not to be a sufficient condition for safeguarding financial stability, in more current discussions, what has been argued is the need to broaden central banks' mandates by including financial stability as another goal for monetary authorities. However, recognising the limitations of monetary policy, extending the mandates of central banks can be seen rather as assigning monetary authorities an additional task that requires a separate set of instruments (Taylor, 2011, pp. 136–138). Irrespective of the ongoing disputes, the most general point that should be uncontroversial for most economists is that monetary policy should serve as a stabilising tool—either in a narrower or a broader sense, depending on whether one also considers financial stability as a monetary policy goal.

These conclusions have been reflected in the monetary policy strategies currently used by central banks. In particular, they have been incorporated into an inflation targeting framework.

1.3 Defining the concept of a monetary policy strategy and its institutional set-ups

Regarding the definition of a monetary policy strategy, as with almost any concept developed within economics, various formulations are possible and no agreement on a specific definition has been reached. In general, a strategy should provide guidance to monetary authorities on how to use policy instruments in order to achieve the final goals (Duwendag et al., 1995, p. 282). In slightly more technical terms, it can also be described as a central bank's reaction function and its communication with the public, together with transparency about the decision-making process (Houben, 2000, p. 2).[33] Taking yet another angle (Borio, 2001, p. 2), a strategy can be seen as a set of central bank objectives (including the final goals, such as price stability or long-term growth) and intermediate targets (such as exchange rates, money, or asset prices). According to Grostal et al. (2016, pp. 12–13), it also includes operating targets (such as short-term money market rates) and monetary policy instruments (such as official interest rates or required reserves) used to reach the specified goals.[34] Thus, it is possible to distinguish between narrower and broader definitions.

To see the full complexity of the basic ideas related to monetary policy, it is also worth looking at different monetary policy rules, listing possible nominal anchors, and noting the importance of various institutional arrangements, as notions closely linked to the concept of a monetary policy strategy.

1.3.1 Monetary policy rules

When considering the essence of monetary policy frameworks, Svensson (1998, 2002) distinguishes between three types of rules that, to some extent, can be regarded as concepts corresponding to monetary strategies. The approach applied by Svensson has been fairly unorthodox, especially when compared with a more traditional use of the term monetary policy rule, but is currently present in the literature (Bénassy-Quéré et al., 2019, pp. 306–307).

The first set of rules encompasses instrument rules, i.e. rules that specify a function governing the changes in monetary policy instruments based on a predetermined (explicit rules) or forward-looking (implicit rules) set of variables, such as inflation and output. However, it is difficult to think about any simple rule that would be able to provide clear and undisputable monetary policy recommendations valid at all times.[35] Thus, the second category of rules—much more plausible—includes targeting rules, i.e. rules advising central banks to minimise a given loss function, by weighting the relevant objectives, such as, again, inflation and output, but this time referred to the specified target values. This approach allows the possible trade-offs between the central banks' goals to be taken into account. The third option—also much more feasible than instrument rules—are intermediate-target rules, i.e. rules according to which monetary authorities try to steer variables that are strongly correlated with their ultimate goals, but which are easier for central banks to control and for that reason may be treated as reasonable intermediate targets.

An example of an instrument rule includes the Taylor rule (Taylor, 1993) that provides a formula for setting a short-term interest rate based on inflation and an output gap estimate. Whereas it is a compelling concept, and, at times, a valuable reference point, it would be difficult to find a central bank that is mechanically following prescriptions given by the Taylor rule. Not least, as an output gap is an unobservable variable whose estimates are subject to considerable uncertainty and revisions. Moreover, it is rather widely accepted that the reaction of monetary policy to shocks should depend on their nature and strength, influencing, among others, shocks' persistence and propagation. Thus, even with a given level of inflation and of output gap, the response of monetary authorities should not always be the same. Put differently, it is far from obvious what the proper monetary policy decision should be, looking at only the two variables.

Another important example of an instrument rule, at least from a historical perspective, is the so-called k-percent rule, proposed by Friedman (1960). It stipulates that monetary authorities should keep a constant growth rate of the money supply, regardless of changing economic conditions (Belka, 1986). The rule is supposed to prevent central banks from introducing disruptive monetary shocks into the economy (White, 1999, pp. 219–222). Other benefits of the rule are to include simplicity, predictability, and credibility in monetary policy, which, indeed, are hard to deny considering the publicly known rule, which leaves little or no scope for modifications. Similarly to the case of the Taylor rule, these apparent advantages are, however, not enough to compensate for the fact that strict policy rules are not accounting for the complexity of the economy and the resulting necessity to consider a lot of factors when conducting monetary policy. For these reasons, the k-percent rule has never been implemented in practice.

In turn, the most prominent example of a targeting rule is inflation targeting, with the loss function typically based on a squared deviation of inflation from the inflation target, and a squared deviation of output from the potential output (Svensson, 1998, pp. 14–15). Compared to instrument rules, targeting rules provide more room for judgement and discretion in making monetary policy decisions, but, at the same time, introduce transparency with respect to the central banks' objectives, directly indicating the potential trade-offs between them. In the case of inflation targeting, it can be quite accurately summarised as a "constrained discretion" (Bernanke and Mishkin, 1997, p. 10).[36] As described by Bernanke (2003), constrained discretion is an approach that allows monetary authorities to conduct monetary policy based on a subjective assessment of all relevant developments, such as economic shocks or financial disturbances, but recognising the need to establish a strong commitment to low and stable inflation. As a result, the trade-off between high employment and price stability should be mitigated, leading to better outcomes along both dimensions, i.e. resulting in limited cyclical fluctuations without scarifying low inflation. This may be the reason behind the still high support for an inflation targeting framework.

Other examples of targeting rules include price-level targeting.[37] The framework assumes that the main aim of monetary authorities would be to stabilise the level of prices around a specified path. The biggest difference compared to inflation targeting is that price-level targeting, in practice, requires that any temporary deviation of inflation from the target would have to be reverted. In turn, nominal gross domestic product (GDP) targeting, which is also often discussed together with price-level targeting as an alternative to IT, was classified by Svensson (1998) as an intermediate-target rule. This approach is based on targeting a given path of nominal GDP, which means that monetary policy would have to be loosened if nominal output is below the targeted value, irrespective of whether it is driven by too low inflation or by too low real GDP growth (the opposite monetary policy reaction would be needed if nominal output is above the targeted value).[38] While these strategies have received a lot of attention, especially in the aftermath of the recent crises, so far they have remained rather theoretical options, partly due to the practical difficulties of implementing them.[39]

A typical example of an intermediate-target rule includes monetary targeting, advocated most strongly in the 1970s and 1980s. It postulates that monetary policy should rely on information derived from changes in monetary aggregates, and announce medium-term targets for the money supply. Introducing targets should provide incentives for central banks to avoid systematic, large deviations from the announced targets, fostering the use of an accountability mechanism (Miskhin, 2006, p. 5). The key advantage of this approach is that data on changes in monetary aggregates are available with only a short lag and, by conveying signals on the monetary policy stance, could be actively used to influence expectations. Looking at the past experiences of the biggest economies with monetary targeting, it seems that not all of them made full use of that element (Grostal and Niedźwiedzińska, 2019, pp. 16–18).[40] Moreover, not least due to financial innovations, in many countries it became clear, especially in the 1980s and 1990s, that a stable relationship between money and inflation no longer held. However, monetary targeting is still in use, although almost never in its pure form. Nowadays, most countries officially declaring to be monetary targeters are simultaneously conducting a policy of stabilising their exchange rate, which could be called an eclectic strategy.[41]

Exchange rate targeting can be regarded as another example of a widely used intermediate-target rule. Under exchange rate targeting, monetary authorities focus on stabilising the nominal exchange rate against a specific currency or a basket of selected currencies at the preannounced level, with the use of foreign exchange (FX) interventions or interest rate changes. As long as an inflexible exchange rate arrangement is credible, which crucially depends on a number of factors, such as the country's competitiveness and its institutional and legislative frameworks, it can effectively stabilise the value of the domestic currency. This, in turn, should reduce inflation expectations and deliver price stability, since typically exchange rates are pegged to the currencies of low-inflation countries. Therefore, exchange rate targeting can simply be seen as a way to import monetary policy credibility from abroad. Its major disadvantage includes, however, the loss of monetary policy autonomy. This strategy still has many followers, mostly within smaller economies, although less numerous than in the past.

1.3.2 Nominal anchors

Examples of actually implemented monetary policy rules, i.e. inflation targeting, monetary targeting, and exchange rate targeting, indicate that all of them are built around some kind of a nominal anchor. In the case of inflation targeting, the announced numerical inflation target is the nominal anchor. In a monetary targeting regime, the announced growth of monetary aggregates serves this purpose. In turn, exchange rate targeting is based on the announced level of exchange rate against another currency or a basket of currencies. As already signalled, there are also cases of combining various nominal anchors, which can be regarded as eclectic frameworks.

Moreover, it is possible to distinguish a monetary policy regime which is using an implicit rather than an explicit nominal anchor. As of relatively recently, the United States was mentioned as a prominent example of a country employing such an approach (Mishkin, 1999, pp. 27–30); however, in

2012 the US Federal Reserve announced an explicit numerical longer-run goal for inflation. Although, prior to 2012, in many respects the US monetary policy framework was similar to inflation targeting, without announcing the desired inflation level it lacked the key ingredient of an IT regime and was sometimes described as a "just-do-it" strategy (Mishkin, 1999, pp. 27–30) or a discretionary regime. Currently, no major central bank follows a strategy that would not make use of an explicit nominal anchor.

As already mentioned, the main benefit of announcing a relatively narrow target for a given nominal variable stems from the fact that it influences the formation of inflation expectations. Technically speaking, a nominal anchor uniquely determines the price level (Mishkin, 1999, p. 1). In a broader sense, it can also be regarded as a way to mitigate the time-inconsistency problem, because publicly known nominal anchors pose a constraint on monetary policy discretion. In fact, nominal anchors can be seen as intermediate targets, because they can be compared to the actual outcomes of the conducted policy, making monetary authorities accountable for their actions. The features of nominal anchors that are important in that respect are predominantly their measurability (including availability with a relatively short lag) and a close link to the final goal.

Overall, although nominal anchors can take many forms, the ultimate reason for employing them is to ensure price stability in the economy. Due to their key role in monetary policy, the term strategy is often understood as being equivalent to the notion of a nominal anchor (Grostal et al., 2016, p. 12).

1.3.3 Institutional set-ups

Treating the terms "strategy", "framework", and "regime" as close synonyms when referring to monetary policy, a particularly useful definition of these concepts is provided by Cottarelli and Giannini (1997, p. 1). The authors understand monetary frameworks as publicly announced basic principles and institutional rules that guide the conduct of monetary policy. The explicit emphasis put on institutional aspects should reflect their importance for the success of any monetary policy regime (Siklos, 2002, pp. 196–200).

Most generally, institutions can be seen as the rules of the game in a society (North, 1990, p. 3). In the context of central banking, institutional set-ups may encompass a number of rules related to pursuing monetary policy, such as formulating the final objective of a monetary authority, governing monetary policy decision-making processes, or setting accountability and transparency requirements. While at first the notion of institutional rules may sound a bit vague, a key concept that is closely associated with it, and that has received a lot of attention in monetary economics, is monetary policy credibility (Wojtyna, 1998, pp. 10–48).

Bordo and Siklos (2014, p. 4) define credibility as a commitment to act according to well-defined and transparent rules and policy goals. Blinder

(1999, p. 4) claims that a central bank is credible if the public believes that it would do what it communicated. A somewhat more precise definition is provided by Mackiewicz-Łyziak (2010, p. 12), who assesses central bank credibility based on whether economic agents have trust in the monetary authorities' determination and ability to deliver the previously announced objectives.

While these formulations differ slightly from each other, in all of them a central bank's reputation is based on its ability to convince the public that monetary policy decisions would be taken in line with the past promises. What is worth noticing is that it is not necessarily equivalent to delivering the intended outcomes. Whereas some authors do point to the benefits of positive track records for enhancing credibility, building expectations via communication is always stressed as essential for establishing a reputation (Bénassy-Quéré et al., 2010, p. 309).

The reason for not treating the actual outcomes of monetary policy as equivalent to credibility is, among others, the presence of uncertainty and the occurrence of unanticipated shocks that may impede delivering the goals. Of course, meeting the objectives significantly strengthens credibility, but there may be material obstacles that prevent central banks from keeping their promises or the costs of keeping such promises could be exceptionally high. In such cases, deviating from past commitments may be advisable, but, at the same time, monetary authorities must take action to protect their reputation, for example, by making use of accountability and transparency mechanisms. Therefore, as already noted, accountability and transparency may be seen as important components of a central bank's institutional set-up. Other institutional arrangements may also be of significance for building trust in a central bank. As Bordo and Siklos (2014, pp. 5–6) notice, institutional rules related, among others, to central banks' mandates, governance, and autonomy, are key determinants of credibility.

The reputation of monetary authorities is important, since it may have an impact on the formation of inflation expectations, which is crucial for maintaining price stability, and thus delivering the final objective of monetary policy (Bofinger, 2001, p. 200). These interdependencies have been discussed in the economic literature ever since arguments related to the dynamic-inconsistency problem, and the resulting inflationary bias, were noticed (Kydland and Prescott, 1977; Barro and Gordon, 1983).

The typically proposed solutions mitigating a potential inflationary bias of monetary policy included making central banks follow non-contingent rules, appointing a Rogoff conservative central banker (Rogoff, 1985), or preparing optimal contracts between political and monetary authorities providing incentives for delivering the agreed goals (Walsh, 1995).[42] Some mechanical rules, which in the past were considered useful in conducting monetary policy, were discussed earlier, together with their main strengths and weaknesses. As already noted, their clear limitations make them an infeasible option. Moving to the second idea, i.e. to select a conservative central banker, while this has not been reflected in the legal requirements on the appointment of governors, some tendency towards choosing candidates with anti-inflationary convictions can, in fact, be noticed (Bénassy-Quéré et al., 2010, p. 310). The reasoning behind it, provided by Rogoff (1985), is that an inflationary bias should be reduced if monetary policy is conducted by a central banker who puts more weight on inflation stabilisation versus employment stabilisation than indicated by the social preference.[43] In turn, incentive contracts that are the third option to choose from in order to reduce an inflationary bias, should foresee the negative consequences for central banks' officials if they do not reach their objectives or, in general, conduct monetary policy in an unsatisfactory way (Walsh, 1995). This solution is rarely practised, and, in fact, the only often-cited case is New Zealand, which—however—stopped being a good example of such an approach in early 2019 due to changes in the bank's institutional set-up.[44] Prior to that date, each new governor of the Reserve Bank of New Zealand signed a contract with the government,[45] agreeing on the monetary policy objectives and acknowledging that he may be dismissed for reasons related directly to his duties.[46] On the surface, this may have seemed quite fair; however, assessing the performance of the governor is far from straightforward, not least because *ex ante* and *ex post* conclusions may be very different.

Overall, all of the proposals for limiting an inflationary bias can be regarded as being related to monetary authorities' independence (Briault et al., 1996, p. 9), which is another keyword associated with the institutional set-ups of central banks. Various aspects of central banks' autonomy and the reasons why it is important will be discussed later, but what should be noticed by now is that the degree of independence affects monetary authorities' reputation, and, in the end, possibly also the ability to influence expectations.

Thus, institutional arrangements, via influencing such aspects of monetary policy as, among others, its independence, accountability, transparency, and, ultimately, credibility, create an environment in which meeting the final goals may be easier or—on the contrary—more difficult. As a consequence, there are good reasons for treating them as important complements to the concept of a monetary policy strategy.

1.4 Most common monetary policy strategies used by central banks

As discussed when introducing the key elements related to the notion of a monetary policy strategy, several options are available regarding the choice of a monetary framework. Their popularity can be, to a great extent, explained by the changing views on the right model of monetary economics. For example, a growing support for monetarism was an important factor promoting monetary targeting in the 1970s. It is also worth noting that some regimes have remained rather theoretical concepts. That group encompasses regimes based not only on strict instrument rules, but also on several frameworks classified as targeting rules, such as price-level targeting, and intermediate-targeting rules, such as nominal GDP targeting. At times, they are actively discussed, but so far without reaching the critical point of being adopted into practice.[47]

Considering strategies that have gained a wider application, it is clear that each of them has its advantages and disadvantages that need to be weighed against each other. Some monetary policy regimes require more preconditions than others to work properly, and this needs to be considered before adopting a given framework. It is therefore interesting to see the recent trends in the use of various monetary policy strategies. This will also be helpful in assessing whether they can be regarded as feasible alternatives to each other.

1.4.1 Historical background

In order to analyse the choices of different monetary policy strategies, it is reasonable to look at the period starting in the early 1970s. Before that date, international settlements were governed by rules established within the Bretton Woods system, including the convertibility of the US dollar into gold. Under such circumstances, the only country that could conduct a quite independent monetary policy was the United States, while other participating economies simply kept fixed exchange rates against the US dollar.[48] The Bretton Woods system was adopted by the United States, Canada, Western Europe, Australia, and Japan, meaning that it applied to all of the main economies except the Soviet Union block. The rest of the countries employed monetary policies aimed, in practical terms, at earning high government revenues from an inflationary tax (Fry et al., 2000, pp. 4–6).

The collapse of the Bretton Woods system in the early 1970s marked a period of monetary instability in many countries, especially since soon afterwards the oil shocks hit the world. In the United States, where reminiscences of the Great Depression were still shaping policies, monetary policy was, at least until the mid-1970s, conducted with the aim to reach full employment (Bordo, 2008, p. 717). Regarding the rest of the world, some countries decided to adopt floating exchange rate regimes, while others—like the Western European economies—continued with a fixed exchange rate regime. In the case of Western Europe, even though it was against the initial idea, the system of mutually pegged exchange rates was soon dominated by the central role of the German currency. In turn, in Germany, the recollections of hyperinflation episodes were influencing the choice of monetary policy priorities, which was therefore much more concerned with inflation (Kokoszczyński, 2004, p. 75).

Around the mid-1970s, together with the growing popularity of the monetarists' arguments advocating a rule-based monetary policy focused

35

exclusively on maintaining price stability as a remedy for high inflation, a number of countries—including Canada, Germany, Switzerland, the United Kingdom, and the United States—started to formally announce their intended monetary targets (Mishkin, 2006, pp. 5–6).[49]

The 1980s was a testing time for monetary targeting, which for Germany and Switzerland was a rather successful undertaking, whereas for Canada, the United Kingdom, and the United States much less so. As already signalled, the approach of monetary targeters to the strategy was not uniform, which, to a significant extent, can explain the different experiences with that policy framework (Mishkin, 2006, pp. 6–11). The successful monetary targeters extensively used the new policy as a communication tool and emphasised long-term considerations related to controlling inflation. At the same time, while they conducted a rather flexible policy, allowing for periods of overshooting the targets, these overshootings were subsequently reversed. In turn, the less successful monetary targeters did not reverse overshootings, artificially lowered the growth rate of targeted monetary aggregates, did not announce their intentions regularly, and targeted various monetary aggregates. All these elements might have weakened the credibility of the strategy. It is worth stressing that none of the countries considered here was driven by monetarist orthodoxy, understood as applying a Friedman-type rule of keeping the money supply growth constant.

However, by the late 1980s, the measurement of the money supply became increasingly problematic due to financial innovations which also meant that the link between monetary aggregates and inflation could no longer be relied on (Bordo, 2008, p. 718). Thus, monetary targeting stopped gaining support and a new applicable strategy was needed. In parallel, recognising the rational expectation hypothesis together with identifying dynamic-inconsistency issues, spoke in favour of monetary regimes that would provide a strong nominal anchor influencing expectations. As a result, at the turn of the 1980s and 1990s, a direct use of the announced numerical target for inflation was tried, with quite an encouraging outcome.

As already signalled, inflation targeting was first introduced in New Zealand[50] as a pragmatic solution to the country's problem of persistently elevated inflation,[51] and despite—or maybe because of—its apparent simplicity, at least on a basic conceptual level, it proved very successful. Since then, over the last 30 years, many other advanced and emerging market economies have become inflation targeters, and other countries are officially announcing preparatory steps to adopt IT in the future.

In many cases, reaching for an IT framework, especially in the initial years, was a decision taken under crisis circumstances—like the European exchange rate mechanism (ERM) crisis of 1992, the Asian currency crisis of 1997–1998, the Czech currency crisis of 1997, and the Latin America financial crisis of 1998. More recently—although there are still exceptions to that rule[52]—adopting an IT strategy is the final stage in a longer preparation process rather than a crisis solution. And, indeed, sometimes it requires considerable time to meet institutional arrangements, build up forecasting capacities, and develop communication tools needed to become a fully fledged inflation targeter. Nevertheless, the effort seems worth it, as almost no country that adopted an IT regime has ever decided to change it for another monetary policy strategy.[53]

1.4.2 Main types of monetary policy strategies

Judging by the regimes that have been used in the recent past and currently, only a few alternatives are considered as most useful—exchange rate targeting, monetary targeting, inflation targeting, and eclectic or discretionary strategies. Since different options are presented only to put the increasing popularity of an IT framework into a broader context, these are summarised rather briefly below (Table 1.1).[54]

Starting with exchange rate targeting, it refers to monetary policy frameworks that use the exchange rate as a nominal anchor. Regarding the choice of the reference currency or the basket of currencies, it is typically based on selecting the most significant trading partner with an established low-inflation reputation. This type of strategy has many variants, depending on how strongly the domestic currency is supposed to be tightened to the reference currency or the basket of currencies. Some arrangements mean fixing the exchange rate at a given level, some set-ups allow for fluctuations within a limited range, and some frameworks are designed to introduce gradual adjustments to the exchange rate level.[55] In that respect, there seems to be a trade-off between the flexibility of the exchange rate arrangement and

Table 1.1 Main characteristics of exchange rate targeting, monetary targeting, and inflation targeting

	Exchange rate targeting	Monetary targeting	Inflation targeting
Final goal	Price stability as the key contribution to the overall macroeconomic stability		
Nominal anchor	Exchange rate level	Growth of monetary aggregate	(Forecast) inflation target
Effectiveness	Medium	Medium	High
Controllability	High	Low	Medium
Flexibility	Low	High	High
Main instrument	FX interventions interest rate	Interest rate monetary base	Interest rate (occasional) FX interventions

Source: Own compilation with the assessment of the effectiveness, controllability, and flexibility of a given strategy taken from Grostal et al. (2016, p. 116).

the transparency of the framework, which possibly influences its sustainability. The more room that is left for changes in the exchange rate, the less understandable the regime becomes for the public, and the more prone it is to speculation.

The advantages of exchange rate targeting include its ability to stabilise inflation even if otherwise domestic monetary policy would lack credibility. In general, it is also a very simple and transparent framework. Monetary authorities generally buy or sell foreign exchange or change interest rates in order to maintain the exchange rate at the intended level, and the outcomes of their actions are instantaneously known, because exchange rates are quoted on a continuous basis.

The disadvantages crucially depend on the size and trade openness of the economy, which influence the degree of its business cycle synchronisation with the reference country. If the synchronisation is weak, the domestic economy may frequently suffer from asymmetric shocks, which cannot be addressed by exchange rate adjustments. Under an exchange rate targeting regime, a country basically imports monetary policy from abroad, and thus has no monetary autonomy.

Another concern is the sustainability of inflexible exchange rate arrangements. As already signalled, many factors affect the credibility of the announced exchange rate target, and thus also the risk of a currency crisis (Koronowski, 2003, pp. 13–91). Overall, unless exchange rate targeting is thought of as a preparatory stage to a currency union, it may be the cause of turbulence in response to speculative attacks triggered by, for example, excessive deficits or self-fulfilling prophecies (Cukierman et al., 2004).

Moving to monetary targeting, it is using the announced targets for the growth of selected monetary aggregates as nominal anchors. The key choice to make is to decide which monetary aggregate to target. There is a rather large variety, with reserve money, M1, M2, or even broad money M3, considered. Each of the aggregates comprises cash and some other financial assets that can be changed into cash without losing much of their value, and—in theory—the broader the scope of the assets included in a given monetary aggregate, the closer may be its potential link to the level of economic activity and to inflation. At the same time, the narrower the aggregate, the more manageable it is for the central bank to control it. Thus, the trade-off here can be seen as between effectiveness in meeting the final goal and delivering the intermediate target, which speaks in favour of treating the announced monetary targets rather flexibly.

Among the strong points of monetary targeting is its transparency that also promotes the accountability of the strategy. Data on monetary aggregates are announced with only a limited lag, so it is easy for the public to keep track of central banks' actions. This may facilitate the process of influencing the formation of inflation expectations. However, this works both ways, so if monetary targets are not reached, expectations may become de-anchored. Therefore, monetary authorities have incentives to meet their objectives, but a possible discrepancy between intermediate and final targets makes it far from easy, and increases the need to explain reasons for deviations from the targets.[56]

The main critique of the monetary targeting framework stems from the empirics. Whereas a stable relationship between some measure of the money supply and inflation is at the centre of monetary targeting, the real data give little support to that notion. Moreover, given the functioning of the banking sector, it is hard to claim that money—especially its broader aggregates— is exogenous, which means that it cannot be fully controlled by monetary authorities with the use of interest rates and monetary base (Szpunar, 2000, pp. 165–166).

Inflation targeting, in turn, can be seen as targeting a specific level of (forecast) inflation as a nominal anchor. It involves a public announcement of a numerical target for inflation, while of key importance is, among others, the choice of inflation measure and the target time horizon. Conceptually, the broader the inflation measure, the closer its link to the perceived inflation and so to inflation expectations. However, it is more difficult for central banks to influence headline inflation encompassing all consumer prices, not least because some prices are more likely to be affected by unanticipated supply shocks. Likewise, the shorter the target time horizon within which inflation should be brought back to the target once it deviates from it, the better in terms of stabilising prices, but more challenging for monetary authorities. The answer to these trade-offs proposed within an inflation targeting regime is flexibility in conducting policy, accompanied by high accountability and transparency requirements that are treated as crucial ingredients of IT.

The benefits of an IT framework should mainly be seen in its considerable flexibility, which allows for attaining better economic outcomes in terms of both inflation and output stabilisation compared to other monetary policy regimes (Grostal et al., 2016, p. 116). Moreover, using the target expressed directly as a specific value for inflation, especially if it is defined with respect to a headline measure, possibly strengthens the anchoring of inflation expectations, facilitating maintaining price stability (Mishkin, 2006, p. 18).

The traditionally recalled drawbacks of inflation targeting include relying on a transmission mechanism that is characterised by long and variable lags.[57] This may significantly impede the process of stabilising inflation at the given level. In addition, prerequisites related to IT that determine, to a great extent, how effective the strategy would be, are rather demanding.[58] From the current point of view, arguments raised against IT encompass insufficient attention paid to financial stability issues, together with its potential inability to effectively revive price dynamics if it is excessively low, which also includes the problem of the possible unsuitability of inflation targeting to cope with the ZLB.

Finally, a mix or none of the above-listed nominal anchors can be used. The first option can be called an eclectic strategy, and the main idea behind it is to make the best use of each considered intermediate target.[59] In turn, the latter framework can be called a discretionary regime, and its superiority should follow from providing flexibility to monetary policy. Both strategies are, however, likely to be rather opaque. For example, using several targets may, in fact, give rise to confusion among the public regarding which one is most important, allowing monetary authorities to manipulate between them, resulting in a rather discretionary monetary policy.

1.4.3 Monetary policy strategy used in the past and currently

Looking at the past decades, some clear trends can be noticed regarding the relative popularity of certain monetary policy regimes, whereas it should be kept in mind that collecting data comparable across countries and time for a broad set of economies is extremely challenging. For example, only in the late 1990s did the International Monetary Fund (IMF) start to conduct its annual reviews of exchange rate arrangements that included information on monetary policy frameworks used worldwide.

Based on Cobham (2018), covering the 59 biggest economies since the mid-1970s, updated with information from the IMF (2015, 2016, 2018), several observations can be made (Chart 1.1).[60] An important caveat is, however, that disregarding smaller economies may heavily influence the proportion of the most popular monetary policy regimes, at least, in a simple country-counting metric. Still, given the difference in the importance of big versus small economies, the picture based on the biggest countries does show the significance of various monetary policy strategies applied around the world.

What is visible among the bigger economies is an apparent termination of systems using direct controls on, for example, direct lending or interest rates. Such frameworks were mainly used by less-developed communist countries and stopped being applied around 1990. Additionally, pure monetary targeting was discontinued, with the last monetary targeters disappearing around the mid-1990s.

Developments related to using exchange rate anchors or eclectic and discretionary strategies have been less dramatic, but evidently their dominance in the analysed sample of countries seems over, especially from the mid-1990s. The attractiveness of exchange rate anchors was heavily undermined by a series of currency crises, such as, for example, the 1994 Mexican crisis, the 1997 Asian crisis, and the 1998 Russian crisis. Likewise, eclectic and discretionary strategies have been losing their status since the late 1990s. The two categories have been combined because, as already noted, they are, in fact, quite similar to each other.

At the same time, the share of countries pursuing an inflation targeting framework has been growing, indicating the high reputation of IT

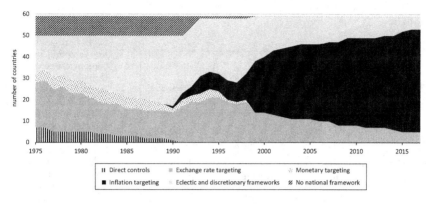

Chart 1.1 Changes in monetary policy strategies used by the 59 largest economies. Notes: Countries included in the chart account for 92% of the world's GDP, based on United Nations data for 2016—the latest available data as of November 2018 (National Accounts Main Aggregates Database available at https://unstats .un.org/unsd/snaama/dnllist.asp, accessed on 15 November 2018). Direct controls include strategies using controls on direct lending, interest rates, etc. Eclectic strategies include strategies using a mix of exchange rate target, monetary target, and inflation target, in different proportions, and are combined in one category with discretionary strategies which include regimes that do not use any explicit nominal anchor. No national framework includes strategies predominantly used by certain European countries before their transition from central planning to free market economies, as well as cases of dollarisation. The rest of the categories indicate the main target used—i.e. either exchange rate target, monetary target, or inflation target. Euro area countries are counted separately (i.e. not as one economy), although since 1999 they have been forming a monetary union with a single monetary policy. Since the date of adopting the euro, euro area countries are classified as inflation targeters, while before joining the euro area they are classified according to their actually used monetary policy strategies. Switzerland, since 2000, and the United States, since 2012, are classified as inflation targeters. Source: Own compilation based on dataset available at www.monetaryframeworks.org, accessed on 15 November 2018 (Cobham, 2018), and IMF (2015, 2016, 2018).

(Chart 1.1). At this point, it is worth noting that while for the majority of countries, especially the smaller ones, being regarded as an inflation targeter is considered a positive attribute,[61] this is not necessarily the case for the major economies. In particular, the euro area, Switzerland, and the United States do not describe their strategies as IT, probably because they want to avoid labelling, which could potentially limit the degree of discretion they may apply.[62] However, as already indicated, since they follow monetary policy regimes that share virtually all the key features of an inflation targeting framework and, in practical terms, are indistinguishable from IT, they are counted as inflation targeters.

Moving to the truly worldwide perspective, one needs to consider around 200 countries (Table 1.4 in Appendix 1). Looking only at the biggest

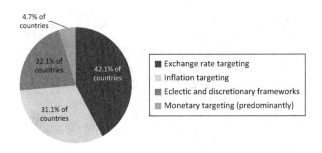

Notes: See notes to
the previous chart.
GDP shares used
for weighting are
computed based on
United Nations data
for 2016—the latest
available data as
of November 2018
(National Accounts
Main Aggregates
Database available
at https://unstats.un
.org/unsd/snaama/
dnllist.asp, accessed
on 15 November
2018). Source: Own
compilation based
on IMF (2018)
and information
from central banks'
websites.

Chart 1.2 Monetary policy strategies used by 190
countries worldwide in 2017 (simple counting).

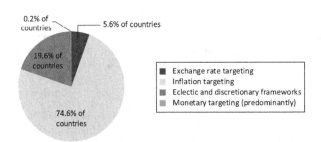

Chart 1.3 Monetary policy strategies used by 190
countries worldwide in 2017 (GDP-weighted counting).

economies may distort the picture, since the preferences of smaller countries regarding the choice of a monetary framework most likely are considerably different than those of the big countries.

Indeed, applying the simplest country-counting metric reveals that, while inflation targeting is still common within the monetary policy strategies used in 2017 (it is used by 60 economies, out of which 19 countries are euro area members counted individually,[63] i.e. 31.1% of countries), it no longer prevails (Chart 1.3). Globally, the most frequently used monetary policy regime is clearly exchange rate targeting (it is used by 80 economies, i.e. 42.1% of countries). Some support can also be seen in the case of eclectic and discretionary frameworks (they are used by 41 economies, i.e. 22.1% of countries), with many of them being *de facto* pegs. Interest in pure monetary targeting is rather weak (it is used by nine economies, i.e. 4.7% of countries).

However, considering a GDP-weighted counting, the pattern is again very much the same as shown by taking into account only the 59 biggest economies (Chart 1.4). Inflation targeting dominates (it is used by countries accounting for almost 75% of the world's GDP), followed by eclectic and

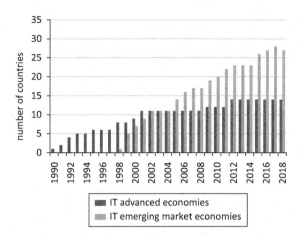

Chart 1.4 Number of IT advanced and emerging market economies.

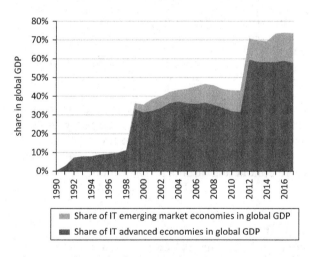

Chart 1.5 Share of inflation targeting economies in global GDP.

Notes: The charts do not include countries that followed an inflation targeting framework but subsequently joined the euro area. Advanced economies include those classified as such by the IMF. Emerging market economies include emerging markets and developing economies together with countries in transition, as classified by the IMF. In 2009, the Czech Republic was reclassified from emerging market economies to advanced economies, which is accounted for in the charts. GDP shares computed based on National Accounts Main Aggregates Database (available at https://unstats.un.org/unsd/snaama/dnllist.asp, accessed on 15 July 2019). Source: Own compilation based on information from central banks' websites, the IMF (2018), and the United Nations' National Accounts Main Aggregates Database.

discretionary strategies (they are used by countries accounting for almost 20% of the world's GDP), and a rather minor fraction of exchange rate targeters (exchange rate anchor is used by countries accounting for less than 6% of the world's GDP). The support for pure monetary targeting is almost non-existent.

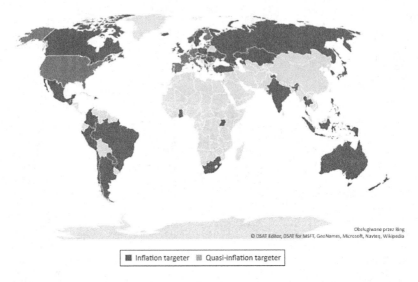

■ Inflation targeter ▦ Quasi-inflation targeter

Chart 1.6 Inflation targeters and quasi-inflation targeters. Notes: Inflation targeters include countries that describe their strategies as IT and are classified as following an inflation targeting regime in the IMF "Annual Report on Exchange Arrangements and Exchange Restrictions 2017" (IMF, 2018). Quasi-inflation targeters include major advanced economies that do not call their strategies IT, but follow monetary policy frameworks that share almost all of the key features of IT and, in practical terms, are indistinguishable from IT. Source: Own compilation based on information from central banks' websites and the IMF (2018).

The comparison indicates that among smaller economies there is a strong preference for strategies based on exchange rate targeting, even at the expense of losing monetary autonomy. At the same time, inflation targeting is found attractive predominantly in somewhat bigger economies (Charts 1.5 and 1.6), where conducting an independent monetary policy is much more advisable.

1.5 Institutional roots of an inflation targeting framework and arguments behind them

Evidently, inflation targeting seems compelling for many different economies. It is, therefore, important to specify what elements can be regarded as crucial for that strategy. Mishkin (2001, p. 9) and similarly Svensson (2008, p. 319) indicate the following key features of the framework: acknowledging price stability as the primary goal of monetary policy; announcing publicly a numerical target for inflation; formulating monetary policy on the basis of a very broad set of information; and applying high accountability and transparency standards to central banks' policies, where accountability and transparency can be seen as complementary elements to granting central banks a high degree of independence. While other formulations are possible (Bofinger, 2001, p. 259), the points listed above well define the idea of IT.

1.5.1 Acknowledging price stability as the primary goal of monetary policy

Following on from the discussed economic theories, it is nowadays rather widely accepted that monetary policy should be made responsible for maintaining price stability, as a way to create a predictable economic environment and reduce uncertainty arising from price changes (Pietrzak, 2008, pp. 89–90). In particular, the new Keynesian model, which in its benchmark version shows that constant inflation is the optimal policy delivering a zero output gap, supports that claim (Blanchard, Dell'Ariccia, and Mauro, 2010, p. 3). High and volatile inflation may influence the decisions of economic agents on investment and consumption, possibly disturbing a proper resource allocation (Grostal and Niedźwiedzińska, 2019, p. 21). Therefore, safeguarding price stability should be a valuable contribution of monetary policy to sustain economic growth. However, in the aftermath of the recent crises, it has been disputed whether caring for price stability with a preference for stable economic growth is enough, or whether central banks should have broader mandates, including financial stability. That issue will be discussed later. Importantly, however, what has been criticised is the too narrow focus of central banks on keeping low inflation, but not the mandate of maintaining price stability itself.

The related problem is associated with the rule: one goal–(at least) one instrument (Tinbergen, 1952), arguing that if central banks should strive for reaching more than one goal, i.e. delivering more than "just" price stability, they should be given more instruments. In the past, i.e. before financial stability considerations became dominant in the debate, what was discussed in that context was the role of exchange rates under IT and the fear of floating (Mohanty, 2013, pp. 1–10). The argument here was that countries— especially emerging market economies—preferred smoother exchange rate movements than the exchange rate changes occurring under a floating regime. Flexible exchange rates may act as a shock absorber and smooth output volatility, but excessive volatility in exchange rates may, in fact, increase output volatility and itself become a source of vulnerability. Thus, despite officially floating their currencies, countries may be reluctant to let exchange rates fluctuate freely in response to macroeconomic shocks (Calvo and Reinhart, 2000, pp. 2–4). From a practical point of view, however, having any kind of exchange rate target might reduce the credibility of the inflation target, as the two objectives may, at times, be in conflict. Therefore, while this is not a formal prerequisite for adopting an IT strategy, it is generally advised to conduct inflation targeting under a floating exchange rate regime, and ensure that any exchange rate interventions are consistent with the monetary policy stance geared towards meeting the inflation target.

When speaking about central banks' mandates, what is also quite broadly supported is the need to grant, at least, instrument independence to monetary authorities.[64] As already noted, the reasoning is that highly discretionary monetary policy—irrespective of previous promises—may generally tend to support higher economic activity at the cost of higher inflation, leading in the longer run simply to higher inflation with no beneficial effects for economic growth (Kydland and Prescott, 1977). By tasking a central bank with one main inflation goal, and making monetary authorities independent in choosing the way they achieve it, an inflationary bias may be minimised. What is worth mentioning is that central banks' instrument independence is postulated as a condition of monetary policy effectiveness not only under an inflation targeting strategy (Bernanke and Mishkin, 1997, pp. 6–8). At the same time, goal independence is not advocated that strongly, as governments also have incentives for choosing price stability as the main aim of their monetary policy (de Haan and Eijffinger, 2016, p. 5).

1.5.2 Public announcement of a numerical target for inflation

As already mentioned, the aim of announcing a numerical target for inflation is to provide a clear nominal anchor. The use of inflation—a commonly known, frequently measured, and generally understood variable—should strengthen the anchoring effect (Bernanke and Mishkin, 1997, pp. 15–16). In this way, monetary policy influences the formulation of inflation expectations, presumably stabilising them close to the announced target. With inflation expectations anchored at the target, maintaining price stability should become easier, especially due to the lower risks of second-round effects occurring in the aftermath of shocks hitting the economy.

However, several factors may limit the ability of central banks to keep inflation at the target. First of all, inflation developments are the outcome of many processes, some of which are beyond any control of monetary policy (e.g. weather conditions affecting crops), and some of which are, to a lesser or greater extent, affected by monetary policy (e.g. the labour market situation). Thus, inflation is by no means directly controlled by monetary authorities, which can only partially influence it by adjusting monetary policy instruments.

Adjusting monetary policy instruments in the right way is easier said than done. All instruments have their limitations, and there are long and variable transmission lags between monetary policy decisions and their strongest impact on the economy. What should help is to focus monetary policy on inflation as expected within the time horizon of monetary policy transmission, which speaks in favour of devoting a lot of attention to forecasts. The problem with forecasts is, however, that they are, by definition, uncertain.

On top of that, economies are frequently hit by unexpected shocks that potentially have significant effects on inflation but cannot be predicted.

Central banks try to overcome these difficulties by formulating their inflation targets in such a way as to minimise potential credibility losses. In particular, one can distinguish between targets specified as a point target or as a target band, and between targets specified for headline or for core inflation.

Regarding the first choice, the target may be set as a point target (with or without an explicit band for deviations) or a band target (with or without an explicit midpoint). The key argument in favour of a point target is that it should more strongly anchor inflation expectations on a specific level of inflation. The key argument against a point target is that it is almost impossible for a central bank to meet it, in the sense of keeping inflation at the announced level. In turn, the big advantage of a target band is that it is easier to steer inflation in-between the lower and the upper limit of the band, and so meeting the target should be easier. The disadvantage of a target band is that it does not give clarity to the public with respect to the level of inflation a central bank aims to achieve. Thus, the compromise here is between the credibility of a central bank stemming from its ability to deliver the target, and its anti-inflation commitment stemming from less acceptance of deviations from the narrowly specified target (Schaechter et al., 2000, pp. 10–11; Debelle, 1997, pp. 14–17).

Moving to the targeted measure, the target may be set for headline inflation or for core inflation (i.e. inflation excluding some categories of prices—typically more volatile and/or influenced, to a large extent, by factors beyond the control of monetary policy). An important benefit of using headline inflation is that it is commonly understood and, in principle, should reflect changes in the general price level as felt by the public. The drawback of headline inflation is that it is potentially significantly influenced by developments not controlled by a central bank. In turn, an appreciated feature of core inflation is that it is more strongly influenced by general economic conditions, and thus monetary policy instruments, since it excludes prices that are driven by other factors (e.g. food prices, administered prices). The shortcoming of core inflation is that it may detach from headline inflation and may not be intuitive for the public. Therefore, the choice here is between the credibility of a central bank stemming from its ability to deliver the target, and its accountability stemming from the public understanding the target (Heenan et al., 2006, pp. 17–21).

Regardless of what kind of targets one considers, what is also important is the time horizon for meeting the target. There can be either end-year targets or continuous ones, meaning valid not only for December of a given year, but at all times. As already noted, it is obviously impossible to "keep" inflation at the target in each period. The idea behind a continuous target is rather to constantly strive to stabilise inflation around the target level in the medium term. The notion of a medium term is very often not defined, giving central banks flexibility to decide how quickly or slowly inflation should be brought back to the target depending on the nature of the shock.

In that respect, two approaches to IT can be distinguished—strict inflation targeting and flexible inflation targeting. The first option means that a central bank fully focuses on meeting the inflation target, irrespective of the costs it can entail in terms of the output level or volatility. Thus, under strict inflation targeting, whenever inflation deviates from the target, the central bank reacts by adjusting monetary policy instruments in order to bring inflation back to the target, as soon as possible. In turn, the second option means that a central bank pays attention to both inflation and output (King, 1997; Ingves, 2011). Therefore, under flexible inflation targeting, whenever inflation deviates from the target, the central bank decides within what time horizon it should be brought back to the target, while minimising the cost for the real economy. There are cases (e.g. negative supply shocks) when extending the time horizon limits the decline in output and employment, as well as mitigates the volatility of real variables, exchange rates, and interest rates (Svensson, 2009; Walsh, 2009). Under the flexible approach, the credibility of monetary authorities may be at risk if the time horizon is too long, but the answer to that problem is clear communication about central banks' intentions rather than moving to strict inflation targeting. In practice, no country is following strict inflation targeting.

Another way to mitigate credibility losses is to explicitly state a list of conditions under which monetary authorities accept temporary deviations of inflation from the target, since striving to meet the target would cause undesirable volatility of output and employment. Such a list is typically called escape clauses and includes, for example, natural disasters, agricultural conditions, and changes in indirect taxes (Heenan et al., 2006, p. 27).

Last but not least, while speaking of numerical targets for inflation, of key significance are their levels. There are arguments advocating for a low, but not too low, level of targeted inflation (Fischer, 1994, pp. 283–285; Mishkin and Schmidt-Hebbel, 2002, pp. 197–201). The target should, on the one hand, allow for preserving the value of money and mitigating distortions caused by changing prices, and, on the other hand, provide room for adjustments, amidst downward nominal rigidities, and limit the risk of hitting an effective lower bound for nominal interest rates—the main instrument of IT central banks.

The frequently recalled costs of high and volatile inflation include several elements.[65] It introduces uncertainty and, in particular, it may provide misleading signals if price changes are wrongly interpreted as reflecting movements in demand (Lucas, 1973). As typical contracts are specified in nominal terms, by affecting the real value of nominal assets and liabilities, elevated inflation means shifting wealth from creditors to debtors, and its higher volatility significantly impedes avoiding these redistribution effects. High and volatile inflation, amidst staggered price adjustments and downward nominal rigidities, may also lead to a misallocation of resources, via the potentially negative influence on expected profits and labour markets. Finally, higher inflation increases the real value of tax obligations and imposes a cost on holding liquid assets, such as cash (Bofinger, 2001, pp. 132–141).

At the same time, too low inflation may be problematic as well (Fischer, 1994, pp. 281–285; Wojtyna, 2001, p. 4). Until recently, the main argument to support that claim was related to the "grease-the-wheels" story. If nominal wages are downwardly rigid, some positive price growth facilitates real wage "cuts", potentially improving labour market efficiency (Tobin, 1972). While this still seems to be a valid point, nowadays more emphasis is given to the ZLB issue.[66] The lower the inflation target, the higher the risk that a central bank will reach the limit of cutting its policy rate, if the economy is hit by a major shock.[67] This restricts the central banks' ability to stimulate the economy with their standard instruments, and may force monetary authorities to use non-standard measures (Bank of Canada, 2011, pp. 10–13; Koronowski, 2005, p. 30). The effectiveness and costs related to these unconventional policy tools are, however, not always easy to assess. A further justification for avoiding excessively low inflation is the risk of deflation that is difficult to combat. In particular, a deflationary spiral may result from debt deflation that raises the real cost of servicing debt, leading to financial distress, which translates into even more downward pressure on prices (Billi and Kahn, 2008, pp. 10–11). Another reason for choosing a positive level of targeted price growth is the likely existence of a positive measurement bias, meaning that inflation may, in fact, be lower than indicated by statistical data (Yates, 1995, pp. 146–148; Mayes and Chapple, 1995, pp. 235–238).[68] Moreover, central banks in emerging market economies should also take into account the consequences of a catching-up process for domestic price developments, and, in particular, a possible Balassa–Samuelson effect, which speaks for somewhat higher inflation targets in that group of countries (Balassa, 1964; Samuelson, 1964).

Regarding a specific numerical level of targeted inflation that could be treated as optimal, various estimates cited in the literature are based on a number of theoretical and empirical studies. They seem, however, highly sensitive to model specifications and assumptions.

Probably the most famous theoretical result is derived from models where the only nominal friction stems from the transactional demand for money. Under such a set-up, the optimal monetary policy, known as the Friedman rule (Friedman, 2006, pp. 1–50), recommends setting the nominal interest rate to zero, which also implies that the optimal level of inflation would be negative and equal—in absolute value—to the real interest rate.

Under changed model assumptions the indications may be different, but still in many variants the advisable inflation should be negative or zero

Table 1.2 Optimal level of inflation implied by alternative classes of models

Class of model	Example of models	Implied optimal rate of inflation
Sticky prices and relative price dispersion	Woodford (2003)	Zero
Sticky wages and productivity growth	Amano et al. (2009)	Deflation (at the rate of productivity growth)
Money demand and asset allocation	Friedman (2006)	Deflation (at the real rate of interest)
Non-indexed pensions	Whitehouse (2009)	Zero or negative
Tax distortions	Feldstein (1997)	Zero

Source: Table taken from Kryvtsov and Mendes (2015, p. 7) with references also taken from Kryvtsov and Mendes (2015, pp. 7–9).

(Table 1.2). This is, however, definitely not in line with the central banks' actual choices, which should reflect some deeper understanding of monetary economics. Schmitt-Grohe and Uribe (2010) try to deliver results closer to 2% optimal inflation by accounting for many frictions, including an incomplete tax system, the existence of foreign demand for domestic currency, sluggish price adjustments, ZLB restrictions, downward nominal rigidities in factor prices, and a quality bias in inflation measurement. They conclude that leading theories of monetary non-neutrality consistently imply that the optimal inflation ranges from minus the real interest rate to levels insignificantly above zero.

The difficulty in constructing a theoretical model that would encompass all relevant effects, encouraged research focused on simply exploring empirical links between inflation and economic growth, with the aim to find a threshold from which the negative effects of inflation would be substantial. For example, Khan and Senhadji (2001) investigated a sample of 140 economies between 1960 and 1998 and found evidence for a threshold level of inflation at 1%–3% for industrial countries, and at 11%–12% for developing countries. According to the authors, two possible factors explain a higher threshold for developing countries—more widespread indexation systems in that group of economies, which mitigate the adverse effects of inflation, and a lower level of conventional taxation in developing countries, which implies that a larger inflation tax is required to cause the same growth-hampering effects.

Other studies include Burdekin et al. (2004) who claimed that for emerging market economies a threshold above which inflation hurts economic activity is close to 3%. In turn, Espinoza et al. (2010) arrived at similar threshold values as Khan and Senhadji (2001), and concluded that they are around 1% for advanced economies and around 10% for emerging market economies. This is also close to the estimates of Kremer et al. (2012) at around 2% and 17%, respectively.

Overall, based on those studies, it seems that inflation values of between 1% and 3% for advanced economies should not have significant negative effects on growth or welfare (Billi and Kahn, 2008, pp. 19–23; Coibion et al., 2012, pp. 29–30).[69] For emerging market economies, that level can potentially be somewhat higher (Błaszczyk, 2019, p. 25).

1.5.3 Formulating monetary policy on the basis of a very broad set of information

As already indicated, an IT strategy does not use intermediate targets, i.e. variables that a central bank can more directly influence than inflation, for which some reference values would be set in order to facilitate meeting the final inflation target.[70] At the same time, for assessing the monetary policy stance that would be appropriate, IT requires looking at many macroeconomic developments that can affect inflation, without specifying any preferred reference values or targets for them. There is no check list, but a standard scope of the analysis encompasses a decomposition of inflation, factors affecting economic activity, the labour market situation, developments in the external environment, and financial market movements.

Formulating monetary policy on the basis of a very broad set of information should help to reinforce its flexibility. This is needed because central banks' reactions to shocks hitting economies should depend, among others, on their sources, persistence, and strength. Not all deviations in inflation from its target require the same policy response, and, in particular, shocks to the demand side of the economy should be addressed differently than supply-side shocks. Assessing these aspects should lead to better decisions, which are by no means mechanical, and should result in forward-looking monetary policy.

A forward-looking orientation means that, apart from inflation itself, its determinants, and factors affecting the monetary transmission mechanism, one of the key elements that should be taken into account while deciding on monetary policy are inflation forecasts. As already noted, to emphasise their importance, an inflation targeting strategy has sometimes been called an inflation-forecast targeting strategy (Svensson, 1997, p. 1111; Woodford, 2007, pp. 7–9).

Forecasts could, in fact, be seen as implicit intermediate targets, as due to transmission lags central banks should try to target inflation within the next few quarters. Policymakers cannot directly influence current price developments, and if in their decisions they also put weight on output stabilisation—which is a rule rather than an exception—the time horizon relevant for them may be even longer. For that reason, it is of great value to have medium-term inflation projections, which in practice means forecasts for the next 2–3 years.

Projections can also be seen as summarising all possible relevant information on current and expected macroeconomic developments influencing inflation (Haldane, 1995, p. 5). They are, however, always based on numerous assumptions and rely on past regularities encompassed by the models used to prepare them. Moreover, there are no guarantees that the models employed to make the forecasts are the right ones. Thus, projections have their limits and should be treated with caution, especially during periods of heightened uncertainty or in times of structural changes. By all means, they offer a useful reference point, to which expert judgement should always be applied.

Therefore, a comprehensive set of information, including forecasts, must be processed by a competent decision maker. It is, however, not clear who would be best in designing monetary policy—a single policymaker or a committee, a committee deciding by a majority vote or a committee deciding consensually, an individualistic committee or a collegial committee, a committee consisting of economists only, or a committee also encompassing other members (Blinder, 2007, pp. 106–123).

Collective decision-making evidently has significant advantages, as it engages people from different backgrounds who have different preferences (i.e. the weight they put on inflation versus economic activity), potentially better reflecting social preferences. Additionally, members may have different understandings of how the economy works (i.e. they may use different models of the economy), which affects the way they process information and reach conclusions. Moreover, because information normally includes some noise, collective decision-making helps, at least, to neutralise noise that is specific to each decision maker, i.e. idiosyncratic noise (Maier, 2010, p. 6). Groups are also presumably better at collecting a broader set of information and collective decision-making reduces the likelihood of extreme positions (Naudon and Pérez, 2017, p. 8).

At the same time, there are also disadvantages to group decision-making. A strong divergence of views may impede reaching decisions, possibly delaying them and increasing policy inertia, which raises the probability of a too late and too weak reaction to macroeconomic developments. In turn, if the group does want to take decisions jointly, some members may choose to follow the group, meaning that one of the biggest strengths of collective decision-making—namely, the heterogeneity of members—is not fully used (Maier, 2010, pp. 14–15).

Simulating monetary policy under uncertainty about the state of the economy shows that group decisions deliver better results, on average, than the decisions of a single policymaker (Lombardelli et al., 2005; Blinder and Morgan, 2007). Empirically, it is, however, not easy to verify whether monetary committees do, indeed, outperform individual policymakers, especially since a dominant member within a committee may start to strongly influence or even control the group, blurring the difference between decisions reached by a single policymaker and a committee.

1.5.4 Applying high accountability and transparency standards as complements to independence

Inflation targeting is not based on applying a simple rule, but rather, as already noted, it is described as a framework of constrained discretion (Bernanke and Mishkin, 1997, pp. 9–10). This means that the strategy allows for a considerable degree of flexibility in deciding how to respond to shocks, but this discretion is constrained by a strong commitment to meeting the inflation target, thereby building the central bank's credibility. Only if the commitment is convincing, and the central bank is credible, do inflation expectations become better anchored (Orphanides and Williams, 2003, p. 26).

In theory, central banks' credibility should, in the first place, stem from meeting the inflation target; however, given the fact that all inflation targeters also put some weight on output stabilisation, i.e. follow a flexible approach to IT, deviating from the target is inevitable during shock periods. Proper communication during these periods is key to influencing expectations and anchoring them at the level of the target which should reduce the need for central banks' action, and thus limit its social cost. In order to make these elements work, not only should policymakers make decisions based on a very broad set of information, but they should also explain how these decisions should contribute to maintaining price stability. As already mentioned, accountability and transparency are therefore helpful in establishing credibility.

The need to explain monetary policy decisions is also related to the already discussed issue of granting central banks a considerable degree of independence. Independence should be accompanied by high accountability standards (Wojtyna, 1998, p. 67), encompassing a periodic release of reports and regular parliamentary hearings. In the case of inflation targeting, it may also be necessary for a central bank to write an open letter explaining the reasons for any sizeable deviation in inflation from the announced target, as well as measures undertaken to bring inflation back to the target. Open letters should predominantly demonstrate the central bank's commitment to maintaining price stability.

Apart from announcing the monetary policy strategy itself, a standard set of information that central banks are nowadays expected to share, in order to enable an assessment of their policies, include analysis of macroeconomic developments, inflation outlook, and the reasoning behind the decisions (Jeanneau, 2009). Inflation reports together with projections and press releases after decision-making meetings, often accompanied by press conferences, are therefore crucial for the accountability and transparency of IT central banks. While it is not straightforward to verify the efficiency of different means of communication, there is quite sizeable homogeneity among inflation targeters not only in what they publish, but also whom they address. The first group to mention would probably be parliament and government, as representatives of the public; the second would encompass professionals, such as financial market analysts or economic journalists; and the third group would be—at least indirectly—the broader public.

The move towards more transparency has been motivated by the belief that it improves the predictability of central banks' actions. Empirical evidence offers some support for that reasoning (Ehrmann et al., 2012), but another aspect to consider is whether too much openness creates confusion by giving the impression that central banks know more than they do or by introducing a cacophony of voices (Blinder, 2007, pp. 119–122; Lustenberger and Rossi, 2017, pp. 26–27). The latter is related to the composition of collegial decision-making bodies.

In general, the more individualistic the committees, the more insights on individual opinions revealed. This may include presenting dissenting views, publishing detailed minutes, giving polemic speeches, and making voting records public. This information should help to better understand monetary policy decisions, but, at the same time, can create confusion about the dominant view. Ultimately, the emphasis on disagreements among committee members may limit the free exchange of opinions or render decision-makers more reluctant to reconsider their views.

Although a high degree of transparency seems indisputable nowadays, it is a relatively new approach to monetary policy. Its popularity spread around the same time as IT, but greater emphasis on communication is not only attributable to inflation targeters. Having said that, from the very beginning inflation targeters occupied the top places in central banks' transparency rankings, which is the best proof of the important role communication plays within the IT framework (Dincer and Eichengreen, 2013, p. 204).

1.5.5 Empirical evidence on inflation targeting effectiveness

The constituting features of an inflation targeting strategy described above are designed to strengthen the commitment of IT monetary authorities to maintaining price stability, and by doing so, to build central banks' credibility. In turn, as already noted, credibility is crucial for anchoring inflation expectations and, ultimately, for meeting the announced inflation targets at the lowest possible cost in terms of output. And, indeed, considering what can be called a traditional metric for assessing monetary policy effectiveness, i.e. a metric taking into account inflation and output developments (Brzoza-Brzezina, 2011, p. 7), an inflation targeting framework turns out to be the right way to deliver price stability while minimising economic growth volatility.

Studies investigating the macroeconomic outcomes of pursuing an IT regime indicate that this framework has proved to be effective. This is especially true in the case of emerging market economies, while much weaker evidence of such beneficial effects can be established for advanced economy inflation targeters.

Regarding inflation (its level, volatility, or persistence), many researchers found that inflation targeting economies were enjoying lower, more stable, or less persistent inflation, with more support for such conclusions visible for emerging market economies. Out of more recent works, it is worth mentioning Vega and Winkelried (2005) who considered 109 countries (out of which 23 were inflation targeters) over the period 1990–2004, and indicated that IT helped to decrease the level and volatility of inflation both in industrial and developing countries, with a stronger effect found for developing inflation targeters. Another example of similar research includes Gonçalves and Salles (2008) who used data for 36 emerging market economies (out of which 13 were inflation targeters) over the period 1980–2005, and found that IT developing countries experienced bigger declines in inflation levels and volatility compared to the control group. Abo-Zaid and Tuzemen (2012) analysed 33 developed and developing countries (out of which 23 were inflation targeters) over the period 1980–2007, and in the case of IT emerging market economies also reported lower and more stable inflation, but not for IT advanced economies. Similarly, Ferreira de Mendonça and de Guimarães e Souza (2012), who covered 180 countries over the period 1990–2007, noted that adopting an IT regime in developing countries resulted in lower inflation levels and volatility, with no evidence for such an effect established for developed economies. In turn, Gerlach and Tillmann (2012) examined the persistence of inflation by looking at eight Asian economies (out of which three were inflation targeters) over the period 1985–2010, and showed a significant reduction in inflation persistence in countries that adopted inflation targeting and no decline in inflation persistence in countries that did not adopt inflation targeting. In addition, Canarella and Miller (2017), studying eight countries (out of which six were inflation targeters), investigated inflation persistence but from a global perspective over the period 1976–2013, and identified that lower inflation persistence in IT advanced economies resulted mainly from lower global inflation (the Great Moderation), whereas the same could not be said for IT emerging market economies, indirectly suggesting that IT might have played a positive role there. At the same time, Ball and Sheridan (2005), who used a sample of 20 developed countries (out of which seven were inflation targeters) over the period 1960–2001, found no evidence of inflation targeting improving economic performance. Likewise, Lin and Ye (2007), who analysed seven advanced economies, concluded that inflation targeting had no significant effect on inflation (neither its level nor its volatility).

Issues related to output (its level, volatility) were sometimes covered in the same studies as discussed above. For example, Gonçalves and Salles (2008) showed that among the analysed emerging market economies, IT countries recorded greater decreases in the volatility of GDP growth rates relative to the control group. In the same vein, Abo-Zaid and Tuzemen

55

(2012) found that IT developing countries experienced higher and more stable GDP growth compared to non-IT developing economies, while IT developed countries enjoyed higher GDP growth, but not less volatile, compared to non-IT developed economies.

Stronger evidence of the beneficial effects of IT to emerging market economies compared to advanced economies can be attributable to the fact that inflation targeting requires important institutional changes in the conduct of monetary policy (Agénor and Pereira da Silva, 2019, pp. 40–42). Given that less advanced economies are typically characterised by weaker institutional arrangements, the need to enhance a monetary policy set-up on the way to become a fully fledged inflation targeter, may have resulted in more pronounced institutional improvements in emerging market economies. Since this can be an essential element behind IT success, it is worth analysing the institutional arrangements in detail, which is the main focus of this study.

The indicated research is only a fraction of the available studies, since the literature investigating the impact of pursuing an inflation targeting strategy on macroeconomic outcomes has already grown considerably. Drawing firm conclusions is, however, difficult due to the changing samples of the reviewed economies, the differences in time coverage, and the various research approaches used. For that reason, it may be interesting to look at the meta-analysis conducted by Balima et al. (2017), who investigated a very broad set of 113 empirical studies. The authors checked for a publication bias favouring research showing the beneficial effects of IT adoption or, at least, results indicating any statistically significant effects, which would suggest that the previously reviewed conclusions should be treated with caution. At the same time, even after correcting for the identified publication biases in their study, meaningful (i.e. genuine) effects of IT adoption could be established for reducing inflation levels and GDP growth volatility, with no significant effects found for inflation volatility and the levels of GDP growth. While the results of meta-analysis are also subject to many caveats, treating these conclusions as a kind of summary findings gives quite a positive assessment of IT effectiveness.

Importantly, while inflation targeting seems to be helpful in keeping low inflation without introducing excessive fluctuations in output or reducing its growth rates, it proved to be insufficient to deliver financial stability (Issing, 2017, p. 340), which currently has been one of the strongest arguments against IT. Looking at the experiences of the 2008 and 2011 crises, this was also the case in countries that had tried to take into consideration some financial stability issues in their monetary policies, i.e. applied a "leaning against the wind" approach (e.g. Sweden). However, the biggest imbalances had been accumulated in countries favouring a "clean-up after" tactic, i.e. reacting only to the consequences of financial asset bubbles once they burst, which may have resulted in a too narrow focus on price stability, possibly even contributing to recent crises (e.g. the United States[71]).[72] As a result, central banks had to introduce a significant degree of monetary policy accommodation into their economies, and since several of them, including many inflation targeters, were faced with the ZLB, they were forced to use unconventional policy measures. For the opponents of inflation targeting, this may be seen as proof of the inability of IT to cope with the ZLB and to revive inflation from deflationary levels. The above observations constitute the most important critique against an inflation targeting regime that is discussed below.

1.6 Challenges related to an inflation targeting framework posed by the recent crises

Until the outbreak of the global and European crises of 2008 and 2011, it seemed that the dominance of an IT regime had been unquestionable, and thus monetary policy debate had concentrated on explaining the reasons behind the Great Moderation period and trying to define, what was called, a science of monetary policy (Mishkin, 2011, p. 2). The crisis that started in the United States in 2007–2008, which in Europe was soon afterwards coupled with a sovereign debt crisis, and the forceful reaction of some central banks to the resulting economic downturn, brought a different set of topics to the attention of macroeconomists. The issues had been partly present in previous discussions, but the debates were much less intense. Furthermore, the conclusions had to be reviewed.

The main topics included two areas: what should be the role of financial stability considerations in monetary policy, and what should be the scope of unconventional monetary policy measures? The first issue relates to the disputes over the proper response of monetary policy to asset price bubbles, whereas the second topic involves arguments for and against treating unconventional measures in the future as conventional ones.

1.6.1 Monetary policy and financial stability considerations

The topic of interactions between monetary policy and financial stability had been discussed before the crises, with two opposing views having their supporters.[73] The "leaning against the wind" fraction advocated the active use of monetary policy to pop or, at least, slow down the build-up of a possible asset price bubble, in order to limit the losses caused to the economy by a bubble burst. Such an approach was recommended, for example, by Cecchetti et al. (2000), Borio and Lowe (2002), as well as Borio, English, and Filardo (2003). In turn, the "clean-up after" camp advised the active use of monetary policy only after a bubble had burst, in order to limit the decline in output and stabilise the economy. This group was composed of, among others, Greenspan (2002), Posen (2006), and Mishkin (2009). The arguments raised in the debate concentrated on evaluating the central banks' ability to detect a bubble, the suitability of using a short-term interest rate as an instrument to address the problem, as well as the effectiveness of potential monetary expansion in dealing with the aftermath of a burst (Sławiński, 2009, pp. 56–61).

In practice, until the mid-2000s, the "leaning against the wind" approach was implemented in Australia, New Zealand, Sweden, and the United Kingdom, where central banks—with an aim to curb housing price increases—had been conducting a somewhat more restrictive monetary policy than could be justified, solely with the view of meeting the price stability objective. The "clean-up after" tactic has been predominantly associated with the monetary policy of the United States.

Past experiences with the "leaning against the wind" policy showed that its opponents had a strong point in claiming that interest rate policy was a rather blunt tool to deal with excessive price rises in specific markets. The related issue followed from the already signalled Tinbergen rule, indicating that to reach one goal, at least one instrument is needed (Tinbergen, 1952). At the same time, the consequences of the recent crises have proved that the "clean-up after" tactic can be extremely costly, not least due to severe financial market tensions persisting after the burst. The tensions have significantly impeded the transmission mechanism of monetary policy measures, which coupled with the apparent limit on additional monetary accommodation that could be introduced with the standard set of instruments, has meant that combating the crises has been exceptionally difficult.

As a result, the need to build up prudential frameworks as the main tool aimed at safeguarding financial stability seems obvious, whereas the views concerning whether, and, if so, how monetary policy strategies should be adjusted to better support financial stability are still diverging. Some argue that monetary policy conducted under flexible inflation targeting, even after considering alternatives in the form of price-level targeting and nominal GDP targeting, provides a robust framework for delivering price and output stability and should maintain focus on these objectives (Bean et al., 2010, pp. 318–319; Svensson, 2010). In turn, other authors recommend more emphasis on "leaning against the wind" policy, and claim that monetary policy should actively support macroprudential policy in ensuring financial stability, which, at the least, may require extending the monetary policy time horizon (Koronowski, 2009, pp. 46–47; Borio, 2011b, pp. 20–22). According to those views, monetary policy should also prevent excessive credit growth, even if credit is not causing an immediate threat to price stability (Ciżkowicz and Rzońca, 2011, pp. 683–686).

1.6.2 Unconventional monetary policy measures

The other topic initiated by the crises is related to the ZLB problem and the resulting need to use unorthodox monetary policy measures to revive inflation. Strictly speaking, unconventional measures are considered warranted when either the room for lowering the central bank interest rates has been exhausted, thus the ZLB has been reached, or when the monetary policy transmission mechanism is no longer working properly. Until the crises, those cases were regarded as rather marginal and theoretical, but became of vital relevance soon after the outbreak of the worldwide economic downturn.

It is useful to start with specifying what is understood by the notion of an unconventional policy measure. A general description could be that these are the tools that are directly targeted at reducing the cost and increasing the availability of external financing to banks, households, and non-financial companies (Bini Smaghi, 2009). However, in order to focus on introducing monetary policy stimulus, and not on pure crisis management, only instruments beyond short-term liquidity-providing measures are considered.[74] At the same time, while some tools can, in principle, be regarded as conventional, their application may speak in favour of treating them as unconventional. This is the case, in particular, for lowering nominal interest rates below zero, committing to an unchanged interest rate policy for some period of time, as well as announcing unlimited FX intervention to weaken the exchange rate (Cukierman, 2019, p. 173). Taking into account the above reasoning, the resulting classification implies that there are five main unconventional measures (Table 1.3): negative interest rates, forward guidance, exchange rate commitment, credit easing, and quantitative easing (QE).

Negative interest rate policy is self-explanatory and is possible because the cost of holding cash is positive, so for some time central banks are able to keep nominal short-term interest rates in a slightly negative territory.

Table 1.3 Classification of monetary policy measures

Monetary policy measure	Remarks	(Un)conventional
Interest rates	Conventional measure	Conventional
Negative interest rates	Unconventional use of a conventional measure	Unconventional
Forward-looking communication	Conventional measure	Conventional
Forward guidance	Unconventional use of a conventional measure	Unconventional
FX interventions	Conventional measure	Conventional
Exchange rate commitment	Unconventional use of a conventional measure	Unconventional
Credit easing	Unconventional measure	Unconventional
Quantitative easing	Unconventional measure	Unconventional

Source: Own compilation.

Forward guidance is a type of central bank communication aimed at influencing expectations on the future evolution of short-term interest rates, and thus on longer-term interest rates. It may take several different forms. One can speak of open-ended, state-contingent, or time-contingent forward guidance, which, in principle, can be seen as a conditional commitment of monetary authorities to keep interest rates at an unchanged low level for a sustained period. This conditional commitment to keep short-term rates at a low level for longer should also help to prevent inflation expectations from declining.

Exchange rate commitment means that a central bank announces its readiness to conduct unlimited FX interventions not only to counteract appreciation pressures, but also to actively weaken the exchange rate, to some extent.

Credit easing includes tools facilitating credit provision by banks via offering them medium-term liquidity in the form of long-term refinancing operations. Bini Smaghi (2009) sees it also as a policy of purchasing private sector assets, such as commercial papers, corporate bonds, or asset-backed securities to address liquidity shortages and increased spreads directly in certain market segments. Such purchases are, however, more typically treated as already constituting a kind of quantitative easing.

Quantitative easing, known also as large-scale asset purchases, is directed at lowering the longer-term interest rates of financial assets, mainly of government bonds. Outright purchases of longer-term assets, financed by central bank reserves, aim to raise the prices of not only the purchased assets, but also—via the portfolio rebalancing channel—of other assets.

During the global financial crisis and the European sovereign crisis, in order to provide additional monetary accommodation, a number of central banks resorted to unconventional monetary policy measures, in fact, in many cases to more than one.[75] This was much more frequent in advanced economies than in emerging market economies, which, to some extent, can be explained by the lower inflation targets prevailing in the first group of countries.[76]

The available evidence, based mainly on event studies, suggests that unorthodox tools were effective in loosening monetary conditions under crisis circumstances, which found reflection, in particular, in lowering longer-term interest rates (Bayoumi et al., 2014, p. 32; Bean et al., 2010, pp. 286–287). Judging by their impact on financial market variables, the effectiveness of unconventional instruments was even comparable to the effectiveness of conventional ones. At the same time, the influence of unorthodox tools on output and inflation has been much less investigated, and thus is harder to compare with conventional instruments, but the direction of the impact is clearly supportive of real activity and prices.

The use of unorthodox tools can, however, be problematic, especially if they are applied for a longer period of time. Apart from their possible diminishing effectiveness and difficulties with implementing exit strategies, the main cost associated with unconventional policies is probably related to the risks they create for central banks' credibility. This issue is relevant particularly in the case of purchases of government securities, because they can be seen as a dangerously close substitute to direct monetary financing (Bayoumi et al., 2014, p. 19). If the actions of monetary authorities start to be regarded as aimed predominantly at ensuring cheap financing for governments, this would mean the fiscal dominance of monetary policy, and the end of central banks' independence.

In the case of other asset purchases, the activities of central banks may, in turn, significantly distort trades, for example, by impairing the price discovery mechanism. The transactions related to private sector assets are conducted in market segments that are generally relatively small compared to the demand coming from a central bank. Buying private sector assets also implies that a monetary authority acts similarly, in many respects, to a typical commercial bank, meaning that it allocates funds to certain industries, companies, or regions. This may be an additional source of distortion, since some entities are selected, while others are not (Bini Smaghi, 2009).

Moreover, a low interest rate environment may contribute to a misallocation of resources, since under such conditions a disproportionate share of funding might be granted to less productive firms (Acharya et al., 2015). If low interest rates are sustained for an extended period of time, it may also increase financial stability risks, by influencing housing prices, the financial situation of insurance companies, pension funds, and the banking sector. Unorthodox tools also have material redistribution effects, and while the same is true for conventional instruments, the effects of unconventional measures may be more difficult to accept, since they may be interpreted as helping debtors at the expense of creditors.

Bean et al. (2010, pp. 281–288) argue for relying in normal times again on short-term interest rates as the primary monetary policy instrument by adding two more elements. First, the monetary transmission mechanism of short-term interest rates is much more understood, and therefore much more predictable compared to the transmission mechanism of unconventional measures. Second, the effectiveness of unorthodox policies may depend on frictions prevailing in crisis circumstances, and it may, in fact, be lower in normal times.

Overall, it seems that there are many arguments for treating unconventional tools as, indeed, unconventional ones. Therefore, while they will be included in an enhanced monetary policy toolkit of monetary authorities, most likely they will remain unused in more tranquil periods (Tucker, 2018, pp. 48–64). This is also suggested by the fact that—prior to the Covid-19 pandemic—many central banks had begun implementing gradual exit strategies from unorthodox policies. Clearly, the pandemic-related global economic shock translated into a worldwide easing of monetary policies, which in many cases involved announcing the use of non-standard instruments.

This is, however, not implying that unconventional tools became part of a standard toolkit during peace times.

1.7 Possible directions of changes to an inflation targeting framework

Given the current state of the discussions on designing monetary policy strategies that would cope with all the identified challenges, it is not easy to foresee their outcomes. Clearly, however, Frankel (2012) who announced the death of inflation targeting after the global financial crisis, did so prematurely.

1.7.1 Proposals related to the identified shortcomings of inflation targeting

As noted above, the strongest accusation against an inflation targeting regime has been that it proved insufficient to safeguard financial stability which became apparent when the global financial crisis broke out. Another issue that the recent crises have brought to the centre of the monetary policy debates has been the ability of an inflation targeting regime to stimulate the economy and revive inflation, especially at the ZLB (Goodhart, 2018, p. 385). Regarding these two aspects, while the discussions on various policy options have yet to reach firm conclusions, the approaches adopted in practice by several central banks seem to indicate a quite widely accepted consensus around two ideas. First, that there is a need to develop macroprudential frameworks involving monetary authorities as the first line of defence against financial stability problems, and second, that central banks need to be ready to reach again for unconventional measures when faced with difficulties in providing adequate monetary policy accommodation.

While it may be claimed that broadening central banks' mandate by adding financial stability to the existing goals, and extending the scope of monetary policy instruments, constitute major changes to the inflation targeting strategy, it may well be argued that these elements can be viewed as complements to IT (Woodford, 2014, pp. 56–57). The latter interpretation would be even less controversial if macroprudential policy is considered as a separate policy and not a part of monetary policy (Viñals et al., 2018, pp. 146–150), and non-standard measures are thought of as a rescue option to be used only in case of severe downturns (Tucker, 2018, pp. 62–63).

Of course, deciding at which point a change already means a new regime is difficult, in particular when analysing inflation targeting, since this strategy from the very beginning has been continuously evolving (Niedźwiedzińska et al., 2019, pp. 42–72). Given the fact that in the 1990s, IT was tried as a pragmatic solution to the problem of heightened inflation without deep theoretical foundations, and only after proving to be quite successful and gaining popularity which motivated economists to look for reasons behind its effectiveness, this constant evolution should not be surprising. Apart from that, when adopting the framework, many inflation targeters were testing some innovative solutions that sometimes turned out to be beneficial and sometimes were abandoned (Ciżkowicz-Pękała et al., 2019, pp. 73–181). For that reasons, although key IT features are commonly known, they are defined in quite general terms and leave room for various interpretations. Indeed, the past three decades have shown that flexibility should be viewed as one of the important aspects of an inflation targeting regime.

Although sometimes it may not be easy to decide what can and what cannot be treated as compatible with IT, some proposals for reforming the currently used monetary policy frameworks clearly do not violate inflation targeting constituting features. Raising inflation targets is definitely one of them (Blanchard et al., 2010; Ball, 2014).[77] Despite not enjoying much support among central bankers (Bernanke, 2019, p. 5), not least due to its likely inconsistency with the mandate of price stability, the idea of increasing the targeted level of inflation in advanced economies from the most typical 2% to 4% has recently been proposed again (Posen, 2019, pp. 68–69).[78] Its key benefit would be to provide more space for lowering nominal interest rates before reaching the ZLB.

At the same time, recognising the fact that inflation targeting was introduced as a framework to fight too high inflation, some economists have raised doubts about whether it can be equally suitable for fighting too low price growth, which would suggest the need to go beyond IT (Heise, 2019, p. 77). Thus, a number of alternative targeting rules have been proposed. Similarly to the case of raising inflation targets, their main motivation is to deal with the problem of the ZLB.

Apart from the already mentioned price-level targeting and nominal GDP targeting, among the discussed options are temporary price-level targeting (Bernanke, 2019, pp. 3–48), i.e. inflation targeting combined with price-level targeting but only at the ZLB, or average inflation targeting[79] (Mertens and Williams, 2019), i.e. where any undershooting of the inflation target would have to be compensated with subsequent overshooting (an overshooting of the target would call for the opposite reaction).[80] Analysing each of them is beyond the scope of this study, but even the supporters of the proposed alternative targeting rules admit that they are not without drawbacks (Blanchard et al., 2014a, pp. 8–9).[81] For example, price-level targeting implies that if inflation is too high, the central bank must tighten monetary policy, even risking a recession to return to the previously announced price-level path, which, in practice, would be highly problematic. In turn, nominal GDP targeting requires that potential output is well specified, otherwise constant revisions of the targeted nominal GDP path would be necessary. Also, other targeting rules may, in fact, result in increasing—instead of decreasing—the instability of the economy. Thus, the implications need to be carefully considered, which will probably take some time. With the US Fed announcing average inflation targeting in August 2020, the trial period has started and will be carefully analysed by other central banks.

Importantly, even if some of the alternative targeting rules are adopted in the future, many of the investigated institutional features of inflation targeting will most likely remain in place. Particularly in the case of the currently discussed more complex rules, aspects related to the accountability and transparency of central banks' frameworks can become even more critical.

However, there are also proposals that constitute more radical solutions to reforming monetary policy frameworks and the current institutional arrangements, including modern monetary theory (Wray, 1998, 2012; Lavoie, 2019) and the abolishment of paper currency (Rogoff, 2017; Stracca, 2018, pp. 92–101). Despite being present in the discussions, at the current juncture they are less likely to find practical applications (Walsh, 2019).

1.7.2 Reviews of monetary policy frameworks in central banks

With the ongoing discussions about feasible alternatives to IT, so far, no visible retreat from inflation targeting can be seen. This is partly explained by the observation that—due to its flexibility and evolving nature—the regime allows for accommodating many of the identified deficiencies without the need to abandon the framework altogether.

Indirectly, the fact that in 2012 the United States decided to officially announce an explicit numerical longer-run goal for inflation, which brought their monetary policy strategy significantly closer to an inflation targeting framework, proved the support for this regime as well. Additionally, also Japan moved in the same direction in 2012. Evidently, at that point, an IT regime was assessed as helpful in reviving inflation, since in these two countries—amidst weak price dynamics—the quantitative inflation targets were supposed to raise inflation expectations.

In 2019, the US Fed launched a comprehensive review of its monetary policy strategy (Fed, 2019), and some voices suggested that the euro area should do the same (Bank of Finland, 2019; ECB, 2019a), which indeed resulted in a European Central Bank (ECB) initiative to reassess its monetary policy framework. The reviews have concentrated on monetary policy instruments and communication, the relationship between inflation and the real economy, and the inflation objective itself, with the view of coping with the consequences of the ZLB in an environment of persistently weak inflationary pressures (Powell, 2019; Fed, 2019; Lagarde, 2020).

In August 2020, the United States concluded its review (Fed, 2020; Powell, 2020, Brainard, 2020; Clarida, 2020). The Fed announced average inflation targeting combined with the asymmetric treatment of the labour market situation by declaring to focus on shortfalls in employment. As already noted, the Fed seems to mean—at least at the current juncture of subdued price developments—asymmetric average inflation targeting, since it explicitly stated that past undershooting of the inflation target would have to be compensated with subsequent acceptance of inflation moderately above its longer-term goal, without indicating that overshooting would also need to be compensated.

The outcome of the ECB considerations is not yet known. The euro area, as of now, has moved in a direction of announcing a symmetry of its inflation aim, which may also be seen as an attempt to strengthen the ECB commitment to fight excessively low inflation (ECB, 2019b).

Interestingly, New Zealand has recently announced changes to its monetary policy framework by introducing a dual mandate—i.e. it has complemented the central bank's price stability objective with an additional aim of supporting maximum sustainable employment.[82] However, the Reserve Bank of New Zealand continues to emphasise that it contributes to public welfare by reducing cyclical fluctuations in economic activity while maintaining price stability over the medium term. The bank also indicates that the maximum sustainable level of employment is largely determined by non-monetary factors, and that adding it as an objective only reinforces the flexibility of the conducted monetary policy. As a result, New Zealand still calls its monetary policy strategy flexible inflation targeting (Reserve Bank of New Zealand, 2019, p. 62).

At the same time, the support for IT among emerging market economies continues to be strong, with a number of countries still preparing to adopt an inflation targeting regime. This seems natural given the fact that emerging market economies have benefited the most from adopting an inflation targeting regime.[83] Recently, only Argentina had to suspend using an IT strategy, but—as already mentioned—it seems that Argentina was simply not prepared to become an inflation targeter.

What is worth noting is that apart from Argentina, to date none of the countries that adopted an inflation targeting regime has ever abandoned it.[84] Even Iceland, which directly after the financial crisis of 2008 focused its monetary policy on stabilising the exchange rate, did not officially stop using an IT framework at that time, and has continued to declare being an inflation targeter.[85]

1.7.3 Empirical comparison of monetary policy regimes with respect to financial stability issues and ZLB

Moreover, also looking at empirical evidence, there may be good reasons not to be too critical about the dominance of IT. Apart from the already discussed traditional literature assessing the effectiveness of various monetary policy frameworks in delivering price stability and limiting output volatility, it is worth mentioning some recent studies dealing with IT in the context of promoting financial stability and coping with the crises.

The findings of preliminary research on the link between pursuing an inflation targeting strategy and accumulating financial imbalances are rather reassuring. In particular, after investigating a rich database of nearly 5500 commercial banks from 70 countries (out of which 22 were inflation targeters) for the period 1998–2012, Fazio et al. (2015) showed that, on average, banking systems of IT countries were more stable, had sounder systemically important banks, and were less distressed than—or at least as distressed as—banking systems from countries following different monetary policy strategies.[86] Considering those results, the authors concluded that inflation targeting cannot be blamed for contributing to financial instability. Similarly, Fouejieu (2017), who analysed emerging market economies based on a sample of 26 countries (out of which 13 were inflation targeters), found that the monetary policy of IT economies was relatively more sensitive to financial risks compared to the monetary policy of economies implementing alternative policy strategies. However, despite this, the financial sector of inflation targeters appeared to be more fragile than that of the control group. Taken together, those results indicate that central banks cannot guarantee the stability of the financial system with their interest rate policies, and thus, should remain focused on controlling inflation, while financial stability should be promoted with the help of macroprudential tools.

Also, initial attempts at assessing the effectiveness of various monetary policy strategies in dealing with the crises suggested that an IT framework is relatively robust. For example, based on a sample of 84 countries (out of which 25 were inflation targeters)[87] analysed over the period 2006–2009, De Carvalho Filho (2010) concluded that IT countries lowered their nominal policy rates by more than other countries and this loosening translated into an even larger differential in real interest rates. Moreover, IT economies were less likely to face deflation scares, and went through deep real depreciations without experiencing a relative deterioration in their risk assessment. The author also found some weak evidence that IT countries outperformed others with respect to unemployment rates, and that IT advanced economies enjoyed relatively stronger industrial production compared to the control group. Finally, advanced economy inflation targeters recorded higher GDP growth rates than advanced economies that followed alternative monetary policy strategies, with no such difference being established in the case of emerging market countries. Similar results were found in De Carvalho Filho (2011) investigating a somewhat smaller sample of 51 advanced and emerging market economies.

It is important to note that the cited empirical works do not allow for comparing theoretical alternatives to inflation targeting, such as the various proposed targeting rules. Moreover, it is too early to draw firm conclusions based on only those few analyses, although they clearly weaken the arguments of IT opponents.

1.8 Concluding remarks

The analysis conducted in Chapter 1 shows that an inflation targeting framework evolved from a pragmatic solution applied in one country in specific circumstances to combat elevated inflation, into a fully fledged monetary policy strategy that, in fact, turned out to be highly flexible. Consequently, inflation targeting has become a dominant regime among big and medium-sized countries.

Inflation targeting incorporates the main conclusions drawn from monetary economics, namely, that there is no long-run trade-off between output and inflation, and that inflation is associated with costs. It also takes into account the role of expectations and the need to use a strong nominal anchor when conducting policies. Within this regime, monetary policy is thought of as a way to stabilise the economy, predominantly by maintaining price stability, but with a preference also for minimising output fluctuations. Thus, it is often stressed that central banks follow a flexible inflation targeting framework, as opposed to strict inflation targeting where monetary authorities would care only for meeting an inflation target, independently of the high costs it would cause.

Looking at elements constituting an inflation targeting strategy, these include clear priority for price stability as a monetary policy objective, public announcement of an inflation target, conducting monetary policy based on a wide range of information, and fulfilling high accountability and transparency requirements, which complement the significant independence granted to monetary authorities. More generally, an IT framework is based on using certain instruments in order to meet specific targets, although it cannot be treated as a simple prescription of predetermined actions needed to reach the final objectives.

It seems that the key feature that makes inflation targeting so compelling to many countries, is that, in practice, it proposes a reasonable balance between inflation and output stabilisation, without, however, sacrificing central banks' credibility. From another perspective, it can also be seen as a compromise between a policy conducted according to rules and a policy allowing for discretion, which is possible owing to the emphasis placed on accountability and transparency within that framework. For these reasons, the notion of constrained discretion appears to be the best way to describe the essence of an IT strategy.

Regarding the critique of an inflation targeting framework related to the recent crises, it concentrated on discussing the need to account for financial stability considerations in monetary policy decisions and to use non-standard measures. The debate on what role financial stability issues should play is ongoing, but it aims at developing proper macroprudential frameworks, accompanied by some "leaning against the wind" in order to limit excessive credit bubbles, rather than at revolutionising monetary policy. Considering instruments, inflation targeting proved fairly robust and, especially compared to other regimes, allowed for providing substantial monetary policy stimulus when it was needed. Indisputably, however, in many economies the additional accommodation had to be introduced with the help of unconventional measures. While it can be seen as stretching the strategy, it turned out that the set of monetary policy tools may be modified well within an IT framework. Overall, a flexible inflation targeting regime still seems to be a quite useful option for central banks, although debates on alternative targeting rules—motivated by the possible lasting consequences of secular stagnation and the flattening of the Phillips curve—are not concluded, as yet.

Irrespective of the outcome of the discussions on monetary policy strategies, many of the institutional arrangements developed as important aspects of an inflation targeting framework will most likely remain in place. These include, in particular, issues related to accountability and transparency mechanisms.

At the same time, when listing the constituting elements of an IT regime, it was indicated that they leave room for different interpretations and can be implemented in various ways. It would, therefore, be useful to check how these key IT features are put into practice, which will be investigated in Chapter 2.

Notes

1 While describing the origins of monetary economics, Schumpeter (1955, pp. 51–59) starts with references to Plato and Aristotle.
2 The quantity theory of money originated from noticing in the mid-1550s that the inflow of precious metals from the Spanish colonies to Europe resulted in higher prices and the depreciation of precious metals. A similar observation was made somewhat earlier by Copernicus (1526; cited after VanLear, 2015, p. 5), who recognised that abundant money usually depreciated.
3 Whereas Wicksell (1898) is commonly referred to while indicating the origins of the concept of a natural interest rate, some economists (Smithin, 2013, p. 52) also cite Thornton (1802). A natural interest rate can be defined as the equilibrium real interest rate consistent with price stability.
4 Those assumptions regarded, among others, limited changes in liquidity preference, marginal productivity of capital, propensity to consume and nominal wages, which in turn depended on expectations and uncertainty about the future.
5 The IS–LM model shows how interactions between the investment–saving curve (the IS curve) and the liquidity preference–money supply curve (LM curve) influence the equilibrium interest rate and real output.
6 Samuelson's textbook titled *Economics* was first published in 1948, and was subsequently revised, appearing in 19 different editions, with many co-authored by Nordhaus, e.g. Samuelson and Nordhaus (1992). The neoclassical synthesis was introduced in the 1955 edition, and its mature version was incorporated in the 1967 edition (Kokoszczyński, 2004, p. 28).
7 Applying theories for making policy recommendations was encouraged by the new econometric model-building techniques developed, among others, by Meade (1951), Tinbergen (1952), Poole (1970), and Blinder and Solow (1973).

8 The term "stagflation" was used for the first time when discussing the economic situation in the United Kingdom in the 1960s, and referred to the combination of high inflation and low GDP growth (House of Commons Official Report, 1965, p. 1165).

9 This is not to disregard that, in general, Keynes was also supporting the idea that price stability should be the main target of monetary policy (Bofinger, 2001, p. 129). Regarding Keynesianism, given its confidence in fiscal policy and its scepticism with respect to monetary policy, combined with the focus on employment goals compared to controlling inflation (Wojtyna, 2000, p. 97), this was, however, a much less emphasised claim.

10 Some economists argued, however, that even the central banks that officially announced targeting monetary aggregates, from the very beginning were in fact controlling interest rates instead of money supply (Moore, 1988; Posen, 1997; Lavoie, 2019).

11 In the short run, firms would have problems in distinguishing whether they faced relative or absolute price changes which would encourage them to produce more. Unemployed, in turn, could mistake higher market wages for higher purchasing power, which would encourage them to accept the job. However, as soon as firms and workers noticed their mistakes, they would return to the previous levels of output and employment.

12 To avoid the Lucas critique, economists started to look for ways to build their models based on microfoundations and take account of rational expectations (Fischer, 2008, p. 21). Moreover, dynamic models have largely replaced static ones, which, to a significant extent, can also be treated as a legacy of the new classicals.

13 In turn, supply-side shocks that would exert a negative impact on output may encompass, for example, unfavourable weather conditions, oil price shocks, stricter environmental rules, or safety regulations.

14 Some other stylised facts related to business cycles were also addressed by the theory (McGrattan, 2008, pp. 10–13). For example, the reason for investment being more volatile than consumption was explained as the outcome of an intertemporal optimisation of consumption-investment decisions. Likewise, the procyclical behaviour of labour was to follow from an intertemporal optimisation of work-leisure trade-offs, with substitution effects related to the choice between work and leisure dominating income effects. However, labour fluctuations seemed to be still too volatile compared to changes in real wages to be fully explained in this way.

15 Economists favouring the neoclassical synthesis treated prices and expectations in the short term as given, i.e. fixed, or adjusting only in line with the adaptive expectation hypothesis, which gave rise to a disequilibrium phenomenon. In turn, economists supporting the new classical way of thinking argued that prices should be seen as perfectly flexible, even in the short term, and expectations should be governed by the rational expectation hypothesis, with deviations from equilibrium being simply the result of the lack of full information (Dixon, 2008, p. 40).

16 Important complementary research included the literature investigating reasons why small menu costs were able to produce disequilibrium outcomes via nominal rigidities. Dixon and Hansen (1999) showed that price stickiness in one sector of the economy may spill over to other sectors, resulting in prices in the whole economy becoming less responsive to shocks. Ball and Romer (1990) provided further support for the notion that prices were not likely to be freely adjusted to a market clearing level, claiming that real rigidities even combined

with small nominal rigidities reduce the scale of menu costs necessary to induce sticky prices.

17 Goodfriend and King (1997) saw incorporating intertemporal optimisation, rational expectations, imperfect competition, and costly price adjustment into macroeconomic models as central for the new neoclassical synthesis.

18 A hybrid variant of the new Keynesian Phillips curve derived by Galí and Gertler (1999) related inflation to real marginal costs, expected future inflation, and lagged inflation, whereas the proxy for real marginal costs could include output gap estimates or a labour income share, with the latter, in fact, favoured by the authors.

19 However, the Taylor rule and its modified versions could only be treated as simplified approximations of central bank policy, since they have not been mechanically followed by monetary authorities when setting nominal rates.

20 The Taylor principle is a necessary condition in most models for a unique equilibrium.

21 As their name indicates, DSGE models are used to analyse the evolution of the economy over time (i.e. are dynamic); allow for random shocks (i.e. are stochastic); encompass the whole economy, meaning firms, households, and monetary authorities (i.e. are general); and recognise the existence of the general steady state (i.e. are of equilibrium). They were first proposed by the economists of the real business cycle school. Only recently, some financial frictions have been added to the analysis.

22 An important development of the 1990s that took place almost in parallel with the emergence of the new neoclassical synthesis, and, in fact, shared many of its assumptions, was the extension of the original DSGE models to deal with open economy issues. It can be viewed as an attempt to formalise the determinants of exchange rate fluctuations within DSGE models based on microfoundations, with nominal rigidities and imperfect competition (Corsetti, 2008, pp. 45–51).

23 However, as noted above, already in the late 1980s, some economists claimed that the variable controlled *de facto* by monetary authorities was interest rate and not money supply (Moore, 1988; Bindseil and König, 2013).

24 While monetary policy was given the primary role, fiscal policy was regarded as less important, and geared towards providing sustainable conditions related to expenditure and taxation (Dixon, 2008, p. 43).

25 The notion of the Great Moderation refers to the reduction in the volatility of business cycle fluctuations accompanied by low inflation, observed in advanced economies starting in the mid-1980s.

26 Several arguments are raised in the literature to explain reasons behind the fall in the natural rate of interest. These include a declining rate of population growth (Bielecki et al., 2018), resulting in a higher propensity to save (Bernanke, 2005; Bofinger and Ries, 2017), and changing the nature of technical progress (Gordon, 2012). Koo (2014) claims that balance sheet recession is another reason for secular stagnation.

27 An effective lower bound used to be called a zero lower bound (ZLB), but since a number of central banks have recently cut their interest rates below zero, the notion of an effective lower bound seems more accurate. Yates (2002, pp. 11–12) reviews reasons why the cost of holding cash may not be zero, resulting in the ZLB falling to a negative territory. Thereafter, the ZLB is also used to indicate an effective lower bound.

28 To address that problem, two main pieces of advice are given—increasing inflation targets or employing unconventional monetary policy measures. Each of the proposed solutions has its drawback, with higher inflation targets threatening

central banks' reputation, not least, due to the difficulty in making them credible amidst a prolong period of inflation undershooting the existing targets in many economies, and unconventional monetary policy measures having their limitations and being, at times, criticised for unfavourable side effects. Some of these arguments are discussed later in more detail.

29 At the same time, it has been argued that households' inflation expectations remain rather sensitive to price changes of frequently purchased goods, such as food or fuel (Coibion et al., 2018).

30 Apart from firmer anchoring inflation expectations, many other explanations of the weaker reaction of prices to output changes have been proposed. Some point to significant inflation inertia or deficiencies in properly estimating the economic slack, while others indicate that—besides central banks' credibility—other structural determinants probably changed as well. Among the often-mentioned factors are stronger globalisation reducing the impact of domestic factors on price developments (Borio and Filardo, 2007; Auer et al., 2017), or the decentralisation of the wage bargaining (Kügler et al., 2018).

31 A weaker reaction of prices to economic activity is equivalent to a higher sacrifice ratio, i.e. a deeper decrease in output is needed to bring inflation down from heightened levels, and in the case of excessively low inflation, a significantly stronger economic upswing is required to revive price growth.

32 Regarding monetary policy instruments, initially changes to the money supply were regarded as key. Currently, the emphasis has clearly been on changes to short-term nominal interest rates. However, adopting a central bank's interest rate as the main monetary policy instrument has become standard practice only with time. For example, in New Zealand, at the time when an IT framework was introduced, the main monetary policy instrument was settlement cash (i.e. the level of commercial banks' reserves at the central bank). In 1997–1999, the Reserve Bank of New Zealand experimented with using the Monetary Condition Index (MCI) as an operating target, and only after negative experiences with that tool moved to treating a short-term interest rate as its operating target (Archer et al., 1999).

33 The latter notion emphasises concepts that have been introduced to central banking relatively recently, such as communication and transparency, while historically the debate about strategies focused on a more fundamental choice between money-supply strategies and interest-rate strategies.

34 In Borio (2001, p. 3), operating targets and monetary policy instruments are classified as belonging to the tactical level of policy implementation, and not to strategy.

35 At the same time, the international gold standard that prevailed before the 1920s could be treated as a "rule-like" regime. Likewise, the currency board arrangements used nowadays by Bulgaria and Hong Kong, among others, can be regarded as "rule-like" frameworks that are still practiced (Bernanke, 2003).

36 It is worth noticing that Bernanke and Mishkin (1997, pp. 8–15) prefer to use the term "framework" rather than a "rule" when speaking of inflation targeting. Similarly, Wojtyna (2004, pp. 256–257) clearly distinguishes between strategies and frameworks, to which inflation targeting is counted, and rules, which are treated as a synonym of instrument rules only.

37 A useful description of price-level targeting can be found, for example, in Mishkin (2006, pp. 22–23). Whereas nominal GDP targeting is discussed, for example, in Bofinger (2001, pp. 274–281).

38 Bofinger (2001, p. 274) and White (1999, pp. 223–225) indicate that the explicit nominal GDP rule is equivalent to the implicit McCallum rule. The McCallum rule gives recommendations to monetary authorities on changing the growth rate

of the monetary base, i.e. a narrow monetary aggregate that encompasses currency outstanding and bank reserves (McCallum, 2000).

39 Only Sweden in the 1930s was following price-level targeting, when the Riksbank was obliged by the government to maintain a constant price level (Błaszczyk, 2019, pp. 149–155).

40 In Germany and Switzerland, monetary targeting was rather successful, especially if compared to the experiences of Canada, the United Kingdom, and the United States.

41 In this work, a regime based on multiple nominal anchors is called an eclectic strategy, whereas a framework that is not making use of any explicit nominal anchor is called a discretionary strategy. In turn, Szpunar (2000, p. 193) uses the term eclectic strategy for regimes that do not use an explicit nominal anchor. Despite the apparent conceptual difference, in practice, eclectic and discretionary regimes are rather close to each other.

42 A critical commentary of all these options can be found in Blinder (1998, pp. 40–48) and Bénassy-Quéré et al. (2010, pp. 296–300).

43 Currently, in an environment of too low inflation persisting in some—predominantly advanced—economies, such an approach should not be valued. Central banks' officials should be equally credible in pursuing policies aimed at avoiding excessively low price growth.

44 In early 2019, the organisation of the decision-making process in the Reserve Bank of New Zealand changed, since a collegial decision-making body was created.

45 The government here is understood as the minister of finance.

46 Until early 2019, the governor of the Reserve Bank of New Zealand was a single decision-maker.

47 As already noted, only Sweden was testing price-level targeting in the 1930s (Błaszczyk, 2019, pp. 149–155).

48 The agreed rules were the first example of a fully negotiated monetary system that was intended to regulate monetary relations between independent states. Under certain conditions, it was also possible to change the exchange rate values.

49 However, overall, the 1970s were characterised by rather infrequent changes in monetary policy frameworks, which can be attributable to the then prevailing view of limited monetary policy effectiveness (Fry et al., 2000, p. 6).

50 Introducing inflation targeting followed from the adoption of the Reserve Bank of New Zealand Act of 1989 that acknowledged price stability as the main objective of the monetary authority. Even though the mandate of the central bank has recently changed, as described below, New Zealand has been still pursuing an IT strategy.

51 As already noted, for over a decade around the 1980s inflation in New Zealand exceeded 10%, which was one of the highest inflation rates among OECD countries at that time.

52 The global financial crisis of 2008 can be seen as a more recent example of exceptional conditions encouraging some central banks to announce inflation targets.

53 As already indicated, the only exception is Argentina.

54 A more comprehensive assessment of the strengths and weaknesses of various monetary policy regimes can be found, for example, in Mishkin (1999, pp. 2–40), Bofinger (2001, pp. 248–268, 414–428), and Szpunar (2000, pp. 130–208).

55 According to the IMF (2018, p. 5), exchange rate targeting regimes include cases of no separate legal tender, currency boards, pegs or stabilised arrangements (with or without bands), crawling pegs or crawl-like arrangements, and other managed arrangements.

56 Other available options, although not always effective, include changing between targeted monetary aggregates, targeting multiple monetary aggregates, or modifying the construction of targeted aggregates. For example, in the euro area in 2001, i.e. before implicitly reducing the importance of the reference value for M3 growth in the ECB strategy in 2003, the ECB started to compute an adjusted M3 (adjusted for all non-euro area residents' holdings of negotiable instruments), claiming that it may be more relevant for the assessment of monetary developments than the previously used M3 aggregate (ECB, 2001, 2003).

57 Monetary transmission mechanism is described in more detail in e.g. Bank of England (1999) and Mishkin (2012).

58 The topic of preconditions for a successful IT adoption is quite broad (Mishkin, 2004, pp. 2–29), but few points are straightforward. First of all, the transmission of monetary impulses to the economy, i.e. mainly of changes to short-term interest rates, although occasionally also of FX interventions, must be working, requiring, in particular, low levels of dollarisation or euroisation (Brzoza-Brzezina, 2011, pp. 87–101). Additionally, a central bank must have extensive forecasting capabilities, since the regular preparation and publication of forecasts is highly recommended. It even found reflection in the strategy being sometimes called an inflation-forecast targeting (Svensson, 1997, p. 1111; Woodford, 2007, pp. 7–9). On top of that, a lot of central banks' resources have to be devoted to meeting high accountability and transparency standards. For these reasons, inflation targeting may not be suitable for all economies.

59 Formulating explicit numerical targets became quite common in the 1990s. The survey conducted by Fry et al. (2000) reveals that in the late 1990s, 95% out of 94 analysed central banks used some kind of an explicit target, and almost half of monetary authorities announced targets for more than one variable (out of a set comprising inflation, money or credit growth, and exchange rate), whereas in the early 1980s such targets were used by only 8% of central banks. In fact, on average, at the end of the surveyed period, each country used 1.5 explicit numerical targets (Fry et al., 2000, pp. 29, 38).

60 The results are broadly in line with the indications of Cottarelli and Giannini (1997, p. 10), that cover a somewhat broader group of 100 countries but only in the period 1970–1994, which makes their study less relevant for analysing developments related to IT.

61 That is why some countries announced well in advanced their plans to adopt an IT strategy.

62 As already noted, this changed in the case of the United States in August 2020, i.e. when modifications to the US monetary policy strategy were announced. At that point, the US Fed admitted that since 2012 it had been pursuing inflation targeting, although previously its framework was not officially named IT.

63 In the study, the euro area is counted as one economy and for that reason the number of analysed inflation targeters is 42.

64 Instrument independence may have many different aspects, including functional, institutional, personal, and financial independence (ECB, 2018, pp. 20–28), which will be discussed later.

65 A comprehensive review of costs related to inflation can be found, for example, in Fischer (1994, pp. 272–274).

66 Available research shows that the probability of hitting a ZLB falls rapidly if an inflation target rises from 0% to around 4% (Billi and Kahn, 2008, p. 13).

67 A prominent example of a major shock is the Covid-19 pandemic which prompted many central banks—both from advanced economies and emerging market economies—to apply non-standard measures (Niedźwiedzińska, 2020).

Whereas the monetary policy response to the pandemic is beyond the scope of this study, it clearly proves that the ZLB became the key aspect to consider.

68 It is often indicated that consumer price inflation may be incorrectly measured, especially since it is difficult to capture price changes adjusted for quality improvements and substitution among products.

69 An overview of arguments for a positive price growth as the optimal rate of inflation can be found, for example, in Yates (1995, pp. 136–148).

70 Examples of intermediate targets include exchange rates or monetary aggregates.

71 While a too narrow focus on inflation is the main line of criticism against inflation targeting, it should be remembered that the United States—where the biggest financial imbalances accumulated, resulting in the global financial crisis of 2008—announced a 2% inflation goal only in 2012. Thus, strictly speaking, they were not following an explicit inflation targeting regime at the time when the build-up of imbalances took place, possibly fuelled by excessively low interest rates (Taylor, 2007; BIS, 2008, pp. 7–9; Taylor, 2009).

72 Investigating reasons behind the outbreak of the global financial crisis is beyond the scope of this study, but evidently many problems stemmed from regulatory shortcomings. Valuable references can be found in, e.g. Taylor (2007), White (2009), Wojtyna (2011), King, (2014), Koppl (2014), Bernanke (2015), and Bernanke, Geithner, and Paulson (2019). An important reference of a more general nature is also Minksy (2008).

73 It is worth noting that the disagreement was about monetary policy reaction to changes in asset prices beyond what was justified by the need to reach the main objectives of central banks in terms of inflation and output stabilisation.

74 Short-term liquidity-providing measures can be thought of as belonging much more to the area related to the lender-of-last-resort role of the central bank.

75 The Covid-19 pandemic and the related monetary policy easing also involved applying unconventional measures in many countries. In fact, the speed at which the central banks reached for non-standard instruments in 2020 indicated that they are becoming less unorthodox than previously thought (Niedźwiedzińska, 2020).

76 This gave rise to the proposal of raising inflation targets in advanced economies, what in principle should limit the risk of hitting the ZLB (Blanchard, Dell'Ariccia, and Mauro, 2010, pp. 10–11). However, this idea has not met with much support within central banks and also many economists pointed out numerous disadvantages of such a change. This issue is discussed a bit broader below.

77 Extending the definition of price stability targets, to include—apart from consumer prices—various asset prices, could be seen as another option (Aydin and Volkan, 2011; Weber, 2015; Heise, 2019, pp. 77–79), but it seems to receive less attention.

78 At the same time, some central banks' announcements can be seen as aimed at lifting inflation targets—at least slightly. In particular, since 2016 the US Fed has been stressing the symmetry of its inflation goal (Fed, 2016). Likewise, the ECB in July 2019 assessed its inflation aim—for the first time in its communication—also as symmetric (ECB, 2019b).

79 Those frameworks can also be called "makeup" strategies (Brainard, 2019, pp. 50–51).

80 Importantly, strictly speaking, when announcing average inflation targeting in August 2020, the US Fed did not mention the symmetry of its approach, and stressed that only undershooting of the inflation target would have to be compensated with subsequent overshooting.

81 A critical appraisal of some of the discussed alternative targeting rules can be found in Bank of Canada (2011, pp. 16–20), Dorn (2018, pp. 193–194), and Thornton (2019, pp. 212–215).

82 Amendments to the monetary policy framework of New Zealand were enacted in 2018 and came into effect in April 2019.

83 Although Agénor and Pereira da Silva (2019) indicate that strong capital flows following the recent crises and subsequent shifts in the monetary policies of major central banks made some emerging market economy inflation targeters review their IT policy frameworks as well. Those reviews were related to increasing the scope for FX interventions to smooth exchange rate volatility, and to acknowledge the fact that when central banks are concerned with maintaining both price and financial stability, monetary and macroprudential policies should be treated as complements.

84 As already mentioned, only some European countries that had pursued an IT strategy in the past (Finland, Spain, the Slovak Republic), but subsequently joined the euro area, dropped out of being counted individually as inflation targeters. However, the euro area has been treated as following an inflation targeting regime.

85 As already noted, shortly after the crisis, the Central Bank of Iceland implicitly admitted that it temporarily departed from IT, but more recently it has stopped indicating that (CBI, 2010, p. 7; 2017, p. 10).

86 In a more recent study, Fazio et al. (2018) analysed data from the banks of 66 countries for the period 1998–2014 to compare how institutional quality impacts financial stability in IT countries compared to the control group. The main finding was that, while banks from IT countries with high-quality institutions did not enjoy significantly higher stability, banks from countries with institutions with average levels of quality seemed to benefit from IT. In addition, in banks from countries with poor-quality institutions, a negative relationship between operating an IT economy and financial stability was reported, indicating that at least some trust in the country's authorities is necessary in order to conduct effective policies.

87 The United States was excluded from the sample, since it was treated as the source of the initial shock. The euro area was not analysed as one economy, instead several of the euro area individual member states were included in the study. Switzerland was counted as an inflation targeter.

References

Abo-Zaid, S., Tuzemen, D. (2012), "Inflation Targeting: A Three-Decade Perspective", *Journal of Policy Modeling*, 34(5), pp. 621–645. https://doi.org/10.1016/j.jpolmod.2011.08.004

Acharya, V., Eisert, T., Eufinger, C., Hirsch, C. (2015), "Whatever It Takes: The Real Effects of Unconventional Monetary Policy", *IMF 16th Jacques Polak Annual Research Conference*, November. www.imf.org/external/np/res/seminars/2015/arc/pdf/Eisert.pdf

Agénor, P.-R., Pereira da Silva, L. A. (2019), *Integrated Inflation Targeting: Another Perspective from the Developing World*, BIS. www.bis.org/publ/othp30.htm

Akerlof, G. A., Yellen, J. L. (1985), "A Near-Rational Model of the Business Cycle, with Wage and Price Inertia", *The Quarterly Journal of Economics*, 100(Supplement), pp. 823–838. http://doi.org/10.1093/qje/100.supplement.823

Amano, R., Moran, K., Murchison, S., Rennison, A. (2009), "Trend Inflation, Wage and Price Rigidities, and Productivity Growth", *Journal of Monetary Economics*, 56(3), pp. 353–364. https://doi.org/10.1016/j.jmoneco.2009.03.001

Archer, D., Brookes, A., Reddell, M. (1999), "A Cash Rate System for Implementing Monetary Policy", *Reserve Bank of New Zealand Bulletin*, 62(1), pp. 51–61.

Auer, R., Borio, C., Filardo, A. (2017), "The Globalisation of Inflation: The Growing Importance of Global Value Chains", *BIS Working Paper, No. 602*, pp. 1–23. www.bis.org/publ/work602.pdf

Aydin, B., Volkan, E. (2011), "Incorporating Financial Stability in Inflation Targeting Frameworks", *IMF Working Paper, No. 11/224*. www.imf.org/external/pubs/ft/wp/2011/wp11224.pdf

Backhouse, R. E., Boianovsky, M. (2016), "Secular Stagnation: The History of a Macroeconomic Heresy", *European Journal of the History of Economic Thought*, 23(6). http://doi.org/10.2139/ssrn.2602903

Balassa, B. (1964), "The Purchasing Power Parity Doctrine: A Reappraisal", *Journal of Political Economy*, 72(6), pp. 584–596. https://doi.org/10.1086/258965

Balima, H. P., Kilama, E. G., Tapsoba, R. (2017), "Settling the Inflation Targeting Debate: Lights from a Meta-Regression Analysis", *IMF Working Paper, No. 213*. www.imf.org/en/Publications/WP/Issues/2017/09/29/Settling-the-Inflation-Targeting-Debate-Lights-from-a-Meta-Regression-Analysis-45253

Ball, L. (2014), "The Case for a Long-Run Inflation Target of Four Percent", *IMF Working Paper, No. 14/9257*, pp. 1–19. www.imf.org/external/pubs/ft/wp/2014/wp1492.pdf

Ball, L., Romer, D. (1990), "Real Rigidities and the Non-Neutrality of Money", *Review of Economic Studies*, 57(2), pp. 183–203.

Ball, L., Sheridan, N. (2005), "Does Inflation Targeting Matter?", in: B. S. Bernanke, M. Woodford (eds.), *The Inflation-Targeting Debate*, University of Chicago Press, pp. 249–276.

Bank of Canada (2011), *Renewal of the Inflation-Control Target*, November. www.bankofcanada.ca/wp-content/uploads/2011/11/background_nov11.pdf

Bank of England (1999), *Quarterly Bulletin*, May.

Bank of Finland (2019), *Bank of Finland Bulletin of 15 March 2019*.

Barro, R. J., Gordon, D. B. (1983), "A Positive Theory of Monetary Policy in a Natural Rate Model", *The Journal of Political Economy*, 91(4), pp. 589–610. https://doi.org/10.1086/261167

Bayoumi, T., Dell'Ariccia, G., Habermeier, K., Mancini-Griffoli, T., Valencia, F. (2014), "Monetary Policy in the New Normal", *IMF Staff Discussion Note*. http://doi.org/10.5089/9781475561784.006

Bean, C., Paustian, M., Penalver, A., Taylor, T. (2010), "Monetary Policy After the Fall", *Proceedings From Economic Policy Symposium—Jackson Hole*, Federal Reserve Bank of Kansas City, pp. 267–328. www.kansascityfed.org/publicat/sympos/2010/Bean_final.pdf

Belka, M. (1986), *Doktryna Ekonomiczno-Społeczna Miltona Friedmana*, PWN.

Bénassy-Quéré, A., Cœuré, B., Jacquet, P., Pisani-Ferry, A. (2010), *Economic Policy: Theory and Practice*, Oxford University Press.

Bénassy-Quéré, A., Coeuré, B., Jacquet, P., Pisani-Ferry, A. (2019), *Economic Policy: Theory and Practice*, Oxford University Press.

Bernanke, B. S. (2003), "'Constrained Discretion' and Monetary Policy", *Remarks Before the Money Marketeers of New York University*, New York, 3 February.

Bernanke, B. S. (2005), "The Global Saving Glut and the U.S. Current Account Deficit", Board of Governors of the Federal Reserve System, *Speech 77*. www.bis .org/review/r050318d.pdf

Bernanke, B. S. (2010), "The Economic Outlook and Monetary Policy", *Speech at the Jackson Hole Economic Policy Symposium.*

Bernanke, B. S. (2015), *The Courage to Act: A Memoir of a Crisis and Its Aftermath*, W. W. Norton & Company.

Bernanke, B. S. (2019), "Monetary Policy in a New Era", in: O. Blanchard, L. H. Summer (eds.), *Evolution or Revolution? Rethinking Macroeconomic Policy after the Great Recession*, MIT Press, pp. 3–48.

Bernanke, B. S., Geithner, T. F., Paulson, H. M., Jr. (2019), *Firefighting: The Financial Crisis and Its Lessons*, Profile Books Ltd.

Bernanke, B. S., Mishkin, F. S. (1997), "Inflation Targeting: A New Framework for Monetary Policy?", *NBER Working Paper, No. 5893*, pp. 1–30. https://doi.org /10.3386/w5893

Bielecki, M., Brzoza-Brzezina, M., Kolasa, M. (2018), "Demographics, Monetary Policy and the Zero Lower Bound", *NBP Working Paper, No. 284*, pp. 1–42. www.nbp.pl/publikacje/materialy_i_studia/284_en.pdf

Billi, R. M., Kahn, G. A. (2008), "What Is the Optimal Inflation Rate?", *Economic Review of the Federal Reserve Bank of Kansas City*, Second Quarter.

Bindseil, U., König, P. J. (2013), "Basil J. Moore's Horizontalists and Verticalists: An Appraisal 25 Years Later", *Review of Keynesian Economics*, 1(4), pp. 383–390

Bini Smaghi, L. (2009), "Conventional and Unconventional Monetary Policy", *Keynote Lecture at the International Center for Monetary and Banking Studies (ICMB)*, Geneva, 28 April. www.ecb.europa.eu/press/key/date/2009/html/sp 090428.en.html

BIS (2008), "78th Annual Report". www.bis.org/publ/arpdf/ar2008e.pdf

Blanchard, O. (2008), "Neoclassical Synthesis", in: S. N. Durlauf, L. E. Blume (eds.), *The New Palgrave Dictionary of Economics*, 2nd Edition, Vol. 5, Palgrave Macmillan, pp. 896–899.

Blanchard, O., Cerutti, E., Summers, L. (2015), "Inflation and Activity—Two Explorations and Their Implications for Monetary Policy", *IMF Working Paper, No. 15/230*, pp. 1–28. www.imf.org/external/pubs/ft/wp/2015/wp15230.pdf

Blanchard, O., Dell'Ariccia, G., Mauro, P. (2010), „Rethinking Macroeconomic Policy", *IMF Staff Position Note, 3*. https://doi.org/10.5089/9781455224982.00 4.a001

Blanchard, O., Dell'Ariccia, G., Mauro, P. (2014a), "Introduction: Rethinking Macro Policy II—Getting Granular", in: G. Akerlof, O. Blanchard, D. Romer, J. Stiglitz (eds.), *What Have We Learnt? Macroeconomic Policy after the Crisis*, MIT Press, pp. 1–28.

Blanchard, O., Furceri, D., Pescatori, A. (2014b), "A Prolonged Period of Low Real Interest Rates?", *Vox CEPR*, 15 August. https://voxeu.org/article/prolonged-peri od-low-real-interest-rates

Blanchard, O., Kiyotaki, N. (1985), "Monopolistic Competition, Aggregate Demand Externalities and Real Effects of Nominal Money", *NBER Working Paper, No. 1770*, pp. 1–38. http://doi.org/10.3386/w1770

Blanchard, O., Summers, L. (2019), "Introduction: Rethinking Stabilisation Policy: Evolution or Revolution?", in: O. Blanchard, L. H. Summer (eds.), *Evolution or Revolution? Rethinking Macroeconomic Policy after the Great Recession*, MIT Press, pp. xi–xliii.

Błaszczyk, P. (2019), "Współczesna Strategia Polityki Pieniężnej w Warunkach Deflacji", *Uniwersytet Ekonomiczny Poznań*.

Blinder, A. S. (1998), *Central Banking in Theory and Practice*, MIT Press.

Blinder, A. S. (1999), "Central Bank Credibility: Why Do We Care? How Do We Build It?", *NBER Working Paper, No. 7161*, pp. 1–23. https://doi.org/10.3386/w7161

Blinder, A. S. (2007), "Monetary Policy by Committee: Why and How?", *European Journal of Political Economy*, 23(1), pp. 106–123. https://doi.org/10.1016/j.ejpoleco.2006.01.003

Blinder, A. S., Morgan, J. (2007), "Leadership in Groups: A Monetary Policy Experiment", *NBER Working Paper, No. 13391*, pp. 1–36. https://doi.org/10.3386/w13391

Blinder, A. S., Solow, R. M. (1973), "Does Fiscal Policy Matter?", *Journal of Public Economics*, 2(4), pp. 319–337. http://doi.org/10.1016/0047-2727(73)90023-6

Bofinger, P. (2001), *Monetary Policy: Goals, Institutions, Strategies, and Instruments*, Oxford University Press.

Bofinger, P., Ries, M. (2017), "Excess Saving and Low Interest Rates: Theory and Empirical Evidence", *CEPR Discussion Paper, 12111*.

Boivin, J., Lane, T., Meh, C. (2010), "Should Monetary Policy Be Used to Counteract Financial Imbalances?", *Bank of Canada Review*, 2010(Summer), pp. 23–36.

Bordo, M. D. (2008), "History of Monetary Policy", in: S. N. Durlauf, L. E. Blume (eds.), *The New Palgrave Dictionary of Economics*, 2nd Edition, Vol. 5, Palgrave Macmillan, pp. 715–721.

Bordo, M. D., Siklos, P. (2014), "Central Bank Credibility, Reputation and Inflation Targeting in Historical Perspective", *NBER Working Paper, No. 20693*. http://doi.org/10.3386/w20693

Borio, C. (2001), "A Hundred Ways to Skin a Cat: Comparing Monetary Policy Operation Procedures in the United States, Japan and the Euro Area", in: *Comparing Monetary Policy Operating Procedures Across the United States Japan and the Euro Area, BIS Paper, No 9*, pp. 1–22. www.bis.org/publ/bppdf/bispap09.pdf

Borio, C. (2011a), "Central Banking Post-Crisis: What Compass for Uncharted Waters?", *BIS Working Paper, No. 353*. www.bis.org/publ/work353.pdf

Borio, C. (2011b), "Rediscovering the Macroeconomic Roots of Financial Stability Policy: Journey, Challenges and a Way Forward", *BIS Working Paper, No 354*. www.bis.org/publ/work354.pdf

Borio, C., English, W., Filardo, A. (2003), "A Tale of Two Perspectives: Old or New Challenges for Monetary Policy?", *BIS Working Paper, No. 127*. www.bis.org/publ/work127.htm

Borio, C., Filardo, A. (2007), " Globalisation and Inflation: New Cross-Country Evidence on the Global Determinants of Domestic Inflation", *BIS Working Paper, No. 227*, pp. 1–48. www.bis.org/publ/work227.pdf

Borio, C., Lowe, P. (2002), "Asset Prices, Financial and Monetary Stability: Exploring the Nexus", *BIS Working Paper, No. 114*. www.bis.org/publ/work114.htm

Borio, C., Zhu, H. (2008), "Capital Regulation, Risk-Taking and Monetary Policy: A Missing Link in the Transmission Mechanism?", *BIS Working Paper, No. 268*. www.bis.org/publ/work268.htm

Brainard, L. (2019), "Rethinking Monetary Policy in a New Normal", in: O. Blanchard, L. H. Summer (eds.), *Evolution or Revolution? Rethinking Macroeconomic Policy after the Great Recession*, MIT Press, pp. 49–60.

Brainard, L. (2020), "Bringing the Statement on Longer-Run Goals and Monetary Policy Strategy into Alignment with Longer-Run Changes in the Economy", *Speech of 1 September 2020 at "How the Fed Will Respond to the COVID-19 Recession in an Era of Low Rates and Low Inflation", an Event Hosted by the Hutchins Center on Fiscal and Monetary Policy at the Brookings Institution*, Washington, DC. www.federalreserve.gov/newsevents/speech/brainard202009 01a.htm

Briault, C., Haldane, A., King, M. (1996), "Independence and Accountability", *Bank of England Working Paper, No. 49*, pp. 1–49.

Brzoza-Brzezina, M. (2011), *Polska Polityka Pieniężna. Badania Teoretyczne I Empiryczne*, C.H. Beck.

Burdekin, R. C. K., Denzau, A. T., Keil, M. W., Sitthiyot, T., Willett, T. D. (2004), "When Does Inflation Hurt Economic Growth? Different Nonlinearities for Different Economies", *Journal of Macroeconomics*, 26(3), pp. 519–532. https:// doi.org/10.1016/j.jmacro.2003.03.005

Cagan, P. (2008), "Monetarism", in: S. N. Durlauf, L. E. Blume (eds.), *The New Palgrave Dictionary of Economics*, 2nd Edition, Vol. 5, Palgrave Macmillan, pp. 677–683.

Calvo, G. A. (1983), "Staggered Prices in a Utility-Maximizing Framework", *Journal of Monetary Economics*, 12(3), pp. 383–398. http://doi.org/10.1016/03 04-3932(83)90060-0

Calvo, G. A., Reinhart, C. M. (2000), "Fear of Floating", *NBER Working Paper, No. 7993*, pp. 1–64. https://doi.org/10.3386/w7993

Canarella, G., Miller, S. (2017), "Inflation Targeting and Inflation Persistence: New Evidence from Fractional Integration and Cointegration", *Journal of Economics of Business*, 92, pp. 45–62. https://doi.org/10.1016/j.jeconbus.2017.05.002

CBI (2010), "Monetary Policy in Iceland after Capital Controls", *Special Publication, No. 11*, Vol. 4.

CBI (2017), "Monetary Policy Based on Inflation Targeting: Iceland's Experience Since 2001 and Post-Crisis Changes", *Special Publication, No. 11*.

Cecchetti, S. G., Genberg, H., Lipsky, J., Wadhwani, S. (2000), "Asset Prices and Central Bank Policy", *Geneva Reports on the World Economy 2*, CEPR, Geneva. https://cepr.org/sites/default/files/geneva_reports/GenevaP135.pdf

Christiano, L., Eichenbaum, M. S., Trabandt, M. (2018), "On DSGE Models", *Journal of Economic Perspectives*, 32(3), pp. 113–140

Ciżkowicz, P., Rzońca, A. (2011), "Dlaczego banki centralne nie powinny podwyższać celu inflacyjnego?", *Ekonomista*, 5, pp. 677–690

Ciżkowicz-Pękała, M., Niedźwiedzińska, J., Stawasz-Grabowska, E., Żuk, P. (2019), "Selected Modifications of an Inflation Targeting Framework", in: J.

Niedźwiedzińska (ed.), *Three Decades of Inflation Targeting, NBP Working Paper, No. 314*, pp. 73–181.

Clarida, R. (2020), "A Federal Reserve's New Monetary Policy Framework: A Robust Revolution", *Speech of 31 August 2020 at the Peterson Institute for International Economics*, Washington, DC. www.federalreserve.gov/newsevents /speech/clarida20200831a.htm

Clarida, R., Galí, J., Gertler, M. (1999), "The Science of Monetary Policy: A New Keynesian Perspective", *Journal of Economic Literature*, 37(4), pp. 1661–1707. https://doi.org/10.3386/w7147

Clower, R. (1967), "A Reconsideration of the Microfoundations of Monetary Theory", *Western Economic Journal*, 6(1), pp. 1–9. https://doi.org/10.1111/j .1465-7295.1967.tb01171.x

Cobham, D. (2018), "A Comprehensive Classification of Monetary Policy Frameworks for Advanced and Emerging Economies", *MPRA Paper, No. 84737*. www.monetaryframeworks.org accessed on 15 November 2018.

Coibion, O., Gorodnichenko, Y., Kumar, S., Pedemonte, M. (2018), "Inflation Expectations—A Policy Tool?", *Conference Proceedings from ECB Forum on Central Banking*, ECB, pp. 93–151. www.ecb.europa.eu/pub/pdf/sintra/ecb.for umcentbank201810.en.pdf

Coibion, O., Gorodnichenko, Y., Wieland, J. F. (2012), "The Optimal Inflation Rate in New Keynesian Models", *NBER Working Paper, No. 16093*. www.nber.org /papers/w16093

Constâncio, V. (2015), "Understanding Inflation Dynamics and Monetary Policy", *Speech at the Jackson Hole Economic Policy Symposium*. www.ecb.europa.eu/pr ess/key/date/2015/html/sp150829.en.html

Copernicus, N. (1526), *De Cudendae Monetae Ratione*.

Corsetti, G. (2008), "New Open Economy Macroeconomics", in: S. N. Durlauf, L. E. Blume (eds.), *The New Palgrave Dictionary of Economics*, 2nd Edition, Vol. 6, Palgrave Macmillan, pp. 45–51.

Cottarelli, C., Giannini, C. (1997), "Credibility Without Rules? Monetary Frameworks in the Post–Bretton Woods Era", *IMF Occasional Paper, 154*, December.

Cukierman, A. (2019), "The Impact of the Global Financial Crisis on Central Banking [in:] Mayes", in: G. G. Mayes, P. Siklos, J.-E. Sturm (eds.), *The Oxford Handbook of the Economics of Central Banking*, Oxford University Press, pp. 171–192.

Cukierman, A., Goldstein, I., Spiegel, Y. (2004), "The Choice of Exchange-Rate Regime and Speculative Attacks", *Journal of the European Economic Association*, 2(6), pp. 1206–1241. http://doi.org/10.1162/1542476042813869

De Carvalho Filho, I. E. (2010), "Inflation Targeting and the Crisis: An Empirical Assessment", *IMF Working Paper, No. 10/45*. www.imf.org/en/Publications/WP /Issues/2016/12/31/Inflation-Targeting-and-the-Crisis-An-Empirical-Assessment -23636

De Carvalho Filho, I. E. (2011), "28 Months Later: How Inflation Targeters Outperformed Their Peers in the Great Recession", *The B.E. Journal of Macroeconomics, De Gruyter*, 11(1), pp. 1–46. https://doi.org/10.2202/1935-1690.2272

de Haan, J., Eijffinger, S. (2016), "The Politics of Central-Bank Independence", *De Nederlandsche Bank Working Paper*, 539, pp. 1–28. https://doi.org/10.2139/ssrn .2888836

Debelle, G. (1997), "Inflation Targeting in Practice", *IMF Working Paper, No. 35*, pp. 1–34. https://doi.org/10.5089/9781451845310.001

Dimand, R. W. (2008), "History of Monetary Economics", in: S. N. Durlauf, L. E. Blume (eds.), *The New Palgrave Dictionary of Economics*, 2nd Edition, Vol. 5, Palgrave Macmillan, pp. 699–708.

Dincer, N. N., Eichengreen, B. (2013), "Central Bank Transparency and Independence: Updates and New Measures", *Bank of Korea Working Paper, No. 21*, pp. 1–56. http://doi.org/10.2139/ssrn.2579544

Dixon, H. D. (2008), "New Keynesian Macroeconomics", in: S. N. Durlauf, L. E. Blume (eds.), *The New Palgrave Dictionary of Economics*, 2nd Edition, Vol. 6, Palgrave Macmillan, pp. 40–44.

Dixon, H. D., Hansen, C. T. (1999), "A Mixed Industrial Structure Magnifies the Importance of Menu Costs", *European Economic Review*, 43(8), pp. 1475–1499. https://doi.org/10.1016/s0014-2921(98)00029-4

Dorn, J. A. (2018), "Monetary Policy in an Uncertain World: The Case for Rules", in: J. A. Dorn (ed.), *Monetary Policy in an Uncertain World*, Cato Institute, pp. 179–206.

Duwendag, D., Ketterer, K.-H., Kösters, W., Pohl, R., Simmert, D. B. (1995), "Teoria pieniądza i polityka pieniężna", *Poltext*.

ECB (2001), *Review of the Quantitative Reference Value for Monetary Growth*, Press Release, 6 December. www.ecb.europa.eu/press/pr/date/2001/html/pr0 11206_2.en.html

ECB (2003), *The ECB's Monetary Policy Strategy*, Press Release, 8 May. www.ecb .europa.eu/press/pr/date/2003/html/pr030508_2.en.html

ECB (2018), *Convergence Report—2018*, May. www.ecb.europa.eu/pub/converge nce/html/ecb.cr201805.en.html

ECB (2019a), "Account of the Monetary Policy Meeting of 5–6 June 2019". www .ecb.europa.eu/press/accounts/2019/html/ecb.mg190711~16eb146254.en.html

ECB (2019b), "Introductory Statement of 25 July 2019". www.ecb.europa.eu/press /pressconf/2019/html/ecb.is190725~547f29c369.en.html

Ehrmann, M., Eijffinger, S., Fratzscher, M. (2012), "The Role of Central Bank Transparency for Guiding Private Sector Forecasts", *The Scandinavian Journal of Economics*, 3(114), pp. 1018–1052. https://doi.org/10.1111/j.1467-9442.201 2.01706.x

Eichengreen, B. (2014), "Secular Stagnation: A Review of the Issues", in: C. Teulings, R. Baldwin (eds.), *Secular Stagnation: Facts, Causes and Cures*, VOX Cepr. https ://voxeu.org/content/secular-stagnation-facts-causes-and-cures,

Espinoza, R., Leon, H., Prasad, A. (2010), "Estimating the Inflation–Growth Nexus. A Smooth Transition Model", *IMF Working Paper, No. 10/76*. www.imf.org /en/Publications/WP/Issues/2016/12/31/Estimating-The-InflationGrowth-Nexus -A-Smooth-Transition-Model-23729

Fazio, D. M., Silvab, T. Ch., Tabak, B., Cajueiro, M., D. O. (2018), "Inflation Targeting and Financial Stability: Does the Quality of Institutions Matter?", *Economic Modelling*, 71, pp. 1–15. https://doi.org/10.1016/j.econmod.2017.09 .011

Fazio, D. M., Tabak, B., Cajueiro, M., D. O. (2015), "Inflation Targeting: Is IT to Blame for Banking System Instability?", *Journal of Banking and Finance*, 59, pp. 76–97. https://doi.org/10.1016/j.jbankfin.2015.05.016

Fed (2016), *Federal Open Market Committee Reaffirms Its "Statement on Longer-Run Goals and Monetary Policy Strategy"*. www.federalreserve.gov/newsevents/pressreleases/monetary20160127b.htm

Fed (2019), "Review of Monetary Policy Strategy, Tools, and Communications—Overview". www.federalreserve.gov/monetarypolicy/review-of-monetary-policy-strategy-tools-and-communications.htm

Fed (2020), *Statement on Longer-Run Goals and Monetary Policy Strategy, as Amended Effective 27 August 2020.* www.federalreserve.gov/monetarypolicy/review-of-monetary-policy-strategy-tools-and-communications-statement-on-longer-run-goals-monetary-policy-strategy.htm

Feldstein, M. (1997), "The Costs and Benefits of Going from Low Inflation to Price Stability", in: C. Romer, D. Romer (eds.), *Reducing Inflation: Motivation and Strategy*, University of Chicago Press, pp. 123–156.

Ferreira de Mendonça, H., de Guimarães, Souza, G. (2012), "Is Inflation Targeting a Good Remedy to Control Inflation?", *Journal of Development Economics*, 98(2), pp. 178–191. https://doi.org/10.1016/j.jdeveco.2011.06.011

Fischer, S. (1994), "Modern Central Banking", in: F. Capic, Ch. Goodhart, S. Fischer, N. Schnadt (eds.), *The Future of Central Banking*, Cambridge University Press, pp. 262–308.

Fischer, S. (2008), "New Classical Macroeconomics", in: S. N. Durlauf, L. E. Blume (eds.), *The New Palgrave Dictionary of Economics*, 2nd Edition, Vol. 6, Palgrave Macmillan, pp. 17–22.

Fisher, I. (1911), *The Purchasing Power of Money*, Augustus M. Kelley Publishers.

Fouejieu, A. (2017), "Inflation Targeting and Financial Stability in Emerging Markets", *Economic Modelling*, 60, pp. 51–70. https://doi.org/10.1016/j.econmod.2016.08.020

Frankel, J. (2012), "The Death of Inflation Targeting", *Commentary of 16 May 2012*, www.project-syndicate.org/commentary/the-death-of-inflation targeting

Friedman, M. (1956), "The Quantity Theory of Money: A Restatement", in: M. Friedman (ed.), *Studies in the Quantity Theory of Money*, University of Chicago Press, pp. 51–68. https://doi.org/10.4324/9781315133607-2

Friedman, M. (1960), *A Program for Monetary Stability*, Fordham University Press.

Friedman, M. (1968), "The Role of Monetary Policy", *The American Economic Review*, 58, pp. 1–17. www.jstor.org/stable/1831652?origin=JSTOR-pdf

Friedman, M. (2006), *Optimum Quantity of Money with a New Introduction by Michael D. Bordo*, Transaction Publishers.

Friedman, M., Schwartz, A. J. (1963), *A Monetary History of the United States, 1867–1960*, Princeton University Press.

Friedrich, C. (2016), "Global Inflation Dynamics in the Post-Crisis Period: What Explains the Puzzles?", *Economics Letters*, 142(2), pp. 31–34. http://doi.org/10.1016/j.econlet.2016.02.032

Fry, M., Julius, D., Mahadeva, L., Roger, S., Sterne, G. (2000), "Key Issues in the Choice of Monetary Policy Framework", in: L. Mahadeva, G. Sterne (eds.), *Monetary Policy Frameworks in a Global Context*, Routledge Press, pp. 1–216.

Galí, J. (2008), *Monetary Policy, Inflation, and the Business Cycle*, Princeton University Press.

Galí, J. (2015), "Hysteresis and the European Unemployment Problem Revisited", *NBER Working Paper, No. 21430*, pp. 1–51. www.nber.org/papers/w21430

Galí, J., Gertler, M. (1999), "Inflation Dynamics: A Structural Econometric Analysis", *Journal of Monetary Economics*, 44(2), pp. 195–222. https://doi.org /10.1016/s0304-3932(99)00023-9

Gerlach, S., Tillmann, P. (2012), "Inflation Targeting and Inflation Persistence in Asia-Pacific", *Journal of Asian Economics*, 23(4), pp. 360–373. https://doi.org /10.1016/j.asieco.2012.03.002

Gonçalves, C., Salles, J. (2008), "Inflation Targeting in Emerging Economies: What do the Data Say?", *Journal of Development Economics*, 85(1–2), pp. 312–318. https://doi.org/10.1016/j.jdeveco.2006.07.002

Goodfriend, M., King, R. G. (1997), "The New Neoclassical Synthesis and the Role of Monetary Policy", *NBER Macroeconomics Annual*, 12, pp. 231–283. http:// doi.org/10.2307/3585232

Goodhart, Ch. (2018), "The Changing Fortunes of Central Banking", in: Ph. Hartmann, H. Huang, D. Schoenmaker (eds.), *The Changing Fortunes of Central Banking*, Cambridge University Press, pp. 376–389.

Gordon, R. (2012), "Is US Economic Growth Over? Faltering Innovation Confronts the Six Headwinds", *NBER Working Paper, No. 18315*, pp. 1–23. www.nber .org/papers/w18315

Greenspan, A. (2002), "Opening Remarks: Rethinking Stabilization Policy", *Proceedings—Economic Policy Symposium in Jackson Hole*, Federal Reserve Bank of Kansas City, pp. 1–10.

Grostal, W., Jabłecki, J., Beniak, P., Ciżkowicz-Pękała, M., Skrzeszewska-Paczek, E., Wesołowski, G., Żuk, P. (2016), "Alternatywne Strategie Polityki Pieniężnej", *NBP*. www.nbp.pl/publikacje/bci/Alternatywne_Strategie_PP.pdf

Grostal, W., Niedźwiedzińska, J. (2019), "Inflation Targeting as a Monetary Policy Framework", in: J. Niedźwiedzińska (ed.), *Three Decades of Inflation Targeting*, *NBP Working Paper, No. 314*, pp. 13–41.

Haldane, A. G. (1995), "Introduction", in: A. G. Haldane (ed.), *Targeting Inflation, A Conference of Central Banks on the Use of Inflation Targets Organised by the Bank of England*, Bank of England, pp. 1–12.

Hansen, A. H. (1939), "Economic Progress and Declining Population Growth", *The American Economic Review*, 29, pp. 1–15

Hansen, A. H. (1953), *A Guide to Keynes*, McGraw Hill.

Heenan, G., Peter, M., Roger, S. (2006), "Implementing Inflation Targeting: Institutional Arrangements, Target Design, and Communications", *IMF Working Paper, No. 278*, pp. 1–57. https://doi.org/10.5089/9781451865387.001

Heise, M. (2019), *Inflation Targeting and Financial Stability*, Springer.

Hicks, J. R. (1937), "Mr. Keynes and the 'Classics': A Suggested Interpretation", *Econometrica*, 5(2), pp. 147–159. https://doi.org/10.2307/1907242

Houben, A. C. F. J. (2000), *The Evolution of Monetary Policy Strategies in Europe*, Kluwer Academic Publishers.

House of Commons Official Report (1965), *Hansard of 17 November 1965*, Vol. 720. https://hansard.parliament.uk/Commons/1965-11-17/debates/06338c6d -ebdd-4876-a782-59cbd531a28a/EconomicAffairs

Hume, D. (1752), "Political Discourses", Printed by R, Fleming for A. Kincaid and A. Donaldson.

IMF (2013), *World Economic Outlook*, April.

IMF (2014), *World Economic Outlook*, April.

IMF (2015), "Annual Report on Exchange Arrangements and Exchange Restrictions 2015", October. www.imf.org/en/Publications/Annual-Report-on-Exchange-A rrangements-and-Exchange-Restrictions/Issues/2017/01/25/Annual-Report-on -Exchange-Arrangements-and-Exchange-Restrictions-2015-42751

IMF (2016), "Annual Report on Exchange Arrangements and Exchange Restrictions 2016", October. www.imf.org/en/Publications/Annual-Report-on-Exchange-A rrangements-and-Exchange-Restrictions/Issues/2017/01/25/Annual-Report-on -Exchange-Arrangements-and-Exchange-Restrictions-2016-43741

IMF (2018), "Annual Report on Exchange Arrangements and Exchange Restrictions 2017", April. www.imf.org/en/Publications/Annual-Report-on-Exchange-A rrangements-and-Exchange-Restrictions/Issues/2018/08/10/Annual-Report-on -Exchange-Arrangements-and-Exchange-Restrictions-2017-44930

Ingves, S. (2011), "Flexible Inflation Targeting in Theory and Practice", *Speech to the Swedish Economics at the Swedish Economics Association*, Stockholm, Sveriges Riksbank, 12 May. http://archive.riksbank.se/en/Web-archive/Publishe d/Speeches/2011/Ingves-Flexible-inflation-targeting-in-theory-and-practice/index .html

Issing, O. (2017), "Financial Stability and the ECB's Monetary Policy Strategy", in: *ECB Legal Conference Shaping a New Legal Order for Europe: A Tale of Crises and Opportunities*, ECB, pp. 340–348. www.ecb.europa.eu/pub/pdf/other/ecb legalconferenceproceedings201712.en.pdf

Jeanneau, S. (2009), "Communication of Monetary Policy Decisions by Central Banks: What Is Revealed and Why", *BIS Working Paper, No. 47*. www.bis.org/ publ/bppdf/bispap47.htm, pp. 1–42.

Keynes, J. M. (1936), *The General Theory of Employment, Interest and Money*, Macmillan Cambridge University Press, reprinted in (1947).

Khan, M. S., Senhadji, A. S. (2001), "Threshold Effects in the Relationship Between Inflation and Growth", *IMF Staff Working Paper No 48*. www.imf.org/External /Pubs/FT/staffp/2001/01a/pdf/khan.pdf

King, M. A. (1997), "Changes in UK Monetary Policy: Rules and Discretion in Practice", *Journal of Monetary Economics*, 39(1), pp. 81–97. https://doi.org/10 .1016/s0304-3932(97)00009-3

King, M. A. (2014), "Monetary Policy during the Crisis: From the Depths to the Heights", in: G. Akerlof, O. Blanchard, D. Romer, J. Stiglitz (eds.), *What Have We Learned?: Macroeconomic Policy after the Crisis*, MIT Press, pp. 45–54.

King, R. G., Plosser, Ch. I. (1984), "Money, Credit, and Prices in a Real Business Cycle", *American Economic Review*, 74, pp. 363–380.

Kokoszczyński, R. (2004), *Współczesna Polityka Pieniężna w Polsce*, PWE.

Koo, R. (2014), "Balance Sheet Recession Is the Reason for 'Secular Stagnation'", in: C. Teulings, R. Baldwin (eds.), *Secular Stagnation: Facts, Causes and Cures*, VOX Cepr. https://voxeu.org/content/secular-stagnation-facts-causes-and-cur es

Koppl, R. (2014), *From Crisis to Confidence: Macroeconomics after the Crash*, Institute of Economic Affairs.

Koronowski, A. (2003), *Czynniki Destabilizacji Rynków Walutowych*, Twigger.

Koronowski, A. (2005), "Skuteczność polityki pieniężnej w obliczu wstrząsów podażowych i popytowych: Nie tylko o pułapce płynności", *Bank i Kredyt*, 36, pp. 29–37

Koronowski, A. (2009), "Polityka pieniężna a kryzysy finansowe", *Gospodarka Narodowa*, 20, pp. 33–48.

Kremer, S., Bick, A., Nautz, D. (2012), "Inflation and Growth: New Evidence From a Dynamic Panel Threshold Analysis", *Empirical Economics*, 44(2), pp. 861–878. https://doi.org/10.1007/s00181-012-0553-9

Krugman, P. (2014), "Four Observations on Secular Stagnation, [in:] Teulings", in: C. Teulings, R. Baldwin (eds.), *Secular Stagnation: Facts, Causes and Cures*, VOX Cepr. https://voxeu.org/content/secular-stagnation-facts-causes -and-cures

Kryvtsov, O., Mendes, R. R. (2015), "The Optimal Level of the Inflation Target: A Selective Review of the Literature and Outstanding Issues", *Bank of Canada Discussion Paper, No. 2015-8.*

Kügler, A., Schönberg, U., Schreiner, R. (2018), "Productivity Growth, Wage Growth and Unions", *Conference Proceedings from ECB Forum on Central Banking*, ECB, pp. 215–247. www.ecb.europa.eu/pub/pdf/sintra/ecb.forumcen tbank201810.en.pdf

Kydland, F., Prescott, E. (1977), "Rules Rather Than Discretion: The Inconsistency of Optimal Plans", *Journal of Political Economy*, 85(3), pp. 473–491. https://doi .org/10.1086/260580

Kydland, F., Prescott, E. (1982), "Time to Build and Aggregate Fluctuations", *Econometrica*, 50(6), pp. 1345–1370. http://doi.org/10.2307/1913386

Lagarde, Ch. (2020), "The Monetary Policy Strategy Review: Some Preliminary Considerations", *Speech at the ECB and Its Watchers XXI Conference, Frankfurt am Main*, 30 September www.ecb.europa.eu/press/key/date/2020/html/ecb.sp2 00930~169abb1202.en.html

Lavoie, M. (2019), "Advances in the Post-Keynesian Analysis of Money and Finance", in: P. Arestis, M. Sawyer (eds.), *Frontiers of Heterodox Economics*, Palgrave Macmillan. www.nbp.pl/badania/seminaria/19vi2019-3.pdf

Lin, S., Ye, H. (2007), "Does Inflation Targeting Really Make a Difference? Evaluating the Treatment Effect of Inflation Targeting in Seven Industrial Countries", *Journal of Monetary Economics*, 54(8), pp. 2521–2533. http://doi .org/10.1016/j.jmoneco.2007.06.017

Lombardelli, C., Proudman, J., Talbot, J. (2005), "Committees Versus Individuals: An Experimental Analysis of Monetary Policy Decision Making", *Bank of England Working Paper, No. 165*, pp. 1–19. https://doi.org/10.2139/ssrn.340560

Lucas, R. E. (1972), "Expectations and the Neutrality of Money", *Journal of Economic Theory*, 4(2), pp. 103–124. http://doi.org/10.1016/0022-0531(72)90142-1

Lucas, R. E. (1973), "Some International Evidence on Output-Inflation Tradeoffs", *American Economic Review*, 63, pp. 326–334.

Lucas, R. E. (1976), "Econometric Policy Evaluation: A Critique", in: K. Brunner, A. Meltzer (eds.), *The Phillips Curve and Labor Markets, Carnegie-Rochester Conference Series on Public Policy. 1*, American Elsevier, pp. 19–46

Lucas, R. E., Sargent, T. J. (1978), "After Keynesian Macroeconomics", in: *After The Phillips Curve: Persistence of High Inflation and High Unemployment, Proceedings a Conference Held at the Federal Reserve Bank of Boston*, pp. 49–72. www.bostonfed.org/news-and-events/events/economic-research-conference-series/after-the-phillips-curve-persistence-of-high-inflation-and-high-unemploym ent.aspx

Lustenberger, T., Rossi, E. (2017), "Does Central Bank Transparency and Communication Affect Financial and Macroeconomic Forecasts?", *SNB Working Paper, No. 12*, pp. 1–58. www.snb.ch/n/mmr/reference/working_paper_2017_12 /source/working_paper_2017_12.n.pdf

Mackiewicz-Łyziak, J. (2010), *Wiarygodność Banku Centralnego*, Difin.

Maier, P. (2010), "How Central Banks Take Decisions: An Analysis of Monetary Policy Meetings", in: P. L. Bohl, M. T. Wohar, M. E. Siklos (eds.), *Challenges in Central Banking: The Current Institutional Environment and Forces Affecting Monetary Policy*, Cambridge University Press. www.mnb.hu/letoltes/maier.pdf

Mankiw, N. G. (1985), "Small Menu Costs and Large Business Cycles: A Macroeconomic Model of Monopoly", *The Quarterly Journal of Economics*, 100(2), pp. 529–538. http://doi.org/10.2307/1885395

Mayes, D., Chapple, B. (1995), "Defining an Inflation Target", in: A. G. Haldane (ed.), *Targeting Inflation, A Conference of Central Banks on the Use of Inflation Targtets Organised by the Bank of England*, Bank of England, pp. 226–245.

McCallum, B. T. (2000), "Alternative Monetary Policy Rules: A Comparison with Historical Settings for the United States, the United Kingdom, and Japan", *NBER Working Paper, No. 7725*, pp. 1–42. https://doi.org/10.3386/w7725

McGrattan, E. R. (2008), "Real Business Cycles", in: S. N. Durlauf, L. E. Blume (eds.), *The New Palgrave Dictionary of Economics*, 2nd Edition, Vol. 7, Palgrave Macmillan, pp. 10–13.

Meade, J. E. (1951), *The Theory of International Economic Policy, Vol. 1, The Balance of Payments. Vol. 2: Trade and Welfare, with Mathematical Supplements*, Oxford University Press.

Mertens, T. M., Williams, J. C. (2019), "Monetary Policy Frameworks and the Effective Lower Bound on Interest Rates", *Federal Reserve Bank of New York Staff Report, No. 877*. www.newyorkfed.org/medialibrary/media/research/staff _reports/sr877.pdf

Mill, J. S. (1848), *Principles of Political Economy, with Some of Their Applications to Social Philosophy*, Charles C. Little & James Brown.

Minsky, H. (2008), *Stabilizing an Unstable Economy*, McGraw-Hill Publishing Company.

Mishkin, F. S. (1995), "The Rational Expectations Revolution: A Review Article of: Preston J Miller Ed, the Rational Expectations Revolution, Readings from the Front Line", *NBER Working Paper, No. 5043*, pp. 1–25. https://doi.org/10.3386/w5043

Mishkin, F. S. (1999), "International Experiences with Different Monetary Policy Regimes", *NBER Working Paper, No. 6965*, pp. 1–46. https://doi.org/10.3386 /w6965

Mishkin, F. S. (2001), "From Monetary Targeting to Inflation Targeting: Lessons from the Industrialized Countries", *Policy Research Working Paper, No. 2684*, World Bank. https://doi.org/10.1596/1813-9450-2684

Mishkin, F. S. (2004), "Can Inflation Targeting Work in Emerging Market Countries?", *NBER Working Paper, No. 10646*, pp. 1–34. https://doi.org/10 .3386/w10646

Mishkin, F. S. (2006), "Monetary Policy Strategy: How Did We Get Here", *NBER Working Paper, No. 12515*, pp. 1–44. https://doi.org/10.3386/w12515

Mishkin, F. S. (2007), "Will Monetary Policy Become More of a Science?", *NBER Working Paper, No. 13566*, pp. 1–41. www.nber.org/papers/w13566

Mishkin, F. S. (2009), "Is Monetary Policy Effective During Financial Crises?", *American Economic Review*, 99(2), pp. 573–577. https://doi.org/10.1257/aer.99 .2.573

Mishkin, F. S. (2011), "Monetary Policy Strategy: Lessons from the Crisis", *NBER Working Paper, No. 16755*, pp. 1–62. www.nber.org/system/files/working_p apers/w16755/w16755.pdf

Mishkin, F. S. (2012), *The Economics of Money, Banking, and Financial Markets*, Prentice Hall.

Mishkin, F. S., Schmidt-Hebbel, K. (2002), "A Decade of Inflation Targeting in the World: What Do We Know and What Do We Need to Know?", in: N. Loayza, R. Soto (eds.), *Inflation Targeting: Design, Performance, Challenges*, Central Bank of Chile, pp. 171–220.

Mohanty, M. (2013), "Market Volatility and Foreign Exchange Intervention in EMEs: What Has Changed?", *BIS Working Paper, No. 73*, pp. 1–10. www.bis .org/publ/bppdf/bispap73a_rh.pdf

Moore, B. J. (1988), *Horizontalists Versus Verticalists: The Macroeconomics of Credit Money*, Cambridge University Press.

Muth, J. F. (1961), "Rational Expectations and the Theory of Price Movements", *Econometrica*, 29(3), pp. 315–335. http://doi.org/10.2307/1909635

National Accounts Main Aggregates Database. https://unstats.un.org/unsd/snaama/ dnllist.asp, accessed on 15 November 2018.

Naudon, A., Pérez, A. (2017), "An Overview of Inflation-Targeting Frameworks: Institutional Arrangements, Decision-Making & the Communication of Monetary Policy", *Banco Central de Chile Working Papers, No. 811*. www.bcentral.cl/es/w eb/central-bank-of-chile/-/an-overview-of-inflation-targeting-frameworks-institu tional-arrangements-decision-making-the-communication-of-monetary-policy

Niedźwiedzińska, J. (2020), "Initial Monetary Policy Response to the COVID-19 Pandemic in Inflation Targeting Economies", *NBP Working Paper, No. 335*. www.nbp.pl/publikacje/materialy_i_studia/335_en.pdf

Niedźwiedzińska, J., Skrzeszewska-Paczek, E., Wesołowski, G., Żuk, P. (2019), "Major Changes to an Inflation Targeting Framework", in: J. Niedźwiedzińska (ed.), *Three Decades of Inflation Targeting, NBP Working Paper, No. 314*, pp. 42–72.

North, D. (1990), *Institutions, Institutional Change and Economic Performance*, Cambridge University Press.

Orphanides, A., Williams, J. C. (2003), "Imperfect Knowledge, Inflation Expectations, and Monetary Policy", *NBER Working Paper, No. 9884*, pp. 1–39. https://doi.org/10.3386/w9884

Phelps, E. S. (1967), "Phillips Curve, Expectations of Inflation and Optimal Unemployment Over Time", *Economica*, 34(135), pp. 254–281. http://doi.org /10.2307/2552025

Phillips, A. W. (1958), "The Relation between Unemployment and the Rate of Change of Money Wage Rates in the United Kingdom, 1861–1957 1", *Economica*, 25(100), pp. 283–299. http://doi.org/10.2307/2550759

Pietrzak, B. (2008), "System Bankowy", in: B. Pietrzak, Z. Polański, B. Woźniak (eds.), *System finansowy w Polsce*, PWN, pp. 69–124.

Poole, W. (1970), "Optimal Choice of Monetary Policy Instruments in a Simple Stochastic Macro Model", *The Quarterly Journal of Economics*, 84(2), pp. 197–216. http://doi.org/10.2307/1883009

Posen, A. S. (1997), "Lessons from the Bundesbank on the Occasion of Its 40th (and Second to Last?) Birthday", *Institute for International Economics Working Paper, No. 97-4.*

Posen, A. S. (2006), "Why Central Banks Should Not Burst Bubbles?", *International Finance,* 9(1), pp. 109–124. https://doi.org/10.1111/j.1468-2362.2006.00028.x

Posen, A. S. (2019), "Monetary Policy in the Wake of the Crisis", in: O. Blanchard, L. H. Summer (eds.), *Evolution or Revolution? Rethinking Macroeconomic Policy after the Great Recession,* MIT Press, pp. 65–70.

Powell, J. H. (2019), "Opening Remarks", *Speech at the Conference on Monetary Policy Strategy, Tools, and Communications Practices,* 4 June. www.federalrese rve.gov/newsevents/speech/powell20190604a.htm

Powell, J. H. (2020), "New Economic Challenges and the Fed's Monetary Policy Review", *Speech of 27.08.2020 at Navigating the Decade Ahead: Implications for Monetary Policy an Economic Policy Symposium Sponsored by the Federal Reserve Bank of Kansas City, Jackson Hole, Wyoming.* www.federalreserve.gov /newsevents/speech/powell20200827a.htm

Rajan, R. G. (2006), "Has Finance Made the World Riskier?", *European Financial Management,* 12(4), pp. 499–533. https://doi.org/10.1111/j.1468-036x.2006 .00330.x

Reserve Bank of New Zealand (2019), *Monetary Policy Handbook,* April.

Ricardo, D. (1951), *The Works and Correspondence of David Ricardo edited by Piero Sraffa with the Collaboration of M. H. Dobb,* Liberty Fund.

Roberts, J. M. (1995), "New Keynesian Economics and the Phillips Curve", *Journal of Money, Credit and Banking,* 27(4), pp. 975–984. http://doi.org/10.2307/2077783

Rogoff, K. (1985), "The Optimal Commitment to an Intermediate Monetary Target", *Quarterly Journal of Economics,* 100(4), pp. 1169–1189. https://doi .org/10.2307/1885679

Rogoff, K. (2017), *The Curse of Cash: How Large Denomination Bills Aid Crime and Tax Evasion and Constrain Monetary Policy,* Princeton University Press.

Samuelson, P. A. (1955), *Economics,* McGraw-Hill Book Company.

Samuelson, P. A. (1964), "Theoretical Notes on Trade Problems", *Review of Economics and Statistics,* 46(2), pp. 145–154. https://doi.org/10.2307/1928178

Samuelson, P. A., Nordhaus, W. D. (1992), *Economics,* McGraw-Hill International Editions.

Samuelson, P. A., Solow, R. M. (1960), "Analytical Aspects of Anti-Inflation Policy", *American Economic Review,* 50, pp. 177–194. www.jstor.org/stable/1815021

Sargent, T. J. (2008), "Rational Expectations", in: S. N. Durlauf, L. E. Blume (eds.), *The New Palgrave Dictionary of Economics,* 2nd Edition, Vol. 6, Palgrave Macmillan, pp. 877–882.

Sargent, T. J., Fand, D., Goldfeld, S. (1973), "Rational Expectations, the Real Rate of Interest, and the Natural Rate of Unemployment", *Brookings Papers on Economic Activity,* 1973(2), pp. 429–472. http://doi.org/10.2307/2534097

Sargent, T. J., Wallace, N. (1975), "Rational Expectations, the Optimal Monetary Instrument, and the Optimal Money Supply Rule", *Journal of Political Economy,* 83(2), pp. 241–254. http://doi.org/10.1086/260321

Sargent, T. J., Wallace, N. (1976), "Rational Expectations and the Theory of Economic Policy", *Journal of Monetary Economics,* 2(2), pp. 169–183. http:// doi.org/10.1016/0304-3932(76)90032-5

Schaechter, A., Stone, M., Zelmer, M. (2000), "Adopting Inflation Targeting: Practical Issues for Emerging Market Countries", *IMF Occasional Paper*, 202, pp. 1–62. https://doi.org/10.5089/9781557759917.084

Schmitt-Grohe, S., Uribe, M. (2010), "The Optimal Rate of Inflation", *NBER Working Paper, No. 16054*, pp. 1–79. http://doi.org/10.3386/w16054

Schumpeter, J. A. (1955), *History of Economic Analysis*, Oxford University Press.

Sheshinski, E., Weiss, Y. (1977), "Inflation and Costs of Price Adjustment", *The Review of Economic Studies*, 44(2), pp. 287–303. http://doi.org/10.2307 /2297067

Sidrauski, M. (1967), "Inflation and Economic Growth", *Journal of Political Economy*, 75(6), pp. 796–810. https://doi.org/10.1086/259360

Siklos, P. (2002), *The Changing Face of Central Banking: Evolutionary Trends Since World War II*, Cambridge University Press.

Sims, Ch. (1972), "Money, Income, and Causality", *American Economic Review*, 62(4), pp. 540–552.

Sławiński, A. (2009), "Ewolucja poglądów na politykę pieniężną", in: W. Przybylska-Kapuścińska (ed.), *Studia z Bankowości Centralnej i Polityki Pieniężnej*, Difin.

Sławiński, A. (2011), "Stabilizowanie inflacji", in: A. Sławiński (ed.), *Polityka pieniężna*, C.H. Beck, pp. 22–50.

Smithin, J. (2013), *Essays in the Fundamental Theory of Monetary Economics and Macroeconomics*, World Scientific Publishing.

Snowdon, B., Vane, H., Wynarczyk, P. (1998), *Współczesne nurty teorii makroekonomii*, WNPWN.

Steuart, J. (1767), *An Inquiry into the Principles of Political Oeconomy*, Printed for A. Millar, and T. Cadell, in the Strand.

Stracca, L. (2018), *The Economics of Central Banking*, Routledge.

Summers, L. (2014), "Reflections on the 'New Secular Stagnation Hypothesis'", in: C. Teulings, R. Baldwin (eds.), *Secular Stagnation: Facts, Causes and Cures*, VOX Cepr. https://voxeu.org/content/secular-stagnation-facts-causes -and-cures

Svensson, L. E. O. (1997), "Inflation Forecast Targeting: Implementing and Monitoring Inflation Targets", *European Economic Review*, 41(6), pp. 1111–1146. https://doi.org/10.1016/s0014-2921(96)00055-4

Svensson, L. E. O. (1998), "Inflation Targeting as a Monetary Policy Rule", *NBER Working Paper, No. 6790*, pp. 1–50. www.nber.org/papers/w6790.pdf

Svensson, L. E. O. (2002), "Inflation Targeting: Should It Be Modeled as an Instrument Rule or a Targeting Rule?", *European Economic Review*, 46(4–5), pp. 771–780. http://doi.org/10.1016/s0014-2921(01)00212-4

Svensson, L. E. O. (2008), "Inflation Targeting", in: S. N. Durlauf, L. E. Blume (eds.), *The New Palgrave Dictionary of Economics*, 2nd Edition, Vol. 4, Palgrave Macmillan, pp. 319–321.

Svensson, L. E. O. (2009), "Flexible Inflation Targeting—Lessons from the Financial Crisis", *Speech at a Seminar: Towards a New Framework for Monetary Policy?, Lessons from the Crisis*, Amsterdam, Netherlands Bank, 21 September. www.bis .org/review/r090923d.pdf

Svensson, L. E. O. (2010), "Where Do Central Banks Go From Here?", *Panel Discussion, Norges Bank Symposium on "What Is a Useful Central Bank?*, 18 November.

Szafranek, K. (2017), "Flattening of the New Keynesian Phillips Curve: Evidence for an Emerging, Small Open Economy", *Economic Modelling*, 63, pp. 334–348. https://doi.org/10.1016/j.econmod.2017.01.009

Szpunar, P. (2000), *Polityka pieniężna. Cele i warunki skuteczności*, PWE.

Taylor, Ch. T. (2011), *A Macroeconomic Regime for the 21st Century: Towards a New Economic Order*, Routledge.

Taylor, J. B. (1979), "Staggered Wage Setting in a Macro Model", *American Economic Review, Papers and Proceedings*, 69(2), pp. 108–113.

Taylor, J. B. (1993), "Discretion versus Policy Rules in Practice", *Carnegie-Rochester Conference Series on Public Policy*, 39, pp. 195–214. http://doi.org/10.1016/01 67-2231(93)90009-1

Taylor, J. B. (2007), "Housing and Monetary Policy", *NBER Working Paper, No. 13682*, pp. 1–16. www.nber.org/papers/w13682

Taylor, J. B. (2009), "The Financial Crisis and the Policy Response: An Empirical Investigation of What Went Wrong", *NBER Working Paper, No. 14631*, pp. 1–30. www.nber.org/papers/w14631

Thornton, D. L. (2019), "Strategies for Conducting Monetary Policy. A Critical Appraisal", in: G. G. Mayes, P. Siklos, J.-E. Sturm (eds.), *The Oxford Handbook of the Economics of Central Banking*, Oxford University Press, pp. 193–227.

Thornton, H. (1802), *An Enquiry into the Nature and Effects of the Paper Credit of Great Britain*.

Tinbergen, J. (1952), *On the Theory of Economic Policy*, North-Holland Publishing Company. https://repub.eur.nl/pub/15884/

Tobin, J. (1972), "Inflation and Unemployment", *American Economic Review*, 62, pp. 1–18

Tucker, P. (2018), "Pristine and Parsimonious Policy: Can Central Banks Ever Get Back to It and Why They Should Try", in: Ph. Hartmann, H. Huang, D. Schoenmaker (eds.), *The Changing Fortunes of Central Banking*, Cambridge University Press, pp. 48–64.

VanLear, W. (2015), "Copernicus and the Quantity Theory of Money", *History of Economic Thought and Policy*, 2(2), pp. 5–20. https://doi.org/10.3280/spe2015 -002001

Vega, M., Winkelried, D. (2005), "Inflation Targeting and Inflation Behavior: A Successful Story?", *International Journal of Central Banking*, 1(3), pp. 153–175. www.ijcb.org/journal/ijcb05q4a5.htm

Viñals, J., Mancini-Griffoli, T., Nier, E. (2018), "Three Cooks of Three Wise Men? The Interplay between Monetary, Macroprudential and Microprudential Policies in Supporting Financial Stability", in: Ph. Hartmann, H. Huang, D. Schoenmaker (eds.), *The Changing Fortunes of Central Banking*, Cambridge University Press, pp. 135–152.

Walsh, C. E. (1995), "Optimal Contracts for Central Bankers", *American Economic Review*, 85, pp. 150–167.

Walsh, C. E. (2009), "Inflation Targeting: What Have We Learnt?", *International Finance*, 12(2), pp. 195–233. https://doi.org/10.1111/j.1468-2362.2009.01236.x

Walsh, C. E. (2019), "Alternatives to Inflation Targeting in Low Interest Rate Environments", *IMES Discussion Paper, No. 2019-E-13*, pp. 1–30.

Weber, A. (2015), "Rethinking Inflation Targeting", *Commentary of 8 June 2012*, www.project-syndicate.org/commentary/rethinking-inflation-targeting-price-s tability-by-axel-weber-1-2015-06

White, L. H. (1999), *The Theory of Monetary Institutions*, Blackwell Publishers.

White, W. R. (2009), "Should Monetary Policy 'Lean or Clean?'", *Federal Reserve Bank of Dallas Working Paper, No. 34*, pp. 1–24.

Whitehouse, E. R. (2009), "Pensions, Purchasing-Power Risk, Inflation and Indexation", *OECD, Social, Employment and Migration Working Paper, No. 77*. https://doi.org/10.1787/227182142567

Wicksell, K. (1898), *Interest and Prices*, Macmillan and Co.

Wojtyna, A. (1998), *Szkice o niezależności banku centralnego*, WNPWN.

Wojtyna, A. (2000), *Ewolucja keynesizmu a główny nurt ekonomii*, PWN.

Wojtyna, A. (2001), "Skuteczność polityki pieniężnej w warunkach niskiej inflacji: Problem zerowej granicy nominalnych stóp procentowych", *Bank i Kredyt, 7*.

Wojtyna, A. (2004), *Szkice o polityce pieniężnej*, PWE.

Wojtyna, A. (2011), *Kryzys finansowy i jego skutki dla krajów na średnim poziomie rozwoju*, PWE.

Wojtyna, A. (2013), *Zmiany instytucjonalne w reakcji na obecny kryzys*, PWE.

Woodford, M. (2001), "The Taylor Rule and Optimal Monetary Policy", *American Economic Review*, 91(2), pp.232–237. http://doi.org/10.1257/aer.91.2.232

Woodford, M. (2003), *Interest and Prices: Foundations of a Theory of Monetary Policy*, Princeton University Press.

Woodford, M. (2007), "The Case for Forecast Targeting as a Monetary Policy Strategy", *Journal of Economic Perspectives*, 21(4), pp. 3–24. https://doi.org/10 .1257/jep.21.4.3

Woodford, M. (2014), "Monetary Policy Targets after the Crisis", in: G. Akerlof, O. Blanchard, D. Romer, J. Stiglitz (eds.), *What Have We Learnt? Macroeconomic Policy after the Crisis*, MIT Press, pp. 55–62.

Wray, L. R. (1998), *Understanding Modern Money: The Key to Full Employment and Price Stability*, Edward Elgar.

Wray, L. R. (2012), "Introduction to an Alternative History of Money", *SSRN Electronic Journal*. http://doi.org/10.2139/ssrn.2050427

Yates, A. (1995), "On the Design of Inflation Targets", in: A. G. Haldane (ed.), *Targeting Inflation, A Conference of Central Banks on the Use of Inflation Targtets Organised by the Bank of England*, Bank of England, pp. 135–169.

Yates, T. (2002), "Monetary Policy and the Zero Bound to Interest Rates: A Review", *ECB Working Paper, No. 190*. www.ecb.europa.eu/pub/pdf/scpwps/ ecbwp190.pdf

Appendix 1: Monetary policy frameworks used worldwide

Table 1.4 Monetary policy frameworks used in the world in 2017

Country	Monetary policy framework	Exchange rate arrangement	Remarks
Afghanistan	Monetary targeting	Floating	
Albania	Inflation targeting	Floating	
Algeria	Monetary targeting	Other managed arrangement	The country maintains a de facto exchange rate anchor to the US dollar
Angola	Exchange rate anchor	Stabilised arrangement	Against US dollar
Antigua and Barbuda	Exchange rate anchor	Currency board	With US dollar
Argentina	Inflation targeting	Floating	Since October 2018 monetary targeting
Armenia	Inflation targeting	Floating	
Aruba	Exchange rate anchor	Conventional peg	Against US dollar
Australia	Inflation targeting	Free floating	
Austria	Other - EMU - inflation-targeting-like framework	Free floating	EMU
Azerbaijan	Other - monetary-targeting-like framework	Other managed arrangement	
Bahrain	Exchange rate anchor	Conventional peg	Against US dollar
Bangladesh	Monetary targeting	Stabilised arrangement	The country maintains a de facto exchange rate anchor to the US dollar
Barbados	Exchange rate anchor	Conventional peg	Against US dollar
Belarus	Monetary targeting	Other managed arrangement	
Belgium	Other - EMU - inflation-targeting-like framework	Free floating	EMU
Belize	Exchange rate anchor	Conventional peg	Against US dollar
Benin	Exchange rate anchor	Conventional peg	Against euro
Bhutan	Exchange rate anchor	Conventional peg	Against other currency

Country	Monetary policy framework	Exchange rate arrangement	Remarks
Bolivia	Monetary targeting	Stabilised arrangement	The country maintains a de facto exchange rate anchor to the US dollar
Bosnia and Herzegovina	Exchange rate anchor	Currency board	With euro
Botswana	Exchange rate anchor	Crawling peg	Against composite
Brazil	Inflation targeting	Floating	
Brunei Darussalam	Exchange rate anchor	Currency board	With other currency
Bulgaria	Exchange rate anchor	Currency board	With euro
Burkina Faso	Exchange rate anchor	Conventional peg	Against euro
Burundi	Monetary targeting	Crawling-like arrangement	The country maintains a de facto exchange rate anchor to the US dollar
Cabo Verde	Exchange rate anchor	Conventional peg	Against euro
Cambodia	Exchange rate anchor	Other managed arrangement	Against US dollar
Cameroon	Exchange rate anchor	Conventional peg	Against euro
Canada	Inflation targeting	Free floating	
Central African Rep.	Exchange rate anchor	Conventional peg	Against euro
Chad Rep. of Congo	Exchange rate anchor	Conventional peg	Against euro
Chile	Inflation targeting	Free floating	
China	Monetary targeting	Stabilised arrangement	the country maintains a de facto exchange rate anchor to a composite
Colombia	Inflation targeting	Floating	
Comoros	Exchange rate anchor	Conventional peg	Against euro
Costa Rica	Other	Crawling-like arrangement	The country maintains a de facto exchange rate anchor to the US dollar
Côte d'Ivoire	Exchange rate anchor	Conventional peg	Against euro
Croatia	Exchange rate anchor	Stabilised arrangement	Against euro

(Continued)

93

Table 1.4 (*Continued*) Monetary policy frameworks used in the world in 2017

Country	Monetary policy framework	Exchange rate arrangement	Remarks
Curaçao and Sint Maarten	Exchange rate anchor	Conventional peg	Against US dollar
Cyprus	Other—EMU—inflation-targeting-like framework	Free-floating	EMU
Czech Rep.	Inflation targeting	Floating	
Democratic Rep. of the Congo	Monetary targeting	Other managed arrangement	The country maintains a *de facto* exchange rate anchor to the US dollar
Denmark	Exchange rate anchor	Conventional peg	Against euro
Djibouti	Exchange rate anchor	Currency board	With US dollar
Dominica	Exchange rate anchor	Currency board	With US dollar
Dominican Rep.	Inflation targeting	Crawling-like arrangement	
Ecuador	Exchange rate anchor	No separate legal tender	US dollar
Egypt	Other—moving towards inflation-targeting-like framework	Floating	The central bank has taken preliminary steps towards inflation targeting
El Salvador	Exchange rate anchor	No separate legal tender	US dollar
Equatorial Guinea	Exchange rate anchor	Conventional peg	Against euro
Eritrea	Exchange rate anchor	Conventional peg	Against US dollar
Estonia	Other—EMU—inflation-targeting-like framework	Free-floating	EMU
Ethiopia	Monetary targeting	Crawling-like arrangement	The country maintains a *de facto* exchange rate anchor to the US dollar
Euro area	Other—inflation-targeting-like framework	Free-floating	EMU
Fiji	Exchange rate anchor	Conventional peg	Against composite
Finland	Other—EMU—inflation-targeting-like framework	Free-floating	EMU
France	Other—EMU—inflation-targeting-like framework	Free-floating	EMU

Country	Framework	Monetary regime	Exchange rate anchor
Gabon	Exchange rate anchor	Conventional peg	Against euro
Georgia	Inflation targeting	Floating	
Germany	Other—EMU—inflation-targeting-like framework	Free-floating	EMU
Ghana	Inflation targeting	Floating	
Greece	Other—EMU—inflation-targeting-like framework	Free-floating	EMU
Grenada, St Kitts, and Nevis	Exchange rate anchor	Currency board	With US dollar
Guatemala	Inflation targeting	Floating	
Guinea	Monetary targeting	Other managed arrangement	
Guinea Bissau	Exchange rate anchor	Conventional peg	Against euro
Guyana	Exchange rate anchor	Stabilised arrangement	Against US dollar
Haiti	Other	Other managed arrangement	
Honduras	Exchange rate anchor	Crawling peg	Against US dollar
Hong Kong SAR	Exchange rate anchor	Currency board	With US dollar
Hungary	Inflation targeting	Floating	
Iceland	Inflation targeting	Floating	
India	Inflation targeting	Floating	
Indonesia	Inflation targeting	Floating	
Iran	Exchange rate anchor	Crawling-like arrangement	Against composite
Iraq	Exchange rate anchor	Conventional peg	Against US dollar
Ireland	Other—EMU—inflation-targeting-like framework	Free-floating	EMU
Israel	Inflation targeting	Floating	
Italy	Other—EMU—inflation-targeting-like framework	Free-floating	EMU
Jamaica	Other	Crawling-like arrangement	The country maintains a *de facto* exchange rate anchor to the US dollar
Japan	Inflation targeting	Free-floating	
Jordan	Exchange rate anchor	Conventional peg	Against US dollar

(Continued)

Table 1.4 (*Continued*) Monetary policy frameworks used in the world in 2017

Country	Monetary policy framework	Exchange rate arrangement	Remarks
Kazakhstan	Inflation targeting	Floating	
Kenya	Other	Stabilised arrangement	The country maintains a *de facto* exchange rate anchor to the US dollar
Kiribati	Exchange rate anchor	No separate legal tender	Other currency
Korea	Inflation targeting	Floating	
Kosovo	Exchange rate anchor	No separate legal tender	Euro
Kuwait	Exchange rate anchor	Conventional peg	Against composite
Kyrgyz Rep.	Other—moving towards inflation-targeting-like framework	Other managed arrangement	The central bank has taken preliminary steps towards inflation targeting
Lao PDR	Other	Stabilised arrangement	The country maintains a *de facto* exchange rate anchor to the US dollar
Latvia	Other—EMU—inflation-targeting-like framework	Free-floating	EMU
Lebanon	Exchange rate anchor	Stabilised arrangement	Against US dollar
Lesotho	Exchange rate anchor	Conventional peg	Against other currency
Liberia	Exchange rate anchor	Other managed arrangement	Against US dollar
Libya	Exchange rate anchor	Conventional peg	Against composite
Lithuania	Other—EMU—inflation-targeting-like framework	Free-floating	EMU
Macedonia	Exchange rate anchor	Stabilised arrangement	Against euro
Madagascar	Monetary targeting	Floating	
Malawi	Monetary targeting	Stabilised arrangement	The country maintains a *de facto* exchange rate anchor to the US dollar
Malaysia	Other	Floating	
Maldives	Exchange rate anchor	Stabilised arrangement	Against US dollar

Country	Monetary policy framework	Exchange rate arrangement	Anchor / notes
Mali	Exchange rate anchor	Conventional peg	Against euro
Malta	Other—EMU—inflation-targeting-like framework	Free-floating	EMU
Marshall Islands	Exchange rate anchor	No separate legal tender	US dollar
Mauritania	Other	Crawling-like arrangement	The country maintains a de facto exchange rate anchor to the US dollar
Mauritius	Other	Floating	The country uses a two pillars approach: economic and monetary pillar
Mexico	Inflation targeting	Free-floating	
Micronesia	Exchange rate anchor	No separate legal tender	US dollar
Moldova	Inflation targeting	Floating	
Mongolia	Other—moving towards inflation-targeting-like framework	Floating	The central bank has taken preliminary steps towards inflation targeting
Montenegro	Exchange rate anchor	No separate legal tender	Euro
Morocco	Exchange rate anchor	Conventional peg	Against composite
Mozambique	Other—moving towards inflation-targeting-like framework	Floating	The central bank has taken preliminary steps towards inflation targeting
Myanmar	Monetary targeting	Other managed arrangement	
Namibia	Exchange rate anchor	Conventional peg	Against other currency
Nauru	Exchange rate anchor	No separate legal tender	Other currency
Nepal	Exchange rate anchor	Conventional peg	Against other currency
New Zealand	Inflation targeting	Floating	
Nicaragua	Exchange rate anchor	Crawling peg	Against US dollar
Niger	Exchange rate anchor	Conventional peg	Against euro
Nigeria	Monetary targeting	Stabilised arrangement	The country maintains a de facto exchange rate anchor to the US dollar
Norway	Inflation targeting	Free-floating	

(Continued)

97

Table 1.4 (*Continued*) Monetary policy frameworks used in the world in 2017

Country	Monetary policy framework	Exchange rate arrangement	Remarks
Oman	Exchange rate anchor	Conventional peg	Against US dollar
Pakistan	Other	Stabilised arrangement	The country maintains a *de facto* exchange rate anchor to the US dollar
Palau	Exchange rate anchor	No separate legal tender	US dollar
Panama	Exchange rate anchor	No separate legal tender	US dollar
Papua New Guinea	Monetary targeting	Stabilised arrangement	The country maintains a *de facto* exchange rate anchor to the US dollar
Paraguay	Inflation targeting	Floating	
Peru	Inflation targeting	Floating	
Philippines	Inflation targeting	Floating	
Poland	Inflation targeting	Free-floating	
Portugal	Other—EMU—inflation-targeting-like framework	Free-floating	EMU
Qatar	Exchange rate anchor	Conventional peg	Against US dollar
Romania	Inflation targeting	Floating	
Russia	Inflation targeting	Free-floating	
Rwanda	Monetary targeting	Crawling-like arrangement	The country maintains a *de facto* exchange rate anchor to the US dollar
Samoa	Other	Conventional peg	The country maintains a *de facto* exchange rate anchor to a composite
San Marino	Exchange rate anchor	No separate legal tender	Euro

Country			
São Tomé and Príncipe	Exchange rate anchor	Conventional peg	Against euro
Saudi Arabia	Exchange rate anchor	Conventional peg	Against US dollar
Senegal	Exchange rate anchor	Conventional peg	Against euro
Serbia	Inflation targeting	Stabilised arrangement	
Seychelles	Monetary targeting	Floating	
Sierra Leone	Monetary targeting	Other managed arrangement	
Singapore	Exchange rate anchor	Stabilised arrangement	Against composite
Slovak Rep.	Other—EMU—inflation-targeting-like framework	Free-floating	EMU
Slovenia	Other—EMU—inflation-targeting-like framework	Free-floating,	EMU
Solomon Islands	Other	Conventional peg	The country maintains a *de facto* exchange rate anchor to a composite
Somalia	Other	Free-floating	No framework
South Africa	Inflation targeting	Floating	
South Sudan	Other	Other managed arrangement	
Spain	Other—EMU—inflation-targeting-like framework	Free-floating	EMU
Sri Lanka	Other	Crawling-like arrangement	The country maintains a *de facto* exchange rate anchor to the US dollar
St Lucia	Exchange rate anchor	Currency board	With US dollar
St Vincent and the Grenadines	Exchange rate anchor	Currency board	With US dollar
Sudan	Other	Stabilised arrangement	The country maintains a *de facto* exchange rate anchor to the US dollar
Suriname	Monetary targeting	Other managed arrangement	
Swaziland	Exchange rate anchor	Conventional peg	Against other currency
Sweden	Inflation targeting	Free-floating	
Switzerland	Other - inflation-targeting-like framework	Floating	
Syria	Exchange rate anchor	Other managed arrangement	Against composite

(Continued)

99

Country	Monetary policy framework	Exchange rate arrangement	Remarks
Tajikistan	Monetary targeting	Stabilised arrangement	The country maintains a *de facto* exchange rate anchor to the US dollar
Tanzania	Monetary targeting	Stabilised arrangement	The country maintains a *de facto* exchange rate anchor to the US dollar
Thailand	Inflation targeting	Floating	
The Bahamas	Exchange rate anchor	Conventional peg	Against US dollar
The Gambia	Monetary targeting	Other managed arrangement	
The Netherlands	Other—EMU—inflation-targeting-like framework	Free-floating	EMU
Timor-Leste	Exchange rate anchor	No separate legal tender	US dollar
Togo	Exchange rate anchor	Conventional peg	Against euro
Tonga	Other	Pegged exchange rate within horizontal bands	The country maintains a *de facto* exchange rate anchor to a composite
Trinidad and Tobago	Exchange rate anchor	Stabilised arrangement	Against US dollar
Tunisia	Other—moving towards inflation-targeting-like framework	Floating	The central bank has taken preliminary steps towards inflation targeting
Turkey	Inflation targeting	Floating	
Turkmenistan	Exchange rate anchor	Conventional peg	Against US dollar
Tuvalu	Exchange rate anchor	No separate legal tender	Other currency
Uganda	Inflation targeting	Floating	
Ukraine	Inflation targeting	Floating	
United Arab Emirates	Exchange rate anchor	Conventional peg	Against US dollar
United Kingdom	Inflation targeting	Free-floating	
United States	Other—inflation-targeting-like framework	Free-floating	
Uruguay	Inflation targeting	Floating	
Uzbekistan	Monetary targeting	Crawling-like arrangement	

Country	Monetary policy framework	Exchange rate arrangement	Remarks
Vanuatu	Other	Other managed arrangement	The country uses elements of monetary targeting and exchange rate targeting
Venezuela	Other	Other managed arrangement	
Vietnam	Exchange rate anchor	Stabilised arrangement	Against composite
Yemen	Monetary targeting	Stabilised arrangement	The country maintains a *de facto* exchange rate anchor to the US dollar
Zambia	Other	Floating	
Zimbabwe	Exchange rate anchor	Other managed arrangement	Against US dollar

Source: Own compilation based on IMF (2018) and information from central banks' websites.

2

DESCRIBING DIFFERENCES IN IMPLEMENTING KEY ELEMENTS OF AN INFLATION TARGETING STRATEGY[1]

2.1 Introductory remarks

The analysis presented in Chapter 2 is conducted based on the elements identified as essential for an inflation targeting (IT) regime. Thus, initially, issues related to treating price stability as the main goal of monetary policy are reviewed. This part mainly discusses the various ways of formulating central banks' mandates, and the possible existence of other goals. Several aspects of central banks' independence are considered crucial in that respect as well. Second, topics associated with announcing a numerical target for inflation are presented, including past changes to targets, their types, time horizons, and levels. Differences in targeted inflation measures are also briefly analysed. Third, a question on how to conduct monetary policy based on a possibly broad set of information is investigated. Within that topic, of particular importance are issues concerning the preparation of forecasts, their ownership and time horizon, as well as the organisation of decision-making processes. The composition of decision-making bodies and rules on releasing voting records are also discussed. Fourth, accountability and transparency requirements are looked at, with the aim to see what main communication tools are used by IT central banks and how much information is disclosed. Finally, the impact of the global financial crisis and the European sovereign crisis on an IT framework is reviewed.

A detailed comparison of rules and practices governing central banks' implementation of inflation targeting required gathering a lot of granular information from various sources. As a result, a very rich and unique data set has been constructed, which is also described. Importantly, using the collected data, it was possible to present many of the aspects analysed in Chapter 2 on charts. This allows for visualising the differences in independence, accountability, and transparency standards among country groups, as well as for detecting changes introduced to inflation targeting over time.

2.2 Collecting information on institutional set-ups of inflation targeting central banks

In order to analyse the institutional set-ups of IT monetary authorities, first, all relevant aspects need to be specified, and second, information on these specified aspects needs to be collected. Both steps are crucial for drawing conclusions regarding the similarities and differences between the monetary policy institutional arrangements used by inflation targeters.

Regarding the first element, it is helpful to look at the various IT features reviewed in the literature, which allows for identifying topics that jointly translate into a central bank's institutional set-up (Debelle, 1997; Mishkin and Posen, 1997; Drop and Wojtyna, 2001; Mishkin, 2001; Heenan et al., 2006; Roger, 2010; Hammond, 2012; Naudon and Pérez, 2017). Following that approach, what has been found of particular importance for the analysis are issues related to formulating central banks' mandates, the level of their independence, the use of forecasts, rules governing decision-making processes, and requirements on accountability and transparency. The scope of the reviewed aspects is very broad, since many arrangements may matter for central banks' overall institutional set-up.

The second element, i.e. gathering information on the specified aspects, requires a considerable amount of work. No database is available that would cover the issues of interest even for a sub-group of the analysed countries, not to mention the history of the arrangements identified as potentially important. At the same time, IT monetary authorities are very open about their procedures and often publish materials enabling checking how they deal with certain topics. To collect the needed information, it is, however, necessary to visit each central bank's website separately and look at many different publications—often archived.

The currently applied practices and the reasons behind them are often described in detail; however, sometimes finding solutions that are used, or were used in the past, is far from straightforward. While, in the case of most central banks, access to documents published several years ago is quite easy, in principle, more historical information is more difficult to find. And even when all documents are collected, it is very time-consuming to enter each of them to see, for example, whether their content visibly changed over time.

Searching for information on 42 central banks' websites is, however, a necessary step to analyse the evolution of the investigated institutional arrangements over the last 30 years, and to produce charts and tables depicting such evolution. Put differently, investing a significant amount of time and effort is essential for the analysis.

Considering all the dimensions—i.e. the scope of the reviewed aspects related to institutional set-ups,[2] the number of IT central banks, and the time frame of the analysis covering the whole period of applying an IT strategy by any monetary authority—resulted in around 45,000 pieces of information that needed to be collected and coded. As a result, a very rich and unique data set has been constructed that allows for a detailed investigation of the institutional arrangements of inflation targeters. The database also enables building indices, proposed later, that are used in the econometric analysis.

2.3 Acknowledging price stability as the primary goal of monetary policy

A look at the legal rules applied to inflation targeters and how they are interpreted reveals important differences among central banks relating to acknowledging price stability as the primary goal of their monetary policy. In fact, quite a few IT central banks turn out to have multiple objectives, which—taken literary—may question monetary authorities' focus on inflation. Apart from the formulation of monetary authorities' mandates, what influences the primacy of price stability in the conduct of monetary policy is also an issue related to the choice of exchange rate regime and the degree of central banks' independence.

2.3.1 Central banks' mandates

Although all the analysed inflation targeting central banks have a price stability objective, contrary to conventional wisdom, their legal mandates are not always formulated in a way that guarantees its primacy (Charts 2.1 and 2.2).

In fact, the central banks of 14 IT countries have multiple objectives, with no priority given to low inflation (this is the case in 5 advanced economy inflation targeters[3] and 9 emerging market economy inflation targeters[4]). The remaining inflation targeters have either price stability as a single objective (this is the case in 6 countries—1 advanced economy, New Zealand,[5] and 5 emerging market economies[6]) or price stability has explicit priority over other goals (this is the case in 22 countries—8 advanced economies[7] and 14 emerging market economies[8]).

Among other goals, the most frequently encountered is an economic activity objective, which may mean contributing to maximum sustainable employment or supporting the policies of the government (30 inflation targeters have mandates including an economic activity objective—12 advanced economies[9] and 18 emerging market economies[10]; Chart 2.2). Nowadays, the second most often stipulated goal is a financial stability objective, which can be seen as a lesson learnt from the recent crises (23 inflation targeters have mandates including a financial stability objective—6 advanced economies[11] and 17 emerging market economies[12]). Regarding other goals, these may include, for example, ensuring a stable payment system.

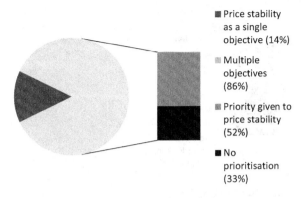

Price stability
as a single
objective (14%)

Multiple
objectives
(86%)

Priority given to
price stability
(52%)

No
prioritisation
(33%)

Notes: A price stability objective is interpreted rather broadly and includes, among others, protecting the value of money. An economic activity objective is interpreted rather broadly and includes, among others, contributing to full employment, supporting the policies of the government, or adding to the nation's welfare. A financial stability objective is interpreted rather broadly and includes, among others, supporting the development of the banking system. Other objectives may include, among others, ensuring a stable payment system. Source: Own compilation based on information from central banks' websites.

Chart 2.1 Objectives of central banks in IT economies.

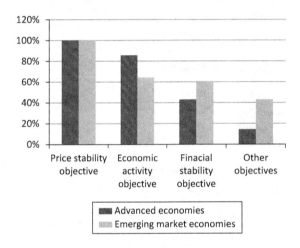

Advanced economies
Emerging market economies

Chart 2.2 Share of IT advanced and emerging market economies with different objectives.

Regarding a comparison between advanced and emerging market economies, selecting price stability as a single objective is more frequent in the latter group of countries, although multiple objectives are quite common in both groups of economies (Charts 2.3 and 2.4).

Importantly, central banks' mandates may include various aims to be achieved, but not necessarily with the use of monetary policy. Monetary policy is regarded as crucial predominantly for delivering price stability and output stability, and for that reason it is worth looking at the hierarchy of these two objectives. In turn, meeting the financial stability goal may be seen as belonging much more to the area of macroprudential policy. And,

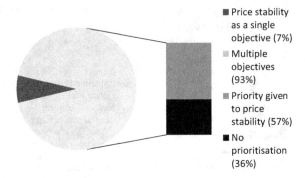

Chart 2.3 Objectives of central banks in IT advanced economies.

Notes: See notes to previous charts. Source: Own compilation based on information from central banks' websites.

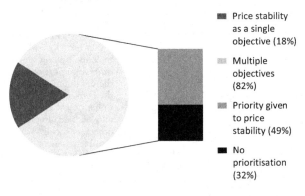

Chart 2.4 Objectives of central banks in IT emerging market economies.

indeed, as indicated below, monetary authorities often engage in conducting macroprudential policy.

2.3.2 Exchange rate regime

Regarding exchange rate regimes, currently all the analysed inflation targeters officially use a floating exchange rate regime (Chart 2.5). Additionally, in the past, the reviewed countries very rarely officially declared applying other exchange rate arrangements. This was the case only for Israel (between 1992 and 2003) and Hungary (between 2001 and 2006). These two economies decided to keep their soft peg arrangements at the early stages of using an inflation targeting strategy, when the fear of floating was still strong and the credibility of the new monetary policy framework not yet established.

This was, however, a source of tension, as the exchange rate targets were not always in line with the inflation targets, creating dilemmas for these central banks (Haldane, 1995, p. 3).

Looking at *de facto* classification, the picture is slightly more nuanced (Chart 2.6; Table 2.1). Although currently the vast majority of IT countries use a floating exchange rate regime (with only the Dominican Republic and Serbia applying soft peg arrangements), in the past there were more

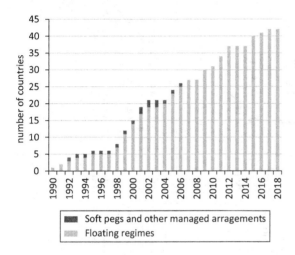

Chart 2.5 De jure classification of exchange rate regimes used by central banks in IT economies.

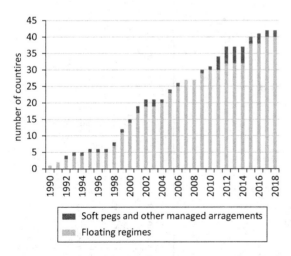

Notes: IMF classification for all countries, based on the end-year regime. Floating regimes include floating (managed floating) and free-floating (independently floating). Soft pegs and other managed arrangements include soft pegs (stabilised arrangement, pegged arrangement, crawl-like arrangement) and other managed arrangements. Source: Own compilation based on information from central banks' websites.

Chart 2.6 De facto classification of exchange rate regimes used by central banks in IT economies.

Table 2.1 Exchange rate regimes (*de facto* classification) used by IT central banks

IT countries using other exchange rate regimes than a floating regime (based on end-year regime)

Before 2009	2009	2010	2011	2012	2013	2014	2015	2016	after 2016
Israel (1992–2003)			Switzerland (2011–2014)		Czech Rep. (2013–2016)				
Hungary (2001–2006)	Georgia	Indonesia		Georgia Indonesia					
			Guatemala		Guatemala (2013–2014)				
				Dominican Rep. (since 2012)					
			Paraguay Peru						
					Armenia (2013–2014)			Serbia (since 2016)	

Source: Own compilation based on information from central banks' websites.
Notes: See notes to previous charts. The upper part refers to advanced economies. The lower part refers to emerging market economies. When other than a floating exchange rate regime was used in a given country for more than one year, the years are indicated in parenthesis. The classification is based on the regime as of end-year, thus dates indicated in the table do not fully correspond to the timing of adopting exchange rate restrictions by a given country. For Armenia—a crawl-like arrangement. For the Czech Republic—other managed arrangement and stabilised arrangement. For the Dominican Republic—crawl-like arrangement. For Georgia—other managed arrangement and stabilised arrangement. For Guatemala—stabilised arrangement and crawl-like arrangement. For Hungary—pegged arrangement. For Indonesia—stabilised arrangement and crawl-like arrangement. For Israel—crawl-like arrangement. For Paraguay—other managed arrangement. For Peru—crawl-like arrangement. For Serbia—stabilised arrangement. For Switzerland— other managed arrangement and crawl-like arrangement.

exceptions to that rule. Apart from Israel and Hungary, at some points—for relatively short periods—other economies also decided to more actively stabilise their exchange rates (the Dominican Republic and Serbia still do it). Looking at the regimes as of end-year, this was the case for Armenia (between 2013 and 2014), the Czech Republic (between 2013 and 2016), Georgia (in 2009 and 2012), Guatemala (in 2011 and between 2013 and 2016), Indonesia (in 2010 and 2012), Paraguay (in 2011), Peru (in 2011), and Switzerland (between 2011 and 2014).

It should, however, be noted that increased financial globalisation has exposed especially emerging market economies to significant capital inflows and outflows, often triggered by external factors. Under such circumstances, over the past two decades, emerging market economies have started to pay more attention to stabilising movements in their exchange rates by pursuing—what has been called by the Bank of International Settlements (BIS)—a controlled floating exchange rate regime (BIS, 2019, pp. 31–52). This is evidenced by the strong rise in the foreign exchange (FX) reserves of emerging market economy inflation targeters, which indicates that only some of them are following a free-floating regime without using FX interventions too actively. At the same time, it is worth recalling that even free-floating does not entirely exclude the possibility of intervening in the exchange rate markets, but this should be on a rare occasion.

Analysing recent developments related to FX interventions undertaken by inflation targeters, the examples of the Czech Republic and Switzerland are worth commenting on. In these countries, in the aftermath of the global financial crisis and the European sovereign crisis, when interest rates reached their lower bound and could no longer be cut, the central banks decided to use the exchange rates as an unconventional instrument. In doing so, they aimed to provide more accommodation to domestic monetary conditions, with the view of avoiding deflation, and thus maintaining price stability. In both cases, the monetary authorities wanted to weaken the exchange rate, which was supposed to support the return of inflation to its target. Therefore, the decisions of these central banks relating to exchange rates were fully in line with their inflation targeting frameworks.

As already mentioned, another noticeable case is Iceland. Following the financial crisis of 2008, Iceland focused its monetary policy on stabilising the exchange rate, and has only recently moved back to more conventional inflation targeting. Interestingly, Iceland did not officially change its monetary policy framework in 2008, nor its *de jure* exchange rate regime, and thus has been continuously counted as an inflation targeter with a floating exchange rate (IMF, 2015, 2016, 2018).

2.3.3 Central banks' goal independence

Central banks' mandates are, as a rule, stipulated in legal acts, which means that they are decided by institutions other than monetary authorities. Formal mandates are, however, formulated in rather general terms, and, as already noted, very often encompass multiple objectives. It is therefore important who is entitled to interpret them, and, in particular, to set a numerical value for targeted inflation which would be in line with the notion of maintaining price stability and delivering other goals expected from monetary policy.

Goal independence means that it is the central bank that translates the legal mandate into a specific inflation target. There are, however, good reasons to advocate for the involvement of government in that process, as it would imply some commitment to the announced target from the fiscal authorities. In some cases, the competence to choose an inflation target lies solely with government.

As far as the details of goal independence are concerned, in half of the countries the target is set jointly by the central bank and the government (this is the case in 21 inflation targeters—7 advanced economies[13] and 14 emerging market economies[14]). In slightly fewer cases (16 countries—5 advanced economies[15] and 11 emerging market economies[16]) the target is set solely by the central bank, and in only a few countries (5 inflation targeters—2 advanced economies,[17] and 3 emerging market economies[18]) the target is set by the government. In looking at the share of countries within advanced and emerging market economies with different authorities responsible for setting the inflation target, the differences are very minor (Charts 2.7 and 2.8).

2.3.4 Central banks' functional and institutional independence

Considering instrument independence, it is useful to distinguish between its different aspects, among others, functional and institutional independence (ECB, 2019, pp. 20–28). Functional independence can be described as providing a central bank with a clear objective, stated in a legally certain way. Institutional independence encompasses a prohibition on giving instructions and approving, suspending, or even invalidating monetary policy decisions by government.

While within IT, central banks' functional independence is less of an issue, as the mandates of inflation targeters are stipulated in their legal acts, and their interpretation is specified rather clearly by setting numerical inflation targets, other areas of independence are worth looking at in more detail.

In many countries, institutional independence is not straightforward. In slightly more than half of the analysed economies (23 inflation targeters—7 advanced economies[19] and 16 emerging market economies[20]), a government representative—most frequently a minister of finance or his/her representative—has the right to attend the meetings of the decision-making body of

110

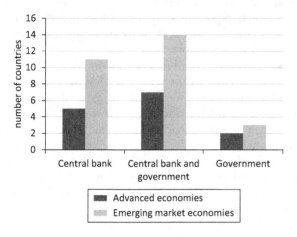

Chart 2.7 Authority responsible for setting an inflation target in IT economies.

Source: Own compilation based on information from central banks' websites.

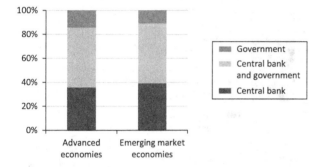
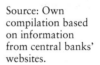

Chart 2.8 Share of IT economies with different authorities responsible for setting an inflation target.

the central bank (Charts 2.9 and 2.10). In almost half of these cases (9 countries where a government representative is attending monetary policy meetings—3 advanced economies[21] and 6 emerging market economies[22]), the government representative is even a member of the decision-making body of the central bank, and in 1 country (Colombia) the minister of finance is even the presiding member of the decision-making body of the central bank.

Being a member means that the government representative has full voting rights at the meetings. The exception here is Canada, where the government representative has no voting rights despite being a committee member. In turn, if the government representative is not a member of the decision-making body, he/she has the right to speak, so potentially also to influence monetary policy decisions, but has no voting rights. The exception here is Russia, where the government representatives are not members of the decision-making body, but in addition to the right to attend the meetings, they also have the right to a consultative vote.

Looking at these issues separately for advanced and emerging market economies, it is apparent that central banks are somewhat more institutionally independent in the first group of countries, with government representatives slightly less involved in decision-making processes (Charts 2.9 and 2.10). However, in a few countries (8 inflation targeters—of which 6 are advanced economies[23] and only 2 are emerging market economies[24]), the government has the right to directly influence monetary policy decisions by suspending or even invalidating them (Table 2.2). As more such cases relate to advanced economies, this may suggest that central banks in emerging market economies are *de jure* more institutionally independent.

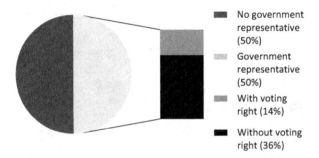

Chart 2.9 Involvement of government in central banks' decision-making in IT advanced economies.

Notes: Government representative means any member of the government or its representative. Source: Own compilation based on information from legal acts on central banks.

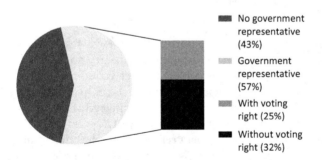

Chart 2.10 Involvement of government in central banks' decision-making in IT emerging market economies.

Table 2.2 IT economies where the government has the right to influence monetary policy decisions

Powers of government representative relating to monetary policy decisions

Canada	The minister of finance may, after consultation with the governor and with the approval of the governor in council, give to the governor a written directive concerning monetary policy.
Japan	The minister of finance or the minister of state for economic and fiscal policy (or a designated official of the ministry of finance or the cabinet office) when attending the board meetings may submit proposals concerning monetary control matters, or request that the board postpones a vote on proposals on monetary control matters submitted at the meeting until the next board meeting. The board decides whether or not to accommodate the request by voting.
Korea	Where the minister of strategy and finance considers the decisions taken by the monetary policy board to be in conflict with the government's economic policy, he may request the board to reconsider them. If the board takes the same decision with at least five members voting for it, the final decision rests with the president of Korea.
New Zealand	The governor-general may, from time to time, by order in council, on the advice of the minister, direct the bank to formulate and implement monetary policy for any economic objective, other than the economic objective of achieving and maintaining price stability, for such a period not exceeding 12 months as shall be specified in the order.
Norway	The king in council may adopt resolutions regarding the operations of the bank. Such resolutions may take the form of general rules or instructions in individual cases.
United Kingdom	The Treasury, after consultation with the governor of the bank, may by order give the bank directions with respect to monetary policy if they are satisfied that the directions are required in the public interest and by extreme economic circumstances.
Chile	The minister of finance has the right to suspend the application of any decision passed by the board for a period not exceeding 15 days and also to veto the resolutions of the board. However, a unanimous favourable vote by the board members means that suspension or veto has no effect.
Uganda	The minister may, after consultation with the governor and subject to this act, give directions of a general nature in writing, relating to the financial and economic policy of the bank.

Source: Own compilation based on information from legal acts on central banks.
Notes: The upper part refers to advanced economies. The lower part refers to emerging market economies.

2.3.5 Decision-makers' personal independence

Personal independence should prevent conflicts of interest, and requires fixed and relatively long terms of office for governors and other members of a central bank's decision-making body,[25] accompanied by restricted

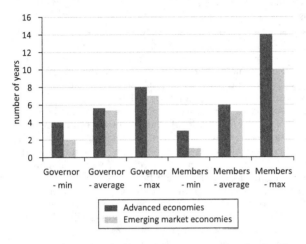

Chart 2.11 Term of office of decision-making bodies in IT advanced and emerging market economies.

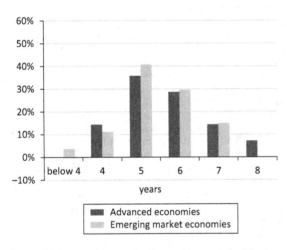

Notes: Members' term of office refers to the term of office of the majority of members. In some cases, there are different kinds of members with different terms of office (e.g. deputy governors in principle have the same term of office as governors, while other members may have a different term of office, and, in particular, government representatives have terms depending on other rules). For the euro area, rules referring to board members are considered (apart from the board members, the governing council consists of the governors of the euro area national central banks who are appointed according to national regulations). Sweden is counted as a country when the term of office is 6 years (in the legal act it is stipulated that the appointment is "for a period of five or six years"). Source: Own compilation based on information from legal acts on central banks.

Chart 2.12 Dispersion in governors' terms of office in IT advanced and emerging market economies.

grounds allowing for their dismissal. Thus, personal independence can be assessed, in particular, by looking at the terms of office of decision-makers[26] (Charts 2.11 and 2.12). The rationale behind this is that the longer the period that governors and other members of decision-making bodies hold office, the more independent they should feel.

The most typical period in office for central banks' decision-makers is 5 years (Chart 2.12). However, the term of office of the governor may be as short as 2 years (in the Dominican Republic) and as long as 8 years (in the euro area). In the case of other members of decision-making bodies, the minimum period is 1–2 years (in the Dominican Republic and Guatemala) and the maximum is 10–14 years (in Chile and the United States). In 1 country (Brazil), the term of office is not specified at all.

In the majority of central banks, the term of office of the governor is the same as that of other members of the decision-making bodies. In some countries (8 inflation targeters[27]), the governor holds office longer than other members, and in a few cases (3 inflation targeters[28]) the governor has a shorter term of office than other members.

Overall, while advanced economies tend to have slightly longer terms of office for decision-makers compared to emerging market economies, the difference is rather minor. In other aspects related to the term of office, advanced and emerging market economies are very similar (Chart 2.12).

Another issue affecting the personal independence of decision-makers is the possibility of their reappointment (Charts 2.13 and 2.14). The argument here is that with the view of being reappointed, decision-makers may be more easily influenced. This would be more of a problem if combined with a relatively short term of office.

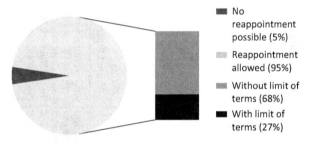

No reappointment possible (5%)

Reappointment allowed (95%)

Without limit of terms (68%)

With limit of terms (27%)

Chart 2.13 Possibility of reappointment of governors in IT economies.

Notes: Rules on the reappointment of members as stipulated in legal acts on central banks are considered. In some cases, there are different kinds of members with different rules applying to their reappointment (e.g. reappointment of government representatives is not regulated). In some legal acts on central banks it is explicitly stated that reappointment is allowed, or that it is not allowed. If no explicit rule on reappointment could be found, it is assumed that reappointment is possible. Source: Own compilation based on information from legal acts on central banks.

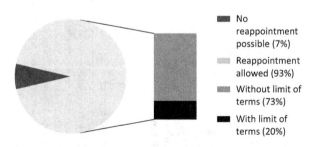

No reappointment possible (7%)

Reappointment allowed (93%)

Without limit of terms (73%)

With limit of terms (20%)

Chart 2.14 Possibility of reappointment of members of decision-making bodies in IT economies.

Table 2.3 Possibility of reappointment of governors and their term of office in IT economies

	Term of office in years							
	No fixed term	2	4	5	6	7	8	Euro area
Reappointment possible	Brazil	Dominican Rep.	Ghana Guatemala	Chile India Paraguay Peru Romania South Africa Thailand Turkey Uganda Japan New Zealand	Argentina Armenia Kazakhstan Mexico Serbia Sweden Switzerland	Albania Georgia Moldova Australia Canada		
Reappointment possible with limits			Colombia Korea	Indonesia Russia Iceland Israel United Kingdom	Hungary Philippines Poland Czech Rep. Norway	Ukraine		
No reappointment			United States					Euro area

Source: Own compilation based on information from legal acts on central banks.
Notes: See notes to previous charts. The upper parts of the respective sections refer to emerging market economies. The lower parts of the respective sections refer to advanced economies. Sweden is counted as a country when the term of office of a governor is 6 years (in the legal act it is stipulated that the appointment is "for a period of five or six years"). In the United States, a member who has completed an unexpired portion of a term may be reappointed, but a member who has served a full term may not be reappointed.

What can be seen is that reappointment is a rule, rather than an exception. In 40 IT countries[29] (12 advanced economies[30] and 28 emerging market economies[31]), governors can be reappointed, and in 28 inflation targeters (6 advanced economies[32] and 22 emerging market economies[33]) there are no limits on how many terms they may serve (Table 2.3). The situation with other members of the decision-making bodies is very similar—in 39 inflation targeters (12 advanced economies[34] and 27 emerging market economies[35]) members can be reappointed, and in 30 central banks (9 advanced economies[36] and 21 emerging market economies[37]) there are no limits on how many terms they may serve. Evidently, rules on reappointments in advanced economies do not materially differ from those in emerging market economies.

If one combines rules regulating terms of office and the reappointment of governors, clearly members of the euro area decision-making body enjoy institutional settings fostering their far-reaching independence (Table 2.3). Without formulating too strong conclusions, on the other end of the scale is Brazil (with no fixed term indicated in legal acts) and the Dominican Republic (with a relatively short term of office and a possibility of unlimited reappointments).

Personal independence also depends on rules on the appointment and dismissal of decision-makers (Chart 2.15). In the vast majority of countries these issues are regulated in legal acts. In many important aspects, such as rules limiting the political involvement of central banks' decision-makers or conflicts of interest, there are no major differences between advanced and emerging market economies.

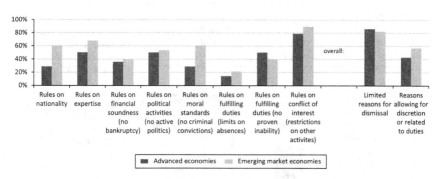

Chart 2.15 Share of IT economies with explicit rules on the appointment and dismissal of policymakers. Notes: Rules related to the appointment and dismissal of governors may differ slightly from rules related to other members of the decision-making bodies (also taking into account different types of members). The chart depicts the rules applying to the majority of decision-makers in a given central bank. The last category "Reasons allowing for discretion or related to duties" includes reasons such as "gross misconduct of their duties", "professional misconduct", "committing an act unbefitting his status", "violating his/her functional obligations", "serious misconduct or gross incompetence in the performance of duties". Source: Own compilation based on information from legal acts on central banks.

Overall, in 35 inflation targeters (12 advanced economies[38] and 23 emerging market economies[39]) the reasons allowing for dismissal of policymakers are explicitly stated in legal acts. However, in 22 countries (6 advanced economies[40] and 16 emerging market economies[41]) the legal acts leave room for discretion in interpreting them, or vaguely relate to the duties of the decision-makers.

2.3.6 Central banks' financial independence

Financial independence means that a central bank has at its autonomous disposal sufficient financial resources to fulfil its mandate and is not required to finance a fiscal deficit (the prohibition of monetary financing). The first thing to notice is that financial independence is difficult to verify. However, the legal rules relating to the financing of the government by the central bank show that this issue is often explicitly regulated.

Table 2.4 Countries with explicit prohibition on monetary financing in IT advanced and emerging market economies

Prohibition of government financing

Czech Republic	Iceland	Norway
Euro area	Israel	Switzerland
Albania	Indonesia	Poland
Armenia	Kazakhstan	Romania
Dominican Rep.	Mexico	Russia
Georgia	Moldova	Serbia
Guatemala	Peru	Turkey
Hungary	Philippines	Ukraine

Source: Own compilation based on information from legal acts on central banks. Notes: The upper part of the table refers to advanced economies. The lower part of the table refers to emerging market economies.

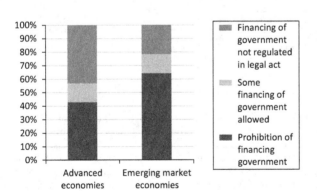

Chart 2.16 Share of IT economies with different rules on monetary financing.

In 24 inflation targeters (6 advanced economies[42] and 18 emerging market economies[43]), the central banks are legally prohibited from financing the government (Table 2.4; Chart 2.16). At the same time, in only 5 countries, of which 2 are advanced economy inflation targeters (Japan and Korea) and 3 are emerging market economy inflation targeters (Argentina, Paraguay, and Uganda), the central banks are formally allowed to finance governments, to some extent. This would suggest that emerging market economies put more weight on financial independence, which could partly be driven by their past negative experiences with the lack of financial independence.

2.3.7 Central banks' instrument independence in legal acts

In many countries, the importance of central banks' instrument independence is reflected in guarantees stipulated in legal acts. In 24 inflation targeters (8 advanced economies[44] and 16 emerging market economies[45]), central banks' instrument independence is explicitly safeguarded (Table 2.5; Chart 2.17). Regarding this aspect, no difference can be seen between advanced and emerging market economies.

2.4 Public announcement of a numerical target for inflation

Central banks do pay attention to the formulation of their targets, as evidenced by the fact that almost all of them have changed it at least once in the past, either with respect to target levels or other features. Beside target levels, among the key characteristics of the targets that are worth analysing are their types, horizon, and the targeted inflation measures.

2.4.1 Previous changes to inflation targets

Only 6 countries have never reformulated their inflation targets (Chart 2.18). They include 4 advanced economies (the euro area,[46] Japan,[47] Switzerland, and the United States) and 2 emerging market economies (Mexico and Uganda). All the others have changed either the level of the target, the type (point, point with a tolerance band, band, or band with a midpoint[48]), the inflation indicator to which the target refers (headline versus core inflation), or the time horizon of the target (end-year versus continuous). Among countries where the targets have been most often modified, i.e. at least eight times (importantly, on one occasion several features of the target might have been changed), are 2 advanced economies[49] and 4 emerging market economies.[50]

If, additionally, one takes into account how long a country has been pursuing an IT strategy, still within the group of advanced economy inflation targeters, 2 countries—Israel and Korea (with an average of 0.4 changes per year)—have most frequently changed their definition of the targets. In the case of emerging market economies, if the same threshold of at least

Table 2.5 Formally independent central banks in IT advanced and emerging market economies

Independence guaranteed in legal act		
Czech Republic	Israel	Sweden
Euro area	Japan	Switzerland
Iceland	Korea	Philippines
Albania	Indonesia	Romania
Armenia	Mexico	Russia
Chile	Moldova	Serbia
Georgia	Paraguay	Turkey
Hungary	Peru	Ukraine

Source: Own compilation based on information from legal acts on central banks. Notes: The upper part of the table refers to advanced economies. The lower part of the table refers to emerging market economies.

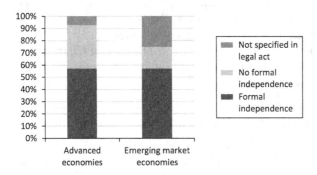

Chart 2.17 Share of IT economies with central bank independence guaranteed in legal act.

0.4 changes per year is used, the group becomes significantly larger. It includes 14 economies, where the targets have been most frequently modified in Ukraine (with an average of one change per year),[51] Indonesia and Ghana (with an average of 0.6 changes per year), Argentina, Colombia, the Dominican Republic, Guatemala, Romania, and the Philippines (with an average of 0.5 changes per year), and Brazil, Hungary, Paraguay, Serbia, and Turkey (with an average of 0.4 changes per year).

Two points should be mentioned here. First, a number of countries adopted an inflation targeting strategy as the final stage of a disinflation process[52] (15 inflation targeters), which almost by definition implied that their targets changed more often (Chart 2.19). This was the case for 2 advanced economies (Israel, Korea) and 13 emerging market economies.[53] With the exception of Ghana, which for many years has been trying to bring inflation down, and Kazakhstan and Ukraine, where the central banks only adopted an IT strategy in 2015–2017, judging by the declining inflation targets, all the other countries managed to sustainably lower their inflation within an IT framework. Initial target levels used for completing disinflation

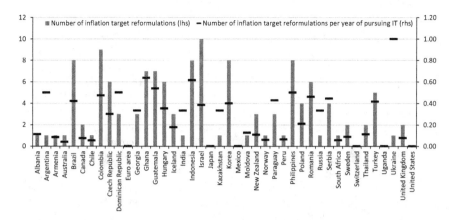

Chart 2.18 Number of reformulations of inflation targets in IT economies until 2018. Notes: Reformulations may include several changes introduced on one occasion. The already announced changes in the target levels that are going to take place in 2019 and in subsequent years are not counted, because they would distort the comparison between countries. Reformulations of the inflation target may include changing the type of target, the level of the target, the width of the tolerance bands around a point target, targeted inflation measures, or the target horizon. Source: Own compilation based on information from central banks' websites.

processes ranged from around 15% in Colombia and Israel to around 6% in the Czech Republic, Georgia, and Indonesia (with an average of 8.8%). The phase of lowering inflation took between 1 year in the Czech Republic, Hungary, Korea, and Romania, up to 7 years in Israel (with an average disinflation process lasting 3.1 years). Overall, looking at subsequent changes to the target levels, the average desired pace of disinflation processes was 1.8 pp. per year.

Second, the most often changed feature of inflation targets has indisputably been their levels (changed on 119 occasions—32 in advanced economies and 87 in emerging market economies), but the type of inflation targets has also been modified relatively frequently (changed 28 times—15 in advanced economies and 13 in emerging market economies). Other modifications have rarely been introduced (Chart 2.20). The target horizon was changed 14 times (3 in advanced economies and 11 in emerging market economies), the width of tolerance bands was adjusted on 11 occasions (4 in advanced economies and 7 in emerging market economies), and changes to the targeted inflation indicator occurred only 8 times (6 in advanced economies and 2 in emerging market economies).

If one considers countries that in the past were more eager to reformulate their targets (Charts 2.21 and 2.22), not much difference can be seen between advanced and emerging market economies in the case of

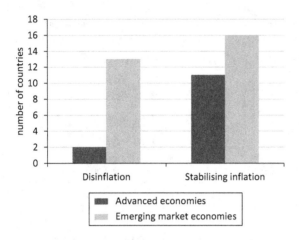

Chart 2.19 Initial motivation for announcing inflation targets in IT economies.

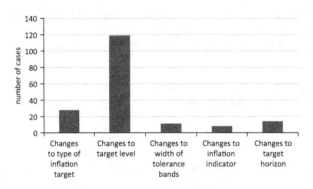

Chart 2.20 Number of reformulations of inflation targets until 2018 in IT economies.

Notes: If the target was changed from a point target with tolerance bands to a point target, this change is counted as a change to the type of inflation target, but not as a change to the width of tolerance bands. If the target was originally formulated as a point target with tolerance bands and the width of the tolerance bands changed, but the point target remained the same, this change is counted as a change to the width of the tolerance bands, but not as a change to the target level. The exception to this rule is Iceland, as tolerance bands were asymmetrical for the first 2 years of implementing an IT strategy there. If the target was originally formulated as a band target and changed to a point target, this change is counted as a change to the target level. The Czech Republic is counted as an emerging market economy on Chart 2.19 (when adopting the IT strategy it was classified as an emerging market economy). Source: Own compilation based on information from central banks' websites.

changes to the type of inflation target (7 advanced economy inflation targeters[54] and 12 emerging market economies[55] changed it at least once), or the width of the tolerance band (2 advanced economies[56] and 5 emerging market economies[57] decided to modify it). At the same time, advanced economies were more willing to modify the targeted inflation measure (5 advanced economies[58] and 2 emerging market economies[59] changed it), which can be attributable to the fact that initially it was much more common that targets referred to some kind of a core inflation measure, and only with time it became more typical to target headline inflation. Since emerging market economies joined the group of inflation targets later, very often they adopted headline inflation targets straight away. In turn, emerging market economies more frequently modified the target levels (in the case of advanced economies such a change occurred in 8 inflation targeters[60] and in emerging market economies in 22 countries[61]) and the target horizon (changed in 3 advanced economies[62] and in 9 emerging market economies[63]), which, to a great extent, may be explained by the already mentioned disinflation processes. To sustainably lower inflation, gradually decreasing end-year targets were announced. If disinflation succeeded and countries moved to stabilising inflation at a constant level, they usually switched to continuous targets.

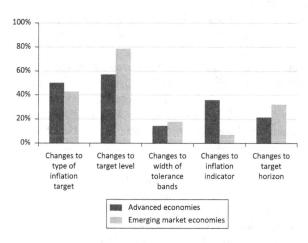

Chart 2.21 Share of IT economies introducing any changes to inflation targets.

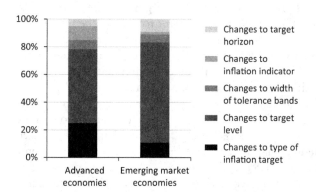

Chart 2.22 Different kinds of reformulations of inflation targets introduced in IT economies.

Notes: See notes to previous charts. Source: Own compilation based on information from central banks' websites.

2.4.2 Types of inflation targets

Looking at the different types of inflation targets, all of them are used (point targets by 14 inflation targeters,[64] point targets with tolerance bands by 23 countries,[65] band targets by 3 countries,[66] and band targets with midpoints by 2 countries[67]), but over time some types have clearly become the more preferred options (Charts 2.23, 2.24, and 2.68 in Appendix 2).

In the case of advanced economies, initially band targets were most commonly used, but over the last 10 years point targets have become dominant (currently 8 advanced economies use point targets). Regarding the choice of the target type, the rest of advanced economy inflation targeters have remained quite diversified, as some of them use point targets with tolerance bands (currently 2 countries—the Czech Republic and Sweden), band targets (currently 2 countries—Australia and Israel), and band targets with midpoints (again, currently 2 countries—Canada and New Zealand).

In turn, in the case of emerging market economies, a strong preference for point targets with tolerance bands has become apparent quite early (currently 21 emerging market economy inflation targeters use point targets with tolerance bands). Nowadays, the second choice for emerging market economies is point targets (currently used by 6 countries—Albania, Argentina, Georgia, Kazakhstan, Russia, and Uganda), with almost no support for the other two target types (currently 1 emerging market economy uses a band target—South Africa).

The proportion of countries with a certain target type often moved in response to incorporating newcomers in the counting, but changing the target type of inflation targeters after some years of pursuing IT was also practised. Within advanced economies, 6 countries decided to switch between different target types at least once (in half of the cases—Israel, Korea, and Sweden—the change occurred more than once, while in the Czech Republic, Iceland, and New Zealand only one reformulation of the target type was decided). The situation looks similar within emerging market economies, out of which 13 countries[68] decided at some point to change the target type (however, in this group only in Hungary was the change reversed, while in other countries if a country decided to switch from a band target to a point target with or without a tolerance band, it stayed with its latter choice).

Among economies using a point target with a tolerance band (23 inflation targeters—2 advanced economies and 21 emerging market economies), the most frequently used tolerance band width is ±1 pp. (preferred by 13 out of the 23 inflation targeters using a point target with a tolerance band—2 advanced economies[69] and 11 emerging market economies[70]; Charts 2.25 and 2.26). Some countries use wider bands of ±1.5 pp. (5 countries—all of which are emerging market economies[71]) or ±2.0 pp. (5 countries—again all of which are emerging market economies[72]), while the previously applied narrower bands of ±0.5 pp. and much wider bands of ±2.5 pp. are no longer used (Chart 2.25; Table 2.6).

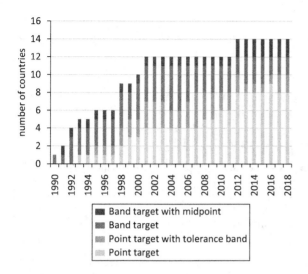

Chart 2.23 Type of inflation targets used by IT advanced economies.

Source: Own compilation based on information from central banks' websites.

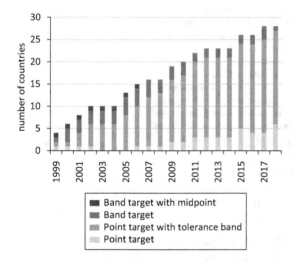

Chart 2.24 Type of inflation targets used by IT emerging market economies.

Apart from the already noted short episode in Iceland (where tolerance bands were asymmetrical for the first 2 years of implementing an inflation targeting strategy, with the lower limit kept at −1.5 pp. and the upper limit decreasing gradually from +3.5 pp. to +1.5 pp.), all countries use

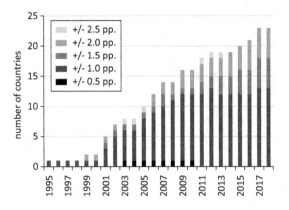

Chart 2.25 Width of tolerance bands used by IT economies.

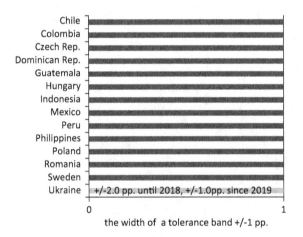

Chart 2.26 Countries with tolerance bands of ±1 pp. among IT economies.

Notes: Only countries with a point target with tolerance bands are included in the charts. Iceland, despite the fact that in the first 2 years it used an asymmetrical tolerance band, in that period was treated as belonging to the group of countries with tolerance bands of "±1.5 pp". Source: Own compilation based on information from central banks' websites.

symmetrical tolerance bands, which signals that deviations both above and below the target are treated the same way.

The symmetry of the target may also be important in the case of other target types than point targets with tolerance bands. Point targets are, as a rule, symmetrical, which some central banks explicitly stress (Fed, 2016), while others do not. Similarly, band targets, irrespective of whether they have indicated a midpoint or not, should be regarded as symmetric. However, in some countries, the targets are specified in a way that suggests their asymmetry, which is the case for the European Central Bank (ECB), with the

Table 2.6 Different widths of tolerance bands used in IT economies

IT countries with a point target with a tolerance band—with the width of a tolerance band other than ±1 pp.

	1999	2000	2001	2002	2003	2004	2005	2006	2007	2008	2009	2010	2011	2012	2013	2014	2015	2016	2017	2018
±0.5 pp.									Korea (2007–2009)											
±1.5 pp.			Iceland (2001–2007)		Colombia (2003–2010)				Armenia (since 2007)				Serbia (since 2011)		Moldova (since 2013)		Thailand (since 2015)		Brazil (since 2017)	
±2.0 pp.	Brazil (1999–2002)							Brazil (2006–2016); Turkey (since 2006)			Serbia (2009–2010)		Ghana (since 2011)			Paraguay (since 2014)		India (since 2016)	Ukraine* (since 2017)	
±2.5 pp.					Brazil (2003–2005)								Paraguay (2011–2013)							

Source: Own compilation based on information from central banks' websites.

Notes: See notes to previous charts. The upper parts of the respective sections of the table refer to advanced economies. The lower parts of the respective sections of the table refer to emerging market economies. Years when a given width of tolerance bands was used in a country are indicated in parenthesis.

* In 2019, Ukraine moved to using a tolerance band of ±1 pp.

127

target formulated as "below, but close to, 2%", and Switzerland, with the target formulated as "below 2%". Recently, the ECB has, however, indicated that it treats its inflation aim as symmetrical (ECB, 2019).

2.4.3 Targeted inflation measure

Regarding the targeted inflation measure, in the early years of IT, when the credibility of the new strategy had not yet been tested, countries tended to use some kind of core inflation measure, or in some other way stressed that

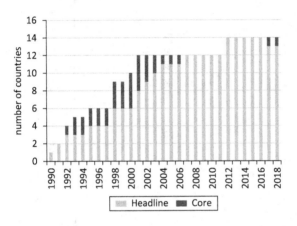

Chart 2.27 Targeted inflation measures in IT advanced economies.

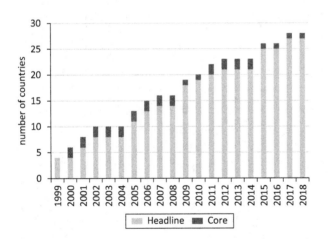

Chart 2.28 Targeted inflation measures in IT emerging market economies.

Notes: The following notation is used: headline—headline measure of consumer price inflation (e.g. CPI in Poland, HICP in the euro area, PCE in the United States); core— any kind of exclusion measure of consumer price inflation (e.g. inflation excluding food and energy prices or inflation excluding mortgage interest payments). In Chile, the target relates to both headline and core inflation, but in the chart Chile is counted as using a headline inflation target. Source: Own compilation based on information from central banks' websites.

monetary policy cannot control the general level of prices (e.g. by using explicit escape clauses).[73] Nowadays, it is rather an exception to the rule, as the vast majority of inflation targeters (40 central banks) express their targets in terms of headline inflation (Charts 2.27 and 2.28). Only Sweden and Uganda are targeting some kind of an exclusion measure. An interesting case is Korea, where first the target referred to headline inflation, then—for a few years—to a core measure, and lately again to headline inflation. In turn, in Chile the target relates to both headline and core inflation.[74] As regards the use of escape clauses, again only 2 countries—1 advanced economy (the Czech Republic) and 1 emerging market economy (Romania)—currently use them, explicitly listing conditions that excuse the central bank from taking action aimed at bringing inflation back to the target.

At the same time, it is important to note that the way inflation is measured is not uniform across countries (and even within countries there might be differences, as is the case in Peru, where the consumer price index (CPI) for Metropolitan Lima is used, and in South Africa, where the CPI for urban areas is used).[75] In particular, headline inflation may include different price categories, depending on the chosen methodology. In some countries, the cost of mortgage interest payments or imputed rents for owner-occupied dwellings are treated as consumer prices, while in other countries these prices do not appear in headline inflation. Likewise, core inflation, which, in principle, is computed by excluding certain types of prices from the headline measure, may encompass various categories of goods, thus having a different meaning, depending on the applied exclusion criteria.[76]

Considering examples of countries that, at some stage, decided to target any kind of core inflation measure, two price categories tended to be excluded from the targeted measure (Table 2.7). The first group consists of prices that are beyond the control of monetary policy, i.e. the price of food and energy or regulated prices. These prices fluctuate due to, for example, weather conditions, the Organisation of the Petroleum Exporting Countries (OPEC) agreements, government policies, and other factors that cannot be influenced by monetary policy decisions. In turn, the second group of prices includes prices that are very strongly affected by monetary policy, for example, the costs of mortgage interest payments. If monetary policy is tightened, these costs almost automatically increase, counter-intuitively leading in the short run to higher headline inflation, which—in principle—when the monetary transmission mechanism is given some time to work through the economy, should decrease as a result of monetary policy tightening (the reverse happens when monetary policy is loosened). Thus, these prices are also often excluded from the targeted inflation measure, as their changes introduce misleading signals (Mayes and Chapple, 1995, p. 232).

In the past, Australia used to target the CPI excluding the price of fruit and vegetables, petrol, interest costs, public sector prices, and other volatile prices (between 1993 and 2003). Other countries decided to exclude

Table 2.7 Different measures of targeted inflation in IT economies

IT countries targeting a measure other than headline inflation

1992	1993–1997	1998	1999–2001	2002	2003	2004	2005	2006	2007	2008	2009–2011	2012–2014	2015	2016	2017	2018
United Kingdom (1992–2003)															Sweden (since 2017)	
	Australia (1993–2003)															
		Czech Rep. (1998–2001)														
			Korea (2000–2006)													
								South Africa (2000–2008)								
									Thailand (2000–2014)							
												Uganda (since 2011)				

Source: Own compilation based on information from central banks' websites.
Notes: The upper part refers to advanced economies. The lower part refers to emerging market economies. Years when some kind of exclusion measure was targeted in a given country are indicated in parenthesis. For Australia—CPI excluding fruit and vegetables, petrol, interest costs, public sector prices, and other volatile prices. For Chile—CPI excluding vegetables, fruit, and fuel. For the Czech Republic—CPI adjusted for regulated prices and for the effect of administrative measures (e.g. indirect tax increases, subsidy cancellations). For Korea—CPI excluding agricultural products and oil. For South Africa—CPI for urban areas excluding mortgage interest costs. For Sweden—CPI with fixed interest rate. For Thailand—CPI excluding raw food and energy prices. For Uganda—inflation excluding food crop prices. For the United Kingdom—retail price index excluding mortgage interest payments.

prices more selectively. The most typically disregarded prices were those of agricultural products and oil, as in Korea (between 2000 and 2006) and Thailand (between 2001 and 2014), mortgage interest payments, as in South Africa (between 2001 and 2008) and the United Kingdom (between 1992 and 2003), and regulated prices, as in the Czech Republic (between 1998 and 2001). Currently, Chile—apart from the headline CPI measure—is also targeting the CPI excluding the price of vegetables, fruit, and fuel; Sweden—the CPI with fixed interest rate (since late 2017); and Uganda—inflation excluding food crop prices (since 2012).

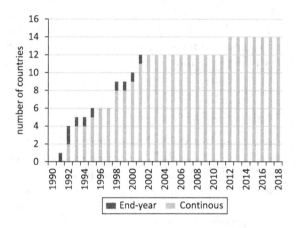

Chart 2.29 Time horizon of inflation targets in IT advanced economies.

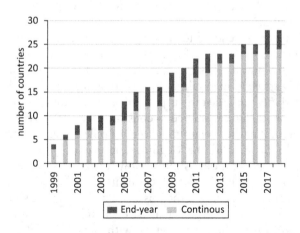

Notes: In a number of cases the initial target was set at a certain inflation level targeted within a few years' horizon. Thus, strictly speaking, in the first years of pursuing an IT strategy, no target was specified. Source: Own compilation based on information from central banks' websites.

Chart 2.30 Time horizon of inflation targets in IT emerging market economies.

2.4.4 Time horizon of inflation targets

Looking at the time horizon of the targets, the dominant choice is a continuous target (Charts 2.29 and 2.30). Continuous target means that inflation should run close to the target at all times, i.e. the target should be met on a continuous basis—each month, quarter, year (currently it is used by all advanced and 24 emerging market economy inflation targeters).[77]

The only 4 countries that keep to end-year targets are Argentina,[78] Ghana, Turkey, and Ukraine. These countries have not yet managed to permanently lower their inflation levels to their longer-term targets, so they may be seen as continuing disinflation processes.

A topic related to the time horizon of the targets is how quickly inflation should be brought back to the target, if it deviates from it (e.g. as a result of an external shock). Here, almost all countries explicitly indicate that they aim at stabilising inflation at the target in the medium term. This reflects the transmission lags of monetary policy and allows for flexibility in reacting to shocks under flexible inflation targeting.

2.4.5 Level of inflation targets

Finally, of key importance is the level of the inflation target (Chart 2.68 in Appendix 2). When comparing target levels,[79] several points are worth mentioning. First of all, there has been a visible decline in target levels across countries over the years, but advanced economies still tend to have lower targets than emerging market economies (Charts 2.31 and 2.32). This holds for both initial target levels (with an average for advanced economies standing at 3.8% compared to an average for emerging market economies standing at 6.0%) and current target levels (with an average of 2.1% for advanced economies compared to an average of 4.3% for emerging market economies; Charts 2.33 and 2.34).

A prominent exception to the trend of lowering inflation targets is New Zealand, which in fact increased its target from an initial level of 0%–2%, first to 0%–3% in 1996, and later to 1%–3% in 2002. After that change, all inflation targeters officially strive to maintain price growth at a positive level (only in the case of Switzerland, with the target specified as "less than 2%", it is not clear if 0% inflation should be considered as consistent with the target).

Higher targets in emerging market economies seem to reflect their lower levels of economic development, and the ongoing convergence process. Higher preferable levels of inflation should simply allow for the catching-up process to take place also via nominal price adjustments. In other words, higher target levels follow from considering the possible Balassa–Samuelson effects. At the same time, as many emerging market economies, often less developed ones, join the group of inflation targeters, with newcomers often using an IT strategy first to finalise a disinflation process, this effect is

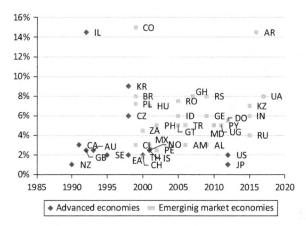

Chart 2.31 Initial target level and date of IT adoption in advanced and emerging market economies.

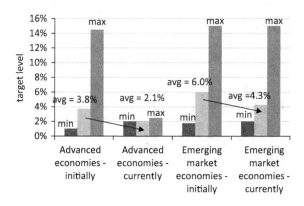

Chart 2.32 Changes in target levels in IT advanced and emerging market economies.

Notes: Target level in the case of point targets is the value of the point target and in the case of target bands—the midpoint of the band. In the case of economies when the target is specified as "below x%" it is assumed that the target is x%. Initial target level is the target announced when an IT strategy was adopted (at times it was not a target for the first year of pursuing IT, but a target with a more distant horizon). Current target level refers to inflation targets for 2018. Two-letter country codes are used. Source: Own compilation based on information from central banks' websites.

exaggerated. Almost by definition, including newcomers increases the average level of inflation targets in that group of countries. However, in many emerging market economies, target levels are already low and comparable to advanced economies (this is the case for Peru with a target of 2% ±1 pp., Poland and Romania with targets of 2.5% ±1 pp., and Thailand with a target of 2.5% ±1.5 pp.).[80]

Moreover, the dispersion of the target levels has decreased over time—for both groups of economies, but much more significantly for advanced economies (12 countries from that group use around a 2% target, and 2

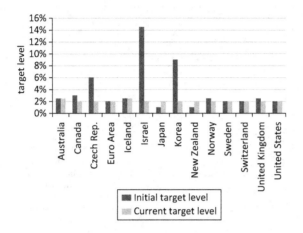

Chart 2.33 Changes to inflation target levels in IT advanced economies.

Notes: See notes to previous charts. Source: Own compilation based on information from central banks' websites.

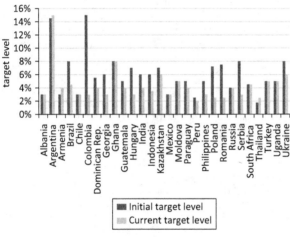

Chart 2.34 Changes to inflation target levels in IT emerging market economies.

countries—Australia and Iceland—use slightly higher targets of around 2.5%; Chart 2.35). Within emerging market economies, the most frequently used targets are around 3% (8 countries[81] from that group opted for around a 3% target) and around 4% (adopted by 6 countries[82]), but the general dispersion of the target levels in emerging market economies is relatively high (ranging from around a 2% target in Peru to around an 8% target in Ghana and around a 15% target in Argentina[83]). The key argument here is that

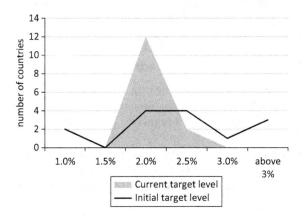

Chart 2.35 Dispersion in inflation target levels in IT advanced economies.

Notes: See notes to previous charts. Source: Own compilation based on information from central banks' websites.

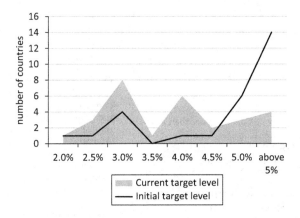

Chart 2.36 Dispersion in inflation target levels in IT emerging market economies.

among emerging market economies there are much more newcomers that—as others in the past—use an IT strategy first to disinflate (Chart 2.36).

2.5 Formulating monetary policy on the basis of a broad set of information

There are many ways in which IT central banks aim at making well-informed policy decisions. First of all, they pay great attention to projections, with inflation and GDP growth being the standard set of forecast variables. Moreover, in order to make use of possible different areas of expertise, typically decision-making bodies are collegial, with a significant share of external members. The frequency of decision-making meetings and rules on the decision-making process also play a role.

2.5.1 Preparation of forecasts

Looking at central banks' use of forecasts, as the crucial element of a comprehensive set of information based on which monetary policy decisions are made, it is clear that all IT central banks regularly publish projections (Charts 2.37 and 2.38).[84]

The majority of central banks prepare projections on a quarterly basis and, in that respect, there is little difference between advanced and emerging market economies. Thirty-two inflation targeters (13 advanced economies

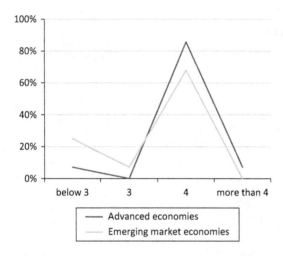

Notes: In Argentina and Uganda the frequency of publishing inflation reports does not correspond to the frequency of publishing forecasts (in Argentina projections are not published, in Uganda not every report includes a forecast). Source: Own compilation based on information from central banks' websites.

Chart 2.37 Share of IT economies with different frequency of publishing projections per year.

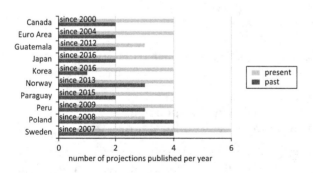

Chart 2.38 Changes to the number of projections published per year in IT economies.

and 19 emerging market economies) publish projections on a quarterly basis. Countries producing less than four forecasts per year include 7 emerging market economies—with 5 countries[85] preparing forecasts biannually and 2 countries[86] preparing three forecasts per year. The only country publishing more than four forecasts per year is Sweden, with six forecasts produced annually.

Regarding the forecast horizon, over the years central banks have tended to extend it. Currently, in most cases, projections cover 2–3 years ahead, which corresponds to the medium-term nature of the inflation targets (Charts 2.39 and 2.40). The forecast horizon is somewhat longer in advanced economies (between 2 and 4 years), and somewhat shorter in emerging market economies (between 1 and 3 years).

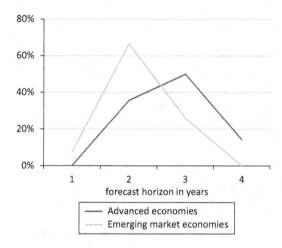

Source: Own compilation based on information from central banks' websites.

Chart 2.39 Share of IT economies with different forecast horizons.

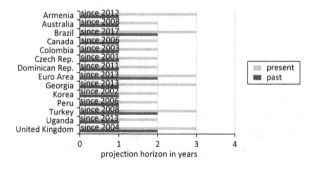

Chart 2.40 Changes to the forecast horizon in IT advanced and emerging market economies.

137

2.5.2 Forecast variables

Considering forecast variables,[87] it is no surprise that all inflation targeters do forecast inflation[88] (in many cases both headline and core inflation; Chart 2.41). Quite frequently, inflation forecasts are accompanied by GDP projections (32 inflation targeters publish projections of both variables—12 advanced economies[89] and 20 emerging market economies[90]), much less often by interest rate projections (published by 7 inflation targeters—5 advanced economies[91] and 2 emerging market economies[92]), and rarely with unemployment rate projections (published by 3 advanced economy inflation

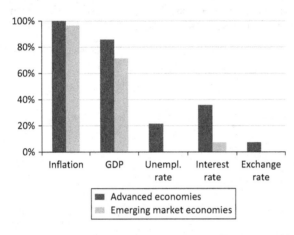

Chart 2.41 Share of IT economies with different forecast variables.

Source: Own compilation based on information from central banks' websites.

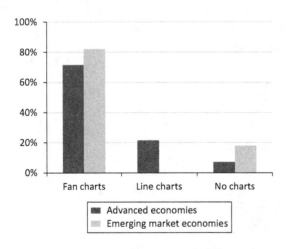

Chart 2.42 Share of IT economies with different forms of presenting forecasts.

138

targeters[93]). Only 1 advanced economy (the Czech Republic) also publishes forecasts of nominal exchange rates against a single currency (the euro).[94]

Over the years, while inflation and GDP have become standard variables to forecast—predominantly in the form of fan charts emphasising forecast uncertainty—the approach to publishing projections of other variables has not been unified (Chart 2.42). In particular, around 2007–2008 some advanced economies decided to communicate their interest rate projections, but since their experiences with those forecasts were mixed, not many followed suit.[95] Among both advanced and emerging market economies, the publication of interest rate forecasts is therefore rare. One of the biggest challenges with publishing interest rate projections seems to be conveying the message that they should not be treated as a commitment by the central bank to follow a certain path in setting future interest rates. Such a disclaimer is valid independent of whether interest rate projections are owned by decision-makers (as is the case in Norway, Sweden, the United States, and Georgia), the central bank (as in New Zealand), or staff (as in the Czech Republic and Guatemala).

At times, central banks decided to discontinue publishing projections of certain variables (Table 2.8). Brazil and Guatemala used to forecast GDP growth, but stopped publishing it a few years ago. Regarding less frequently forecast variables, the United Kingdom published forecasts of 3-month interest rates, Norway released forecasts of import-weighted exchange rates, and Moldova prepared forecasts of exchange rates against the euro and US dollar and interest rates on 91-day T-bills.

2.5.3 Ownership of forecasts and involvement of staff in a decision-making process

In some central banks, it is openly communicated that projections are owned by decision-makers or by staff (Chart 2.43). In the latter case, decision-makers do not have to share the assessment of staff. In turn, in some central banks, it is indicated that the forecasts are the bank's forecasts, which, in fact, does not give clarity to whose assessment the projections are supposed to show.

In most cases, projections are owned by the bank or staff, which means that they do not necessarily reflect the views of decision-makers (this is the case in 31 inflation targeters—9 advanced economies[96] and 22 emerging market economies[97]; Chart 2.43). Only in 10 countries—5 advanced economies[98] and 5 emerging market economies[99]—are forecasts owned by decision-makers. Therefore, in advanced economies it is slightly more frequent that projections are shaped by decision-makers rather than by staff.

Staff are, however, involved in decision-making not only via producing forecasts, but also by formulating formal recommendations for the decisions (Chart 2.44). While in many cases (18 countries), no information is

Table 2.8 Forecast variables other than inflation and GDP in IT economies

	Before 2000	2001–2004	2005	2006	2007	2008	2009	2010–2011	2012	2013–2014	2015	2016	After 2016
Australia											Unemployment rate (since early 2015)		
Czech Rep.						Interest rate path (since 2008)	Koruna-euro nominal exchange rate (since 2009)						
New Zealand	90-day bank bill rate (until late 2016)												Official cash rate (since late 2016)
Norway			Interest rates—sight deposit rate (in late 2005) / Import-weighted exchange rate (in late 2005)		Interest rates—key policy rate (since 2007)								
Sweden					Repo rate (since 2007)								
United Kingdom	3-month interest rate (from mid-1997 to early 2000)									Unemployment rate (since mid-2013)			
United States	Unemployment rate								Federal funds rate (since 2012)				
Georgia												Monetary policy rate (since mid-2016)	
Guatemala									Monetary policy rate (since 2012)				

Source: Own compilation based on information from central banks' websites.
Notes: The upper part refers to advanced economies. The lower part refers to emerging market economies.

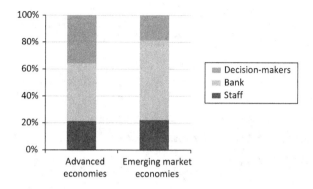

Chart 2.43 Share of IT economies with different ownership of forecasts.

Source: Own compilation based on information from central banks' websites.

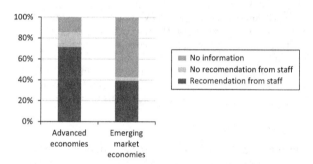

Chart 2.44 Involvement of staff in decision-making processes in IT economies.

available on how monetary policy meetings proceed, in the vast majority of countries where such information is given, staff recommendations are part of the decision-making process. This is the case in 21 countries—10 advanced economies[100] and 11 emerging market economies.[101] Only in 2 advanced economies (Korea and the United Kingdom) and in 1 emerging market economy (Armenia), where information on the decision-making process is revealed, it seems that no formal recommendations are prepared. This would suggest that the involvement of staff in decision-making processes is, in fact, somewhat heavier in advanced economies.

In some countries, recommendations are formulated by staff working in economic departments as part of preparations for the decision-making meetings. However, in some countries, a formal committee meets shortly before the decision-making body to discuss and formulate official recommendations for the monetary policy actions. Examples include not only Georgia

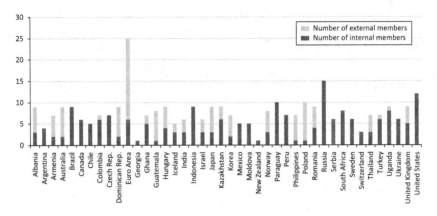

Chart 2.45 Composition of decision-making bodies in IT advanced and emerging market economies. Notes: Internal members are members from inside the central bank. Representatives of the government are treated as external members. In countries where the size of the committee may vary, the maximum allowed number of members is assumed. In Hungary, the committee may consist of between five and nine members. In Indonesia, the committee may consist of between six and nine members. In Paraguay, the committee consists of around 10 members. In Uganda, the committee may consist of between seven and nine members. Source: Own compilation based on information from central banks' websites and legal acts on central banks.

and New Zealand,[102] where governors are single decision-makers, but also Canada, Kazakhstan, and the Philippines, where decisions are taken anyway by the collegial decision-making bodies. Additional committees can also be found in Romania and Ukraine, but their competencies are somewhat different, as they include the formulation of the strategy, objectives, and guidelines for the central bank.

2.5.4 Decision-making bodies

In looking at decision-makers themselves, a few points can be made (Chart 2.45). First, with only 2 exceptions—1 advanced economy (New Zealand[103]) and 1 emerging market economy (Georgia)—monetary policy decisions are taken by committees, which shows a strong preference for collegial decision-making (this is the case in 40 inflation targeters). And, as already mentioned, also in Georgia and New Zealand there are collegial advisory bodies helping governors to formulate the decisions (a monetary policy committee consisting of 12 internal members in Georgia and an advisory committee consisting of 12 members, including 2 external members, in New Zealand).[104]

Second, with relatively few exceptions, the committees include between 5 and 10 members, which shows a clear inclination for a relatively broad spectrum of opinions, but still manageable from an organisational point of view (35 out of 40 countries with committees belong to this group— 10 advanced economies[105] and 25 emerging market economies[106]). Apart from cases of a single decision-maker, only Switzerland and Argentina have smaller committees (with 3 and 4 members, respectively), while on the other end of the scale is the euro area (with 25 members)[107], Russia (with 15 members), and the United States (with 12 members).[108]

Third, with a number of exceptions, committees consist of both internal and external members, which should allow for combining decision-makers with different backgrounds. Out of all inflation targeters with committees, 17 countries (5 advanced economies[109] and 12 emerging market economies[110]) have committees with no external members. Out of the remaining 23 countries with collegial decision-making bodies, in many cases the ratio of external members to internal members is substantial. It can be as high as 86% in the Philippines, 88% in Guatemala, and 90% in Poland (in 16 countries, it is 50% or more, out of which 6 are advanced economies[111] and 10 are emerging market economies[112]).

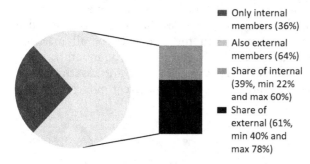

Chart 2.46 Share of IT advanced economies with different composition of decision-making bodies.

Notes: See notes to previous charts. Source: Own compilation based on information from central banks' websites and legal acts on central banks.

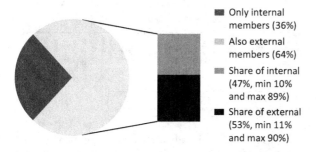

Chart 2.47 Share of IT emerging market economies with different composition of decision-making bodies.

Regarding the composition of committees, there are minor differences between advanced and emerging market economies (Charts 2.46 and 2.47). However, on average, the share of internal members is slightly lower in the decision-making bodies of advanced economies compared to emerging market economies.

2.5.5 Frequency of decision-making meetings

Considering the frequency of decision-making meetings, the most typical number among inflation targeters is currently 8 per year—24 of the analysed decision-making bodies meet with semi-quarterly frequency (11 advanced economies[113] and 13 emerging market economies[114]; Chart 2.48). Only 6 countries have a lower number of meetings (2 advanced economies—Switzerland with 4 meetings per year and Sweden with 6 meetings per year, and 4 emerging market economies—Ghana, India, South Africa, and Uganda with 6 meetings per year), and 12 countries (1 advanced economy—Australia[115] and 11 emerging market economies[116]) have a higher number of meetings (ranging from 9 to 24 meetings per year). Thus, on average, monetary policy meetings are somewhat more frequently held by emerging market economies compared to advanced economies.

What is interesting is that in many countries the number of scheduled decision-making meetings is lower than the frequency of all meetings required by law (which is either quarterly, semi-quarterly, monthly, semi-monthly, or even—in some cases—weekly). This is not necessarily inconsistent, since not all meetings must be devoted to current monetary policy

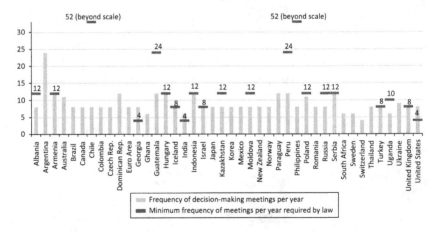

Chart 2.48 Frequency of meetings per year in IT advanced and emerging market economies. Notes: In many cases no information was available on the minimum frequency of meetings required by law. Source: Own compilation based on information from central banks' websites and legal acts on central banks.

issues, and evidently in many cases they are not. In Korea, for example, it is clearly communicated that some meetings are designed to discuss financial stability issues.

In all the analysed central banks, apart from scheduled meetings, there is a possibility to call an extraordinary decision-making meeting, if the need arises. It is a rarely used option, but at times very important. In particular, following the collapse of Lehman Brothers, on 8 October 2008, the central banks of Canada, the euro area, Japan, Sweden, Switzerland, the United Kingdom, and the United States, called extraordinary monetary policy meetings and issued an unprecedented joint statement showing their continuous close cooperation in reducing strains in financial markets.[117]

The dominant practice of eight decision-making meetings per year is a rather new phenomenon. In the past, it was much more often that monetary policy decisions were taken 12 times per year, i.e. on a monthly basis (Charts 2.49 and 2.50). Many countries, predominantly emerging market economies, moved to a semi-quarterly frequency around 2010–2013, and a

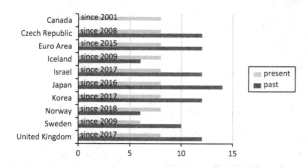

Chart 2.49 Changes to the meeting schedules in IT advanced economies.

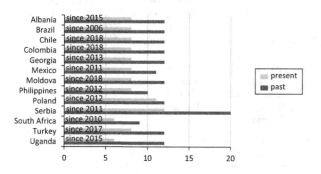

Chart 2.50 Changes to the meeting schedules in IT emerging market economies.

Notes: Until 2000, in Canada there was no fixed schedule for meetings. Until 2011, Norway had between eight and nine meetings per year. Until 2006, the Philippines had between 11 and 15 meetings per year. Until 2009, South Africa had between five and nine meetings per year. Until 2008, Sweden had between 7 and 10 meetings per year. Source: Own compilation based on information from central banks' websites.

number of advanced economies have recently followed suit. Apparently, the majority of IT central banks came to the conclusion that in normal times there is no need to review their monetary policy stance more often.

2.5.6 Decision-making process

Another important aspect of the decision-making process is how the decisions are taken (Chart 2.51; Table 2.9). In the past, especially before the inflation targeting strategy became widespread, most central banks had a single decision-maker—the governor. But starting in the 1990s, collegial

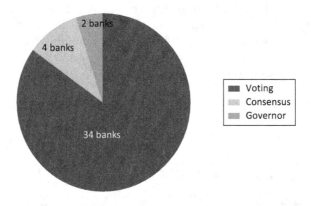

Chart 2.51 Decision-making processes in IT economies.

Table 2.9 IT economies with different approaches to decision-making

Source: Own compilation based on information from central banks' websites.
Notes: The upper parts of the respective sections of the tables refer to advanced economies. The lower parts of the respective sections of the tables refer to emerging market economies. In Paraguay and Switzerland, no information is available on how decisions are taken. *In 2019, a collegial decision-making body was created in New Zealand.

Decision-making process			
Voting			
Australia	Israel	Norway	United States
Czech Rep.	Japan	Sweden	Serbia
Iceland	Korea	United Kingdom	South Africa
Albania	Dominican Rep.	Moldova	Thailand
Argentina	Guatemala	Peru	Turkey
Armenia	Hungary	Philippines	Uganda
Brazil	India	Poland	Ukraine
Chile	Kazakhstan	Romania	
Colombia	Mexico	Russia	

Consensus		*Governor*	
Canada	Euro area	New Zealand*	
Ghana	Indonesia	Georgia	

146

decision-making bodies have been established in many countries (examples include Brazil, Japan, Norway, Sweden, Switzerland, and the United Kingdom), and thus voting has become standard practice.

Currently, 34 IT central banks have committees deciding by majority voting (10 advanced economies[118] and 24 emerging market economies[119]). Only 4 banks look for consensus among collegial decision-makers (Canada and the euro area—from advanced economies, and Ghana and Indonesia—from emerging market economies, whereas in Indonesia if no consensus can be reached, the governor decides as a single decision-maker). Only in 2 cases—1 advanced economy (New Zealand[120]) and 1 emerging market economy (Georgia)—are the decisions from the very beginning with the governor. However, as already noted, their collegial advisory bodies also prepare recommendations for decisions. Looking at the share of countries with different decision-making processes, not much difference can be seen between advanced and emerging market economies. In Paraguay and Switzerland, no information is available on their decision-making process.

Considering changes related to committees' proceedings, in the past there was somewhat more support for consensus-based decision-making, although its popularity was always much lower than that of voting. Judging by information on the ratio of votes, recently, 3 countries have changed their way of reaching decisions from consensus to majority voting (Table 2.10). These include 1 advanced economy (Norway) and 2 emerging market economies (Brazil and South Africa).

It seems that voting is a more efficient way of making decisions, in particular, as the requirements on the composition of decision-making bodies (i.e. involving members with expert knowledge) favour the individualism of decision-makers.[121] This in itself is not a disadvantage, but can significantly impede the formulation of a consensus view.

2.5.7 Releasing voting records

In distinguishing between collegial and individualistic committees, it is helpful to look at information on voting records (Charts 2.52 and 2.53). In many countries, no voting records are made public (this is the case in 16 out of 34 countries with voting—with only 1 advanced economy, Australia, and 15 emerging market economies[122]), and in many cases where they are released, it is a relatively new practice (Table 2.11).

Reservations about the disclosure of insights from decision-making meetings can be explained by the desire to enable discussions "behind closed doors", possibly encouraging free exchange of views with the aim of making the best use of committee expertise. In turn, reasons behind publishing voting records include strengthening the accountability of decision-makers and supporting the general understanding of the decision-making process.

147

Table 2.10 Changes to decision-making processes in IT advanced and emerging market economies

	Decision-making process	Rules on making the decisions	
Norway	Voting, although consensus is preferred	Consensus (until mid-2017)	Voting (since mid-2017)
Brazil	Voting, although consensus is preferred	Consensus (until late 2006)	Voting (since late 2006)
South Africa	Voting, although consensus is preferred	Consensus (until late 2014)	Voting (since late 2014)

Notes: The upper part of the table refers to advanced economies. The lower part of the table refers to emerging market economies. Information in the table on when the rules on decision-making processes changed is based on the dates when any kind of voting records became available. Regarding information on voting records, only countries where decisions are made by voting are considered. Ratio of votes means a ratio of votes for and against the decision. Full voting records mean voting records with names. Source: Own compilation based on information from central banks' websites.

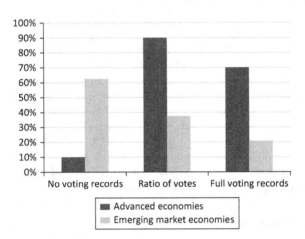

Chart 2.52 Share of IT economies with different approaches to publishing voting records.

Out of 34 countries where decisions are a result of voting (Table 2.9), 18 central banks reveal some kind of voting records—6 only a ratio of votes (2 advanced economies[123] and 4 emerging market economies[124]), and 12 banks additionally also full voting records (7 advanced economies[125] and 5 emerging market economies[126]; Chart 2.54). In many countries, either the ratio of votes or simply full voting records are published.[127] However, in some cases, first the ratio of votes is released, and then the full voting records (as in the Czech Republic and the United Kingdom).

The most typical way of releasing voting records is to include them in press releases or minutes (this is practised in 13 inflation targeters—6 advanced economies[128] and 7 emerging market economies[129]; Table 2.11). Other publications used for that purpose include inflation reports and annual reports

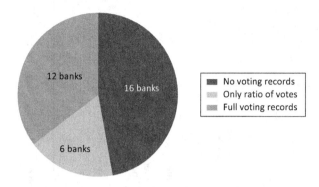

Chart 2.53 Disclosing information on voting records in IT economies.

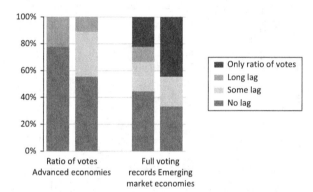

Chart 2.54 Share of IT economies with different timing of publishing voting records.

Notes: See notes to previous charts. In Thailand, no voting records are available, but sometimes a ratio of votes is included in press releases or in minutes. No lag means following the decision—e.g. in press releases, press conference. Some lag means a few weeks after the decision—e.g. in minutes. Long lag means a few months after the decision—e.g. in inflation reports, annual reports. Source: Own compilation based on information from central banks' websites.

(which is the case in 2 advanced economies—Iceland and Israel, and in 1 emerging market economy—Moldova). In rare instances, press conferences (Korea) and the central bank's website (Poland[130]) are used.

2.6 Applying high accountability and transparency standards

The emphasis placed on accountability and transparency is one of the most characteristic features of an IT strategy. Most of the analysed central banks provide a lot of information to the public on the considerations behind their decisions. This includes, among others, publishing press releases and inflation reports, but—in some countries—also open letters. Since the

Table 2.11 Publishing voting records in IT advanced and emerging market economies

	Ratio of votes			Full voting records		
	No lag (following the decision, e.g. in statement, press conference)	Some lag (few weeks after the decision, e.g. in minutes)	Long lag (few months after the decision, e.g. in inflation reports)	No lag (following the decision, e.g. in statement, press conference)	Some lag (few weeks after the decision, e.g. in minutes)	Long lag (few months after the decision, e.g. in inflation reports)
Czech Republic	Statements				Minutes (since 2008)	
Iceland						Annual report
Israel			Annual report	Statements		
Japan	Statements		Annual report	Statements		
Korea	Press conference (since 2014)			Press conference (since 2014)		
Norway	Statements (since 2017)	Minutes (since 2017)			Minutes (since 2003)	
Sweden	Statements (since 2009)	Minutes (since 2003)		Statements (since 2009)	Minutes (since 1997)	
United Kingdom	Statements (since 2015)					
United States	Statements			Statements		
Brazil	Statements	Minutes		Statements (since 2012)	Minutes (since 2012)	
Chile	Statements (since 2018)	Minutes (since 2017)		Statements (since 2018)	Minutes (since 2017)	
Colombia	Statements (since 2016)	Minutes (since 2016)				
Hungary		Minutes			Minutes (since 2005)	
India	Statements (since 2016)		Inflation reports (since 2013)		Minutes (since 2016)	
Moldova			Inflation reports (since 2001)	Statements (since 2017)		
Poland		Website (since 2011)			Website (since 2011)	Inflation reports (since 2001)
Romania		Minutes				
South Africa	Statements (since 2014)					

Source: Own compilation based on information from central banks' websites.
Notes: The upper part refers to advanced economies. The lower part refers to emerging market economies. If no date is indicated, it means that a given publication since the very beginning included voting records.

accountability of central banks closely relates to their independence, this is no surprise.

2.6.1 Main central banks' publications on monetary policy

All inflation targeters announce their monetary policy strategy, most frequently as a separate document, but in some cases as a description on their website. They also publish annual reports (although in Mexico and Paraguay annual reports were substituted by a compilation of quarterly reports in 2013 and 2014, respectively) and inflation reports (Chart 2.55).

With only four exceptions (Argentina, Israel, Uganda, and the United States),[131] the frequency of publishing inflation reports corresponds to the frequency of publishing forecasts, since projections—together with the assessment of the current macroeconomic environment and the description of monetary policy—are standard parts of almost all inflation reports. Thus, regarding the share of countries releasing publications mentioned here, there are no material differences between advanced and emerging market economies.

2.6.2 Central banks' communication on monetary policy decisions

Press releases are nowadays a primary way in which to communicate monetary policy decisions (Charts 2.56 and 2.57). They inform the public not only about monetary policy decisions, but also about the rationale behind them, and often include information on the monetary policy stance (in only 5 inflation targeters, all of which are emerging market economies, this element is rather vague,[132] while in other cases press releases encompass a rather explicit forward-looking monetary policy stance). Currently, a standard practice is to publish a press release on the day of the meeting, or—in rare cases—on the day following the meeting.

Press releases are used by all inflation targeters; however, this was not always the case. In Canada, press releases have been published after each decision-making meeting since 1996 (previously press releases were issued only when the interest rate was changed). Likewise, in Mexico press releases have been prepared regularly since 2003, in New Zealand since early 2006, and in Australia since late 2007. In the United Kingdom, press releases have only started to be published after each decision-making meeting since mid-2015 (previously they were issued, in principle, only when the rate was changed, as following the decision the committee discussed whether or not it wished to issue a press release).

Press releases are often presented during press conferences which also include Q&A sessions (21 inflation targeters—7 advanced economies[133] and 14 emerging market economies[134]—hold press conferences after each decision-making meeting). Some banks have chosen to hold press conferences

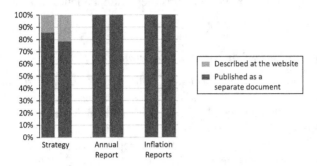

Chart 2.55 Share of IT economies publishing different documents on monetary policy.

Source: Own compilation based on information from central banks' websites.

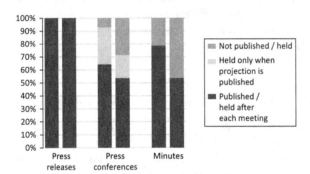

Chart 2.56 Share of IT economies using different ways of communicating monetary policy decisions.

less frequently, i.e. only when the new forecast is published (10 central banks—5 advanced economies[135] and 5 emerging market economies[136]—assessed that such a frequency would be more suitable), or even less often (central banks of Hungary and Switzerland).

Similar to press releases, press conferences were not as popular in the past as they are now. Many countries started organising them around 2010, or only very recently. In Sweden, until 2007, press conferences were held only after meetings when the level of the key policy rate was changed. In Serbia, this is still the case. Eight inflation targeters, i.e. 1 advanced economy and 7 emerging market economies,[137] do not use that communication tool at all.

A slightly less commonly used tool of communication is minutes, which describe in more detail the discussions held at the monetary policy meetings (Charts 2.56 and 2.58). Sweden and the United Kingdom were the first inflation targeters to publish minutes, in the late 1990s, followed by a number of advanced and emerging market economies.[138] A big group of countries started publishing minutes in the mid-2000s, some joined the group

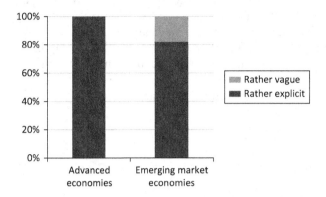

Chart 2.57 Share of IT economies with forward-looking elements included in press releases.

Source: Own compilation based on information from central banks' websites.

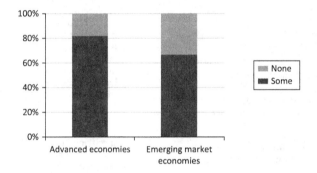

Chart 2.58 Share of IT economies publishing minutes with different approaches to revealing disagreements.

around 2010, and another wave was visible around 2015. Currently, 25 inflation targeters regularly publish minutes (10 advanced economies[139] and 15 emerging market economies[140]).

The content of minutes differs between countries, as some indicate a divergence of views among decision-makers, more or less explicitly (19 out of 25 banks publishing minutes reveal at least some indication of a discrepancy of views—9 advanced economies[141] and 10 emerging market economies[142]), while the rest do not. This follows from a different assessment of the possible disadvantages of such openness.

2.6.3 Central banks' reporting to parliaments

Moving to the accountability mechanisms, the central banks of the vast majority of countries report to parliament—both by attending regular hearings and submitting cyclical reports.

In 31 inflation targeters (13 advanced economies[143] and 18 emerging market economies[144]), representatives of monetary authorities regularly attend either plenary hearings of parliament or hearings at parliamentary commissions (Chart 2.59). At the same time, all advanced economy inflation targeters and almost all emerging market economy inflation targeters regularly submit reports to parliament (Chart 2.60). The most frequently applied practice is to do it one or two times per year, but quite a number of banks do it three or four times per year.

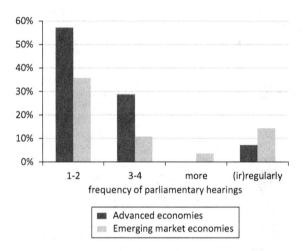

Notes: The notion of "(ir)regularly" applies to countries where reporting to parliament is part of the accountability mechanism, but no information could be found on its frequency (some central banks declare that they report regularly, but without specifying how often). If no information on reporting to parliament could be found, it is assumed that it is neither required nor practiced. Source: Own compilation based on information from central banks' websites.

Chart 2.59 Share of IT economies with different frequency per year of parliamentary hearings.

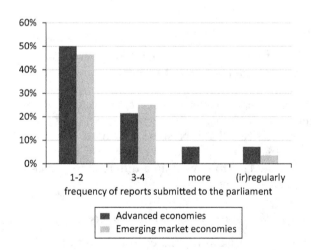

Chart 2.60 Share of IT economies with different frequency per year of submitting reports to parliament.

In rather rare cases, inflation targeters do not declare using that form of accountability mechanism, suggesting that reporting to parliament is not necessary. Regarding attending parliamentary hearings, this is the case in 11 countries—1 advanced economy (Switzerland) and 10 emerging market economies.[145] Considering submitting reports to parliament, it is not required in 9 countries—2 advanced economies (Australia and Canada) and 7 emerging market economies.[146]

2.6.4 Central banks' open letters

While communicating a central bank's assessments of inflation developments and corresponding policy actions is a rather standard practice among inflation targeters, in some countries—if inflation significantly or persistently deviates from the target—a more formal explanation is required in the form of an open letter or a similar document.

An open letter should show the central bank's commitment to the announced target (Table 2.12). The key elements to be included in an open letter encompass the reasons why inflation deviated from the target, the expected inflation outlook, and possible actions to be taken by the central bank in order to bring inflation back to the target. To write an open letter under certain circumstances, 13 inflation targeters are required out of which 5 are advanced economies[147] and 8 are emerging market economies.[148]

2.6.5 Decision-makers' background materials

Nowadays, a number of central banks publish other materials from their decision-making meetings, such as presentations, staff memos, or chart packs. These additional publications should facilitate understanding the monetary policy decisions, and support the accountability of decision-makers. This is, however, a much less common practice than publishing press releases, holding press conferences, and preparing inflation reports. Currently, 23 inflation targeters (8 advanced economies[149] and 15 emerging market economies[150]) expand publicly available materials to staff background reports.

2.7 Accounting for financial stability considerations and unconventional measures

As already noted, two major topics that the recent crises brought to the attention of IT central banks were the significance of financial stability considerations and the use of unconventional monetary policy measures. Especially regarding the latter, there are considerable differences between advanced and emerging market economies.

Table 2.12 Publishing open letters in IT advanced and emerging market economies

Open letters	
Iceland	A report must be submitted to the government if inflation exceeds 4% or falls below 1%.
Korea	An explanation must be given through various means, e.g. the governor's press conference, if inflation deviates from the target by more than 0.5 percentage point in either direction for 6 consecutive months (if inflation subsequently remains more than 0.5 percentage point above or below the target, the Bank of Korea provides further explanations every 3 months).
New Zealand	An explanation must be given on occasions when the annual rate of inflation is outside the medium-term target range, or when such occasions are projected.
Norway	If there are significant deviations between actual price inflation and the target, the annual report includes a thorough assessment of that issue (particular emphasis should be placed on any deviations outside the interval of ±1 percentage point).
United Kingdom	An open letter must be submitted to the chancellor if the inflation target is missed by more than 1 percentage point on either side.
Brazil	An open letter must be written if inflation breaches the target.
India	A report must be submitted to the government if average inflation remains above (below) the upper (lower) tolerance level of the inflation target for any three consecutive quarters.
Indonesia	An explanation must be submitted to the government if the inflation target is not achieved during any given year (this explanation is a basis for open explanations presented jointly by the government and the Bank of Indonesia to the Indonesian parliament and the public).
Moldova	A plan of corrective actions must be published if there is a deviation of the inflation rate exceeding the variation interval.
Philippines	An open letter must be submitted to the president in case the central bank fails to achieve the inflation target.
Serbia	A notification must be submitted to the government if the departure of inflation from the set target lasts for more than 6 consecutive months.
Thailand	An explanation must be given if headline inflation breaches the announced target (the progress of policy actions must be reported to the minister of finance in a timely manner).
Turkey	An open letter must be submitted to the government, in case of a breach or a probable breach of the inflation target.

Source: Own compilation based on information from central banks' websites and legal acts on central banks.
Notes: The upper part refers to advanced economies. The lower part refers to emerging market economies.

2.7.1 Central banks and financial stability

When analysing the attitude of central banks to financial stability, it is worth looking at the issue of who bears the formal responsibility for safeguarding it in a given country (Chart 2.61). Traditionally, banking—or

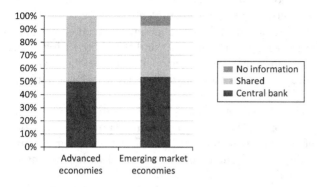

Chart 2.61 Share of IT economies with different authorities responsible for financial stability.

Source: Own compilation based on information from central banks' websites.

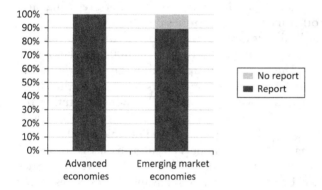

Chart 2.62 Share of IT central banks publishing reports on financial stability.

more generally financial supervision—has been considered as key in that respect, while nowadays it is a much more macroprudential policy.[151] Both can be placed within a central bank, or can be conducted by separate institutions.[152]

In 22 inflation targeters (7 advanced economies[153] and 15 emerging market economies[154]) the full responsibility for financial stability is with the monetary authority, whereas in 18 countries (7 advanced economies[155] and 11 emerging market economies[156]) the responsibility is shared, which means that macroprudential policy is conducted by a body comprising several institutions.[157] Most typically, such a body includes representatives of the central bank, the ministry of finance, and the supervisory authority (if it is separate from the central bank). There are no significant differences in that respect between advanced and emerging market economies.

While financial supervision has a comparatively long tradition, in most countries regulations concerning macroprudential policy have been introduced only recently, i.e. in the aftermath of the global financial crisis. This has been, in particular, the case in the euro area and the United Kingdom. However, although some institutional arrangements, including a set of macroprudential measures, are quite new, issues linked to the stability of the financial system had already been monitored by central banks for some time before the recent crises. This is evidenced by the fact that almost all of the analysed monetary authorities have been publishing reports regularly on financial stability, independently of whether responsibility for safeguarding it has rested only with the central bank or has been shared with other institutions (Charts 2.62 and 2.63).

Until recently, within advanced economies only the US Federal Reserve was not publishing reports on financial stability, but it started to do so in late 2018.[158] Within emerging market economies, the central banks of the Dominican Republic, Ghana, and Guatemala are still not preparing such reports, while all the other monetary authorities do.

The practice of cyclically reviewing the shape of the financial system by central banks became common around the 2000s, i.e. before the global financial crisis.[159] The first reports appeared in the late 1990s, with Norway, Sweden, and the United Kingdom the first to move in this direction. Advanced economies were very soon joined by monetary authorities from emerging market economies in analysing financial stability issues, with the biggest group starting to publish reports around the mid-2000s.

Currently, the dominant practice among IT central banks is to publish reports on financial stability on a semi-annual frequency (Chart 2.64). Such timing has been chosen by 29 countries—11 advanced economies[160] and 18 emerging market economies.[161] The only 3 central banks within the first group of countries publishing one report per year are those of the Czech Republic, Norway, and Switzerland.[162] Within the latter group, the central banks of 6 countries publish reports annually,[163] while 1 country (Moldova) publishes more often.[164]

Overall, the central banks acknowledged the importance of financial stability considerations well before the recent crises, which is reflected in their regular publications. However, in many cases, only since the crisis have IT central banks been assigned more formal responsibilities for the condition of the financial system, in particular, by being engaged in conducting macroprudential policy.

2.7.2 Unconventional monetary policy measures

Before moving to discuss unorthodox monetary policy measures, it is useful to see what instruments IT central banks regard as conventional. Considering a standard set of monetary policy tools typical for an inflation

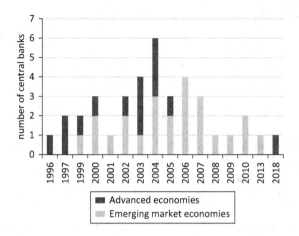

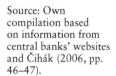

Chart 2.63 Number of IT central banks starting to regularly publish reports on financial stability in a given year.

Source: Own compilation based on information from central banks' websites and Čihák (2006, pp. 46–47).

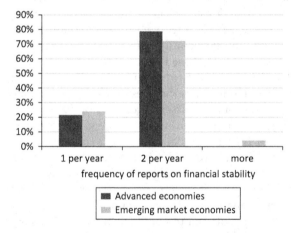

Chart 2.64 Share of IT central banks with different frequency of publishing reports on financial stability.

targeting regime, in the vast majority of IT countries, it comprises of only one measure, namely, a short-term interest rate (Chart 2.65). This instrument is reported by all the analysed central banks.

At times, but relatively rarely, FX interventions are also mentioned. This is the case in 8 countries—3 advanced economies (Iceland, Israel, and Norway) and 5 emerging market economies (Peru, Poland, Serbia, Turkey, and Uganda). It is important to note that not all countries that consider occasional FX interventions as a monetary policy tool, use them, and—vice versa—not all countries that do not list occasional FX interventions as a monetary policy tool restrain from using them. In particular, the Czech Republic between late 2013 and early 2017, and Switzerland between late 2011 and early 2015, massively intervened in the exchange rate markets, whereas Poland in the recent two decades conducted FX interventions only on single occasions.

In some countries, other measures are indicated as belonging to a standard policy toolkit. For example, in Japan this is the amount of funds in the money market, and in the United States, it is the size and composition of the Federal Reserve's asset holdings and communications with the public about the likely future course of monetary policy. Regarding these two countries, the indicated elements can, however, be seen as already referring to less conventional measures.

Regarding instruments classified as unconventional, there are several points to make. First, lowering interest rates to a negative territory has often been accompanied by the change in the interest rate being treated as the main policy rate by a given central bank.[165] Second, FX commitment refers only to cases when monetary authorities—in order to provide more policy accommodation—undertook actions to weaken the domestic currency. Thus, it does not include cases when FX interventions were conducted for other purposes, for example, to limit the volatility of the exchange rate or to combat its strong depreciation.[166] Third, some IT central banks used or have been using forward guidance with respect to instruments other than their main interest rate. In particular, monetary authorities may provide guidance on how long they are going to continue asset purchases, or FX commitment.[167] However, these cases are not taken into account in the overview. At the same time, all kinds of forward guidance referring to interest rates are included, such as open-ended forward guidance, calendar-based forward guidance, and conditional forward guidance (Niedźwiedzińska et al., 2019, pp. 67–72). Fourth, credit easing comprises all programmes designed to support the provision of external financing to the private sector, mainly via longer-term refinancing operations offered to commercial banks. On single occasions, such measures had also been used prior to the crises to enhance credit supply, but generally on a much smaller scale.[168] Fifth, quantitative easing includes cases when a central bank purchased securities (outright), even if such operations were conducted only temporarily and on a very limited scale.[169]

Looking at the use of non-standard tools across the analysed central banks until 2018, i.e. in the period covered in the study, clearly they were employed much more often in advanced economies than in emerging market economies. This followed from the fact that advanced economies—with generally lower levels of interest rates—had less room for providing the needed monetary policy accommodation using only their standard

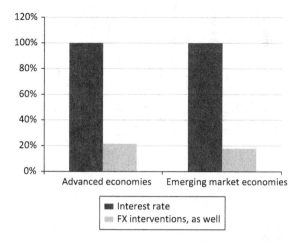

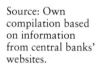

Source: Own compilation based on information from central banks' websites.

Chart 2.65 Share of IT economies with interest rate and FX interventions as main policy instruments.

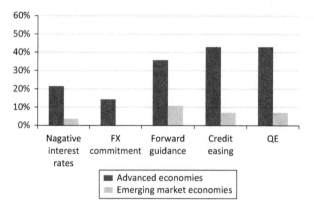

Chart 2.66 Share of IT economies using unconventional monetary policy instruments.

instrument due to the zero lower bound (ZLB). As already mentioned, the unorthodox monetary policy tools were requested mainly after the central banks were faced with the ZLB restriction, i.e. after short-term rates were lowered to very low levels. In the past, this was much more frequently the case in advanced economies, with some of them being at the centre of the crises, and others—not least due to strong links to the United States and the euro area—quite severely affected by the crises (Chart 2.66; Table 2.13). However, several emerging market economies also made use of certain unconventional measures, although on a much more limited scale compared to advanced economies (Chart 2.66; Table 2.14). This description

Table 2.13 Unconventional monetary policy measures in IT advanced economies

	Negative interest rates	FX commitment	Forward guidance	Credit easing	Quantitative easing
Canada			From April 2009 to March 2010		
Czech Republic		From November 2013 to April 2017			
Euro area	Since June 2014		Since July 2013	TLTRO I—June 2014 TLTRO II—March 2016	APP (expanded asset purchase programme) consisted of CBPP3 (third covered bond purchase programme): from October 2014 to end 2018 ABSPP (asset-backed securities purchase programme): from November 2014 to end 2018 PSPP (public sector purchase programme): from March 2015 to end 2018 CSPP (corporate sector purchase programme): from June 2016 to end 2018

Israel	Since November 2015		
Japan		Fund-Provisioning Measure to Support Strengthening the Foundations for Economic Growth: since June 2010 Fund-Provisioning Measure to Stimulate Bank Lending: January–March 2014 to January–March 2019	Interventions in the secondary market of local government bonds: from February 2009 to August 2009 QE: since late 1980s QQE (quantitative and qualitative monetary easing): since April 2013, expanded in October 2014, introduced supplementary measures in December 2015 QQE with a negative interest rate: since January 2016, and introduced enhanced monetary easing in July 2016 QQE with yield curve control: since September 2016
Korea		Bank Intermediated Lending Support Facility: Loans extended to banks based on their SME loan performances (operating since 1994): since 2012 the aggregate ceiling for the facility was systematically increased	

(Continued)

Table 2.13 (Continued) Unconventional monetary policy measures in IT advanced economies

	Negative interest rates	FX commitment	Forward guidance	Credit easing	Quantitative easing
Sweden	From February 2015 to December 2019			Fixed rate loans for banks for up to 12 months: since October 2009	Purchases of Swedish government bonds: from February 2015 to December 2017
Switzerland	Since December 2014	From September 2011 to until January 2015		Purchases of Swiss franc bonds issued by domestic private sector borrowers: from March 2009 to February 2010 (the bonds were sold back into the market between March and August 2010)	
United Kingdom			From August 2013 to January 2014	Funding for Lending Scheme: from April 2013 to January 2018	New Asset Purchase Facility: from March 2009 to June 2017 Term Funding Scheme: from September 2016 to February 2018 Corporate Bond Purchase Scheme: since August 2016
United States			From December 2008 to December 2014		QE1: from December 2008 to March 2010 QE2: from November 2010 to June 2011 QE3: from September 2012 to October 2014

Source: Own compilation based on information from central banks' websites.

164

Table 2.14 Unconventional monetary policy measures in IT emerging market economies

	Negative interest rates	FX commitment	Forward guidance	Credit easing	Quantitative easing
Albania					
Hungary	From January 2017 to February 2020		Since August 2014 From July 2014 to May 2018	2-year collateralised loan tenders: February 2012 to April 2013 Funding for Growth Scheme: from June 2013 to March 2017 (in three tranches) Market-based Lending Scheme: January 2016 to December 2018	Government bond sale and purchase in the secondary market: autumn 2008 mortgage bond purchase programme: since March 2010
Poland			From September 2013 to June 2014		
Russia				Many special refinancing mechanisms	
Turkey					Some purchases of government securities—since 2010

Source: Own compilation based on information from central banks' websites.

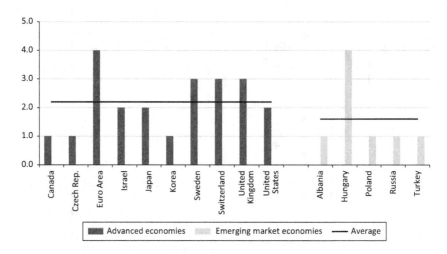

Chart 2.67 Number of unconventional measures used in a given IT economy.
Source: Own compilation based on information from central banks' websites.

refers to the period following the global financial crisis and the European sovereign crisis. At the same time, the Covid-19 pandemic of 2020 proved that unconventional instruments were also in high demand in a number of emerging market economies (Grostal, 2020; Niedźwiedzińska, 2020).

Considering the period up to 2018, among advanced economies, the most popular non-standard instruments included credit easing and quantitative easing, used by 6 countries.[170] Forward guidance was also quite frequently requested, with 5 countries incorporating it in their communication.[171] These measures were followed by negative interest rates, implemented in 3 advanced economies,[172] and FX commitment used by 2 countries.[173]

Within emerging market economies, the preferences were somewhat different, with the most frequently used measure being forward guidance, employed by 3 countries.[174] Credit easing and quantitative easing were implemented in 2 countries.[175] Interest rates were lowered to negative levels only in Hungary, while FX commitment was not used at all.

Prior to the Covid-19 crisis, in the case of advanced economies, some countries employed only one unconventional instrument, some took advantage of using two or three, and one—the euro area—used four non-standard measures (Chart 2.67). Among emerging market economies, with the prominent exception of Hungary, all other countries reaching for unorthodox tools were selecting only one non-standard instrument that they considered the most appropriate to address the identified market tensions. In turn, Hungary made use of almost all available options, employing four measures. Looking at the countries that used any unconventional measures, the average number of unorthodox tools applied by IT central banks was higher for advanced economies compared to emerging market economies (standing at 2.2 and 1.6, respectively).

Considering the timing, advanced economies started to use non-standard measures somewhat earlier than emerging market economies, and—partly because of that—they were implementing them for a longer period. However, the differences in that respect are not very big.

With only few exceptions, the majority of unconventional measures had already been discontinued when the pandemic-related crisis hit the global economy, indicating that they were treated as needed only during a crisis period. This observation would suggest that the significance of the short-term interest rate as the main policy tool of IT central banks in tranquil times does not seem threatened. At the same time, as already noted, the developments brought about by Covid-19 and the resulting necessity to significantly loosen monetary conditions, led even more central banks to resort to non-standard instruments, proving that those have become a feasible option to consider whenever a situation turns out to be severe. Moreover, the ongoing debates on the design of monetary policy strategies that focus on finding a way to cope with the ZLB, will most likely result in confirming an important role for unorthodox tools in central banks' toolkits.

2.8 Concluding remarks

The analysis conducted in Chapter 2 indicates that, while there are many similarities, there are also visible differences in the institutional arrangements used in IT central banks.

In particular, the review shows that, regarding almost all institutional features of an IT strategy, as practised by all the analysed central banks, there is no single way to go. This holds, for example, in formulating central banks' mandates, defining committee composition, or deciding how much insight from decision-making processes should be revealed. However, it also shows a lot of similarities among central banks' practices. This is clearly visible in choosing a floating exchange rate regime, publishing regular inflation forecasts, and putting significant emphasis on accountability mechanisms.

While investigating many important IT institutional arrangements, numerous examples of changes in central banks' practices introduced in the past 30 years were discussed. These relate, in particular, to defining various features of inflation targets, moving towards collective decision-making, and allowing for greater central bank accountability by publishing more documents on monetary policy.

Of particular interest for the review was the comparison between advanced and emerging market economies. Assessing the distribution of certain institutional arrangements among these two groups indicates that, while in many instances there is hardly any difference to be noted, in some aspects the approach of advanced economies to IT differs significantly from that of emerging market economies.

Key similarities among advanced and emerging market economies include, to a great extent, formulating the central bank's mandates, choosing the exchange rate regime, selecting the targeted inflation measure, indicating the target horizon, deciding on the size and composition of decision-making bodies, safeguarding personal independence, designing the main features of an accountability mechanism—including the use of certain communication tools (e.g. press releases, inflation reports, annual reports), and publishing inflation projections.

Some, but no major, discrepancies between advanced and emerging market economy inflation targeters can be seen in the case of frequency of meetings, organisation of decision-making processes, guaranteeing financial independence, holding regular press conferences, and publishing minutes or open letters.

In turn, the most visible differences between advanced and emerging market economies concern such features as target types and levels, releasing voting records, involvement of government representatives in decision-making process, ownership of forecasts, and publishing projections of other variables than inflation.

Regarding the consequences of the recent crises, the approach of IT central banks to financial stability issues is not much different between advanced and emerging market economies. At the same time, the use of non-standard monetary policy measures was—at least until the outbreak of Covid-19 in 2020—much more frequent in the first group of countries, not least since they have been confronted with the ZLB more often than emerging market economies. However, the discontinuation of many unorthodox policies and the implementation of exit strategies from unconventional instruments before the pandemic-related crisis made them again highly requested, indicate that these tools were, indeed, treated as non-standard, and thus they should be applied only under special circumstances.

The main finding of Chapter 2 is that the rules and practices of inflation targeters related to the analysed institutional features have not been homogeneous—neither across time nor across countries. It would be useful to conduct a more systematic comparison of the institutional set-ups of IT central banks, based on indices summarising the reviewed aspects of pursuing monetary policy within an inflation targeting regime, which will be the aim of Chapter 3.

Notes

1 Parts of Chapter 2 rely heavily on Niedźwiedzińska (2018).
2 The same procedure applies to collecting information on topics related directly to central banks' institutional arrangements, and to topics related to financial

stability considerations and the use of unconventional measures in the conduct of monetary policy.

3　Australia, Canada, Switzerland, the United Kingdom, and the United States.

4　Argentina, Brazil, Chile, the Dominican Republic, Guatemala, Paraguay, Russia, Thailand, and Uganda.

5　In early 2018, a new Policy Targets Agreement stipulated that monetary policy in New Zealand should "be directed at achieving and maintaining stability in the general level of prices over the medium term and supporting maximum sustainable employment". However, the Reserve Bank of New Zealand Act of 1989 was not amended at that time, so the primary function of the Reserve Bank was still to achieve and maintain stability in the general level of prices. The Reserve Bank of New Zealand Act of 1989 was changed only in early 2019, which—due to the given cut-off date for the analysis—is not accounted for in the review.

6　Colombia, Kazakhstan, Peru, the Philippines, and Romania.

7　The Czech Republic, the euro area, Iceland, Israel, Japan, Korea, Norway, and Sweden.

8　Albania, Armenia, Georgia, Ghana, Hungary, India, Indonesia, Mexico, Moldova, Poland, Serbia, South Africa, Turkey, and Ukraine.

9　All advanced economy inflation targeters apart from New Zealand and Sweden. Although, in the case of New Zealand, as already indicated, the 2018 Policy Targets Agreement included an objective of supporting maximum sustainable employment, which in 2019 was reflected in the Reserve Bank Act.

10　Albania, Argentina, Brazil, Georgia, Ghana, Guatemala, Hungary, India, Indonesia, Moldova, the Philippines, Poland, Serbia, South Africa, Thailand, Turkey, Uganda, and Ukraine.

11　The Czech Republic, Iceland, Israel, Korea, Norway, and the United Kingdom.

12　Albania, Argentina, Armenia, Brazil, the Dominican Republic, Georgia, Ghana, Hungary, Mexico, Moldova, Paraguay, the Philippines, Russia, Serbia, Thailand, Uganda, and Ukraine.

13　Australia, Canada, the Czech Republic, Iceland, Israel, Korea, and New Zealand.

14　Argentina, Armenia, Brazil, Ghana, Guatemala, Hungary, India, Kazakhstan, the Philippines, Romania, Serbia, Thailand, Turkey, and Ukraine.

15　The euro area, Japan, Sweden, Switzerland, and the United States.

16　Albania, Chile, Colombia, the Dominican Republic, Mexico, Moldova, Paraguay, Peru, Poland, Russia, and Uganda.

17　Norway and the United Kingdom.

18　Georgia, Indonesia, and South Africa.

19　Australia, Canada, the Czech Republic, the euro area, Japan, Korea, and the United Kingdom.

20　Albania, Armenia, Chile, Colombia, the Dominican Republic, Guatemala, Indonesia, Kazakhstan, Mexico, Moldova, the Philippines, Romania, Russia, Serbia, Turkey, and Uganda.

21　Australia, Canada, and Korea.

22　Colombia, Guatemala, Kazakhstan, the Dominican Republic, the Philippines, and Uganda.

23　Canada, Japan, Korea, New Zealand, Norway, and the United Kingdom.

24　Chile and Uganda.

25　A decision-making body of the central bank may mean either the governor—in countries where the governor is a single decision-maker, or some kind of a committee—in countries were decision-making is with collegial bodies (these may include boards, councils, committees).

26　Members' term of office refers to the term of office of the majority of members of the decision-making body.

27 Australia, Norway, and the United Kingdom—from advanced economies, and Armenia, Guatemala, India, Thailand, and Uganda—from emerging market economies.

28 The United States—from advanced economies, and Chile and Mexico—from emerging market economies.

29 If no explicit rule on reappointment could be found, it is assumed that reappointment is possible. Brazil (with no fixed term) is counted as a country, when reappointment is possible.

30 All advanced economy inflation targeters apart from the euro area and the United States, although in the United States a member who completed an unexpired portion of a term may be reappointed.

31 All emerging market economy inflation targeters.

32 Australia, Canada, Japan, New Zealand, Sweden, and Switzerland.

33 All apart from Colombia, Hungary, Philippines, Poland, Russia, and Ukraine.

34 All advanced economy inflation targeters apart from the euro area and the United States.

35 All emerging market economy inflation targeters apart from Poland.

36 All advanced economy inflation targeters in which reappointment is possible apart from the Czech Republic, Israel, and Norway.

37 All emerging market economy inflation targeters in which reappointment is possible apart from Colombia, Indonesia, Philippines, Russia, Thailand, and Ukraine.

38 All advanced economy inflation targeters apart from New Zealand and the United States, whereas in New Zealand the reasons used to be stipulated in an agreement signed between each new governor and the government.

39 All emerging market economy inflation targeters apart from Brazil, Ghana, India, Kazakhstan, and South Africa.

40 Australia, the Czech Republic, Israel, Japan, Korea, and New Zealand.

41 Albania, Argentina, Armenia, Brazil, Chile, Ghana, India, Kazakhstan, Mexico, Moldova, Peru, the Philippines, Romania, Serbia, Thailand, and Ukraine.

42 The Czech Republic, the euro area, Iceland, Israel, Norway, and Switzerland.

43 Albania, Armenia, the Dominican Republic, Georgia, Guatemala, Hungary, Indonesia, Kazakhstan, Mexico, Moldova, Peru, the Philippines, Poland, Romania, Russia, Serbia, Turkey, and Ukraine.

44 The Czech Republic, the euro area, Iceland, Israel, Japan, Korea, Sweden, and Switzerland.

45 Albania, Armenia, Chile, Georgia, Hungary, Indonesia, Mexico, Moldova, Paraguay, Peru, the Philippines, Romania, Russia, Serbia, Turkey, and Ukraine.

46 Though in 2003 the ECB slightly changed the wording of its definition of price stability from "below 2%" to "below, but close to, 2%", claiming that this was not a change of the target, but its clarification.

47 In 2012, when announcing, for the first time, a numerical value for targeted inflation, the Bank of Japan announced a price stability goal in the medium to long term at "a positive range of 2% or lower" and a goal at 1% "for the time being", but already in 2013 the bank announced a price stability target simply at 2%. This is not treated as changing the target, because from the very beginning the 2% goal was envisaged.

48 As already noted, there are some differences in interpreting the targets depending on their types. Point targets indicate a single number at which inflation expectations should be anchored. Point targets with tolerance bands indicate a number at which inflation expectations should be anchored (a point target) with a surrounding interval (a tolerance band) that should make it clear for the public that some upward and downward deviations of inflation from the

point target are inevitable, and as long as they are small, monetary authorities may not react to them. Band targets indicate an interval within which inflation should hover, without pointing to any single number preferred by the central bank. Band targets with midpoints indicate not only an interval within which inflation should hover, but also a number (a midpoint) preferred by the central bank at which inflation expectations should be anchored.

49 Israel and Korea.
50 Brazil, Colombia, Indonesia, and the Philippines.
51 Ukraine adopted an IT strategy only in 2017.
52 Disinflation is understood as lowering targeted inflation from a relatively high level to below 6%, even if some countries subsequently strived for lower levels of inflation and currently have much lower targets. The threshold of 6% is somewhat arbitrary, but given the fact that many emerging market economies have around 4%–5% targets, it seems reasonable.
53 Argentina, Brazil, Colombia, the Czech Republic (when the Czech Republic was adopting an IT strategy it was still classified as an emerging market economy, and was reclassified to advanced economies only in 2009), Georgia, Ghana, Hungary, Indonesia, Kazakhstan, Poland, Romania, Serbia, and Ukraine.
54 The Czech Republic, Iceland, Israel, Korea, New Zealand, Sweden, and the United Kingdom.
55 Albania, Argentina, Armenia, Chile, Colombia, Ghana, Guatemala, Hungary, India, the Philippines, Poland, and Thailand.
56 Iceland and Korea.
57 Brazil, Colombia, Moldova, Paraguay, and Serbia.
58 Australia, the Czech Republic, Korea, Sweden, and the United Kingdom.
59 South Africa and Thailand.
60 Canada, the Czech Republic, Iceland, Israel, Korea, New Zealand, Norway, and the United Kingdom.
61 All emerging market economy inflation targeters apart from Albania, Mexico, Moldova, Russia, South Africa, and Uganda.
62 Canada, the Czech Republic, and New Zealand.
63 Armenia, Guatemala, Hungary, India, Peru, Poland, Romania, Russia, and Serbia.
64 The euro area, Iceland, Japan, Korea, Norway, Switzerland, the United Kingdom, and the United States—from advanced economies, and Albania, Argentina, Georgia, Kazakhstan, Russia, and Uganda—from emerging market economies.
65 The Czech Republic and Sweden—from advanced economies, and Armenia, Brazil, Chile, Colombia, the Dominican Republic, Ghana, Guatemala, Hungary, India, Indonesia, Mexico, Moldova, Paraguay, Peru, the Philippines, Poland, Romania, Serbia, Thailand, Turkey, and Ukraine—from emerging market economies.
66 Australia and Israel—from advanced economies, and South Africa—from emerging market economies.
67 Canada and New Zealand.
68 Albania, Argentina, Armenia, Chile, Colombia, Ghana, Guatemala, Hungary, India, Kazakhstan, the Philippines, Poland, and Thailand.
69 The Czech Republic and Sweden.
70 Chile, Colombia, the Dominican Republic, Guatemala, Hungary, Indonesia, Mexico, Peru, the Philippines, Poland, and Romania.
71 Armenia, Brazil, Moldova, Serbia, and Thailand.
72 India, Ghana, Paraguay, Turkey, and Ukraine.
73 At times, it was not entirely clear what inflation measure the target referred to. This was, in particular, the case for New Zealand (Mishkin and Posen, 1997, pp. 29, 31–34).

74 The central bank of Chile does not specify which inflation indicator it considers more relevant for evaluating its actions—headline CPI or CPI excluding the price of vegetables, fruit, and fuel. This should not make much difference, if shocks related to the excluded price categories are random. In such circumstances, it can be expected that headline inflation hovers around core inflation, so while deviations from the target of headline inflation are generally bigger than those of core inflation, the average of the two measures should be more or less equal. This is, however, not always the case.

75 In these two countries, apart from difficulties with measuring prices in the whole country, an important argument for using an inflation measure with limited geographical coverage, is the fact that their populations are concentrated in regions included in the restricted inflation measure.

76 The often applied exclusion criteria include disregarding the price of food and energy, excluding the most volatile prices, or eliminating administered or regulated prices.

77 As already noted, in the past, in many countries, especially those that used an IT strategy for finalising a disinflation process, in the first years of pursuing IT the targets were set as end-year targets. It was rather a standard practice to move to a continuous target once the longer-run level of the inflation target was announced.

78 It needs to be recalled that Argentina stopped using an IT regime in late 2018.

79 Target level is understood as the midpoint of the target, independent of the target type.

80 Beginning from 2020, the inflation target in Thailand was changed to a band target of between 1% and 3%. Given the cut-off date for the analysis, this is, however, not accounted for in the review.

81 Albania, Chile, Colombia, Georgia, Hungary, Mexico, the Philippines, and Serbia.

82 Armenia, the Dominican Republic, Guatemala, India, Paraguay, and Russia.

83 It should once again be recalled, though, that in late 2018, Argentina changed its monetary policy strategy from inflation targeting to monetary base targeting.

84 The only exception is Argentina, which was not publishing projections, even when it was officially pursuing an inflation targeting regime between 2016 and late 2018. This can be treated as an indication that Argentina was, in fact, not prepared to become an inflation targeting country.

85 The Dominican Republic, Ghana, India, Kazakhstan, and South Africa.

86 Guatemala and Poland.

87 Only the main forecast variables are considered.

88 As already mentioned, the only exception is Argentina, which is not publishing any projections.

89 Australia, Canada, the Czech Republic, the euro area, Israel, Japan, Korea, New Zealand, Norway, Sweden, the United Kingdom, and the United States.

90 Albania, Armenia, Chile, Colombia, the Dominican Republic, Georgia, Ghana, Hungary, India, Indonesia, Kazakhstan, Mexico, Moldova, Peru, Poland, Russia, Serbia, South Africa, Thailand, and Ukraine.

91 The Czech Republic, New Zealand, Norway, Sweden, and the United States.

92 Georgia and Guatemala.

93 Australia, the United Kingdom, and the United States.

94 Although during the period of an asymmetric exchange rate commitment and a few quarters afterwards, the forecast of the korona nominal exchange rate was not published. It became available again starting from projections published in 2018.

95 Besides difficulties with agreeing on the projected interest rate path by decision-makers, the other issues that became evident during the global financial

crisis included credibility losses occurring when financial market expectations of policy rates proved better than the central bank's own forecasts (Carlstrom, 2013). Moreover, publishing interest rate projections, by reducing the perceived uncertainty, may have encouraged economic agents to take more risk (Niedźwiedzińska et al., 2019, p. 49).

96 Australia, Canada, the Czech Republic, the euro area, Iceland, Israel, Korea, New Zealand, and Switzerland.

97 Albania, Armenia, Colombia, the Dominican Republic, Guatemala, Hungary, India, Indonesia, Kazakhstan, Mexico, Moldova, Paraguay, Peru, the Philippines, Poland, Romania, Russia, Serbia, South Africa, Turkey, Uganda, and Ukraine.

98 Japan, Norway, Sweden, the United Kingdom, and the United States.

99 Brazil, Chile, Georgia, Ghana, and Thailand.

100 Australia, Canada, the Czech Republic, the euro area, Iceland, Israel, New Zealand, Norway, Sweden, and the United States.

101 Albania, Brazil, Chile, Colombia, Georgia, India, Peru, the Philippines, Romania, Thailand, and Ukraine.

102 In early 2019, the Reserve Bank of New Zealand Act of 1989 was amended stipulating that a collegial decision-making body should be formed, which started operating in April 2019. Given the cut-off date for the analysis this is, however, not accounted for in the review.

103 As already noted, as of 2019, New Zealand moves to the group where decision-making is with a collegial body.

104 Until 2010 also in Israel monetary policy decisions were made by the governor, but in 2011 a monetary committee was established.

105 Australia, Canada, the Czech Republic, Iceland, Israel, Japan, Korea, Norway, Sweden, and the United Kingdom.

106 Albania, Armenia, Brazil, Chile, Colombia, the Dominican Republic, Ghana, Guatemala, Hungary, India, Indonesia, Kazakhstan, Mexico, Moldova, Paraguay, Peru, the Philippines, Poland, Romania, Serbia, South Africa, Thailand, Turkey, Uganda, and Ukraine.

107 Since 2015, the euro area governing council (a decision-making body of the ECB) acts within a rotation system concerning the allocation of voting rights—all members of the governing council have the right to speak, but voting rights rotate.

108 The Federal Open Market Committee (FOMC, a decision-making body of the US Federal Reserve) acts within a rotation system concerning the allocation of voting rights—all members of the FOMC have the right to speak, but voting rights rotate.

109 Canada, the Czech Republic, Sweden, Switzerland, and the United States.

110 Argentina, Brazil, Chile, Indonesia, Mexico, Moldova, Paraguay, Peru, Russia, Serbia, South Africa, and Ukraine.

111 Australia, the euro area, Israel, Japan, Korea, and Norway.

112 Albania, Armenia, the Dominican Republic, Guatemala, Hungary, India, the Philippines, Poland, Romania, and Thailand.

113 Canada, the Czech Republic, the euro area, Iceland, Israel, Japan, Korea, New Zealand, Norway, the United Kingdom, and the United States.

114 Albania, Brazil, Chile, Colombia, Georgia, Kazakhstan, Mexico, Moldova, the Philippines, Romania, Russia, Thailand, and Turkey.

115 Australia has 11 meetings per year.

116 Argentina has 24 scheduled meetings per year, of which 12 should be devoted to discussing the monetary policy rate and the other 12 to setting the cut-off rate on open market operations. Poland has 11 meetings per year. Armenia,

the Dominican Republic, Guatemala, Hungary, Indonesia, Paraguay, Peru, and Serbia have 12 per year, and Ukraine has 9 per year.

117 Another occasion when the necessity to resort to unscheduled meetings became apparent—in fact, even on a broader scale—was the need for an urgent policy response to the Covid-19 pandemic in early 2020 (Niedźwiedzińska, 2020).

118 Australia, the Czech Republic, Iceland, Israel, Japan, Korea, Norway, Sweden, the United Kingdom, and the United States.

119 Albania, Argentina, Armenia, Brazil, Chile, Colombia, the Dominican Republic, Guatemala, Hungary, India, Kazakhstan, Mexico, Moldova, Peru, the Philippines, Poland, Romania, Russia, Serbia, South Africa, Thailand, Turkey, Uganda, and Ukraine.

120 As already indicated, starting in 2019, New Zealand changed its decision-making process by creating a collegial decision-making body.

121 The rule is that each member has one vote, with the governor (chairperson) having a casting vote in the case of a tie.

122 Albania, Argentina, Armenia, the Dominican Republic, Guatemala, Kazakhstan, Mexico, Peru, the Philippines, Russia, Serbia, Thailand, Turkey, Uganda, and Ukraine.

123 Israel and Norway.

124 Colombia, Moldova, Romania, and South Africa.

125 The Czech Republic, Iceland, Japan, Korea, Sweden, the United Kingdom, and the United States.

126 Brazil, Chile, Hungary, India, and Poland.

127 In Iceland, Israel, Japan, Korea, Norway, Sweden, the United States—from advanced economies, and in Brazil, Chile, Colombia, Hungary, India, Moldova, Poland, Romania, and South Africa—from emerging market economies.

128 The Czech Republic, Japan, Norway, Sweden, the United Kingdom, and the United States.

129 Brazil, Chile, Colombia, Hungary, India, Romania, and South Africa.

130 In Poland, the motions put forward at decision-making meetings related to interest rates, together with full voting records, are published on the central bank's website: if the motion was not passed—after 6 weeks from the date of voting, and if the motion was passed—after the voting records have been published in the *Court and Economic Monitor* (external official publication).

131 In Argentina no projections are published. In Israel projections are owned by staff (published four times a year), while inflation reports are a monetary committee document (published twice a year). The Bank of Uganda publishes six reports per year, but not every report includes a forecast. In the United States, projections are owned by decision-makers (published four times a year), while inflation reports (Monetary Policy Reports) are a document prepared by staff (published twice a year).

132 The Dominican Republic, Guatemala, Moldova, Romania, and Serbia.

133 The Czech Republic, the euro area, Iceland, Japan, Korea, Norway, and Sweden. Starting in 2019, the United States also joined that group of countries.

134 Albania, Colombia, Ghana, Guatemala, India, Mexico, Moldova, Peru, Poland, Romania, Serbia, South Africa, Thailand, and Ukraine.

135 Canada, Israel, New Zealand, the United Kingdom, and the United States. As already noted, the United States moved to holding press conferences after each decision-making meeting in 2019.

136 Chile, Georgia, the Philippines, Russia, and Turkey.

137 Australia—from advanced economies, and Armenia, Brazil, the Dominican Republic, Indonesia, Kazakhstan, Paraguay, and Uganda—from emerging market economies.

138 The United States and Japan also started publishing minutes quite early—in fact even before they announced their explicit inflation targets.

139 Australia, the Czech Republic, the euro area, Iceland, Israel, Japan, Korea, Sweden, the United Kingdom, and the United States.

140 Armenia, Brazil, Chile, Colombia, Guatemala, Hungary, India, Mexico, Moldova, Paraguay, the Philippines, Poland, Romania, Thailand, and Turkey.

141 The Czech Republic, the euro area, Iceland, Israel, Japan, Korea, Sweden, the United Kingdom, and the United States.

142 Brazil, Chile, Colombia, Guatemala, Hungary, India, Mexico, Poland, Romania, and Thailand.

143 All advanced economy inflation targeters apart from Switzerland.

144 Armenia, Brazil, Chile, Colombia, Georgia, Guatemala, Hungary, Indonesia, Kazakhstan, Mexico, Moldova, Peru, Poland, Russia, Serbia, South Africa, Turkey, and Ukraine.

145 Albania, Argentina, the Dominican Republic, Ghana, India, Paraguay, the Philippines, Romania, Thailand, and Uganda. In Ghana, if the target is not achieved, the governor may be summoned to parliament to explain developments within the economy, but otherwise there are no regular parliamentary hearings.

146 Armenia, Brazil, Chile, Ghana, India, Paraguay, and Peru.

147 Iceland, Korea, New Zealand, Norway, and the United Kingdom.

148 Brazil, India, Indonesia, Moldova, the Philippines, Serbia, Thailand, and Turkey.

149 Australia, the Czech Republic, the euro area, Israel, Japan, Norway, Sweden, and the United States.

150 Argentina, Brazil, Chile, Colombia, Georgia, Ghana, Hungary, India, Indonesia, Kazakhstan, Peru, Romania, South Africa, Thailand, and Ukraine.

151 The aim of financial supervision is to supervise individual financial entities. In turn, the aim of macroprudential policy is to oversee the financial system as a whole, and thus to monitor systemic risks.

152 When checking what institution is responsible for financial stability, whenever possible the emphasis is put on macroprudential policy. However, in some cases, it is not easy to find rules on the arrangements related to macroprudential policy. Therefore, in order to apply a possibly uniform approach across all the analysed countries, no strict division between micro- and macroprudential policies is introduced.

153 Canada, the Czech Republic, Israel, Japan, Korea, the United Kingdom, and the United States.

154 Albania, Argentina, Armenia, Brazil, Georgia, Hungary, India, Indonesia, Kazakhstan, Peru, the Philippines, Russia, Serbia, South Africa, and Thailand.

155 Australia, the euro area, Iceland, New Zealand, Norway, Sweden, and Switzerland. Whereas in New Zealand it is the central bank but in consultation with other institutions.

156 Chile, Colombia, the Dominican Republic, Guatemala, Mexico, Moldova, Poland, Romania, Turkey, Uganda, and Ukraine.

157 No information on the involvement of central banks in macroprudential policy was easily available for Ghana and Paraguay.

158 The first report prepared by the US Federal Reserve was published in November 2018.

159 Currently, the central banks of more than 60 countries, predominantly advanced economies, regularly publish financial stability reports (Horváth and Vaško, 2016, p. 46).

160 Australia, Canada, the euro area, Iceland, Israel, Japan, Korea, New Zealand, Sweden, the United Kingdom, and the United States.

161 Albania, Argentina, Armenia, Brazil, Chile, Colombia, Hungary, India, Indonesia, Paraguay, Peru, the Philippines, Poland, Romania, Russia, South Africa, Turkey, and Ukraine.
162 In the past, Iceland and Israel also used to publish one report annually.
163 Georgia, Kazakhstan, Mexico, Serbia, Thailand, and Uganda.
164 In the past, Albania, Armenia, and Poland also used to publish one report annually.
165 This was, in particular, the case in the euro area and Hungary.
166 This was, in particular, the case in Iceland and Turkey.
167 This was, in particular, the case in the Czech Republic—with respect to FX commitment, and in the euro area and the United States—with respect to asset purchases.
168 This was, in particular, the case in Korea and Russia.
169 This was, in particular, the case in Israel.
170 The first tool was used by the euro area, Japan, Korea, Sweden, Switzerland, and the United Kingdom, and the second tool by the euro area, Israel, Japan, Sweden, the United Kingdom, and the United States.
171 Canada, the euro area, Israel, the United Kingdom, and the United States.
172 The euro area, Sweden, and Switzerland.
173 The Czech Republic and Switzerland.
174 Albania, Hungary, and Poland.
175 The first tool was implemented in Hungary and Russia, and the second in Hungary and Turkey.

Bibliography

Bank Indonesia, www.bi.go.id/en/Default.aspx, accessed several times between 1 April and 20 December (2018).

Bank of Albania, www.bankofalbania.org/, accessed several times between 1 April and 20 December (2018).

Bank of Canada, www.bankofcanada.ca/, accessed several times between 1 April and 20 December (2018).

Bank of England, www.bankofengland.co.uk/, accessed several times between 1 April and 20 December (2018).

Bank of Ghana, www.bog.gov.gh/, accessed several times between 1 April and 20 December (2018).

Bank of Guatemala, www.banguat.gob.gt/, accessed several times between 1 April and 20 December (2018).

Bank of Israel, www.bankisrael.org.il/, accessed several times between 1 April and 20 December (2018).

Bank of Japan, www.boj.or.jp/en/index.htm/, accessed several times between 1 April and 20 December (2018).

Bank of Korea, www.bok.or.kr/eng/main/main.do, accessed several times between 1 April and 20 December (2018).

Bank of Mexico, www.banxico.org.mx/, accessed several times between 1 April and 20 December (2018).

Bank of Thailand, www.bot.or.th/English/Pages/default.aspx, accessed several times between 1 April and 20 December (2018).

Bank of the Republic, Colombia, www.banrep.gov.co/en, accessed several times between 1 April and 20 December (2018).

Bank of Uganda, www.bou.or.ug/bou/home.html, accessed several times between 1 April and 20 December (2018).

BIS (2019), *Annual Economic Report 2019*.

Board of Governors of the Federal Reserve System, www.federalreserve.gov/, accessed several times between 1 April and 20 December (2018).

Canada (1985), "The Bank of Canada Act" with Possible Amendments, Canada.

Carlstrom, J. (2013), *Economists Foiled by Guidance Pioneered by Riksbank*, Bloomberg, 15 October.

Central Bank of Argentina, www.bcra.gob.ar/default.asp, accessed several times between 1 April and 20 December (2018).

Central Bank of Armenia, www.cba.am/am/SitePages/Default.aspx, accessed several times between 1 April and 20 December (2018).

Central Bank of Brazil, www.bcb.gov.br/en/#!/home, accessed several times between 1 April and 20 December (2018).

Central Bank of Chile, www.bcentral.cl/es/web/central-bank-of-chile/home, accessed several times between 1 April and 20 December (2018).

Central Bank of Iceland, www.sedlabanki.is/, accessed several times between 1 April and 20 December (2018).

Central Bank of Norway, Norges Bank, www.norges-bank.no/, accessed several times between 1 April and 20 December (2018).

Central Bank of Paraguay, www.bcp.gov.py/, accessed several times between 1 April and 20 December (2018).

Central Bank of the Dominican Republic, www.bancentral.gov.do/, accessed several times between 1 April and 20 December (2018).

Central Bank of the Philippines (Bangko Sentral ng Pilipinas), www.bsp.gov.ph/, accessed several times between 1 April and 20 December (2018).

Central Bank of the Republic of Turkey, www.tcmb.gov.tr/, accessed several times between 1 April and 20 December (2018).

Central Bank of the Russian Federation, www.cbr.ru/eng/, accessed several times between 1 April and 20 December (2018).

Central Reserve Bank of Peru, www.bcrp.gob.pe/, accessed several times between 1 April and 20 December (2018).

Čihák, M. (2006), "How Do Central Banks Write on Financial Stability?", *IMF Working Paper, No. 163.* www.imf.org/external/pubs/ft/wp/2006/wp06163.pdf

Commonwealth of Australia (1959), "The Reserve Bank Act" with Possible Amendments, Australia.

Czech National Bank, www.cnb.cz/en/index.html, accessed several times between 1 April and 20 December (2018).

Czech Republic (1993), "The Act on the Czech National Bank" with possible amendments, the Czech Republic.

Debelle, G. (1997), "Inflation Targeting in Practice", *IMF Working Paper, No. 35*, pp. 1–34. https://doi.org/10.5089/9781451845310.001

Dominican Republic (2002), "The Monetary and Financial Law" with possible amendments, the Dominican Republic.

Drop, J., Wojtyna, A. (2001), "Strategia Bezpośredniego Celu Inflacyjnego: Przesłanki Teoretyczne i Doświadczenia Wybranych Krajów", *Materiały i Studia NBP, 118*.

ECB (2019), "Introductory Statement of 25 July 2019". www.ecb.europa.eu/press/pressconf/2019/html/ecb.is190725~547f29c369.en.html

European Central Bank, www.ecb.europa.eu/home/html/index.en.html, accessed several times between 1 April and 20 December (2018).

European Union (2012), "'The Treaty on the Functioning of the European Union' with Possible Amendments", the European Union.

Fed (2016), *Federal Open Market Committee Reaffirms Its "Statement on Longer-Run Goals and Monetary Policy Strategy"*. www.federalreserve.gov/newsevents/pressreleases/monetary20160127b.htm.

Federative Republic of Brazil (1964), "The Law on the National Financial System" with possible amendments, Brazil.

Georgia (2009), "'The Organic Law of Georgia on the National Bank of Georgia' with Possible Amendments, Georgia".

Grostal, W. (2020), "Monetary Policy Across the World in Response to the COVID-19 Pandemic", *Bezpieczny Bank/Safe Bank*, 2(79), pp. 7–24.

Haldane, A. G. (1995), "Introduction", in: A. G. Haldane (ed.), *Targeting Inflation, A Conference of Central Banks on the Use of Inflation Targtets Organised by the Bank of England*, Bank of England, pp. 1–12.

Hammond, G. (2012), *State of the Art of Inflation Targeting*, Centre for Central Banking Studies, Bank of England. www.bankofengland.co.uk/ccbs/state-of-the-art-of-inflation-targeting

Heenan, G., Peter, M., Roger, S. (2006), "Implementing Inflation Targeting: Institutional Arrangements, Target Design, and Communications", *IMF Working Paper, No. 278*, pp. 1–57. https://doi.org/10.5089/9781451865387.001

Horváth, R., Vaško, D. (2016), "Central Bank Transparency and Financial Stability", *Journal of Financial Stability*, 22, pp. 45–56. https://doi.org/10.1016/j.jfs.2015.12.003.

Hungary (2013), "The Act CXXXIX on the Magyar Bank, Nemzeti" with possible amendments, Hungary.

IMF (2015), "Annual Report on Exchange Arrangements and Exchange Restrictions 2015", October. www.imf.org/en/Publications/Annual-Report-on-Exchange-Arrangements-and-Exchange-Restrictions/Issues/2017/01/25/Annual-Report-on-Exchange-Arrangements-and-Exchange-Restrictions-2015-42751

IMF (2016), "Annual Report on Exchange Arrangements and Exchange Restrictions 2016", October. www.imf.org/en/Publications/Annual-Report-on-Exchange-Arrangements-and-Exchange-Restrictions/Issues/2017/01/25/Annual-Report-on-Exchange-Arrangements-and-Exchange-Restrictions-2016-43741

IMF (2018), "Annual Report on Exchange Arrangements and Exchange Restrictions 2017", April. www.imf.org/en/Publications/Annual-Report-on-Exchange-Arrangements-and-Exchange-Restrictions/Issues/2018/08/10/Annual-Report-on-Exchange-Arrangements-and-Exchange-Restrictions-2017-44930

Japan (1997), "The Bank of Japan Act" with Possible Amendments, Japan.

Kingdom of Norway (1985), "The Norges Bank Act" with possible amendments, Norway.

Kingdom of Sweden (1988), "The Sveriges Riksbank Act" with possible amendments, Sweden.

Kingdom of Thailand (1942), "The Bank of Thailand Act" with possible amendments, Thailand.

Magyar Nemzeti Bank (Central Bank of Hungary), www.mnb.hu/en/, accessed several times between 1 April and 20 December (2018).

Mayes, D., Chapple, B. (1995), "Defining an Inflation Target", in: A. G. Haldane (ed.), *Targeting Inflation, A Conference of Central Banks on the Use of Inflation Targtets Organised by the Bank of England*, Bank of England, pp. 226–245.

Mishkin, F. S. (2001), "From Monetary Targeting to Inflation Targeting: Lessons from the Industrialized Countries", *Policy Research Working Paper, No. 2684*, World Bank. https://doi.org/10.1596/1813-9450-2684.

Mishkin, F. S., Posen, A. S. (1997), "Inflation Targeting: Lessons from Four Countries", *NBER Working Paper, No. 6126*, pp.1–133. www.nber.org/papers /w6126.

National Bank of Georgia, www.nbg.gov.ge/index.php?m=2, accessed several times between 1 April and 20 December (2018).

National Bank of Kazakhstan, https://nationalbank.kz/?&switch=kazakh, accessed several times between 1 April and 20 December (2018).

National Bank of Moldova, www.bnm.md/en, accessed several times between 1 April and 20 December (2018).

National Bank of Poland, www.nbp.pl/, accessed several times between 1 April and 20 December (2018).

National Bank of Romania, www.bnro.ro/Home.aspx, accessed several times between 1 April and 20 December (2018). accessed several times between 1 April and 20 December, 2018.

National Bank of Serbia, www.nbs.rs/internet/english/, accessed several times between 1 April and 20 December (2018).

National Bank of Ukraine, www.bank.gov.ua/control/uk/index, accessed several times between 1 April and 20 December (2018).

Naudon, A., Pérez, A. (2017), "An Overview of Inflation-Targeting Frameworks: Institutional Arrangements, Decision-Making & the Communication of Monetary Policy", *Banco Central de Chile Working Papers, No. 811*. www.b central.cl/es/web/central-bank-of-chile/-/an-overview-of-inflation-targeting-fra meworks-institutional-arrangements-decision-making-the-communication-of -monetary-policy.

New Zealand (1989), "The Reserve Bank of New Zealand Act" with possible amendments, New Zealand.

Niedźwiedzińska, J. (2018), "Inflation Targeting—Institutional Features of the Strategy in Practice", *NBP Working Paper, No. 299*. www.nbp.pl/publikacje/ materialy_i_studia/299_en.pdf.

Niedźwiedzińska, J. (2020), "Initial Monetary Policy Response to the COVID-19 Pandemic in Inflation Targeting Economies", *NBP Working Paper, No. 335*. www.nbp.pl/publikacje/materialy_i_studia/335_en.pdf.

Niedźwiedzińska, J., Skrzeszewska-Paczek, E., Wesołowski, G., Żuk, P. (2019), "Major Changes to an Inflation Targeting Framework", in: J. Niedźwiedzińska (ed.), *Three Decades of Inflation Targeting, NBP Working Paper, No. 314*, pp. 42–72.

Republic of Albania (1997), "The Law on Bank of Albania" with possible amendments, Albania.

Republic of Armenia (2008), "The Law on the Central Bank of the Republic of Armenia" with possible amendments, Armenia.

Republic of Chile (1989), "The Basic Constitutional Act Central Bank of Chile" with possible amendments, Chile.

Republic of Colombia (1993), "The Decree, 2520/1993" with possible amendments, Colombia.

Republic of Ghana (2002), "The Bank of Ghana Act" with possible amendments, Ghana.

Republic of Guatemala (2002), "The New Organic Law of the Banco De Guatemala" with possible amendments, Guatemala.

Republic of Iceland (2001), "The Act on the Central Bank of Iceland" with possible amendments, Iceland.

Republic of India (2016), "The Reserve Bank 1934" with Possible Amendments, India.

Republic of Indonesia (2004), "The Bank Indonesia Act" with possible amendments, Indonesia.

Republic of Kazakhstan (1995), "The Law of the Republic of Kazakhstan" with possible amendments, Kazakhstan.

Republic of Korea (1997), "The Bank of Korea Act" with possible amendments, Korea.

Republic of Moldova (1995), "The Law on the National Bank of Moldova" with possible amendments, Moldova.

Republic of Paraguay (1995), "The Organic Law of Banco Central Del Paraguay" with possible amendments, Paraguay.

Republic of Peru (1922), "The Organic Law" with possible amendments, Peru.

Republic of Philippines (1993), "The New Central Bank Act" with possible amendments, the Philippines.

Republic of Poland (1997), "The Act on Narodowy Bank Polski" with possible amendments, Poland.

Republic of Serbia (2003), "The Law on the National Bank of Serbia" with possible amendments, Serbia.

Republic of South Africa (1989), "The South African Reserve Bank Act of 1989" with Possible Amendments, South Africa.

Republic of Turkey (1970), "The Law on the Central Bank of the Republic of Turkey" with possible amendments, Turkey.

Republic of Uganda (2000), "The Bank of Uganda Act" with possible amendments, Uganda.

Reserve Bank of Australia, www.rba.gov.au/, accessed several times between 1 April and 20 December (2018).

Reserve Bank of India, www.rbi.org.in/home.aspx, accessed several times between 1 April and 20 December (2018).

Reserve Bank of New Zealand, www.rbnz.govt.nz/, accessed several times between 1 April and 20 December (2018).

Riksbank, Sveriges, www.riksbank.se/en-gb/, accessed several times between 1 April and 20 December (2018).

Roger, S. (2010), "Inflation Targeting Turns 20", *Finance and Development*, 47(1), pp. 46–49.

Romania (2004), "The Law on the Statute of the National Bank of Romania" with Possible Amendments, Romania.

"Russian Federation" (2002), "The Federal Law on the Central Bank of the Russian Federation" with possible amendments, Russia.

South African Reserve Bank, www.resbank.co.za/, accessed between 1 and 30 June (2018).

"State of Israel" (2010), "The Bank of Israel Law" with possible amendments, Israel.

Swiss Confederation (2003), "The National Bank Act" with possible amendments, Switzerland.

Swiss National Bank, www.snb.ch/en/, accessed several times between 1 April and 20 December (2018).

Ukraine (1999), "The Law of Ukraine on the National Bank of Ukraine" with possible amendments, Ukraine.

United Kingdom of Great Britain and Northern Ireland (1998), "The Bank of England Act" with possible amendments, the United Kingdom.

United Mexican States (1993), "The Banco De Mexico Law" with possible amendments, Mexico.

United States of America (1913), "The Federal Reserve Act" with possible amendments, the United States.

Appendix 2: Inflation targets used by inflation targeting central banks

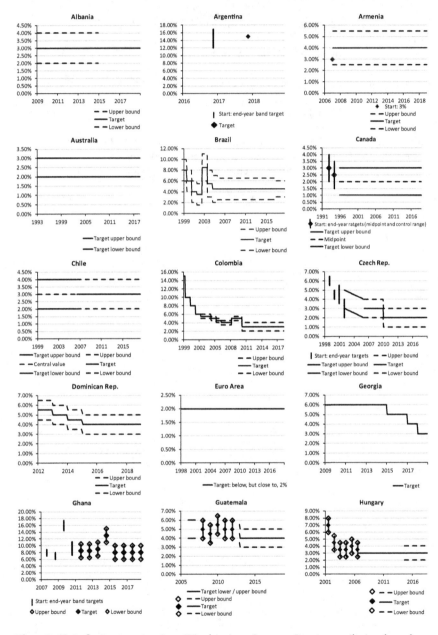

Chart 2.68 Inflation targets since IT adoption. Source: Own compilation based on information from central banks' websites.

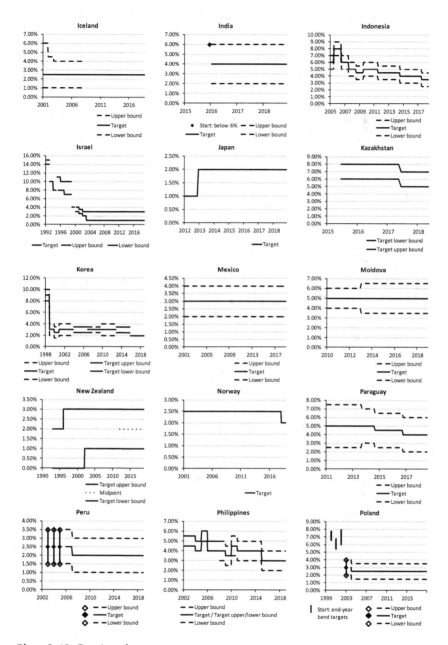

Chart 2.68 Continued

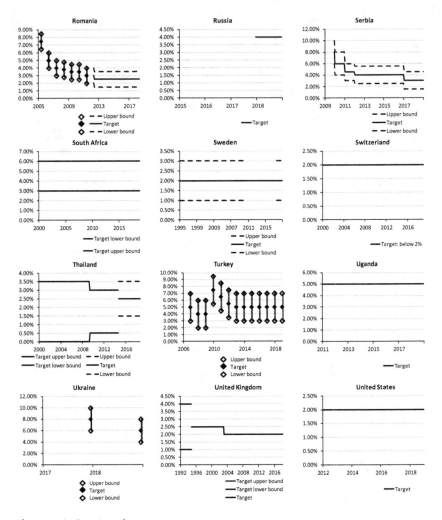

Chart 2.68 Continued

3

CONSTRUCTING INDICES COMPARING INSTITUTIONAL SET-UPS OF INFLATION TARGETING CENTRAL BANKS

3.1 Introductory remarks

The aim of Chapter 3 is to group institutional aspects into topic areas which will allow for their more systematic comparison. However, first, arguments behind the importance of central banks' institutional set-ups are discussed, since this will be helpful in understanding why the issues reviewed in Chapter 2 are of interest. This is followed by an overview of the existing literature on indices comparing central banks' independence, accountability, and transparency as the keywords related to the institutional arrangements of central banks. Against this background, a number of indices are proposed summarising such aspects of central banks' set-ups as: how experienced a country has been with pursuing an inflation targeting (IT) strategy (the Mature_IT index); how much independence an IT central bank has been granted (the Independent_IT index); how well informed decision-makers have been in an IT central bank (the Informed_IT index); how understandable a decision-making process has been at an IT central bank (the Explicatory_IT index); how transparently monetary policy has been conducted in an IT central bank (the Transparent_IT index); and how high accountability standards have been employed in an IT central bank (the Accountable_IT index). These individual indices should be helpful in assessing the credibility of a monetary authority, which is, in a way, captured by a summary index being the average of all the listed individual indices (the Fully-fledged_IT index). Separately, also an index reviewing differences in IT central banks' approach to financial stability and the use of standard and non-standard monetary policy measures is presented (the Stretched_IT index).

The proposed indices are used to investigate, in particular, whether some clear tendencies across economies and time can be noticed, with the expectation to see a move towards an improvement in the analysed aspects of central banks' institutional set-ups.

3.2 Arguments behind the importance of central banks' institutional set-ups

As already noted, institutional set-ups under which central banks act most probably influence the way monetary policy is conducted. For that reason, the topic has received a lot of attention, as evidenced by the rich literature dealing with such aspects as central banks' independence, accountability, and transparency. The sequence of the listing corresponds to the historical evolution of economists' thinking on these issues that first focused on the importance of central banks' independence, then emphasised the need for central banks' accountability as a natural complement to their increasing independence, and later moved to analysing the benefits and costs of central banks' growing transparency.

3.2.1 Central banks' independence

Regarding independence, typically its two key dimensions are distinguished: goal independence, also called political independence, and instrument independence, also called economic independence (Grilli et al., 1991, pp. 365–370; Debelle and Fischer, 1994, p. 197). The first notion refers to a situation in which it is the central bank that determines its policy objectives without interference from the government, while the second concept describes a situation in which the central bank—given the objectives—has the freedom to conduct its monetary policy without interference from the government.

Goal independence can be important, but it is not advocated that strongly, since in democratic societies, there may be good reasons for making the government responsible for setting the ultimate objectives for policies, including monetary policy. Although central banks' officials are generally appointed by elected political authorities, they are not directly accountable to the electorate, which may speak in favour of leaving the decision on monetary policy objectives to the government. However, whereas considering price stability as the right goal for a central bank should not be controversial either for political or for monetary authorities, when it comes to specifying more precisely what price stability means, the unanimity is not that certain. Granting goal independence may result in a lower level of preferable inflation, if a central bank values price stability more than the government. A situation in which a central bank puts more weight on an inflation stabilisation objective than the government can be seen as leaving monetary policy in the hands of a Rogoff conservative central banker (Rogoff, 1985).

Regarding instrument independence, there is currently a rather broad consensus on the need to entrust the conduct of monetary policy to monetary authorities that are not subject to political pressures (de Haan and Eijffinger, 2016, pp. 1–5). Looking more closely, as already mentioned, instrument independence can have several important aspects, namely, functional, institutional, personal, and financial (ECB, 2018, pp. 20–28). Functional independence means that monetary policy has clear objectives, and central banks have the instruments to achieve these objectives independently of other authorities. Institutional independence deals with the issue of other authorities giving instructions to central banks' officials, as well as other authorities requesting or accepting instructions from central banks' officials which is banned. It also requires that monetary policy decisions are not subject to any approving, suspending, annulling, or deferring, and that the legal frameworks ensure the stable functioning of a central bank. Personal independence relates predominantly to the security of tenure for decision-makers, but it can also be seen more broadly—as providing such rules on term of office, reasons for dismissal, and the possibility of the reappointment of central banks' officials that limits the possible influence of the government on monetary policy decisions. Finally, financial independence implies that a central bank has sufficient financial resources to fulfil its objectives and is not obliged to provide monetary financing. All these areas seem important, and thus many of these issues are often explicitly regulated in the legal acts on central banks.[1]

While central banks' independence may have various dimensions, most generally it can be described as insulating monetary authorities from political influence. This is advisable because the time horizon on which politicians focus may be shorter than relevant for evaluating the full effects of monetary policy decisions, favouring goals related to economic activity gains rather than maintaining price stability. As already indicated, Kydland and Prescott (1977) and Barro and Gordon (1983) showed that the resulting inflationary bias would deliver unintended outcomes—higher inflation, but no systematically higher output. Another reason for a possible inflationary bias includes the temptation for politicians to issue money to finance government spending, or to earn revenues from seigniorage (Cukierman, 1992, pp. 117–135). The result would be similar, since it would lead to time-inconsistent monetary policy at the expense of higher inflation.

The rules versus discretion debate clearly advocated for finding a way that would eliminate an inflationary bias, and thus—indirectly—political influence on central banks (de Haan and Eijffinger, 2016, pp. 1–5). The frequently cited solutions to the problem included the already noted options: applying non-contingent rules, such as the Friedman rule (Friedman, 2006, pp. 1–50), appointing a Rogoff conservative central banker (Rogoff, 1985), or making optimal performance contracts between political and monetary authorities (Walsh, 1995). In practical terms, granting central banks a higher degree of autonomy seemed to be the most feasible, and thus the most compelling choice mitigating an inflationary bias, although one needs to note that all the listed ideas, to some extent, could also be seen as being related to central banks' independence (Briault et al., 1996, p. 9).

3.2.2 *Central banks' accountability*

As the idea of granting monetary authorities a considerable degree of independence gained support in the 1980s and 1990s, so was the notion that central banks should be kept accountable for reaching their objectives, i.e.—slightly simplifying—monitored by elected political authorities. To better explain their understanding of accountability, some authors distinguished between its different aspects. And so, one can speak of *de jure* and *de facto* accountability (Briault, Haldane, and King, 1996, pp. 11–12), *ex ante* and *ex post* accountability (Bini-Smaghi and Gros, 2000, p. 152), accountability on objectives, procedural accountability, and information accountability (Siklos, 2002, p. 228). These concepts placed emphasis on various elements related to monetary policy, such as defining central banks' objectives, monetary authorities' reporting to government, or the possibility of overriding monetary policy decisions by political authorities.

The requirement that independence should be accompanied by democratic control can be seen as a way to strengthen central banks' commitment to meeting their goals, since, in general, in the context of monetary policy, accountability focuses on evaluating policy outcomes. Providing the public with information on the reasoning behind monetary policy decisions and their consequences can be regarded as a tool to increase central banks' commitment, in particular, to a no-surprise policy and—by reducing an inflationary bias—enhance their credibility. Thus, it allows monetary authorities to conduct less restrictive policies than would otherwise be needed to meet monetary policy objectives. Additional reasons speaking in favour of providing some kind of controlling mechanisms to central banks' policies stem from the fact that these policies affect real variables, even if predominantly in the short run, and income distribution within society (Bini Smaghi and Gros, 2000, pp. 147–151). Accountability lowers the likelihood of unanticipated monetary policy decisions that may be associated with significant unintended redistribution effects between creditors and debtors. Moreover, it enables economic agents to predict central banks' reactions to major shock, which may foster a cooperative equilibrium, for example, by reducing excessive wage demands or too expansionary fiscal policy. All these mechanisms should deliver Pareto-superior social welfare. Investing in accountability should therefore bring an increase in overall welfare (Bini Smaghi and Gros, 2000, pp. 147–151).

Scrutiny by others should be supported, not least, by regular reporting on central banks' actions with the view to facing negative consequences if these actions are considered unsatisfactory (Geraats, 2009, p. 135).

However, evaluating policy outcomes is challenging. Speaking about various monetary policy frameworks, already specifying a monetary policy objective which can be seen as a benchmark against which a central bank should be assessed, may give rise to difficulties. This is especially the case if objectives are not clearly stated, which allows for various interpretations. Also a situation when there are multiple objectives that can potentially be in conflict with each other, especially if no indication of their prioritisation is provided, is highly problematic. And even if monetary policy is targeted at a specific goal, stipulated by a single number for a certain variable, like a numerical target for inflation, the assessment of policy outcomes is far from straightforward.[2]

Analysing the effects of monetary policy decisions on the economy is not easy, since many processes simultaneously influence each other, making the identification of policy outcomes complicated. Moreover, due to variable transmission lags and inherent uncertainty about future economic developments, it is not clear what policy should be considered the appropriate one. In particular, *ex post* comparisons of the realised outcomes with the targets would disregard, for example, the effects of unanticipated shocks, and as such may be of limited help. A more justified approach would try to evaluate central banks' decisions taking an *ex ante* point of view, i.e. analyse the anticipated outcomes of monetary policy considering the information available to the central banks' officials at the time of acting. While this is not an easy task, high accountability standards can substantially facilitate such an assessment.

3.2.3 Central banks' transparency

Accountability is very closely related to transparency, although transparency has become a much broader concept. Following Geraats (2002, p. F533), specific aspects of transparency related to different elements of policymaking are often distinguished. These include political transparency, economic transparency, procedural transparency, policy transparency, and operational transparency. Political transparency describes a relationship between monetary and political authorities, by looking, among others, at how central banks' mandates are defined. This should provide the public with a clear idea of monetary policy objectives, and their prioritisation in the case of multiple goals. Economic transparency is assessed based on how much information, including data and forecasts, that serves as inputs to monetary policy decision-making processes is revealed. Procedural transparency relates to the issue of whether information on how decisions are made is available, among others, by publishing transcripts, minutes, and—in the case of collegial decision-making bodies that arrive at decisions by voting—also voting records. Policy transparency concerns the timely communication of monetary policy decisions and an explanation of their backgrounds, as well as some guidance on the likely direction of future decisions. Similarly as in the case of economic transparency, this allows the public not only to assess central banks' actions, but also to form expectations on a future policy course. Finally, operational transparency is understood as providing *ex post* evaluations of

189

the conducted policies. This covers reviewing by the central banks the accuracy of their past forecasts and accounting for their past errors, which help to explain the role of unanticipated shocks for policy outcomes. In this way, the public has the possibility to form their own informed opinion on how good monetary authorities have been in delivering their goals. Looking at the different aspects of transparency, it is clear that they are covering various stages of conducting monetary policy. However, all of them should simply support greater understanding of central banks' policies, which, in turn, should be beneficial for the central banks themselves.

A rationale for higher transparency includes several arguments (Laurens, Arnone, and Segalotto, 2009, pp. 108–111).[3] By strengthening understanding of monetary policy, central banks may, in a way, teach the private sector how they are likely to react to different economic developments and unanticipated shocks (Mishkin and Schmidt-Hebbel, 2007, pp. 23–26; Dincer and Eichengreen, 2013, p. 191). By doing this, monetary authorities enable the public to better predict monetary policy decisions, which in turn should accelerate monetary policy transmission. This is important both in normal times, when economic agents may realistically assume what policy to expect, accommodating it in their decisions, as well as in the presence of shocks when central banks' communication may provide the public with new information enabling swifter adjustment to changed economic conditions.

The most compelling argument for transparency is, indeed, related to shaping private sector expectations, among others, by reducing information asymmetries and uncertainty (Blinder, 1998, pp. 70–75). This seems key, since central banks generally have direct control only over the very short-term end of the yield curve, while, for the economy, more important are long-term interest rates, exchange rates, asset prices, etc. All these variables are influenced, to a great extent, by expectations on future monetary policy. Thus, educating the public on what drives central banks' decisions is crucial for the transmission mechanism to work (Fracasso et al., 2003, p. 4). In turn, the lack of transparency can lead to expectations-driven fluctuations, destabilising the economy.

Transparency can also be seen as a tool used by central banks to build trust in their actions (Geraats, 2001, pp. 7–8). If central banks' communication is convincing in explaining how monetary policy decisions should support reaching their final objective, the private sector is more likely to believe these announcements and to adapt its expectations in line with central banks' intentions. At the same time, by clearly communicating monetary policy objectives and decisions aimed at reaching these objectives, central banks enable the public to assess whether the two are consistent. Such scrutiny will, in turn, reduce a possible inflationary bias of decision-makers and provide incentives for monetary authorities not to deviate from the targets.

Transparency is, however, also useful in minimising credibility losses if central banks' objectives have not been reached. By providing the public with information, for example, on expected economic developments and the intended policy outcomes, monetary authorities may show the reasoning behind their decisions, even if subsequently they do not deliver the projected results. Apart from cases when a central bank was clearly wrong in its policies, the failure to reach the objectives may result from factors that are beyond the control, or even influence, of monetary policy. A high degree of transparency simply allows central banks to be evaluated not only based on the achieved results but also based on the logic of their actions.

The additional benefits of transparency stem from the fact that it may be helpful in protecting central banks' independence. First, it is an important element of an accountability mechanism, and thus supports the legitimisation of monetary policy actions. Second, it enables possible political pressures to be more easily identified. At the same time, better communication by central banks' allows political authorities to verify whether monetary policy is conducted in line with its mandate. Transparency may also enhance fiscal and monetary policy coordination.

3.2.4 Limits to independence, accountability, and transparency

Despite numerous theoretical arguments supporting central banks' independence, accountability, and transparency, other issues should also be taken into account when deciding what should be the recommended institutional set-up for monetary authorities. Regarding independence, one may argue that leaving monetary policy to an independent central bank that focuses on inflation may result in a higher variability of output, unemployment, and interest rates (Eijffinger and de Haan, 1996, pp. 13–15). In turn, more emphasis put on higher accountability requirements may be regarded as limiting monetary authorities' independence (Fry et al., 2000, pp. 72–73). Finally, the main drawbacks of greater transparency encompass risks that the private sector will start to attach too much weight to central banks' forecasts (Ueda, 2010), and that it will get confused by the amount of information it receives (van der Cruijsen et al., 2010). Thus, there are possibly limits to the desired degree of independence, accountability, and transparency.

Overall, however, these concepts can be regarded as helpful in building monetary authorities' credibility (Pietrzak, 2008, pp. 89–90) and, for that reason, much attention is devoted to them.

3.3 Selected literature on indices comparing central banks' institutional set-up

Ever since economists started to see the possible consequences of the different institutional set-ups in the area of central banking, they have tried to find measures of central banks' independence, accountability, and transparency. Thus, a number of indices of each of these concepts have been proposed. Despite similarities in the basic ideas behind the constructions of many measures, no uniform approach has been developed so far to assess monetary authorities' institutional arrangements. As a result, many authors have created their own indices and correlations between them have turned out to be rather low (Laurens et al., 2009, pp. 33–34, 105–106, 121–122).

3.3.1 Measures of central banks' independence

As already noted, central banks' independence was the first topic that attracted significant attention, and thus a number of its measures have been proposed in the literature. These include indices used, among others, in Bade and Parkin (1988), Grilli et al. (1991), Cukierman et al. (1992) which is probably the most widely cited overview of measures of central banks' independence, Alesina and Summers (1993), and Fry et al. (2000, pp. 70–71). What is interesting is that the authors quite early on started to distinguish between formal and actual independence.

Most measures are based on assessing formal independence, i.e. analysing legal acts governing monetary authorities in order to detect regulations related to selected issues that seem significant for central banks' goal or instrument independence (Bade and Parkin, 1988; Grilli et al., 1991; Cukierman et al., 1992). These indices typically cover such aspects as rules on the formulation of the main monetary policy objectives, procedures for appointing and dismissing central banks' decision-makers (predominantly governors), and restrictions on financial relationships between monetary authorities and the government.

The level of detail being analysed within different measures is not homogeneous, since sometimes a narrow subset of relatively precisely formulated legal rules is considered, while in other cases a wider list of legal regulations is included. From a practical point of view, the measures are constructed as weighted averages of indices that are the coded answers to questions related to central banks' independence.

The strength of these indices is that they may take into account many important characteristics of the institutional set-ups, and so, may encompass both goal and instrument independence, with the latter being investigated in all its relevant aspects—i.e. functional, institutional, personal, and financial. Moreover, after applying a simple coding method, these measures can be calculated for all countries for which legal acts on central banks are available.

However, indicators based on legal acts also have their shortcomings. While legal acts provide foundations for the functioning of monetary authorities in a given country, they do not necessarily regulate all possibly important aspects. And even when explicit rules do exist, practice may deviate from legal requirements, which may be a consequence of many different factors, such as informal links between central banks' decision-makers and government, or the overall approach of public institutions to obeying law. Moreover, as not all issues are regulated in the same way in different countries, at times, reading legal acts requires some interpretation which introduces subjectivism into the measurement. Also, deciding on what features should be analysed and whether they should be given the same weight in the overall index is subject to judgement.

To more accurately capture actual independence, other indices have been proposed. A measure that seems quite straightforward is the actual turnover of central banks' governors, or a governor's turnover relative to his/her official term of office (Cukierman et al., 1992). Cukierman and Webb (1995) developed another version of the turnover indicator by analysing the probability of a governor's dismissal shortly after a change of government. The higher the turnover, the less independent a given central bank, because it implies that political authorities, independently of the legal regulations on the term of office, tend to substitute central banks' governors for those who are more responsive to their preferences. While this intuition is compelling, the critics of turnover indicators point to the fact that low turnover rates may simply mean that selected governors are "accommodative" enough to government's needs, and exactly for that reason are not replaced.

Another approach used to assess central banks' autonomy is to construct indices based on questionnaires that include questions related to both formal and actual independence. As in the case of formal independence indicators, in practice these measures are weighted averages of indices that are coded answers to a list of questions. The big difference is that the answers to the questionnaires are provided by the analysed central banks themselves, which in theory should be the best possible source of information on their independence. Also combining formal and actual independence in one indicator should be considered as its clear advantage. However, these indices may be very judgemental, not only because the list of included questions is arbitrary, but also because the answers may be biased, if central banks like to present themselves as more autonomous than they really are. Also, the knowledge of the person filling in the questionnaire may not be complete regarding all aspects covered by the questionnaires, or his/her interpretation of the questions may not be uniform across all central banks.

Since all independence measures have some shortcomings, many papers use the averages of the described indices (Alesina and Summers, 1993; Hall and Franzese, 1998). This should allow for combining all available information in a single index, possibly alleviating some of the indicated problems. An overview of many independence measures can be found in Masłowska (2012, pp. 50–72).

3.3.2 *Measures of central banks' accountability*

Looking at the measures of accountability proposed in the literature, they are, to a great extent, constructed in a similar way as the indices of formal independence. Examples include Briault et al. (1996), de Haan et al. (1998), Bini-Smaghi and Gros (2000, pp. 153–154), Fry et al. (2000, p. 77), and Siklos (2002, pp. 248–251).

Defining accountability shows that it builds strongly on central banks' independence and transparency, and, in a way, combines elements of these two concepts. For that reason, the majority of the existing accountability indices cover such aspects as who decides on the ultimate objectives of monetary policy and how these objectives are defined, how transparent actual monetary policy is and, in particular, whether minutes of decision-making meetings and reports on monetary policy are regularly published, as well as who bears the final responsibility for monetary policy outcomes. The last point is understood as the rules on a governor's appointment and dismissal, the possibility to override monetary policy decisions by the government, and requirements related to central bank's regular reporting to political authorities via written reports or hearings. Thus, democratic control can be seen as a mix of rules and practices related to monetary authorities' autonomy and communication.

Similarly, as in the case of the indices related to central banks' formal independence, the measures of accountability are constructed as the weighted averages of indices that are the coded answers to a list of questions related to monetary authorities' democratic control. The level of detail being analysed may substantially differ, as shown by a significant discrepancy in the number of questions used to assess how accountable central banks are. From a practical point of view, a slight difference compared to the independence measures is that accountability indices are based not only on legal acts, but also on observing central banks' practices. The major strengths and weaknesses of these measures are the same as those of the formal independence indices.

3.3.3 *Measures of central banks' transparency*

Moving to measures of transparency, again, they are derived similarly as the indices discussed earlier. This is even less surprising when one notices that accountability and transparency indices were, in many instances, proposed by the same authors. The key references include Fry et al. (2000, pp. 78–79),[4] Siklos (2002, pp. 252–255),[5] de Haan and Amtenbrink (2003), and Eijffinger and Geraats (2006).

Transparency is associated with communication tools used by central banks, primarily to announce and clarify monetary policy decisions to the public, but also to guide expectations on the likely future policy directions. The first measures of transparency were based on information whether a prompt explanation of monetary policy decisions was revealed (possibly including minutes and voting records); whether regular forward-looking analyses were published (preferably together with forecasts' risk assessments and explanations of errors); and whether cyclically produced reports, speeches, and research publications were made available. More recent indices cover a broader range of topics and communication channels in order to capture political transparency, economic transparency, procedural transparency, policy transparency, and operational transparency. In particular, they additionally investigate such issues as how monetary policy objectives are defined, whether macroeconomic models used to produce forecasts are disclosed, whether explicit policy rules or monetary policy strategy are published, and whether regular evaluations of policy outcomes against objectives are provided. Since transparency is closely related to accountability, clearly there is a significant overlap between the two concepts.

Again, the proposed indices are weighted averages of the coded answers to questions related to monetary authorities' transparency, with visible heterogeneity in the level of detail being reviewed. The answers are mainly based on assessing central banks' practices in the area of communication policy. The strengths and weaknesses of these measures are the same as the indices of formal independence and accountability constructed in an analogous way.

A significant additional difficulty in measuring transparency is whether, and—if yes—how to account for the quality of central banks' communication. In fact, while the issue of clarity has received some attention, so far the available studies dealing with that topic analyse only selected communication tools, for example, inflation reports or press releases, and not the comprehensive communication policies of the central banks. Examples of such research include Fracasso et al. (2003), Jansen (2010), and Bulíř et al. (2012). The authors use various methods to measure the readability of the analysed publications—including appointing readers to rate a number of the characteristics of the assessed materials, or applying simple indices, like the so-called Flesch–Kincaid grade level, that inform how many years of education are needed to sufficiently understand a text (Kincaid et al., 1975). Each of the approaches has its disadvantages and limitations, but not surprisingly, the existing evidence shows that quality does matter, for example, for the predictability of central banks' decisions. Having said that, none of the indices of transparency proposed in the literature takes the issue of clarity into account, which is most probably due to the difficulty in its objective and easy assessment.

3.4 Constructing indices assessing institutional set-ups of inflation targeting central banks

In order to analyse IT central banks' institutional set-ups, a number of indices are proposed, each of them summarising a selected aspect of conducting monetary policy. Indices are derived based on the methodology of constructing independence, accountability, and transparency measures discussed earlier. Thus, they are coded answers to a list of questions related to a given issue of interest.

However, the proposed indices do not directly follow any of the definitions used in other studies, since the indices already present in the literature were designed to assess the institutional arrangements of central banks pursuing monetary policy under various monetary regimes. At the same time, as the focus of the analysis is to examine central banks' acting only within an inflation targeting framework, it was advisable to construct an original set of indices that would most accurately capture material similarities and differences between the reviewed inflation targeters. Put differently, regarding institutional set-ups, there are reasons to believe that IT central banks are, in a way, special, not least since applying high accountability and transparency standards is considered to be one of the key elements constituting inflation targeting.[6] Therefore, the selected indices try to take that issue into account and detect areas where solutions applied by IT central banks are not homogeneous (Chart 3.79 in Appendix 3; Table S in Supplement).

An additional argument for developing a new set of indices stemmed from the fact that the values of the indices already present in the literature were often not available for the entire analysed group of countries and for the entire period covered by the study.

The construction of the indices is based on information collected in a unique database produced by the author while reviewing IT central banks' institutional set-ups over the last 30 years.

3.4.1 Key considerations on the constructed indices

Most of the analysed questions are closely associated with the notions of independence, accountability, and various aspects of transparency, but they do not necessarily encompass the same set of questions as the indices present in the literature. As already noted, a consensus view on how to measure independence, accountability, and transparency has not yet been reached, so even fully applying any of the previously used concepts would be subject to an arbitrary choice, and thus problematic. The key consideration is, therefore, to construct indices most adequate for analysing IT central banks.

The proposed indices assess several aspects of IT central banks' institutional set-ups and include the Mature_IT index describing how experienced a country has been with pursuing an IT strategy; the Independent_IT index informing how much independence has been granted to a central bank; the Informed_IT index showing how well informed decision-makers have been in a central bank; the Explicatory_IT index reviewing how understandable a decision-making process has been at a central bank; the Transparent_IT index assessing how transparent monetary policy has been in a central bank;

and the Accountable_IT index capturing how high accountability standards have been employed in a central bank. A summary index, the Fully-fledged_ IT index, being the average of all the listed individual indices, is thought to be helpful in valuing the credibility of a monetary authority.

Each index ranges from 1 to 10 and for all the categories, and except the Fully_fledged_IT index, is a sum of the coded answers to 10 questions associated most closely with a given aspect of conducting monetary policy within an IT framework. In some cases, the same information is included in more than one index. This means that these issues are given more attention, and thus more significance, especially since the Fully_fledged_IT index is an average of the other indices, so replicated information is counted more than once. This is a conscious decision that should allow for capturing the relative importance of the analysed issues for the overall assessment of an IT institutional framework in a given country. If a given issue is influencing many aspects of monetary policy, there are reasons to assign more significance to it than to other topics. However, repeating exactly the same specific question is rare (it concerns one question in the Mature_IT index and the Independent_IT index, one question in the Informed_IT index and the Explicatory_IT index, and one question in the Transparent_IT index and the Accountable_IT index).

For each question a list of possible answers is set, ranked from the most to the least preferred ones, which is also reflected in the corresponding scores, equally distributed among answers. The better the assessment of a central bank's institutional set-up, the higher the scores. The highest score is associated with a practice or a rule considered as the most advisable one in view of the existing literature. In cases when it is not evident what the most advisable answer should be, the highest score is given to a practice or a rule most commonly used among the analysed central banks, assuming that there must be important reasons if it is considered desirable by most inflation targeters themselves. When no information on an investigated practice or a rule is available for a given monetary authority, the lowest score is assumed. This means that, in some cases, central banks are ranked lower than they should be, but it can be seen as a consequence of them not being too open about their proceedings which in itself should not be rewarded by higher scores.

Evaluating the answers based on arguments raised in the literature favouring certain solutions over others, or—in the absence of a broader discussion of some issues—based on the dominant practice suggesting arrangements preferred for pragmatic reasons by decision-makers, allows for assessing central banks' institutional set-ups and ranking the IT countries with the help of the proposed indices.

Except for the index related to independence, all other indices have a time-series dimension, which means that they reflect changes introduced to central banks' policies over the years.

The scores are assigned based on publicly available information regarding a point of interest. To limit subjectivity and the amount of judgement, they do not reflect any qualitative assessment of the "content" of policies, procedures, publications, etc. Weighting all questions equally also reduces the potential for arbitrariness, although, as indicated earlier, including the same information in more than one index assigns more weight to the selected issues.

The scope of the proposed indices is somewhat different than the measures already existing in the literature, in order to capture all relevant aspects related to the institutional set-ups of IT central banks. The idea is also to make the fullest use of the issues reviewed in Chapter 2. Despite the differences, as already indicated, the proposed indices are closely linked to past independence, accountability, and transparency measures.

3.4.2 Mature_IT index

The Mature_IT index (Table 3.1) values experienced inflation targeters who have a clearly stated priority for price stability in their mandates, and are autonomous in setting their inflation targets (goal independence). Preferably their targets are permanent, specified in terms of headline inflation, continuous, low (up to 3%), and narrow (point targets). These features should be beneficial in strengthening the anchoring of inflation expectations, because they are reducing possible uncertainty on what is, and is likely to continue to be, the precise level of targeted inflation. In turn, frequent announcements of targets, wide tolerance bands, or the use of escape clauses increase the ambiguity of the level of targeted inflation. For the same reasons, any changes to the formulation of targets are not welcomed, nor exchange rate arrangements that could possibly become a source of conflict with a price stability objective. The Mature_IT index, in many respects, corresponds to the measure of political transparency present in the literature.

3.4.3 Independent_IT index

The Independent_IT index (Table 3.2) favours monetary authorities who enjoy autonomy in setting their inflation targets (goal independence) and have a single mandate focused on price stability (functional independence). Regarding the decision-making bodies of the central banks, these should preferably be headed by governors appointed for a relatively long term of office (above 6 years), with the majority of members not eligible for reappointment. At the same time, once appointed, decision-makers should not be easily dismissed, with only limited reasons for dismissal—neither allowing for discretion nor related to duties—being stipulated in legal acts (personal independence). Giving decision-makers long and non-renewable terms of office should limit the risk of reappointing compliant governors. Also valued are explicit rules limiting the possibility of encountering conflicts of interest by monetary policy decision-makers, and, in particular, a requirement that

Table 3.1 Construction of Mature_IT index

1. Mature_IT—questions and answers	Scores	Source of information
1.1 Inflation targeting in place		Information from website
(a) For more than 10 years	1	
(b) For more than 5 years and up to 10 years	0.5	
(c) For less than 5 years	0	
1.2 Price stability in a central bank mandate		Provision in legal act
(a) Price stability as a single objective	1	
(b) Priority given to price stability in the case of multiple objectives	0.5	
(c) Multiple objectives and no priority given to price stability	0	
1.3 Authority setting the target		Information from website
(a) Bank	1	
(b) Bank together with the government	0.5	
(c) Government	0	
1.4 Frequency of announcing the target		Information from website
(a) Permanent target	1	
(b) Every few years	0.5	
(c) Each year	0	
1.5 Targeted measure		Information from website
(a) Headline inflation	1	
(b) Headline inflation + escape clauses	0.5	
(c) Core inflation	0	
1.6 Target horizon		Information from website
(a) Continuous target	1	
(b) End-year target	0	
1.7 Target level (midpoint)		Information from website
(a) Up to 3%	1	
(b) Above 3% and up to 4%	0.5	
(c) Above 4%	0	
1.8 Width of the target		Information from website
(a) Point target	1	
(b) Point target with tolerance bands of up to ±1 pp. or a band target with width of the band up to 2 pp.	0.5	
(c) Point target with tolerance bands wider than ±1 pp. or a band target with width of the band above 2 pp.	0	
1.9 Changes to the formulation of the target in the past 3 years		Information from website
(a) None within the last 3 years	1	
(b) At least 1 within the last 3 years	0.5	
(c) Still disinflation	0	
1.10 Exchange rate arrangement		Information from website (IMF classification)
(a) Floating	1	
(b) Other managed	0.5	
(c) Soft pegs	0	

Source: Own compilation.

Table 3.2 Construction of Independent_IT index

2. Independent_IT—questions and answers	Scores	Source of information
2.1 Authority setting the target		Information from website
(a) Bank	1	
(b) Bank together with the government	0.5	
(c) Government	0	
2.2 Single or multiple bank's mandate		Provision in legal act
(a) Price stability as a single objective	1	
(b) Multiple objectives (with or without prioritisation)	0	
2.3 Term of office of the governor		Provision in legal act
(a) Above 6 years	1	
(b) Above 4 years and up to 6 years	0.5	
(c) Up to 4 years or no fix term	0	
2.4 Reappointment of members*		Provision in legal act
(a) Reappointment not possible	1	
(b) Reappointment allowed but with a limit of terms	0.5	
(c) Reappointment allowed without a limit of terms or no fix term	0	
2.5 No conflict of interest and no political activity required at appointment		Provision in legal act
(a) Both included as rules related to appointment	1	
(b) One of the above included as rules related to appointment	0.5	
(c) Not required or no information	0	
2.6 Rules on dismissal		Provision in legal act
(a) Limited reasons for dismissal not allowing for discretion nor related to duties	1	
(b) Reasons allowing for discretion or related to duties	0.5	
(c) No limits to dismissal or no information	0	
2.7 Government representative in a monetary policy committee		Provision in legal act
(a) None	1	
(b) Yes—but without voting rights	0.66	
(c) Yes—with voting rights	0.33	
(d) Yes—chairing the committee	0	
2.8 Possibility of influencing monetary policy decisions by the government		Provision in legal act
(a) No	1	
(b) Yes—but monetary policy committee has the final word (only postponement)	0.5	
(c) Yes	0	
2.9 Lending to the government		Provision in legal act
(a) Prohibited	1	
(b) Allowed to a limited extent	0.5	
(c) Allowed or not regulated in legal acts	0	
2.10 Instrument independence granted in the law to the central bank		Provision in legal act
(a) Explicit independence	1	
(b) No explicit independence	0	

Source: Own compilation.
Note: * In countries with the governor being a single decision-maker, rules on reappointing the governor.

they are not engaged in political activities. Moreover, the involvement of government representatives in monetary policy decision-making processes should be minimised, likewise any other possibility to influence monetary policy decisions by the government (institutional independence). Finally, lending to the government should be prohibited (financial independence). Ideally, the explicit instrument independence of the central bank should be granted in law. The Independent_IT index is similar to the existing measures of formal independence.

Answers to almost all questions related to the Independent_IT index are based on provisions stipulated in legal acts. Since it is very difficult, even impossible, to check all the analysed countries if their central banks' acts have been amended with respect to the provisions of interest, it is assumed that the regulations have not changed since the beginning of the imple-mentation of an inflation targeting strategy by a given central bank. This assumption should, in most cases, be uncontroversial, since many coun-tries treated the amendment of their legal acts consisting of granting their monetary authorities more independence, as a necessary preparatory stage for adopting an IT framework. However, especially for countries that have been pursuing an inflation targeting strategy for a long time, some changes to legal acts were introduced in between the date when they became infla-tion targeters and now. In these cases, the Independent_IT index, which also forms a part of the Fully-fledged_IT index, is biased upwards. Since it is not easy to fix this issue, it can be treated as an additional positive premium for more experienced inflation targeters.[7]

3.4.4 Informed_IT index

The Informed_IT index (Table 3.3) rewards central banks where decision-making processes benefit from involving knowledgeable decision-makers, also from outside the bank, so that individuals with possibly diversified backgrounds are engaged in reaching the decisions. Thus, the highest scores are given to including legal requirements related to expertise as a condi-tion for being appointed as a central bank decision-maker, as well as to a significant share of external members in a decision-making body. Voting is preferred, as it should offer the best chance for a free exchange of views during the meetings. Since monetary policy conducted under an inflation targeting framework should be forward-looking, a lot of attention is given to projections. If they are owned by decision-makers, meaning that they should reflect decision-makers' assessments, this makes them potentially very use-ful in designing policies. Also, the more frequently projections are prepared, the longer their time horizon, and the more encompassing the list of fore-cast variables, the better informed are monetary policy decisions. Including uncertainty intervals is also valued, since it reveals, for example, whether risks around the central projection are balanced or skewed to the upside or

Table 3.3 Construction of Informed_IT index

3. Informed_IT—questions and answers	Scores	Source of information
3.1 Decision-making process		Information from website
(a) Voting	1	
(b) Consensus	0.66	
(c) Governor as a single decision-maker	0.33	
(d) No information	0	
3.2 External members in a monetary policy committee		Provision in legal act
(a) Many (more than a half of the committee)	1	
(b) Some (up to a half of the committee)	0.5	
(c) None	0	
3.3 Expertise required at appointment		Provision in legal act
(a) Included as a rule related to appointment	1	
(b) Not included as a rule related to appointment or no information	0	
3.4 Ownership of forecasts		Information from website
(a) Committee	1	
(b) Bank	0.66	
(c) Staff	0.33	
(d) No forecasts	0	
3.5 Frequency of publishing inflation reports with forecasts		Information from website
(a) Every second decision-making meeting or more often	1	
(b) Less often	0.5	
(c) No forecasts	0	
3.6 Forecast horizon		Information from website
(a) Above 2 years	1	
(b) Above 1 year and up to 2 years	0.66	
(c) Up to 1 year	0.33	
(d) No forecasts	0	
3.7 Forecast variables		Information from website
(a) Inflation, GDP, and interest rate	1	
(b) Inflation and GDP	0.66	
(c) Inflation only	0.33	
(d) No forecasts	0	
3.8 Forecast presentation		Information from website
(a) Fan Charts—showing central projections and uncertainty intervals	1	
(b) Line Charts—showing central projections	0.66	
(c) No Charts—only description	0.33	
(d) No forecasts	0	
3.9 Forecast presentation at press conferences		Information from website
(a) Yes	1	
(b) No or no forecasts	0	
3.10 Recommendation from staff for the committee		Information from website
(a) Yes	1	
(b) No or no information	0	

Source: Own compilation.

to the downside, which, at times, may be important. Moreover, explaining projections at press conferences is thought to improve their quality, since allowing for scrutiny by others should be a motivating factor for constructing them in a proper way. At the same time, as central banks' staff is generally well prepared to regularly analyse issues relevant for monetary policy, since this is their main responsibility, the recommendations from staff for decision-making bodies are also considered beneficial. The Informed_IT index has a lot in common with the measure of economic transparency.

3.4.5 Explicatory_IT index

The Explicatory_IT index (Table 3.4) relates to the ease with which one can follow monetary policy.[8] Therefore, it rewards regular—not too frequent and not too infrequent—decision-making meetings, whereas the dominant practice of eight meetings per year is given the highest score. Likewise, the size of a decision-making body should be big enough to allow for involving individuals with different expertise, and small enough to allow for a proper exchange of views. The role of the governor should be neither too strong nor too weak, so that collegial decision-making can show its strengths, but with the voice of the governor worth listening to, as guidance for the committee's view. In line with that reasoning, simple majority voting with a quorum including the governor is believed to be the most advisable option for reaching decisions. To allow for the assessment of a possible divergence of opinions among decision-makers, voting records, information on dissenting views, and the projections of individual committee members are considered useful. In order to better understand the decisions, again ownership of forecasts is important, as well as possible recommendations from staff. Holding press conferences after each decision-making meeting and publishing staff background reports clearly additionally facilitate understanding policy actions.

It is worth noting that the Explicatory_IT index does not simply value using certain types of publications by central banks as a part of their communication policies. Rather, the index focuses on the content of available materials that should enable the public to understand monetary policy. It can be seen as relating to the measures of procedural transparency proposed in the literature.

Perhaps somewhat counter-intuitively, the Explicatory_IT index does not include speeches. The reason is that due to language issues it is difficult to check, in a unified way across the analysed central banks, the extent to which speeches are used. At the same time, there are many arguments that make that omission less problematic. Some of them relate to the fact that most speeches are thought of as an instrument to spread the message coming from a given central bank to different audiences. Therefore—apart from rare cases when they are used as a tool to clarify or correct some misunderstandings—speeches should remain in line with other communication instruments

Table 3.4 Construction of Explicatory_IT index

4. Explicatory_IT—questions and answers	*Scores*	*Source of information*
4.1 Frequency of decision-making meetings		Information from website
(a) Eight per year	1	
(b) More than eight per year	0.66	
(c) Less than eight per year	0.33	
(d) No fixed schedule	0	
4.2 Size of a monetary policy committee		Provision in legal act
(a) Above 5 members and up to 10 members	1	
(b) Up to 5 members	0.5	
(c) Above 10 members	0	
4.3 Role of the governor in decision-making processes		Provision in legal act
(a) Strong position of the governor—chair, casting vote, and less than four other members	1	
(b) Very strong position of the governor—a single decision-maker	0.5	
(c) Less strong position of the governor	0	
4.4 Rules on quorum and voting		Provision in legal act
(a) Simple rules (quorum with the governor and simple majority voting)	1	
(b) Complicated rules on quorum or voting	0.5	
(c) No information	0	
4.5 Ownership of forecasts		Information from website
(a) Committee	1	
(b) Bank	0.66	
(c) Staff	0.33	
(d) No forecasts	0	
4.6 Forecast of individual decision-makers		Information from website
(a) Published	1	
(b) Not published	0	
4.7 Press conferences after decision-making meetings		Information from website
(a) Yes—after each decision-making meeting	1	
(b) Yes—but less often, e.g. only when a new forecast is published*	0.5	
(c) No	0	
4.8 Voting records		Information from website
(a) Full voting records available with a short lag**	1	
(b) Only ratio of votes available with a short lag	0.66	
(c) Any voting records available with a longer lag	0.33	
(d) No voting records or no information on decision-making processes	0	

(Continued)

Table 3.4 (*Continued*) Construction of Explicatory_IT index

4. Explicatory_IT—questions and answers	Scores	Source of information
4.9 Revealing dissenting views—in press releases, press conferences, minutes, etc.		Information from website
(a) Yes—dissenting views presented explicitly (with names)	1	
(b) Yes—dissenting views presented, but without indicating names	0.5	
(c) No revealing of dissenting views (all documents present views of the committee)	0	
4.10 Recommendation from staff for the committee and publishing staff background reports		Information from website
(a) Both recommendations and staff reports	1	
(b) Either recommendations or staff reports	0.5	
(c) None or no information	0	

Source: Own compilation.
Notes: * Or every second meeting, as in the case of Switzerland. ** Or decisions are taken either by the governor as a single decision-maker, or by a committee by consensus. Short lag means before the next decision-making meeting.

employed by the central bank, such as, for example, press releases or press conferences, and thus should not bring too much news. Other arguments relate to the difficulty in assessing whether more speeches are advisable, or—on the contrary—less speeches are advisable. First, having said what should be the aim of most speeches, the speeches of individual members of collegial decision-making bodies may, indeed, give more insights on their individual opinions. However, this is not necessarily beneficial for the public, since it can give rise to the cacophony issues. Second, analysing speeches may, in fact, require significant resources, in terms of time and knowledge, in order to read all of them, which in itself may be problematic, especially if all speeches are not made available to the observers of central banks' actions in a language understandable to them. All in all, valuing speeches that would do justice to all of these considerations would be challenging.

3.4.6 Transparent_IT index

The Transparent_IT index (Table 3.5) assesses communication policy of a central bank, understood as using certain types of publications or, more broadly, certain communication tools for sending the message on monetary policy to the public. Thus, publishing monetary policy strategy, annual reports, press releases (best with a forward-looking component), inflation reports, minutes (best with an indication of dissenting views), and staff background reports is valued. Also, holding press conferences, as well as short lags in revealing voting records, is thought to increase the transparency of a central bank. Again, speeches are not included for the reasons

Table 3.5 Construction of Transparent_IT index

5. Transparent_IT—questions and answers	Scores	Source of information
5.1 Publishing monetary policy strategy and annual reports		Information from website
(a) Yes—both publications available as separate documents	1	
(b) Yes—one publication available as a separate document	0.66	
(c) Annual report as a compilation of other reports and strategy described only at the website	0.33	
(d) Not published	0	
5.2 Press releases		Information from website
(a) Yes—after each decision-making meeting	1	
(b) Yes—but only after some decision-making meetings	0.5	
(c) No	0	
5.3 Forward-looking component of press releases		Information from website
(a) Yes—rather explicit	1	
(b) Yes—but rather vague	0.5	
(c) No or no press releases	0	
5.4 Frequency of publishing inflation reports with forecasts		Information from website
(a) At least four per year	1	
(b) Three per year	0.66	
(c) Below three per year	0.33	
(d) No forecasts	0	
5.5 Press conferences—any		Information from website
(a) After each decision-making meeting	1	
(b) When a new projection is published or every second meeting	0.66	
(c) Only after a decision-making meeting when the policy was changed	0.33	
(d) None	0	
5.6 Publishing minutes		Information from website
(a) Yes	1	
(b) No	0	
5.7 Revealing dissenting views in minutes		Information from website
(a) Yes—indicating individual views (with names)	1	
(b) Yes—indicating some divergence of views, but without indicating names	0.5	
(c) No indication of divergence of views or no minutes	0	
5.8 Lags in releasing ratios of votes		Information from website
(a) No lag in releasing ratios of votes (in press releases/press conferences)	1	
(b) Some lag in releasing ratios of votes (in minutes/inflation reports)	0.66	
(c) Long lag in releasing ratios of votes (in annual reports)	0.33	
(d) No voting records available	0	

(*Continued*)

Table 3.5 (Continued) Construction of Transparent_IT index

5. Transparent_IT—questions and answers	Scores	Source of information
5.9 Lags in releasing full voting records		information from website
(a) No lag in releasing full voting records (in press releases/press conferences)	1	
(b) Some lag in releasing full voting records (in minutes/inflation reports)	0.66	
(c) Long lag in releasing full voting records (in annual reports)	0.33	
(d) No full voting records available	0	
5.10 Publishing staff background reports		information from website
(a) Yes – published with a very short lag (up to a few days)	1	
(b) Yes – but published with some lag (after a week or later)	0.5	
(c) No or no information	0	

Source: Own compilation.

mentioned earlier. The Transparent_IT index seems more closely linked to the measures of policy transparency present in the literature.

3.4.7 Accountable_IT index

The Accountable_IT index (Table 3.6), apart from rewarding transparent monetary policy, also includes questions related to regular reporting to parliaments, either via written reports or via hearings. Also, a special form of democratic control, i.e. a requirement to prepare an open letter once inflation breaches the target,[9] is treated as a way to increase accountability. Including rules related to the appointment of decision-makers that limit the possibility of conflicts of interest, as well as rules on dismissal related to absences of committee members should additionally support conducting monetary policy in a responsible manner.

3.4.8 Fully_fledged_IT index

The Fully-fledged_IT index (Table 3.7), as an average of the discussed individual indices, summarises all the institutional issues indicated earlier. It can be interpreted as a proxy for the credibility of a central bank, stemming from acting within an advisable institutional set-up, i.e. institutional arrangements involving a considerable degree of independence, as well as high accountability and transparency standards.

Before looking at the proposed indices in more detail, it is useful to be aware of what sources of information they are based on, and what aspects they most value.

Table 3.6 Construction of Accountable_IT index

6. Accountable_IT—questions and answers	Scores	Source of information
6.1 Publishing monetary policy strategy		Information from website
(a) Yes—as a separate document	1	
(b) Yes—only as a description at the website	0.5	
(c) Not published	0	
6.2 Publishing annual report		Information from website
(a) Yes—as a separate document	1	
(b) Yes—as a compilation of other reports	0.5	
(c) Not published	0	
6.3 Parliamentary hearings		Provision in legal act
(a) Yes	1	
(b) No or no information	0	
6.4 Submitting written reports to parliament		Provision in legal act
(a) Yes	1	
(b) No or no information	0	
6.5 Frequency of reporting to parliament (via reports or hearings)		Information from website
(a) At least three times per year	1	
(b) Less than three times per year or no information on frequency	0.5	
(c) No reporting or no information	0	
6.6 Open letters		Information from website
(a) Yes	1	
(b) No	0	
6.7 Rules on dismissal related to absences		Provision in legal act
(a) Indicated as a reason for dismissal	1	
(b) No or no information	0	
6.8 No conflict of interest required at appointment		Provision in legal act
(a) Included as a rule related to appointment	1	
(b) No or no information	0	
6.9 Frequency of publishing inflation reports with forecasts		Information from website
(a) At least four per year	1	
(b) Three per year	0.66	
(c) Below three per year	0.33	
(d) No forecasts	0	
6.10 Publishing press releases, minutes, and holding press conference after each decision-making meeting		Information from website
(a) Yes—all of the above	1	
(b) Two of the above	0.5	
(c) Otherwise	0	

Source: Own compilation.

Table 3.7 Construction of Fully_fledged_IT index

7. *Fully_fledged_IT index—construction*	
1. Mature_IT index	
2. Independent_IT index	
3. Informed_IT index	Average of all the
4. Explicatory_IT index	indices
5. Transparent_IT index	
6. Accountable_IT index	

Source: Own compilation.

Regarding the first topic, the share of legal provisions in individual indices is rather small, with the prominent exception of the Independent_IT index (Charts 3.1 and 3.2). In turn, the majority of indices are based on information taken from central banks' websites. This means that they reflect changes occurring in a specific area over years, and have a time-series dimension.

Regarding the aspects that are most valued, one can distinguish between questions related to the following main topics: mandate (who specifies it, how it is formulated, how often it is announced, what the target level and time horizon are, etc.); decision-makers (what rules govern the appointment and dismissal of decision-makers, what the composition of a decision-making body is, what the frequency of decision-making meetings is, etc.); forecasts (how often forecasts are prepared, what variables are forecast, what the forecast horizon is, whether forecasts of individual decision-makers are published, etc.); communication (what the standard communication channels used at a given central bank are, what additional materials are useful in understanding monetary policy, whether voting records are made available, etc.); or other (there are only four questions put in that category—1.1 on how experienced with IT is a given country, and 2.8, 2.9, and 2.10 related most directly to possible political influences on monetary authorities). Sometimes including a question in a selected category is based on an arbitrary assessment, but in most cases the assignment is rather straightforward.

Distinguishing between the different topics seems useful in getting an idea of what elements are considered most important and shape the levels of the proposed indices (Charts 3.3 and 3.4). Clearly, the issues related to communication are greatly valued, with their shares being very high especially for the Transparent_IT index and the Accountable_IT index, which—given the scope of the two indices—should not be surprising. A bit less, but still much weight is associated with rules referring to decision-makers, questions dealing with mandates, and issues related to forecasts. However, whereas rules referring to decision-makers

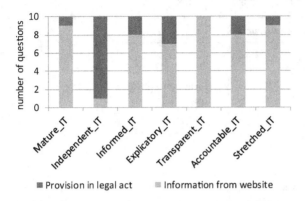

Chart 3.1 Sources of information used to construct the proposed individual indices.

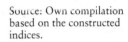

Source: Own compilation based on the constructed indices.

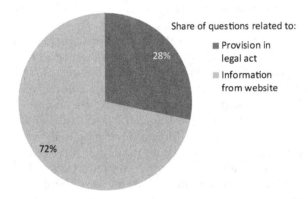

Chart 3.2 Sources of information used to construct Fully_fledged_IT index.

are present in different indices (with their highest share visible in the Independent_IT index), questions dealing with mandates are concentrated in the Mature_IT index, and issues related to forecasts value most in the Informed_IT index.

Moving to the Fully_fledged_IT index, it looks rather balanced, with the most prominent, but not dominating role of communication, followed with equal importance by the other three topics. This speaks in favour of calling that index a summarising index.

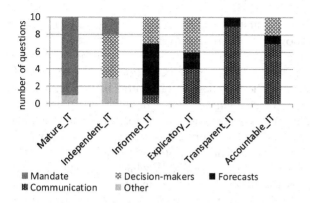

Source: Own compilation
based on the constructed
indices.

Chart 3.3 Topics included in the proposed individual
indices.

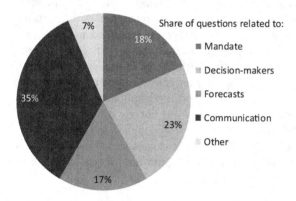

Chart 3.4 Topics included in Fully_fledged_IT index.

3.5 Comparing inflation targeting central banks' institutional set-ups

Before analysing the proposed indices, it is important to recall that the first inflation targeters originated from advanced economies. At the same time, only in the first decade of IT expansion, the majority of newcomers stemmed from advanced economies. Despite the fact that emerging market economies joined the group of inflation targeters somewhat later, since the early 2000s they have already constituted the majority of inflation targeting economies.

3.5.1 General trends

Regarding individual indices, a first look at the scattered plots of all observations shows that a clear move towards an improvement of institutional set-ups for both advanced and emerging market economies can only be seen in the case of the Mature_IT index (Chart 3.28 in Appendix 3). For the Transparent_IT index, a tendency to increase the openness of IT central banks can also be noted, although in the case of emerging market economies it is much more muted (Chart 3.32 in Appendix 3). In advanced economies, upward-sloping time trends can also be detected for the Informed_IT index, the Explicatory_IT index (Charts 3.30 and 3.31 in Appendix 3), and—although marginal—the Accountable_IT index (Chart 3.33 in Appendix 3), while in emerging market economies the fitted trends are almost flat for these indices.

For the Independent_IT index (Chart 3.29 in Appendix 3), which, as already mentioned, has no time-series dimension, what can be noted is that judging by the levels of the index, no general trend towards greater independence can be observed that would result in newcomers' independence being higher than that of more experienced inflation targeters. Importantly, since independence levels for a given country are assumed not to change over the analysed period, it is not possible to investigate them in more detail.

A second observation to make is that differences in the levels of the indices between advanced and emerging market economies can be quite easily detected in the case of the Mature_IT index, the Explicatory_IT index, and the Transparent_IT index. The case is less clear cut for the Accountable_IT index, and no material differences can be seen looking at the Independent_IT index and the Informed_IT index. This would suggest that advanced economies enjoy better institutional set-ups in many, but not all, analysed aspects.

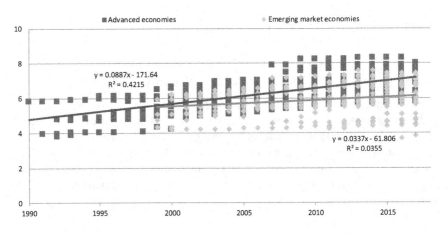

Chart 3.5 Evolution of Fully_fledged_IT index in IT advanced and emerging market economies. Source: Own compilation based on the constructed indices.

The summary index indicates that combining the information from all the individual indices related to central banks' institutional arrangements results in the Fully_fledged_IT index that has an upward-sloping time trend, although it is much more steep for advanced economies (Chart 3.5). Moreover, it is evident that emerging market economies are characterised by the lower levels of the Fully_fledged_IT index, which would imply their weaker institutional set-ups, possibly translating into lower credibility.

3.5.2 Changes at the country level

Scatter plots are, however, somewhat blurred by newcomers that often, when adopting an IT framework, were only developing some communication tools or forecasting capacities, which is reflected in the generally

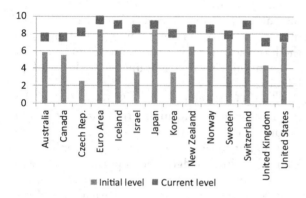

Chart 3.6 Changes of Mature_IT index in IT advanced economies.

Source: Own compilation based on the constructed indices.

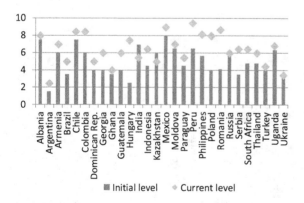

Chart 3.7 Changes of Mature_IT index in IT emerging market economies.

213

lower levels of their indices. To see more clearly the dimension of this issue, a comparison of the initial and current levels of the analysed indices can be useful, which is possible for all the indices apart from the Independent_IT index. The Independent_IT index is, however, reported to discuss some apparent differences in its levels between advanced and emerging market economies.

Considering the Mature_IT index (Charts 3.6 and 3.7), its initial levels for advanced economies were rather diversified among countries, while its current levels are close to 8 for most of the advanced economy inflation targeters. In turn, in emerging market economies, while the dispersion of the initial levels of the Mature_IT index was comparable to that of advanced economies, which means it was sizeable, the current dispersion is by no means lower. Looking at the changes of the Mature_IT index, they were quite pronounced in many countries, with somewhat bigger improvement recorded among advanced economies.[10] As a consequence, the current levels of the Mature_IT index are, on average, significantly higher in advanced economies compared to emerging market economies. In the latter group they are close to 7, whereas also among emerging market economies there are countries with very high levels of the Mature_IT index.

Regarding the Independent_IT index (Charts 3.8 and 3.9), its dispersion is very high both in advanced and in emerging market economies, and its levels are comparable in both groups of countries, with an average even somewhat higher for emerging market economies. This may signal that these countries acknowledged the importance of central banks' independence while drafting legal acts on their monetary authorities, possibly, not least, due to previous negative experiences with the lack of central banks' autonomy. What needs to be stressed, however,

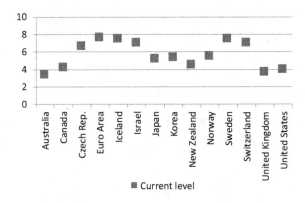

■ Current level

Chart 3.8 Levels of Independent_IT index in IT advanced economies.

Source: Own compilation based on the constructed indices.

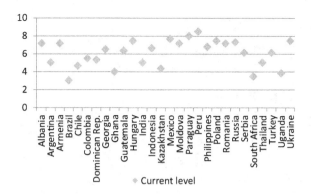

Chart 3.9 Levels of Independent_IT index in IT
emerging market economies.

is that the Independent_IT index measures only formal independence, which may not always correspond to the actual monetary authorities' autonomy.

Moving to the Informed_IT index (Charts 3.10 and 3.11), its initial levels were highly diversified among advanced economies, while its current levels are, similarly as for the Mature_IT index, close to 8 for most of them. In emerging market economies, the dispersion of the Informed_IT index was and remains high, but mainly due to outliers, with many emerging market economy inflation targeters scoring close to 7. Comparing the changes of the Informed_IT index, its improvement was considerable in many advanced economies, and only in some emerging market economies. However, the current level of the Informed_IT index is, on average, only somewhat higher in advanced economies compared to emerging market economies.

Concerning the Explicatory_IT index (Charts 3.12 and 3.13), for both groups of economies its initial levels were rather diversified and are still far from being homogeneous. That said, its improvement in many advanced and emerging market economies was substantial, with an average somewhat higher for advanced economies. However, what is most noticeable is that the levels of the Explicatory_IT index are visibly lower than those of the previously discussed indices. This holds even for the best performers that do not exceed 8, while levels around 6 are already a good score.

Analysing the Transparent_IT index (Charts 3.14 and 3.15) reveals that its dispersion remains rather high both in advanced and in emerging market economies, with not much difference in that respect between the two groups of countries. This is so, despite spectacular improvements recorded over time in some economies. Looking at the averages, they are significantly higher for advanced economies, with one of

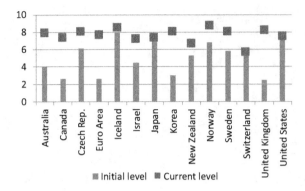

Chart 3.10 Changes of Informed_IT index in IT advanced economies.

Source: Own compilation based on the constructed indices.

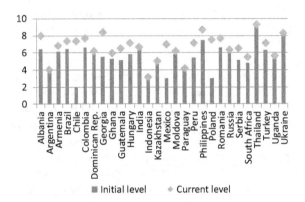

Chart 3.11 Changes of Informed_IT index in IT emerging market economies.

them—Sweden—hitting the score of 10. However, also for many other countries, including some emerging market economies, the Transparent_IT index reaches levels close to 8–9.

The initial levels of the Accountable_IT index (Charts 3.16 and 3.17) were much less diversified in advanced economies compared to emerging market economies, which remains valid for the current levels of the index as well. What is also evident in the case of the Accountable_IT index is that its levels have not improved much over time. Only in a very few countries can some increases of the index be reported. Regarding its averages, they are not much different for advanced and emerging market economies, since in both cases they are close to 7.

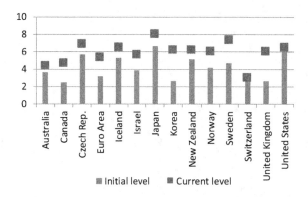

Chart 3.12 Changes of Explicatory_IT index in IT advanced economies.

Source: Own compilation based on the constructed indices.

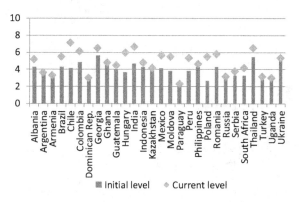

Chart 3.13 Changes of Explicatory_IT index in IT emerging market economies.

Finally, the Fully_fledged_IT index (Charts 3.18 and 3.19), as an average of all the above individual indices, is not very diversified, which holds both for its initial and its current levels, irrespective of which group of economies is considered. Looking at the changes, the summary index improved much more in advanced economies than in emerging market economies, reaching levels close to 7–8 for most of the advanced economies. The difference in the scale of changes means that emerging market economies are characterised, on average, by lower levels of the index. While there are also emerging market economies with the Fully_fledged_IT index close to 8, the majority hovers around 6.

Since changes in the Fully_fledged_IT index result from changes in individual indices, it is also worth looking at the main drivers for an

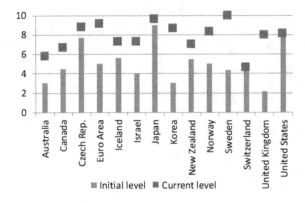

Chart 3.14 Changes of Transparent_IT index in IT advanced economies.

Source: Own compilation based on the constructed indices.

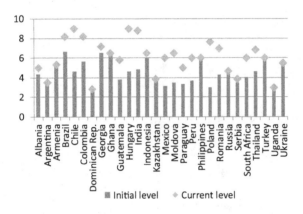

Chart 3.15 Changes of Transparent_IT index in IT emerging market economies.

improvement of the summary index in each of the analysed countries (Charts 3.20 and 3.21).

For certain countries, the only, or predominant, factor that drove the improvement was the move in the Mature_IT index, but for the majority of economies the improvement stemmed from a mix of factors (Charts 3.22 and 3.23). Apart from changes in the Mature_IT index, other visible contributors to higher scores in the Fully_fledged_IT index included the Transparent_IT index, the Informed_IT index, and the Explicatory_IT index, with relatively little contribution from changes in the Accountable_IT index. In these patterns, there are no material differences between advanced and emerging market economies.

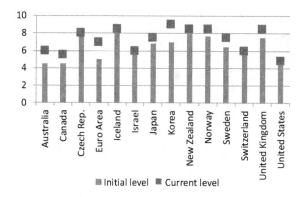

Chart 3.16 Changes of Accountable_IT index in IT advanced economies.

Source: Own compilation based on the constructed indices.

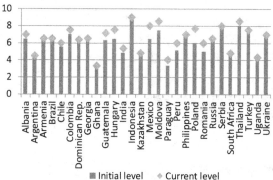

Chart 3.17 Changes of Accountable_IT index in IT emerging market economies.

The fact that, in the past, many inflation targeters improved their institutional set-ups is important, and, in particular, may mean that new-comers significantly influence the computed averages. Thus, to make a more fair comparison between advanced and emerging market economies, a more detailed analysis is warranted. Especially since a number of emerging market economies, in many respects, are characterised by already favourable institutional set-ups, which is not clearly visible looking at the averages.

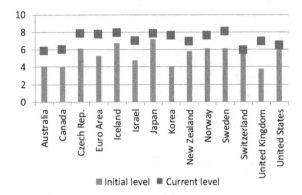

Chart 3.18 Changes of Fully_fledged_IT index in IT advanced economies.

Source: Own compilation based on the constructed indices.

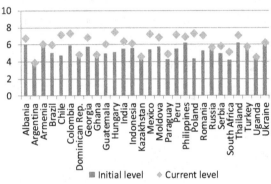

Chart 3.19 Changes of Fully_fledged_IT index in IT emerging market economies.

3.5.3 Comparison of advanced and emerging market economies

It seems justified to look at inflation targeters divided into three distinct "age" categories: the ones that adopted an IT framework in the 1990s, the ones that did it in the 2000s, and the ones that joined the group most recently, meaning in 2010 or later.

The first group, for simplicity called the "old" inflation targeters, includes 9 advanced economies and 4 emerging market economies (dates of IT adoption by a given country are indicated in parenthesis): Australia (1993), Canada (1991), the Czech Republic (1998),[11] the euro area (1998),[12] Israel (1992), Korea (1998), New Zealand (1990), Sweden (1995), and the United Kingdom (1992)—from advanced economies, and Brazil (1999), Chile (1999), Colombia (1999), and Poland (1999)—from emerging market economies.

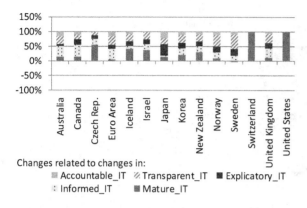

Changes related to changes in:
▨ Accountable_IT ▨ Transparent_IT ■ Explicatory_IT
⁙ Informed_IT ■ Mature_IT

Chart 3.20 Sources of changes to Fully_fledged_IT index in IT advanced economies.

Source: Own compilation based on the constructed indices.

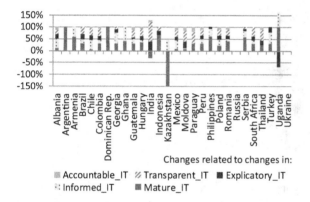

Changes related to changes in:
▨ Accountable_IT ▨ Transparent_IT ■ Explicatory_IT
⁙ Informed_IT ■ Mature_IT

Chart 3.21 Sources of changes to Fully_fledged_IT index in IT emerging market economies.

The second group, called the "middle-aged" inflation targeters, comprises 3 advanced economies and 15 emerging market economies: Iceland (2001), Norway (2001), and Switzerland (2000)—from advanced economies, and Albania (2009), Armenia (2006), Georgia (2009), Ghana (2007), Guatemala (2005), Hungary (2001), Indonesia (2005), Mexico (2001), Peru (2002), the Philippines (2002), Romania (2005), Serbia (2009), South Africa (2000), Thailand (2000), and Turkey (2006)—from emerging market economies.

Finally, the last group, called the "new" inflation targeters, consists of 2 advanced economies and 9 emerging market economies: Japan (2012) and the United States (2012)—from advanced economies, and Argentina (2016),[13] the Dominican Republic (2012), India (2015), Kazakhstan (2015),

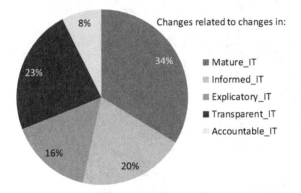

Chart 3.22 Sources of overall changes to Fully_fledged_
IT index in IT advanced economies.

Source: Own
compilation based
on the constructed
indices.

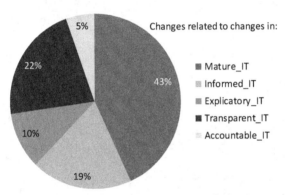

Chart 3.23 Sources of overall changes to Fully_fledged_
IT index in IT emerging market economies.

Moldova (2010), Paraguay (2011), Russia (2015), Uganda (2011), and
Ukraine (2017)—from emerging market economies.

What should be kept in mind is that a country is included in the averages
from the moment it adopted an IT framework. This means that the changes
in the averages partly reflect the evolution of a certain aspect related to central banks' institutional set-ups over time, and partly the inclusion of newcomers—if newcomers were characterised by institutional arrangements not
very close to the average when joining the group of inflation targeters.

For the Mature_IT index (Chart 3.34 in Appendix 3), there has been a
quite significant discrepancy between the averages covering all advanced
and all emerging market economies, with no clear convergence visible in
the data. The picture looks, however, very different in the case of the "old"
inflation targeters (Chart 3.35 in Appendix 3). For these countries, which

anyway—from the very beginning—were not much distanced from each other, one can see almost full convergence, with the current average level of the Mature_IT index for the "old" emerging market economy inflation targeters being very close to the average level of the index for the "old" advanced economy inflation targeters. In turn, for the "middle-aged" and the "new" inflation targeters, the distance between the two group of economies has remained significant, with no signs of diminishing (Charts 3.36 and 3.37 in Appendix 3).

What is also notable is that currently the average level of the Mature_IT index for advanced economies is almost the same (around 8) for all "age" groups, whereas for emerging market economies it declines from around 8 for the "old", to around 7 for the "middle-aged", and to around 5 for the "new" inflation targeters.

Considering the Independent_IT index (Chart 3.38 in Appendix 3), both the "old" and the "middle-aged" inflation targeters seem homogeneous with respect to formal independence levels (Charts 3.39 and 3.40 in Appendix 3), regardless of whether they are advanced or emerging market economies. Only in the case of the "new" inflation targeters this cannot be said (Chart 3.41 in Appendix 3), with emerging market economies characterised by somewhat higher average levels of the index, with not much convergence of advanced economies observed, at least so far.

Interestingly, currently the average level of the Independent_IT index for all "age" groups is close to 6, except for the "new" advanced economy inflation targeters, where it is lower, at around 4.

Moving to the Informed_IT index (Chart 3.42 in Appendix 3), when looking at the averages across all inflation targeters, it seems that following the global financial crisis some divergence can be observed between advanced and emerging market economies. However, for the "old" inflation targeters the convergence between the two groups of countries, which in fact have never been much distanced from each other, is now complete (Chart 3.43 in Appendix 3). For the "middle-aged" inflation targeters, some small difference persists, but it does not rise over time (Chart 3.44 in Appendix 3). Only for the "new" inflation targeters is the discrepancy significant (Chart 3.45 in Appendix 3). This clearly shows that, in fact, there is no effect related to the global financial crisis *per se*. The crisis might have simply pushed some countries to adopt an IT framework, which—especially in the case of emerging market economies—concerned economies with somewhat weaker institutional set-ups, as evidenced by the lower average level of their Informed_IT index.

Similarly as in the case of the Mature_IT index, currently the average level of the Informed_IT index for advanced economies in all "age" groups is around 8, whereas for emerging market economies it declines from the score of 8 by around 1 point when moving from the "old" to the "middle-aged" inflation targeters, and by another 1 point when moving from the "middle-aged" to the "new" inflation targeters.

Regarding the Explicatory_IT index (Chart 3.46 in Appendix 3), again, the averages across all inflation targeters could suggest that following the global financial crisis some divergence appeared between advanced and emerging market economies, which is not the case. The "old" inflation targeters have always been and continue to be fully converged, with the averages for the two groups of countries at around 6 (Chart 3.47 in Appendix 3). The situation with the "middle-aged" inflation targeters is the same, except for the average level of the Explicatory_IT index for advanced and emerging market economies which is slightly lower, at around 5 (Chart 3.48 in Appendix 3). In turn, for the "new" inflation targeters the average for advanced economies that currently stands at around 7, is significantly higher than the average for emerging market economies, at around 4 (Chart 3.49 in Appendix 3).

This indicates that the average levels of the Explicatory_IT index within "age" groups are not homogeneous in either group of economies. A prominent feature is that the "new" advanced economy inflation targeters are the best performers with respect to the Explicatory_IT index, whereas the "new" emerging market economy inflation targeters score the worst.

As in the case of the previous two indices, the averages of the Transparent_IT index for the full sample would wrongly suggest divergence after 2008 (Chart 3.50 in Appendix 3), whereas advanced and emerging market economy inflation targeters classified as "old" and "middle-aged", which have never been much different from each other, are currently fully converged—at a score of around 8 for the "old" and a score of around 6 for the "middle-aged" ones (Charts 3.51 and 3.52 in Appendix 3). Only the "new" inflation targeters are displaying significant differences between advanced and emerging market economies, with the averages at around 9 and 5, respectively (Chart 3.53 in Appendix 3).

Again, the average levels across "age" groups show that they are quite diverged within both groups of economies, with the "new" advanced economy inflation targeters scoring the best with respect to the Transparent_IT index, and the "new" emerging market economy inflation targeters being the worst.

The averages of the Accountable_IT index are almost flat across most of the subgroups, with no signs of either convergence or divergence noted (Chart 3.54 in Appendix 3). Overall, the discrepancies between advanced and emerging market economies are rather small, across all categories.

However, the levels of the averages are not the same for all countries across the "age" groups. Within advanced economies, currently the average for the "old" inflation targeters stands at around 7 (Chart 3.55 in Appendix 3), for the "middle-aged" ones it rises to around 8 (Chart 3.56 in Appendix 3), and for the "new" ones it declines to around 6 (Chart 3.57 in Appendix 3).

Within emerging market economies, currently the averages for both the "old" and the "middle-aged" inflation targeters are close to 7, and for the "new" inflation targeters it approaches 6.

The Fully_fledged_IT index is, by definition, somewhere in between, as evidenced by the comparison of the averages across countries and time (Chart 3.58 in Appendix 3).

For the "old" inflation targeters there has never been any divergence between advanced and emerging market economies with respect to the Fully_fledged_IT index, with the averages for both groups currently standing at around 7 (Chart 3.59 in Appendix 3). For the "middle-aged" and the "new" advanced economy inflation targeters, the averages are the same. At the same time, the averages for emerging market economies are decreasing by around 1 point when moving from the "old" to the "middle-aged" ones, and by another 1 point when moving from the "middle-aged" to the "new" inflation targeters. As a result, the discrepancies between advanced and emerging market economies in the case of the "middle-aged" and the "new" inflation targeters rise visibly (Charts 3.60 and 3.61 in Appendix 3).

Overall, for the "old" inflation targeters there are either no or only small differences between advanced and emerging market economies regarding all the analysed aspects of central banks' institutional set-ups (Table 3.8). For the "middle-aged" inflation targeters merely in the case of the Mature_IT index the discrepancy is somewhat bigger, with all other indices being almost homogeneous. In turn, for the "new" inflation targeters the gaps between advanced and emerging market economies are sizeable.

What is somewhat surprising is that it seems that only in the case of the "old" inflation targeters has there been a clear convergence between advanced and emerging market economies regarding institutional aspects where the indices at the beginning were not homogeneous across these two groups of countries. At the same time, for the "middle-aged" and the "new" inflation targeters, no convergence between advanced and emerging market economies can be observed. If the averages of the initial levels of the indices were close to each other, they stayed close, and if they were distanced from each other, they stayed distanced. This is especially worrisome for the "new" emerging market economy inflation targeters, since they greatly diverge from advanced economy inflation targeters and also significantly from the "old" and the "middle-aged" emerging market economy inflation targeters.

Looking again at the averages across the "age" groups within advanced and emerging market economies, it is clear that advanced economies are much more converged with each other than emerging market economies. Advanced economies, irrespective of when they became inflation targeters, are either fully or almost fully converged in the case of the Mature_IT index (Chart 3.62 in Appendix 3) and the Informed_IT index (Chart 3.66 in Appendix 3), while some discrepancies between them can be noted in the Independent_IT index (Chart 3.64 in Appendix 3), the Explicatory_IT

Table 3.8 Convergence of indices in IT advanced and emerging market economies

		Mature_IT	Independent_IT	Informed_IT	Explicatory_IT	Transparent_IT	Accountable_IT	Fully-fledged_IT
All	Distance	Some	Small	Some	Some	Some	Small	Some
	Convergence	No	No	No	No	No	No	No
"Old"	Distance	Small	Small	None	None	None	Small	None
	Convergence	Yes	No	Yes	No	No	No	No
"Middle-aged"	Distance	Some	None	Small	None	Small	Small	Small
	Convergence	No		No	No	No	No	No
"New"	Distance	High	Some	Some	High	High	Small	Some
	Convergence	No	No	No	No	No	No	No
Description of coding used:								
Assessing convergence	No—no visible convergence			Assessing distance	High—high differences in levels	High—high differences in levels	Small—small differences in levels	
	Yes—visible convergence				Some—some differences in levels	Some—some differences in levels	No—no differences in levels	

Source: Own compilation based on the constructed indices.

index (Chart 3.68 in Appendix 3), the Transparent_IT index (Chart 3.70 in Appendix 3), and the Accountable_IT index (Chart 3.72 in Appendix 3). For emerging market economies, some major differences between the "age" groups can be seen in all indices, without any visible signs of convergence over time (Charts 3.63, 3.65, 3.67, 3.69, 3.71, and 3.73) in Appendix 3.

As a result, the summary index indicates that advanced economy inflation targeters are generally fully converged, whereas the same cannot be said for emerging market economies (Charts 3.74 and 3.75 in Appendix 3). While the average level of the Fully_fledged_IT index for the "middle-aged" group seems quite close to the average for the "old" emerging market economy inflation targeters, the distance between them and the "new" inflation targeters has been substantial and is not diminishing over time.

3.6 Constructing an index on approach to financial stability and on policy instruments

The construction of an index related to central banks' response to the recent crises (the Stretched_IT index) is presented separately, because—despite many similarities with the previously discussed indices—conceptually it differs significantly from them. For that reason, it is not included in the Fully_fledged_IT index.

3.6.1 Stretched_IT index

The Stretched_IT index is thought to capture differences in IT central banks' approaches to financial stability and their use of standard and non-standard monetary policy measures (Table 3.9). It is again a sum of the coded answers to 10 questions associated with the issues of interest, and thus ranges from 1 to 10. The answers are derived from information taken from central banks' websites, and in the case of most questions have a time-series dimension.[14]

However, contrary to indices reflecting the selected aspects of central banks' institutional set-ups, the Stretched_IT index does not value the answers based on their advisability. The given scores simply reflect the extent to which a monetary authority is responsible for financial stability and the extent to which it reached for unorthodox policy measures in the aftermath of the recent crises. The broader the responsibility and the broader the unconventional toolkit used, the higher the scores, but this does not mean a better assessment of a given country. Countries that decided to make several institutions in charge of macroprudential policy and did not face the ZLB problem, do receive lower scores, but this is not an evaluation of their policies. Differences in scores only show how much IT central banks differ between each other with respect to the analysed issues, but should not be used for ranking the countries.

Table 3.9 Construction of Stretched_IT index

8. Stretched_IT—questions and answers	Scores	Source of information
8.1 Responsibility for financial stability		Information from website
(a) With the central bank	1	
(b) Shared—with central bank involved	0.5	
(c) No information	0	
8.2 Publishing financial stability report		Information from website
(a) Yes	1	
(c) No	0	
8.3 Frequency of publishing financial stability report		Information from website
(a) At least two per year	1	
(b) One per year	0.5	
(c) No report	0	
8.4 Main monetary policy instrument		Information from website
(a) Interest rate and FX interventions	1	
(b) Interest rates	0	
8.5 Unconventional monetary policy measures		Information from website
(a) Used	1	
(b) Not used	0	
8.6 Negative interest rates used as an unconventional measure		Information from website
(a) Yes	1	
(b) No	0	
8.7 Forward guidance used as an unconventional measure		Information from website
(a) Yes	1	
(b) No	0	
8.8 FX interventions used as an unconventional measure		Information from website
(a) Yes	1	
(b) No	0	
8.9 Credit easing used as an unconventional measure		Information from website
(a) Yes	1	
(b) No	0	
8.10 Quantitative easing used as an unconventional measure		Information from website
(a) Yes	1	
(b) No	0	

Source: Own compilation.

3.6.2 Main features of Stretched_IT index

Clearly, since the Stretched_IT index is reviewing, in particular, central banks' use of unconventional instruments in response to the recent crises up to 2018, for most countries, in that respect, it is a constant, since only relatively few economies decided to reach for non-standard measures until the

Covid-19 pandemic. As already indicated, advanced economies, on average, were more actively using non-standard tools. For 10 advanced and 5 emerging market economies that prior to the pandemic employed unorthodox policies (Tables 2.13 and 2.14), the parts of the Stretched_IT index related to unconventional monetary policy instruments increased over time, but at the end of the analysed period—in line with the implemented exit strategies—started to decline.

It is, however, interesting to look also at the remaining components of the Stretched_IT index, and compare them between advanced and emerging market economies. These components deal with more institutional issues, and therefore are even less volatile, being either constant or increasing only slightly if a given central bank started to release reports on financial stability during the analysed period or increased the frequency of this publication.

As evidenced by the comparison of arrangements related to assigning the responsibility for financial stability to certain institutions, there is little differences between advanced and emerging market economies (Chart 3.24). In some countries, the responsibility is with the central bank (this is the case for 7 advanced economies and 15 emerging market economies), and in some it is shared by several institutions, involving the central bank (this is the case for 7 advanced economies and 11 emerging market economies). As already indicated, for 2 emerging market economies (Ghana and Paraguay) information indicating how macroprudential policy is conducted is not available.

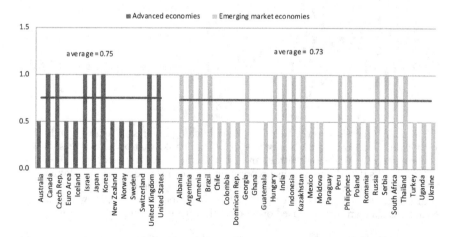

Chart 3.24 Question on assigning the responsibility for financial stability to the central bank in IT economies. Notes: 1—for assigning the responsibility for financial stability to the central bank. 0.5—for shared responsibility. 0—for no information. Source: Own compilation based on information from central banks' websites.

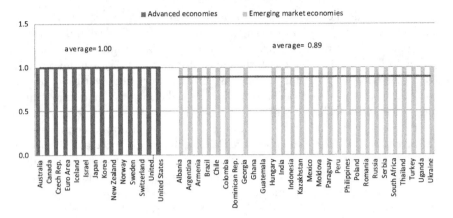

Chart 3.25 Question on publishing reports on financial stability by a given IT central bank. Notes: 1—for central banks that publish reports on financial stability. 0—for central banks that do not publish reports on financial stability. Source: Own compilation based on information from central banks' websites.

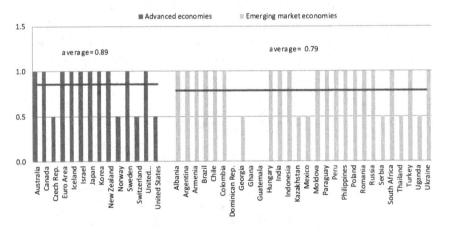

Chart 3.26 Question on the frequency of publishing reports on financial stability by a given IT central bank. Notes: 1—for central banks that publish at least two reports per year. 0.5—for central banks that publish one report per year. 0—for central banks that do not publish reports on financial stability. For the United States it has been assumed that the Federal Reserve will publish two reports per year (the first two reports were published in November 2018 and May 2019). Source: Own compilation based on information from central banks' websites.

Looking at the publication of financial stability reports by the analysed central banks, the vast majority of the reviewed countries regularly prepare such reports (Chart 3.25). As already mentioned, until late 2018, a prominent exception to that rule within advanced economies was the US Federal Reserve, but this changed after the publication of its first report in

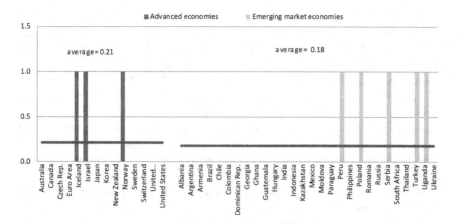

Chart 3.27 Question on the main policy instruments in a given IT economy.
Notes: 1—for central banks pointing to interest rates and FX interventions as the main instruments. 0—for central banks pointing to interest rates only as the main instrument. Source: Own compilation based on information from central banks' websites.

November 2018. Currently, the only IT central banks that do not prepare financial stability reports are those of the Dominican Republic, Ghana, and Guatemala.

Considering the frequency of publishing financial stability reports, the differences between advanced and emerging market economies are marginal (Chart 3.26). Most central banks prepare such reports twice a year (this is the case for 10 advanced economies and 18 emerging market economies), with one country (Moldova) publishing three or four reports annually. The rest of the IT central banks that do prepare a regular overview of financial stability issues do it once a year (this is the case for 3 advanced economies and 6 emerging market economies). This clearly shows that these reports are significantly less frequently published than inflation reports, which may reflect differences in the importance assigned to these two communication tools by the monetary authorities in pursuing their main policy goals. Assuming this optic, this can imply that IT central banks do see price stability as their main task, and believe in the crucial role of communication related to monetary policy for influencing inflation expectations.

Regarding the main policy instruments indicated by the analysed central banks, little difference between advanced and emerging market economies is to be noted (Chart 3.27). All IT countries focus on the use of a short-term interest rate, with only a few mentioning occasional FX interventions in that respect (this is the case for 3 advanced economies and 5 emerging market economies).

Overall, looking at the evolution of the Stretched_IT index (Chart 3.76 in Appendix 3), hardly any difference between the averages covering all advanced and all emerging market economies could be seen prior to the global financial crisis. After the onset of the crisis, the discrepancy became significant and even increased over time up until 2015. This follows from the fact that unconventional monetary policy instruments were—at least during the global financial crisis and the European sovereign crisis—applied more often in advanced economies than in emerging market economies. At the end of the analysed period, however, the discrepancy began to decline, reflecting exit strategies from unorthodox tools being implemented at that time in a number of countries.

Within the "age" groups, the pattern is broadly the same, with the index averages for emerging market economies remaining lower than for advanced economies (Charts 3.77 and 3.78 in Appendix 3).

Considering the "age" groups separately within advanced and emerging market economies, the differences are not major (Charts 3.77 and 3.78 in Appendix 3). Currently, the average levels of the Stretched_IT index for advanced economies are almost the same, at around 4, for all "age" categories. Likewise, for emerging market economies there is no material difference across the "age" groups to be reported, with the average levels of the index for all groups remaining around 3.

3.7 Concluding remarks

The analysis presented in Chapter 3 is based on indices encompassing a very broad set of aspects related to IT central banks' institutional set-ups. Overall, the comparison of their levels across countries and time shows that institutional arrangements do differ between countries and do evolve over time. Thus, they can capture potentially significant developments that may affect the way monetary policy has been conducted.

Importantly, when constructing the indices assessing rules and practices governing the reviewed IT central banks, higher scores are assigned to solutions regarded as preferable in light of the existing research or the prevailing practice. This allows for ranking the institutional set-ups used in different countries.

A few points can be made after analysing the indices. First, a move towards a general improvement of institutional set-ups can be noted both for advanced and emerging market economies, especially when looking at the evolution of the indices at individual country levels over time. On average, advanced economies are characterised by more favourable institutional arrangements compared to emerging market economies, in almost all respects. At the same time, significant differences at the country level can be seen, with some emerging market economies scoring very high in a number of areas related to the analysed institutional set-ups. Interestingly, the recent crises do not seem to influence the evolution in the proposed indices, as evidenced by the fact that the observed tendencies have not changed in recent years, compared to a more distant past.

Moreover, the comparison of advanced and emerging market economies within the distinguished "age" groups indicates that, in fact, the division line is more likely to be related to how long a country has been pursuing an IT strategy, and not so much whether it is classified as an advanced or an emerging market economy. In particular, it seems that in the case of the "old" and the "middle-aged" inflation targeters there has been a clear convergence between advanced and emerging market economies. In turn, the "new" emerging market economy inflation targeters significantly diverge both from advanced economy inflation targeters and also from the "old" and the "middle-aged" emerging market economy inflation targeters.

Finally, comparing approaches to financial stability issues by the analysed central banks reveals that, looking at the averages across country groups, there are no major differences between advanced and emerging market economies in that respect. At the same time, the use of non-standard monetary policy measures was in the analysed period much more intense within the first group of countries. Overall, the index capturing these developments shows that prior to the global financial crisis, hardly any difference between the averages covering all advanced and all emerging market economies could be seen, whereas later the discrepancy became significant. At the end of the reviewed period, however, the implementation of exit strategies from unorthodox tools resulted in a decline in the difference. Importantly this description is referring to the period up until the Covid-19 pandemic which is already beyond the scope of the study.

After developing the indices describing IT central banks' institutional arrangements, the final step of the analysis would be to use them for verifying whether aspects concerning independence, accountability, and transparency significantly affect the outcomes of monetary policy. This will be done in Chapter 4.

Notes

1 However, other factors may influence the actual level of central banks' independence, such as informal relationships between monetary and political authorities.
2 Only in the case of exchange rate targets, the assessment whether a central bank managed to deliver its goal is quite simple, since an exchange rate is a variable that can, in principle, be directly and immediately controlled by monetary authorities.
3 An overview of theoretical models supporting or questioning arguments for central banks' transparency can be found in Geraats (2002).
4 Although in their report Fry et al. (2000, pp. 76–80) stress that they construct a measure of policy explanations, which does not cover all aspects related to transparency.
5 Siklos (2002, p. 235) uses the term "disclosure", treating is as a synonym of "transparency".

6 A similar approach was adopted in Al-Mashat et al. (2018), where the authors also proposed their own list of questions, but their index was computed only for one country—the Czech Republic.

7 The upward bias is consistent with the observation that in the vast majority of cases it is unquestionable that the amendments introduced to legal acts have been aimed at strengthening central banks' independence. Unfortunately, there are also exceptions to that rule, as exemplified with the case of Hungary. These are, however, very rare cases.

8 The thresholds considered in answers to some questions used for constructing the Explicatory_IT index are somewhat arbitrary, but were set based predominantly on the dominant practices among central banks.

9 As already noted, the cases when a central bank is required to prepare an open letter are often more narrowly defined. For example, it can be stated that an open letter is needed when the departure of inflation from the target lasts for more than 6 consecutive months.

10 There are also three cases where the Mature_IT index decreased. These include Sweden—from advanced economies, and India and Kazakhstan—from emerging market economies. The reason is that the index punishes revising targets, especially upwards, changing from a point target to a target with wider tolerance bands, and moving from targeting a headline inflation measure to some kind of an exclusion measure. All of these changes took place in the indicated countries.

11 As already mentioned, the Czech Republic was reclassified to advanced economies only in 2009, but for simplicity it is included in the "old" advanced economy inflation targeters throughout the whole analysed period.

12 The euro was introduced in 1999, but the ECB was established in mid-1998. Also in 1998, the governing council of the ECB adopted a quantitative definition of price stability. Therefore, 1998 is treated as the starting date of the ECB monetary policy strategy.

13 It is worth recalling that in October 2018, Argentina decided to adopt monetary base targeting.

14 Only for Question 8.1. on responsibility for financial stability and Question 8.4. on the main policy instrument, it is assumed that the current state has been valid since IT adoption.

References

Alesina, A., Summers, L. (1993), "Central Bank Independence and Macroeconomic Performance: Some Comparative Evidence", *Journal of Money, Credit, and Banking*, 25(2), pp. 151–162. https://doi.org/10.2307/2077833

Al-Mashat, R. A., Bulíř, A., Nergiz Dinçer, N., Hlédik, T., Holub, T., Kostanyan, A., Laxton, D., Nurbekyan, A., Portillo, R. A., Wang, H. (2018), "An Index for Transparency for Inflation-Targeting Central Banks: Application to the Czech National Bank", *IMF Working Paper, No. 18/210*. https://www.imf.org/~/media/Files/Publications/WP/2018/wp18210.ashx

Bade, R., Parkin, M. (1988), *Central Bank Laws and Monetary Policy*, Department of Economics, University of Western Ontario, Canada.

Barro, R. J., Gordon, D. B. (1983), "A Positive Theory of Monetary Policy in a Natural Rate Model", *The Journal of Political Economy*, 91(4), pp. 589–610. https://doi.org/10.1086/261167

Bini Smaghi, L., Gros, D. (2000), *Open Issues in European Central Banking*, Palgrave Macmillan.

Blinder, A. S. (1998), *Central Banking in Theory and Practice*, MIT Press.

Briault, C., Haldane, A., King, M. (1996), "Independence and Accountability", *Bank of England Working Paper, No. 49*, pp. 1–49.

Bulíř, A., Čihák, M., Šmídková, K. (2012), "Writing Clearly: The ECB's Monetary Policy Communication", *German Economic Review*, 14(1), pp. 50–72. https://do i.org/10.1111/j.1468-0475.2011.00562.x

Cukierman, A. (1992), *Central Bank Strategy, Credibility, and Independance: Theory and Evidence*, MIT Press.

Cukierman, A., Webb, S. B. (1995), "Political Influence on the Central Bank: International Evidence", *The World Bank Economic Review*, 9(3), pp. 397–423. https://doi.org/10.1093/wber/9.3.397

Cukierman, A., Webb, S. B., Neyapti, B. (1992), "Measuring the Independence of Central Banks and Its Effect on Policy Outcomes", *The World Bank Economic Review*, 6(3), pp. 353–398. https://doi.org/10.1093/wber/6.3.353

de Haan, J., Amtenbrink, F. (2003), "A Non-Transparent European Central Bank? Who Is to Blame?", *SSRN Electronic Journal*, pp. 1–38. http://doi.org/10.2139/ssrn.1138224

de Haan, J., Amtenbrink, F., Eijffinger, S. (1998), "Accountability of Central Banks: Aspects and Quantifications", *SSRN Electronic Journal*, pp. 1–27. http://doi.org /10.2139/ssrn.1307581

de Haan, J., Eijffinger, S. (2016), "The Politics of Central-Bank Independence", *De Nederlandsche Bank Working Paper*, 539, pp. 1–28. https://doi.org/10.2139/ssrn .2888836

Debelle, G., Fischer, S. (1994), "How Independent Should a Central Bank Be?", in: J. C. Fuhrer (ed.), *Goals, Guidelines and Constraints Facing Monetary Policymakers*, Federal Reserve Bank of Boston, pp. 195–225.

Dincer, N. N., Eichengreen, B. (2013), "Central Bank Transparency and Independence: Updates and New Measures", *Bank of Korea Working Paper, No. 21*, pp. 1–56. http://doi.org/10.2139/ssrn.2579544

ECB (2018), "Convergence Report—2018", May. https://www.ecb.europa.eu/pub/ convergence/html/ecb.cr201805.en.html

Eijffinger, S., de Haan, J. (1996), "The Political Economy of Central-Bank Independence", *Special Papers in International Economics*, 19, pp. 1–92

Eijffinger, S., Geraats, P. (2006), "How Transparent Are Central Banks?", *European Journal of Political Economy*, 22(1), pp. 1–21. https://doi.org/10.1016/j.ejpo leco.2005.09.013

Fracasso, A., Genberg, H., Wyplosz, Ch. (2003), "How Do Central Banks Write? An Evaluation of Inflation Targeting Central Banks", *Geneva Reports on the World Economy Special Report 2*, Geneva and CEPR. https://cepr.org/sites/de fault/files/geneva_reports/GenevaP161.pdf

Friedman, M. (2006), *Optimum Quantity of Money with a New Introduction by Michael D. Bordo*, Transaction Publishers.

Fry, M., Julius, D., Mahadeva, L., Roger, S., Sterne, G. (2000), "Key Issues in the Choice of Monetary Policy Framework", in: L. Mahadeva, G. Sterne (eds.), *Monetary Policy Frameworks in a Global Context*, Routledge Press, pp. 1–216.

Geraats, P. (2001), "'Why Adopt Transparency? The Publication of Central Bank Forecasts", *ECB Working Papers*, 41, pp. 1–42. https://www.ecb.europa.eu/pub/ pdf/scpwps/ecbwp041.pdf?a1cb4280848b9c3557120a146468f3ab

Geraats, P. (2002), "Central Bank Transparency", *The Economic Journal*, 112(483), pp. F532–F565. http://doi.org/10.1111/1468-0297.00082

Geraats, P. (2009), "Accountability, Transparency and Oversight", *Issues in the Governance of Central Banks, A Report from the Central Bank Governance Group, BIS*, pp. 135–150. https://www.bis.org/publ/othp04.htm

Grilli, V., Masciandaro, D., Tabellini, G., Malinvaud, E., Pagano, M. (1991), "Political and Monetary Institutions and Public Financial Policies in the Industrial Countries", *Economic Policy*, 6(13), pp. 342–392. https://doi.org/10.2307/1344630

Hall, P. A., Franzese, R. J. (1998), "Mixed Signals: Central Bank Independence, Coordinated Wage Bargaining, and European Monetary Union", *International Organization*, 52(3), pp. 505–535. https://doi.org/10.1162/002081898550644

Jansen, D.-J. (2010), "Has the Clarity of Central Bank Communication Affected Financial Markets? Evidence from Humphrey-Hawkins Testimonies", *Contemporary Economic Policy*, 29, pp. 494–509. https://doi.org/10.1111/j.1465-7287.2010.00238.x

Kincaid, J., Jr., Fishburne, R., Rogers, R., Chissom, B. (1975), *Derivation of New Readability Formulas (Automated Readability Index, Fog Count, and Flesch Reading Ease Formula) for Navy Enlisted Personnel*, Memphis, Naval Air Station. https://doi.org/10.21236/ada006655

Kydland, F., Prescott, E. (1977), "Rules Rather Than Discretion: The Inconsistency of Optimal Plans", *Journal of Political Economy*, 85(3), pp. 473–491. https://doi.org/10.1086/260580

Laurens, B. J., Arnone, M., Segalotto, J.-F. (2009), *Central Bank Independence, Accountability, and Transparency. A Global Perspective*, Palgrave Macmillan.

Masłowska, A. (2012), *Studies on Institutions and Central Bank Independence*, Turku School of Economics.

Mishkin, F. S., Schmidt-Hebbel, K. (2007), "Does Inflation Targeting Make a Difference?", *NBER Working Paper, No. 12876*, pp. 1–64. http://doi.org/10.3386/w12876

Pietrzak, B. (2008), "System Bankowy", in: B. Pietrzak, Z. Polański, B. Woźniak (eds.), *System Finansowy w Polsce*, PWN, pp. 69–124.

Rogoff, K. (1985), "The Optimal Commitment to an Intermediate Monetary Target", *Quarterly Journal of Economics*, 100(4), pp. 1169–1189. https://doi.org/10.2307/1885679

Siklos, P. (2002), *The Changing Face of Central Banking: Evolutionary Trends Since World War II*, Cambridge University Press.

Ueda, K. (2010), "Central Bank Communication and Multiple Equilibria", *International Journal of Central Banking*, 6, pp. 145–167. https://www.ijcb.org/journal/ijcb10q3a5.pdf

van der Cruijsen, C., Eijffinger, S., Hoogduin, L. (2010), "Optimal Central Bank Transparency", *Journal of International Money and Finance*, 29(8), pp. 1482–1507. https://doi.org/10.1016/j.jimonfin.2010.06.003

Walsh, C. E. (1995), "Optimal Contracts for Central Bankers", *American Economic Review*, 85, pp. 150–167.

Appendix 3: Indices of institutional set-ups in inflation targeting central banks

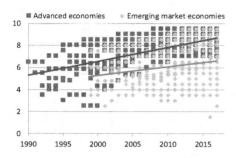

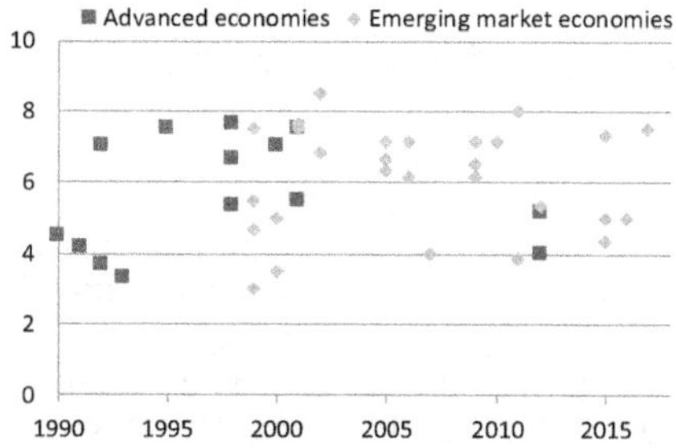

Chart 3.28 Evolution of Mature_IT index in IT advanced and emerging market economies.

Chart 3.29 Levels of Independent_IT index at the time of an IT adoption by a given economy.

Source: Own compilation based on the constructed indices.

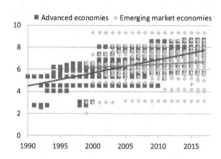

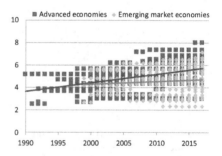

Chart 3.30 Evolution of Informed_IT index in IT advanced and emerging market economies.

Chart 3.31 Evolution of Explicatory_IT index in IT advanced and emerging market economies.

Source: Own compilation based on the constructed indices.

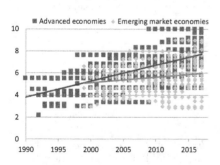

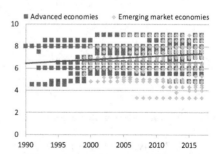

Chart 3.32 Evolution of Transparent_IT index in IT advanced and emerging market economies.

Chart 3.33 Evolution of Accountable_IT index in IT advanced and emerging market economies.

Source: Own compilation based on the constructed indices.

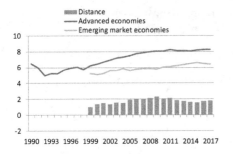

Chart 3.34 Average Mature_IT index in IT advanced and emerging market economies—all economies.

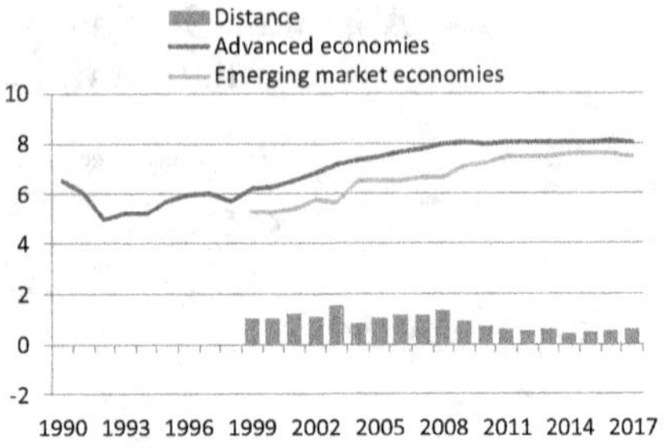

Chart 3.35 Average Mature_IT index in "old" IT advanced and emerging market economies.

Source: Own compilation based on the constructed indices.

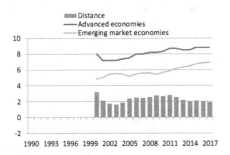

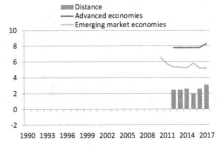

Chart 3.36 Average Mature_IT index in "middle-aged" IT advanced and emerging market economies.

Chart 3.37 Average Mature_IT index in "new" IT advanced and emerging market economies.

Source: Own compilation based on the constructed indices.

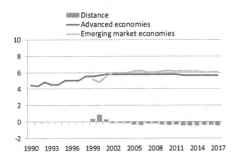

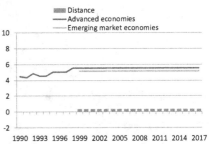

Chart 3.38 Average Independent_IT index in IT advanced and emerging market economies—all economies.

Chart 3.39 Average Independent_IT index in "old" IT advanced and emerging market economies.

Source: Own compilation based on the constructed indices.

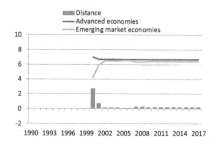

Chart 3.40 Average Independent_IT index in "middle-aged" IT advanced and emerging market economies.

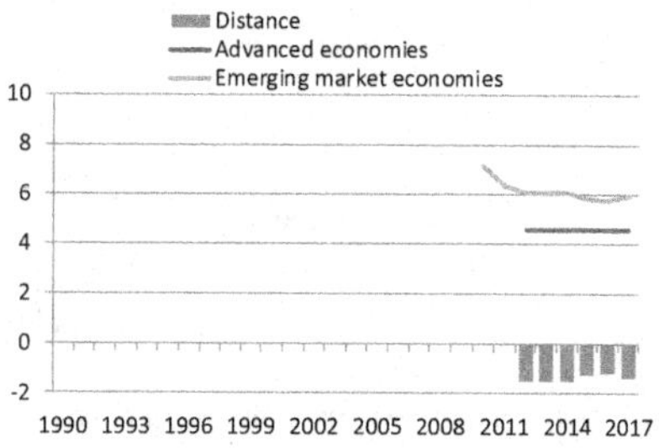

Chart 3.41 Average Independent_IT index in "new" IT advanced and emerging market economies.

Source: Own compilation based on the constructed indices.

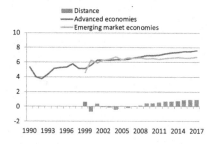

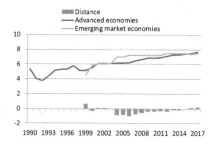

Chart 3.42 Average Informed_IT index in IT advanced and emerging market economies—all economies.

Chart 3.43 Average Informed_IT index in "old" IT advanced and emerging market economies.

Source: Own compilation based on the constructed indices.

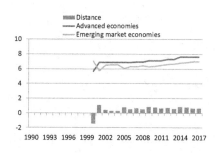

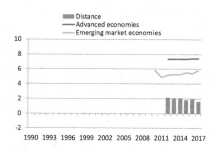

Chart 3.44 Average Informed_IT index in "middle-aged" IT advanced and emerging market economies.

Chart 3.45 Average Informed_IT index in "new" IT advanced and emerging market economies.

Source: Own compilation based on the constructed indices.

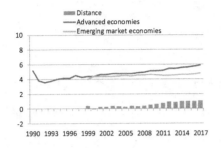

Chart 3.46 Average Explicatory_IT index in IT advanced and emerging market economies—all economies.

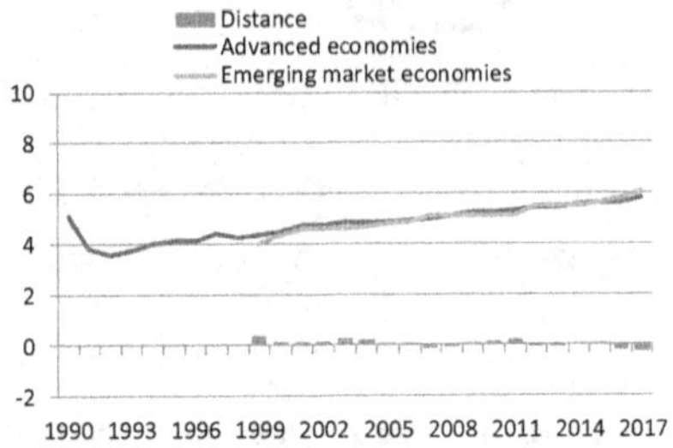

Chart 3.47 Average Explicatory_IT index in "old" IT advanced and emerging market economies.

Source: Own compilation based on the constructed indices.

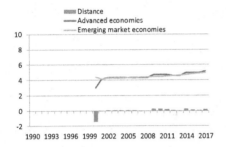
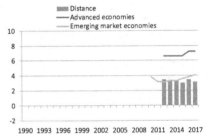

Chart 3.48 Average Explicatory_IT index in "middle-aged" IT advanced and emerging market economies.

Chart 3.49 Average Explicatory_IT index in "new" IT advanced and emerging market economies.

Source: Own compilation based on the constructed indices.

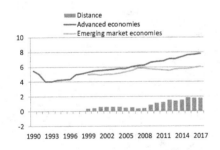
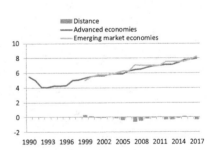

Chart 3.50 Average Transparent_IT index in IT advanced and emerging market economies—all economies.

Chart 3.51 Average Transparent_IT index in "old" IT advanced and emerging market economies.

Source: Own compilation based on the constructed indices.

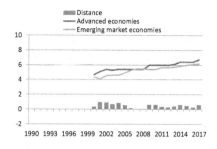 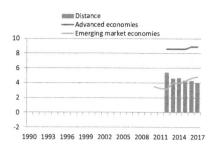

Chart 3.52 Average Transparent_IT index in "middle-aged" IT advanced and emerging market economies.

Chart 3.53 Average Transparent_IT index in "new" IT advanced and emerging market economies.

Source: Own compilation based on the constructed indices.

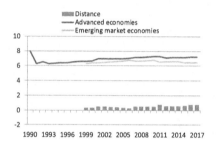 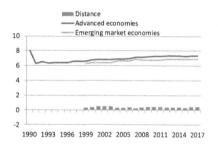

Chart 3.54 Average Accountable_IT index in IT advanced and emerging market economies—all economies.

Chart 3.55 Average Accountable_IT index in "old" IT advanced and emerging market economies.

Source: Own compilation based on the constructed indices.

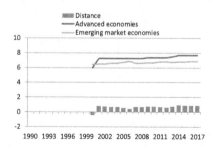 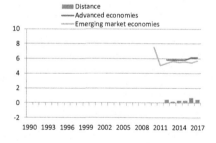

Chart 3.56 Average Accountable_IT index in "middle-aged" IT advanced and emerging market economies.

Chart 3.57 Average Accountable_IT index in "new" IT advanced and emerging market economies.

Source: Own compilation based on the constructed indices.

241

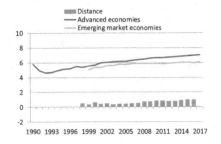

Chart 3.58 Average Fully_fledged_IT index in IT advanced and emerging market economies—all economies.

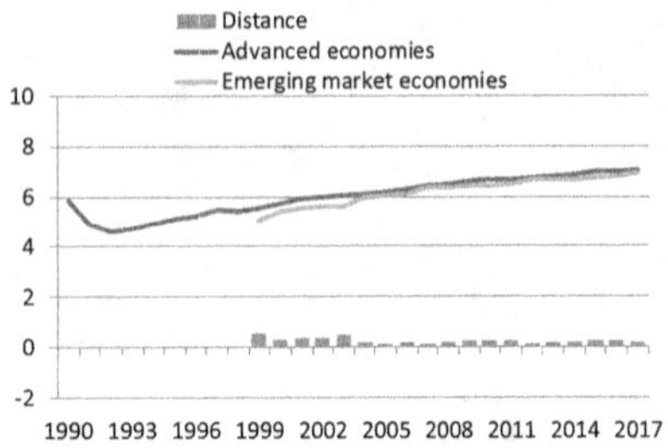

Chart 3.59 Average Fully_fledged_IT index in "old" IT advanced and emerging market economies.

Source: Own compilation based on the constructed indices.

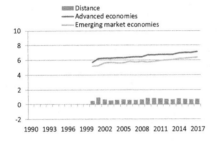
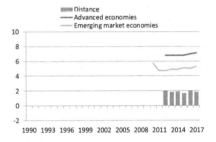

Chart 3.60 Average Fully_fledged_IT index in "middle-aged" IT advanced and emerging market economies.

Chart 3.61 Average Fully_fledged_IT index in "new" IT advanced and emerging market economies.

Source: Own compilation based on the constructed indices.

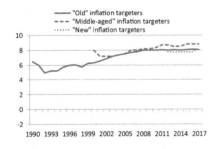
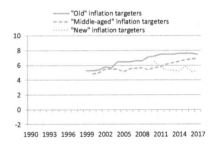

Chart 3.62 Averages of Mature_IT index in IT advanced economies within "age" groups.

Chart 3.63 Averages of Mature_IT index in IT emerging market economies within "age" groups.

Source: Own compilation based on the constructed indices.

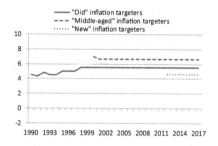

Chart 3.64 Averages of Independent_IT index in IT advanced economies within "age" groups.

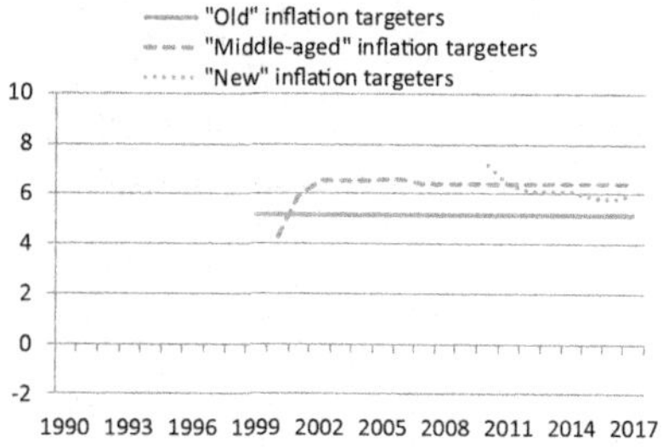

Chart 3.65 Averages of Independent_IT index in IT emerging market economies within "age" groups.

Source: Own compilation based on the constructed indices.

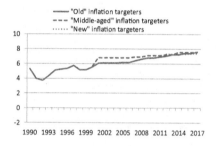

Chart 3.66 Averages of Informed_IT index in IT advanced economies within "age" groups.

Chart 3.67 Averages of Informed_IT index in IT emerging market economies within "age" groups.

Source: Own compilation based on the constructed indices.

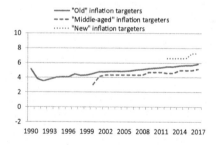
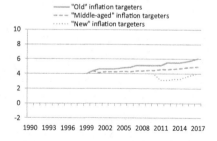

Chart 3.68 Averages of Explicatory_IT index in IT advanced economies within "age" groups.

Chart 3.69 Averages of Explicatory_IT index in IT emerging market economies within "age" groups.

Source: Own compilation based on the constructed indices.

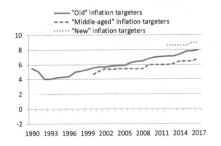

Chart 3.70 Averages of Transparent_IT index in IT advanced economies within "age" groups.

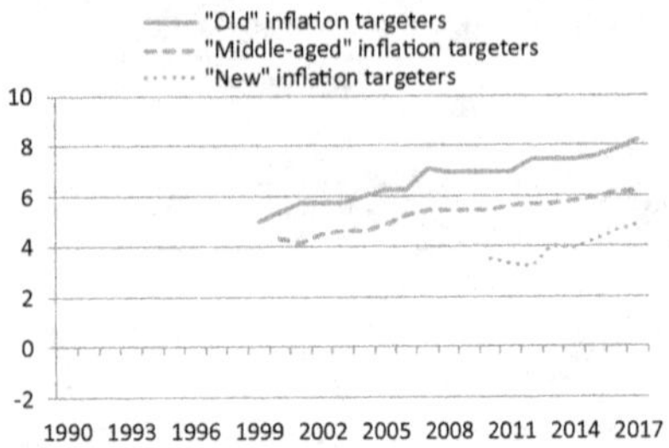

Chart 3.71 Averages of Transparent_IT index in IT emerging market economies within "age" groups.

Source: Own compilation based on the constructed indices.

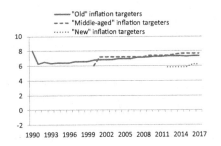
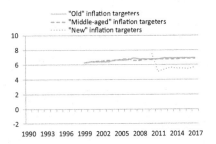

Chart 3.72 Averages of Accountable_IT index in IT advanced economies within "age" groups.

Chart 3.73 Averages of Accountable_IT index in IT emerging market economies within "age" groups.

Source: Own compilation based on the constructed indices.

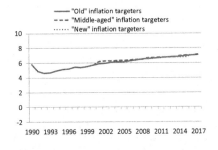
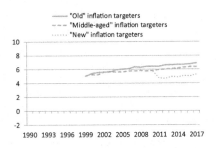

Chart 3.74 Averages of Fully_fledged_IT index in IT advanced economies within "age" groups.

Chart 3.75 Averages of Fully_fledged_IT index in IT emerging market economies within "age" groups.

Source: Own compilation based on the constructed indices.

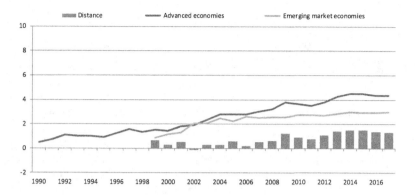

Chart 3.76 Average Stretched_IT index in IT advanced and emerging market economies. Source: Own compilation based on the constructed indices.

Chart 3.77 Averages of Stretched_IT index in IT advanced economies within "age" groups.

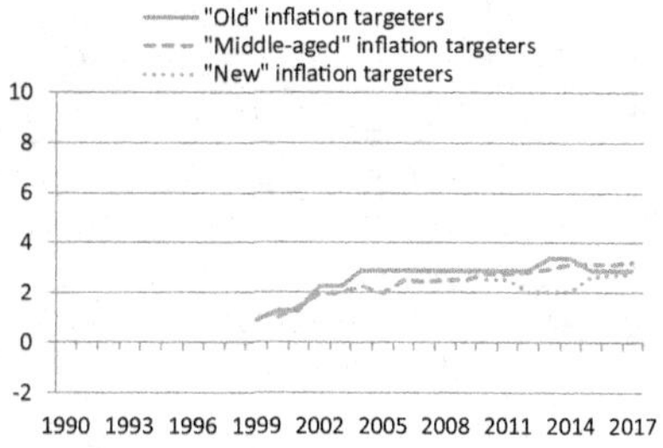

Chart 3.78 Averages of Stretched_IT index in IT emerging market economies within "age" groups.

Source: Own compilation based on the constructed indices.

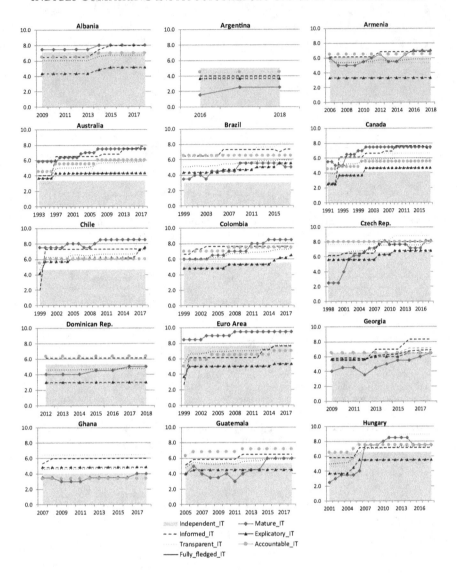

Chart 3.79 Indices of institutional set-ups in IT central banks since IT adoption. Source: Own compilation based on information from central banks' legal acts and central banks' websites.

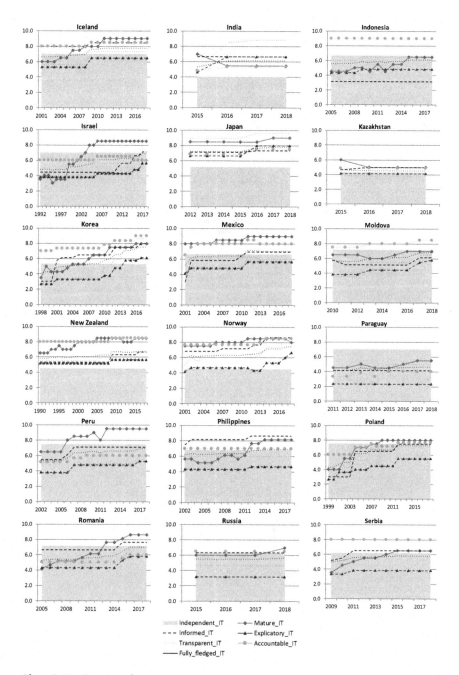

Chart 3.79 Continued

247

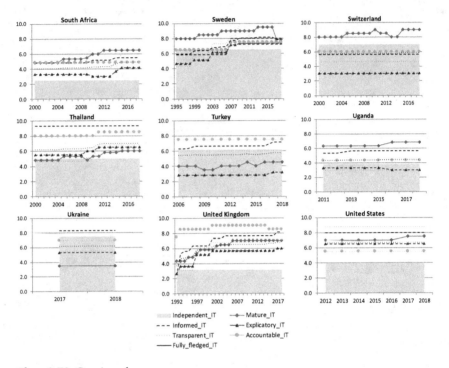

Chart 3.79 Continued

4

ANALYSING THE IMPLICATIONS OF DIFFERENCES IN INSTITUTIONAL SET-UPS OF INFLATION TARGETING CENTRAL BANKS

4.1 Introductory remarks

In order to provide a background for the analysis, Chapter 4 starts with presenting a review of the literature dealing with links between central banks' institutional set-ups and policy outcomes. The main findings, together with a brief evaluation of the past conclusions, are discussed. This is followed by reporting some stylised facts related to the issues of interest. A closer look at the data shows that selecting the analysed period can significantly influence the findings, which speaks in favour of employing a panel set-up instead of a cross-section approach. The final step consists of proposing models that can be used to answer the key question asked in this study, namely, to check if the identified differences in the institutional set-ups of inflation targeting (IT) central banks have an impact on monetary policy effectiveness understood as safeguarding price stability, while also taking into account output developments.

Policy effectiveness is assessed by looking at the inflation level and volatility, and inflation deviations from the targets, as well as by analysing the gross domestic product (GDP) growth level and volatility, and output gap estimates. A panel approach is used to specify models describing the developments of the indicated dependent variables with the help of regressors capturing the structural and cyclical characteristics of the analysed economies, together with some common global factors that can be treated as control variables. On top of such baseline specifications, the proposed indices of institutional set-ups are added. Based on the sign and the significance of the estimated coefficients related to the indices describing IT central banks' institutional arrangements, an attempt is made to answer the question of whether they have a meaningful impact on the ability of monetary policy to meet its goals.

4.2 Selected literature on links between central banks' institutional set-ups and policy outcomes

Not surprisingly, the indices of independence, accountability, and transparency proposed in the literature were used to see whether the differences in central banks' institutional set-ups affect policy outcomes. So far, however, the conclusions stemming from available analysis have been rather mixed.

4.2.1 Importance of central banks' independence

As already indicated, monetary authorities' autonomy was the first topic related to institutional arrangements that received considerable attention among economists. Recognising its potential importance already in the 1970s and 1980s encouraged many authors to investigate how increasing the degree of independence granted to central banks affected inflation or output developments in different countries. As a result, nowadays a very rich empirical research is available on the relationship between monetary policy autonomy and inflation and economic growth.[1] Below, some seminal papers are recalled to indicate how the consensus view on the need to make central banks immune from political influences has been formed.

One of the first analyses in that area was conducted by Bade and Parkin (1988). Using a very simple equation, the authors analysed the experiences of 12 industrial economies and legal rules governing their central banks over the 1972–1986 period. Their results showed that independence was associated with lower, but not necessarily less, volatile inflation.

A slightly bigger group of 18 industrial economies and a somewhat longer period of 1950–1989 were covered by the study of Grilli et al. (1991). With the help of a rather elementary specification, the impact of monetary policy autonomy on macroeconomic variables was examined, but apart from looking only at the impact on inflation, the authors also explored the impact on GDP growth and its volatility. The research broadly confirmed a significant inverse relationship between central bank's independence and inflation, whereas regarding output growth and the volatility of inflation and GDP growth, no systematic links were detected.

An important extension of the analysis was offered by Cukierman et al. (1992). Their paper included 72 economies—both industrial and developing ones—that were studied over the 1950–1989 period. The authors constructed measures of central banks' independence for all these countries at four different dates (corresponding to the analysed four decades). The aim of this undertaking was to check how monetary authorities' autonomy affected inflation and its volatility. The results, obtained after employing a very plain econometric equation, suggested that in industrial countries a higher degree of monetary policy independence led to lower and less volatile inflation, whereas no such relationship could be identified for developing economies.

In an influential paper by Alesina and Summers (1993), the authors restricted their sample again to industrial countries only, and analysed 18 economies over the 1955–1988 period and the 1973–1988 sub-period. The study looked at correlations between a measure of monetary policy autonomy and a number of variables, such as inflation, GDP growth, unemployment, and interest rate—considered both in levels and variances—in the selected group of countries. Using simple scatter plots, the conclusions that were drawn supported the view that greater central bank independence was associated with lower and less volatile inflation, with no large benefits or costs in terms of real variables.

Several remarks are worth making when discussing the findings of the above-mentioned studies. First, the indicated results were in line with the intuition behind the concept of an inflationary bias of politicians that spoke in favour of protecting central banks from pressures potentially stemming from governments. Thus, to a great extent, the cited papers shaped the way economists and many decision-makers viewed the issue of monetary policy autonomy. Second, the common interpretation given to the conclusions made a very strong case for central banks' independence, arguing that sound institutional arrangements separating monetary authorities from other influences would deliver low and less volatile inflation without any significant impact on real variables, which could be seen as offering a "free lunch" (Walsh, 2008, p. 730). Third, problems in finding a significant relationship between central banks' autonomy and policy outcomes in developing countries were mostly explained as related to the difficulty in adequately measuring the independence of the monetary authorities in these economies. The reasoning was based on reckoning that legal rules in less developed economies may, in fact, be much weaker than in advanced economies, due to deficiencies in following the rule of law there. This assumption could be partly supported by research indicating a positive correlation between the turnover rates of central banks' governors—which, as already mentioned, can be seen as reflecting the actual dependence of monetary policy on governments—and inflation levels.[2] Fourth, the discussed studies were mainly based on bivariate cross-section regressions, which did not account for variables that could simultaneously affect central banks' autonomy and the analysed macroeconomic variables. This made them highly susceptible to critique, as more robust econometric techniques became widely used.

Subsequent papers reported rather mixed results, with many suggesting weak or no support for the negative relationship between independence and inflation outcomes. In particular, after considering additional explanatory variables, the impact of central banks' autonomy on inflation was found insignificant in studies conducted by Posen (1993) that analysed 32 economies over the 1960–1989 period, Campillo and Miron (1996) that considered 62 countries over the 1973–1994 period, Fuhrer (1997) that covered

251

70 economies over the 1950–1989 period, and Sturm and de Haan (2001) that included 82 countries over the 1980–1989 period.

At the same time, even after accounting for a number of control variables, a rather robust evidence of the importance of independence was indicated by Oatley (1999) who studied 21 industrial economies over the 1970–1990 period, and after applying somewhat different econometric methods also Brumm (2002) who examined 42 countries over the 1973–1994 period, Crowe and Meade (2008) who encompassed 56 countries over the 1987–1991 and 2002–2006 sub-periods, and Posso and Tawadros (2013) who used the same sample as Crowe and Meade (2008).[3]

Finally, Dincer and Eichengreen (2013), having constructed independence indices for 100 countries over the 1998–2010 period, and after including some control variables, concluded that the response of both the level and the volatility of inflation to rising independence are significantly negative. However, the authors indicated that it was difficult to disentangle the impact of the two factors that they analysed jointly in their study, which were the growing independence and transparency of central banks.

4.2.2 *Importance of central banks' accountability and transparency*

The issue of accountability has generally not been treated as a separate topic in empirical research, probably since it is very closely related to the concept of transparency. Thus, what follows is a short description of the most recognised papers dealing with the significance of central banks' communication in delivering monetary policy goals. Since this issue has been investigated starting only in the late 1990s and the early 2000s, the scope of the available analysis is somewhat less ample compared to the studies on monetary authorities' independence.

One of the earliest contributions was the paper of Cecchetti and Krause (2002) who used the results of the Bank of England survey of central banks, reported in Fry et al. (2000), to examine how central banks' institutional arrangements related to independence, accountability, and transparency affected their macroeconomic performance. Considering data for the 1985–1989 period for 63 countries, the authors concluded that more transparent central banks delivered better macroeconomic outcomes in terms of inflation and output volatility, while independence and accountability did not seem to explain much of the cross-country variation in the analysed variables.

The effects of transparency were also studied by Demertzis and Hughes Hallett (2007). Based on a transparency index constructed by Eijffinger and Geraats for nine industrial economies, and taking into account data from the early 1990s till the end of 2001, the authors showed that the averages of inflation and output gap estimates were not affected by the levels of transparency, whereas about 50% of the variability in inflation could be explained by differences in transparency scores between countries. The link between transparency and output gap volatility was rather ambiguous.

Again using the survey results of Fry et al. (2000), Sterne et al. (2002) focused on analysing transparency related to releasing forecasts for 87 countries. Considering data for the 1995–1999 period, their main finding was that there was a statistically significant negative correlation between transparency and the inflation level and no statistically significant correlation between transparency and GDP growth variance.

Stasavage (2003) also analysed the survey of Fry et al. (2000), but restricted his sample to 44 countries for which he calculated sacrifice ratios using data covering the 1990–1999 period. According to his results, countries with more transparent central banks incurred lower disinflation costs, while accountability had no clear effect on sacrifice ratios.

Some caveats that should be kept in mind when recalling those early results are similar to the ones indicated with respect to the studies investigating the effects of central banks' independence on policy outcomes. First, whereas a positive impact of increased transparency on monetary policy effectiveness was consistent with a number of plausible arguments, the conclusions in many papers were neither too strong nor consistent. Nevertheless, the results were instrumental in advocating for a broader openness in the conduct of monetary policy. Second, findings were often based on model specifications that did not take into account some potentially important control variables, putting in question the robustness of the results. At times, the authors openly admitted that their analysis should be seen as an attempt to identify correlations rather than causal relationships between the investigated phenomena, which is, however, not always noted when referring to those contributions. Third, one of the major difficulties was to correctly measure accountability and transparency, preferably in a uniform way across time and countries. Collecting relevant information required a lot of effort and was anyway subject to a critique on selectivity. For that reason, most authors used the same survey results reported in Fry et al. (2000), and followed a cross-section approach.

Most recent research, while, to a large extent, facing the same measurement difficulties, added a time-series dimension to the picture, although sometimes at the expense of limiting the number of analysed countries.[4] In general, new evidence broadly confirmed the positive effects of transparency on macroeconomic stability, though some studies suggested that there were limits to how open central banks should be to make the best use of their communication policies.[5]

An important step in broadening the country and time coverage of research related to accountability and transparency was made in the paper by Dincer and Eichengreen (2007), and the already mentioned study of Dincer and Eichengreen (2013) that encompassed virtually all central banks over a relatively long period. Their contributions gave rise to a new wave of research based, predominantly, on panel models.

In Dincer and Eichengreen (2007), transparency indices were constructed for 100 monetary authorities over the 1998–2005 period, which resulted in a very rich sample of countries. In Dincer and Eichengreen (2013), again 100 monetary authorities were covered, but the period analysed was extended until 2010, and instead of looking only at transparency scores, independence indices were also built. This allowed the identification of clear trends towards greater openness and autonomy of central banks over the years, and to explore the effects of these changes on macroeconomic outcomes. In both studies, the authors took into account some control variables. Their results broadly supported a negative, although relatively weak, impact of central banks' openness on inflation and output volatility.

Weber (2018) also built on Dincer and Eichengreen's data on central bank transparency and independence for the 1998–2005 period, but employed a much richer set of additional variables that could potentially play an important role in explaining inflation developments, and thus their omission could distort the estimation results. Using a panel data approach, the author concluded that, even after controlling for more regressors, transparency significantly lowered inflation levels and volatility.

4.2.3 The relevance of the existing literature for the analysis of IT central banks' institutional set-ups

As can be seen from the above overview, especially the early contributions were often based on a rather small selection of countries, predominantly industrial economies, which spoke in favour of remaining cautious when trying to draw more general conclusions. Caution was also advised due to the fact that simple, mainly cross-section models were used that neither accounted for possible endogeneity issues, nor tested the direction of causality. Despite that, many of the results were quite influential in the discussions on the advisable shape of central banks' institutional arrangements.

Extending country coverage was a noteworthy development, not least, since it allowed for comparing arrangements between advanced and emerging market economies. Likewise, providing measures evaluating the analysed dimensions of central banks' institutional set-ups over time offered the possibility to see whether any trends in their evolution could be noted. Moreover, constructing different indices assessing various aspects of independence, accountability, and transparency helped to verify the robustness of the earlier findings.

Looking at the existing literature from the perspective of the main question asked in this study, a few additional remarks should be made. For obvious reasons, the time coverage of the reported analyses was not the same, with many papers encompassing periods when inflation targeting was not yet so popular. Also regarding country coverage, an important observation to make is that it was standard practice to include countries with different monetary policy strategies in one sample—sometimes controlling for that by adding a variable indicating a monetary policy regime used, but often disregarding that issue. These two elements decrease the relevance of the past research for formulating conclusions for IT economies.

At the same time, as discussed earlier, some authors examined the link between following an inflation targeting regime and economic performance.[6] To some extent, those studies could be treated as asking about the relationship between central banks' increased autonomy, democratic control, and enhanced communication efforts and policy outcomes, since—as already noted—employing high accountability and transparency standards as complements to monetary authorities' substantial independence is one of the key features of an inflation targeting framework. However, while such a parallel in many cases is uncontroversial,[7] it ignores the fact that inflation targeters are not independent, accountable, or transparent in the same way and to the same degree, as clearly shown in this study. Since the beneficial effects of IT adoption were found to be stronger for emerging market economies compared to advanced economies, possibly due to the greater enhancement in institutional set-ups required to become an inflation targeter in the first group of countries, distinguishing between better and worse set-ups may be of importance. Thus, investigating how differences in institutional arrangements governing inflation targeting central banks affect the ability of monetary policy to meet its goals is justified.

Moreover, restricting the sample to inflation targeters only offers additional advantages. First, analysing economies following the same monetary policy strategy eliminates the problem of disentangling the impact of the effectiveness of a given monetary policy regime, and the effectiveness of specific institutional arrangements used within this monetary policy regime.[8] Second, the existing literature is focused on examining policy outcomes understood as inflation and GDP growth levels and volatility, sometimes supplemented with output gap estimates. Among inflation targeting central banks, in turn, apart from these aspects, deviations in inflation from the target should also be treated as relevant for evaluating monetary policy effectiveness. The approach adopted in the empirical analysis builds on these considerations.[9]

4.3 Stylised facts on links between central banks' institutional set-ups and policy outcomes

The early contributions dealing with the significance of central banks' institutional arrangements for policy outcomes were heavily based on analysing simple correlations. While this strategy has many shortcomings, it is useful to look at the collected data at their face value (i.e. without any modifications or employing models). This may be helpful in verifying some stylised facts that are commonly referred to when discussing issues related to independence, accountability, and the transparency of monetary authorities.

4.3.1 A cross-section set-up for analysing the relevance of institutional arrangements

As indicated above, a number of studies analysed the relationships between institutional arrangements (described using indices of independence, accountability, and transparency in their various dimensions) and monetary policy outcomes (understood as levels and/or the volatility of inflation and output) in a cross-section set-up. Such an approach means viewing the data at a specific point in time (though both single observations as well as multi-year averages can be used) across a group of countries, and drawing conclusions based on the differences between those countries at that very moment. Taking such an optic, it seems interesting to look at correlations between the proposed indices and several variables related to inflation and output developments.

To allow for a brief comparison with the discussed literature, it is useful to consider the inflation level and its variance, as well as the GDP growth and its variance (Charts 4.9–4.12 and 4.15–4.18 in Appendix 4). At the same time, as already mentioned, for the purpose of the current study, also of importance are inflation deviation from the target and GDP deviation from the potential output, i.e. the output gap (Charts 4.13, 4.14, 4.19 and 4.20 in Appendix 4). Thus, all these variables are graphed against various features of IT central banks' institutional set-ups. To mitigate a problem of selecting atypical observations, all macroeconomic variables are presented as three-year averages (for the 2015–2017 period[10]). Consequently, the proposed indices of institutional arrangements refer to 2014, which means they are lagged three periods, so that they depict central banks' set-ups prior to the realised inflation and output outcomes.

Individual indices of institutional arrangements show diversified relationships with the analysed macroeconomic variables (Table 4.1). Moreover, in many instances, the direction of the link differs between IT advanced and IT emerging market economies. In the case of the Fully_fledged_IT index, it is, in fact, a rule rather than an exception, but other indices often show divergences as well (Table 4.1). However, before drawing any conclusions, it should be noted that many of the depicted relationships are not statistically meaningful. Thus, the estimated correlation coefficients linking the institutional set-ups to variables related to inflation and output are not different from 0 at a typically used 5% significance level.

To check whether there is any robust relationship between the proposed indices and policy outcomes that would allow for detecting potential structural differences between advanced and emerging market economies, a look at correlations at various points in time is warranted (Table 4.1).

Table 4.1 Correlations between the proposed indices and macroeconomic variables in selected years

		Mature_IT (lag 3)		Independent_IT (lag 3)		Informed_IT (lag 3)		Explicatory_IT (lag 3)		Transparent_IT (lag 3)		Accountable_IT (lag 3)		Fully_fledged_IT (lag 3)	
		Advanced economies	Emerging market economies	Advanced economies	Emerging market economies	Advanced economies	Emerging market economies	Advanced economies	Emerging market economies	Advanced economies	Emerging market economies	Advanced economies	Emerging market economies	Advanced economies	Emerging market economies
Inflation—three-year average	2008 All inflation targeters		−0.6	Corr.(+)	Corr.(−)		Corr.(−)	Corr.(+)	Corr.(−)				Corr.(+)		Corr.(−)
	Sub-samples	Corr.(−)	Corr.(−)			Corr.(+)	Corr.(−)	Corr.(+)	Corr.(−)		Corr.(−)	Corr.(+)	Corr.(−)	Corr.(+)	−0.5
	2011 All inflation targeters	Corr.(−)	−0.6		Corr.(−)	Corr.(+)	Corr.(−)	Corr.(+)	−0.5	Corr.(−)	Corr.(−)	Corr.(+)	Corr.(−)		−0.6
	Sub-samples	Corr.(−)	−0.6	Corr.(−)	−0.5	Corr.(+)	Corr.(−)	Corr.(+)	Corr.(−)						−0.6
	2014 All inflation targeters	Corr.(−)	−0.5	Corr.(−)	−0.4	Corr.(+)	Corr.(−)	Corr.(+)	Corr.(−)	Corr.(+)	Corr.(−)	Corr.(+)	Corr.(−)	Corr.(+)	−0.6
	Sub-samples		−0.5	Corr.(+)		0.8	Corr.(−)	Corr.(+)	Corr.(−)		Corr.(−)		Corr.(+)	Corr.(+)	−0.4
	2017 All inflation targeters		−0.4	Corr.(−)	−0.4	Corr.(+)	Corr.(−)	Corr.(+)	Corr.(−)	Corr.(+)		Corr.(+)	Corr.(−)	Corr.(+)	−0.4
	Sub-samples	Corr.(−)	Corr.(−)	Corr.(+)		Corr.(+)	Corr.(−)	Corr.(+)	Corr.(−)	Corr.(−)		Corr.(+)	Corr.(+)	Corr.(+)	Corr.(−)
Inflation variance—three-year variance	2008 All inflation targeters	Corr.(−)	Corr.(−)	Corr.(+)			Corr.(−)	Corr.(+)	Corr.(−)	Corr.(−)		Corr.(+)	Corr.(−)	Corr.(+)	Corr.(−)
	2011 All inflation targeters	Corr.(−)	Corr.(−)			Corr.(+)	Corr.(−)	Corr.(+)	Corr.(−)			Corr.(+)	Corr.(+)	Corr.(+)	Corr.(−)
	2014 All inflation targeters		Corr.(−)	Corr.(+)	Corr.(−)	Corr.(+)		Corr.(+)	Corr.(−)		−0.4	Corr.(+)	−0.3	Corr.(+)	−0.4
	Sub-samples	Corr.(+)	Corr.(−)	Corr.(+)	Corr.(−)	Corr.(+)	Corr.(−)	Corr.(+)	Corr.(−)	Corr.(+)	Corr.(−)	Corr.(+)	Corr.(−)	Corr.(+)	Corr.(−)
	2017 All inflation targeters	Corr.(−)	Corr.(−)	Corr.(+)	Corr.(−)	Corr.(+)	Corr.(−)	Corr.(+)	Corr.(−)	Corr.(+)	Corr.(−)	Corr.(+)	Corr.(−)	Corr.(+)	Corr.(−)
	Sub-samples	Corr.(−)	Corr.(−)	Corr.(+)		Corr.(+)		Corr.(+)		Corr.(+)		Corr.(+)		Corr.(+)	

(Continued)

Table 4.1 (*Continued*) Correlations between the proposed indices and macroeconomic variables in selected years

		Mature_IT (lag 3)		Independent_IT (lag 3)		Informed_IT (lag 3)		Explicatory_IT (lag 3)		Transparent_IT (lag 3)		Accountable_IT (lag 3)		Fully_fledged_IT (lag 3)	
		Advanced economies	Emerging market economies	Advanced economies	Emerging market economies	Advanced economies	Emerging market economies	Advanced economies	Emerging market economies	Advanced economies	Emerging market economies	Advanced economies	Emerging market economies	Advanced economies	Emerging market economies
Inflation deviation from target—three-year average	2008 All inflation targeters	−0.4			Corr.(+)		Corr.(+)		Corr.(+)		Corr.(+)		Corr.(+)		
	Sub-samples	Corr.(−)	Corr.(−)	Corr.(+)		Corr.(+)	Corr.(−)	Corr.(+)		Corr.(+)		Corr.(+)		Corr.(−)	Corr.(−)
	2011 All inflation targeters				Corr.(+)				Corr.(−)		Corr.(−)		Corr.(+)		
	Sub-samples	Corr.(−)	Corr.(+)	Corr.(−)	Corr.(+)	Corr.(+)		Corr.(+)	Corr.(−)	Corr.(−)	Corr.(−)	Corr.(+)	Corr.(+)	Corr.(+)	Corr.(−)
	2014 All inflation targeters	Corr.(−)			Corr.(−)			Corr.(+)	Corr.(−)	Corr.(−)	Corr.(−)	Corr.(+)		Corr.(+)	Corr.(−)
	Sub-samples	Corr.(−)	Corr.(−)	Corr.(−)	Corr.(−)	Corr.(+)	Corr.(−)	Corr.(+)	Corr.(−)	Corr.(+)	Corr.(−)	Corr.(+)		Corr.(+)	Corr.(−)
	2017 All inflation targeters	Corr.(−)		Corr.(−)		Corr.(+)		Corr.(+)	Corr.(−)	Corr.(+)	Corr.(−)	Corr.(+)		Corr.(+)	Corr.(−)
	Sub-samples	Corr.(−)	Corr.(−)	Corr.(−)	Corr.(−)	Corr.(−)	Corr.(−)	Corr.(−)	Corr.(−)	Corr.(−)	Corr.(−)	Corr.(−)	Corr.(−)	Corr.(−)	Corr.(−)
GDP growth—three-year average	2008 All inflation targeters		Corr.(−)	0.8		0.8	Corr.(−)	0.6		0.5	Corr.(−)		Corr.(−)	Corr.(+)	Corr.(−)
	Sub-samples	Corr.(−)	Corr.(−)	Corr.(−)	Corr.(+)	Corr.(−)		Corr.(−)		Corr.(−)	Corr.(−)	Corr.(−)	Corr.(−)	Corr.(+)	Corr.(−)
	2011 All inflation targeters	Corr.(−)		Corr.(+)	Corr.(−)	Corr.(−)	Corr.(−)	Corr.(−)	Corr.(−)	Corr.(−)		Corr.(−)	Corr.(−)	Corr.(−)	Corr.(−)
	Sub-samples		Corr.(−)	Corr.(−)	Corr.(−)	Corr.(−)	Corr.(−)	Corr.(−)	Corr.(−)	Corr.(−)	Corr.(−)	Corr.(−)	Corr.(−)	Corr.(−)	Corr.(−)
	2014 All inflation targeters	Corr.(−)	Corr.(−) −0.5	Corr.(−)	Corr.(−)	Corr.(−)	Corr.(+)	Corr.(−)	Corr.(+)	Corr.(−)	Corr.(+)	Corr.(−)	Corr.(+)	Corr.(−) −0.4	Corr.(−)
	Sub-samples	Corr.(−)	Corr.(−)	Corr.(−)	0.4	Corr.(−)	Corr.(−)	Corr.(−)	Corr.(+)	Corr.(+)	Corr.(+)		Corr.(+)	Corr.(−)	Corr.(−)
	2017 All inflation targeters	Corr.(−)	Corr.(−)	Corr.(−)	Corr.(−)	Corr.(−)	Corr.(−)	Corr.(+)	Corr.(−)	Corr.(+)	Corr.(−)		Corr.(−)	Corr.(−)	Corr.(−)
	Sub-samples	Corr.(−)	Corr.(−)	Corr.(+)	Corr.(+)	Corr.(+)	Corr.(−)	Corr.(+)	Corr.(+)	Corr.(+)	Corr.(+)	Corr.(+)	Corr.(+)	Corr.(+)	Corr.(−)
GDP growth variance—three-year variance	2008 All inflation targeters	Corr.(+)		Corr.(+)		Corr.(−)		Corr.(+)		Corr.(+)		Corr.(+)		Corr.(+)	Corr.(+)
	Sub-samples	Corr.(−)	Corr.(−)	Corr.(+)	Corr.(+)	Corr.(+)	Corr.(+)	Corr.(+)	Corr.(+)	Corr.(+)		Corr.(+)	Corr.(+)	Corr.(+)	Corr.(+)
	2011 All inflation targeters	Corr.(−)		Corr.(+)		Corr.(−)		Corr.(+)		Corr.(+)		Corr.(+)		Corr.(+)	Corr.(+)
	Sub-samples		Corr.(+)	Corr.(+)	Corr.(+)	Corr.(+)	Corr.(+)	Corr.(+)	Corr.(+)	Corr.(+)		Corr.(+)		Corr.(+)	Corr.(+)
	2014 All inflation targeters	Corr.(+)	Corr.(−)	Corr.(+)		Corr.(+)		0.6	Corr.(−)	Corr.(+)		Corr.(+)	Corr.(+)	0.7	Corr.(+)
	Sub-samples	Corr.(+)	Corr.(+)	Corr.(+)	Corr.(+)	Corr.(+)	Corr.(+)	Corr.(+)	Corr.(+)	Corr.(+)	Corr.(+)	Corr.(+)	Corr.(+)	Corr.(+)	Corr.(+)
	2017 All inflation targeters	Corr.(+)	Corr.(−)	Corr.(+)		Corr.(−)		0.6	Corr.(−)	Corr.(+)		Corr.(+)	Corr.(−)	0.7	Corr.(+)
	Sub-samples	Corr.(+)	Corr.(−)	Corr.(+)	Corr.(−)	Corr.(+)	Corr.(−)	Corr.(+)	Corr.(−)	Corr.(+)	Corr.(−)	Corr.(+)	Corr.(−)	Corr.(+)	Corr.(−)

		Mature_IT (lag 3)		Independent_IT (lag 3)		Informed_IT (lag 3)		Explicatory_IT (lag 3)		Transparent_IT (lag 3)		Accountable_IT (lag 3)		Fully_fledged_IT (lag 3)	
		Advanced economies	Emerging market economies	Advanced economies	Emerging market economies	Advanced economies	Emerging market economies	Advanced economies	Emerging market economies	Advanced economies	Emerging market economies	Advanced economies	Emerging market economies	Advanced economies	Emerging market economies
Output gap—three-year average	2008 All inflation targeters	Corr.(-)		Corr.(+)		Corr.(+)		Corr.(+)		Corr.(+)		Corr.(+)		Corr.(+)	
	Sub-samples	Corr.(+)	Corr.(-)	Corr.(+)	Corr.(+)	Corr.(+)	Corr.(+)	Corr.(+)	Corr.(+)	Corr.(+)	Corr.(+)	Corr.(+)	Corr.(-)	0.6	Corr.(-)
	2011 All inflation targeters		Corr.(+)	Corr.(+)	Corr.(-)	Corr.(+)	Corr.(-)	Corr.(+)	Corr.(+)	Corr.(+)	Corr.(-)			Corr.(-)	-0.5
	Sub-samples	Corr.(+)		Corr.(+)	Corr.(-)	Corr.(-)	Corr.(-)	Corr.(-)	Corr.(-)	Corr.(-)	Corr.(-)	Corr.(-)	Corr.(-)	Corr.(-)	
	2014 All inflation targeters	-0.4	-0.5	-0.4	-0.5	-0.6		-0.8	Corr.(+)	-0.7	Corr.(+)		Corr.(+)	-0.9	
	Sub-samples			-0.5				Corr.(+)	Corr.(+)	Corr.(+)	Corr.(+)	Corr.(+)	Corr.(+)		
	2017 All inflation targeters	Corr.(-)	Corr.(+)	Corr.(+)	Corr.(+)	Corr.(+)		Corr.(+)		Corr.(+)		Corr.(+)		Corr.(+)	
	Sub-samples														
Description of coding used:		Corr.(-)—statistically insignificant negative correlation		Corr.(-)—statistically insignificant correlation		Blank - no visible relationship		Corr.(+)—statistically insignificant positive correlation		Corr.(+)—statistically positive correlation		Positive number—statistically significant positive correlation			

Source: Own compilation based on the constructed indices and macroeconomic variables (sources indicated in Table 4.12).
Notes: See notes to Charts 4.9–4.24. Numbers indicated in the table are correlation coefficients (only coefficients significantly different from 0 at a 5% significance level are reported).

The years 2008, 2011, 2014, and 2017 are selected, so that they cover periods when the number of inflation targeters was already big enough to analyse within a cross-section approach.[11] Moreover, the indicated years represent quite different global macroeconomic conditions which make them especially useful reference points. Again the proposed indices of institutional arrangements lagged three periods, and three-year averages of various indicators related to inflation and GDP are taken into account.

If only correlation coefficients that are different from 0 are considered (at a 5% significance level), not many meaningful relationships can be detected (Table 4.1). Neither can any apparent regularity be seen regarding the strength and the direction of the links, as suggested by cross-section data for the selected years. Only in the case of the Mature_IT index and the Fully_fledged_IT index, when the inflation level is looked at, are statistically negative correlation coefficients consistently found for several sub-samples. Otherwise, the remaining correlation coefficients are significant merely in single instances. Overall, in almost all cases, the connection between the proposed indices and the analysed macroeconomic variables is not stable over time and depends on the period covered by the data (in a specific year it can turn out to be positive or negative, but in other periods it is non-existent).

That instability of the relationships concerns both advanced and emerging market economies, with no clear pattern evident. In particular, no strong cases support a claim that there is any structural difference between IT advanced and emerging market economies in how their central banks' institutional arrangements affect variables related to inflation and output. Moreover, any potential discrepancy between advanced and emerging market economies may simply reflect the heterogeneous economic conditions of the two groups of countries, stemming from factors other than monetary authorities' institutional set-ups.

A cross-section perspective for any given point in time ignores the fact that countries may be in different phases of their respective business cycles, which clearly impacts the analysed macroeconomic variables. For example, an economy in a recession should be characterised by weak price and demand pressures, independently of the institutional arrangements governing its central bank. Also, the global context can be substantially different depending on the studied period, which may affect economies in various ways. For instance, independently of institutional set-ups governing central banks, in an environment of high oil prices, countries that are oil importers would probably experience higher price pressures and sluggish economic growth. At the same time, oil exporters would most likely see rising demand, with buoyant economic growth possibly translating into higher price pressure as well, but clearly for other reasons than in oil-importing economies. Therefore, a cross-section approach may be insufficient to capture the relationships underlying the investigated phenomenon.

In order to make the findings of a cross-section analysis more reliable, it is advisable to use longer multi-year averages that would encompass periods covering a full business cycle. The applied three-year averages would probably be too short for that purpose, but deciding an appropriate time dimension is far from straightforward. The problem with selecting the right duration of a business cycle for a single economy is not trivial, and picking a multi-year average that would do justice to the length of business cycle fluctuations in many economies that are, in various respects, very different from each other is even more doubtful.[12] Thus, instead of trying to fix a cross-section approach, the next step was to use a panel analysis.

4.3.2 A panel set-up for analysing the relevance of institutional arrangements

To address some of the shortcomings of a cross-section approach, it is useful to add a time dimension to the analysis and to move in the direction of a panel set-up. Considering the full sample, the relationships between the proposed indices and the macroeconomic variables seem much more alike within advanced and emerging market economies (Charts 4.21–4.32 in Appendix 4), but again many of them turn out not to be statistically meaningful (at a 5% significance level).

Importantly, the number of observations included in the full sample is around 500, while for each of the sub-samples consisting of only advanced or only emerging market economies it is around 250. Thus, detecting statistically significant correlation coefficients is easier compared to a cross-section analysis based on a much lower number of observations.

Indeed, if again a 5% significance level is applied, much more meaningful links can be seen compared to the above-discussed cross-section analysis. Interestingly, more correlation coefficients considerably different from 0 are recorded for variables related to inflation than for variables related to output. Nevertheless, the difference is not strong enough to argue that central banks' institutional arrangements do affect inflation processes, but do not impact output developments.

Looking at individual indices, it seems that the Mature_IT index and the Transparency_IT index exert a negative impact on many of the analysed variables, with other indices characterised by much more diversified links with policy outcomes. Overall, in most of the cases, central banks' institutional set-ups are negatively correlated with the inflation level and variance, as well as with the GDP growth. Somewhat weaker evidence is found for a negative link between institutional arrangements and inflation deviation from the target, whereas a rather mixed picture can be seen for the GDP growth variance, and virtually no trace of any relationship can be established for output gap estimates (Table 4.2).

Table 4.2 Correlations between the proposed indices and macroeconomic variables over the full sample

		Mature_IT (lag 3)		Independent_IT (lag 3)		Informed_IT (lag 3)		Explicatory_IT (lag 3)		Transparent_IT (lag 3)		Accountable_IT (lag 3)		Fully_fledged_IT (lag 3)	
		Advanced economies	Emerging market economies	Advanced economies	Emerging market economies	Advanced economies	Emerging market economies	Advanced economies	Emerging market economies	Advanced economies	Emerging market economies	Advanced economies	Emerging market economies	Advanced economies	Emerging market economies
Inflation—three-year average	All inflation targeters		-0.5		-0.1		-0.1		-0.2		-0.1		-0.2		-0.3
	Sub-samples	-0.4	-0.4		-0.3		-0.2		-0.3		-0.1		-0.1	-0.1	-0.4
Inflation variance—three-year variance	All inflation targeters	-0.3					-0.1		-0.1	-0.2			-0.1		-0.3
	Sub-samples	-0.2	-0.2	0.2	-0.2		-0.2		Corr.(-)	-0.1					
Inflation deviation from target—three-year average	All inflation targeters	-0.2	-0.2		-0.1			Corr.(+)	-0.2						-0.1
	Sub-samples	-0.1	-0.2		-0.2							0.2			-0.2
GDP growth—three-year average	All inflation targeters	-0.3					-0.1	-0.3	-0.2	-0.4	-0.2		-0.1	-0.4	-0.3
	Sub-samples	-0.5		0.3		0.1	0.1		0.1			Corr.(-)	Corr.(-)		Corr.(-)
GDP growth variance—three-year variance	All inflation targeters	-0.1						0.2				0.2		0.2	
	Sub-samples		Corr.(-)		Corr.(-)	0.1	Corr.(+)	Corr.(-)	Corr.(-)						
Output gap—three-year average	All inflation targeters									Corr.(-)					
	Sub-samples	Corr.(-)													
Description of coding used:	Negative number—statistically significant negative correlation	Corr.(-)—statistically insignificant negative correlation				Blank—no visible relationship		Corr.(+)—statistically insignificant positive correlation				Positive number—statistically significant positive correlation			

Source: Own compilation based on the constructed indices and macroeconomic variables (sources indicated in Table 4.12).
Notes: See notes to Table 4.1. Rows related to all inflation targeters denote relationships indicated by including observations for all countries for all years (i.e. for each country, a period from the adoption of an IT strategy until 2018), which are later divided into sub-samples of advanced and emerging market economies.

However, many of the reservations raised with respect to the cross-section perspective, still hold. Simple correlations are not able to detect robust relationships between the proposed indices of central banks' institutional set-ups and policy outcomes, since many additional factors that affect inflation and output performance may be at play. In particular, based on the conducted analysis, it is not possible to positively verify the conclusions from the early research on central banks' independence, accountability, and transparency, suggesting that better institutional set-ups should be helpful in delivering price stability, without having much bearing on output. In order to check the validity of that claim, it seems necessary to employ a panel regression approach that would account for a number of control variables, featuring structural differences between economies and accounting for their various cyclical conditions.

4.4 Data and empirical methodology used to analyse policy outcomes

When referring to the policy outcomes of inflation targeters, two dimensions should be considered. First, the ability of IT central banks to meet the inflation targets, and second, the ability of IT central banks to stabilise output. As already indicated, the reason for looking at both inflation and output performance in assessing policy outcomes is that all the analysed monetary authorities pursue a flexible inflation targeting strategy that is not focused solely on price stability, but also cares about output stability and overall macroeconomic stability. A similar understanding of what constitutes proper monetary policy was presented in Brzoza-Brzezina (2011, p. 7). In line with that reasoning, in order to assess central banks' policies, apart from looking at inflation and GDP growth (levels and volatility), deviations of inflation from the target as well as output gap estimates are also analysed.

4.4.1 Model used to analyse policy outcomes

The empirical analysis is based on a panel data set covering both advanced and emerging market economy inflation targeters. In the baseline estimations almost all inflation targeters, as of 2018, are included, with the exception of countries that adopted an IT framework less than five years prior to the end of the sample period.[13] This means that 37 economies are studied.

Since, as already noted, different countries adopted an IT strategy in different years (beginning with New Zealand in 1990), they are included in the sample starting at different points in time, and thus the panel is unbalanced. The time series used are of annual frequency. Generally, the period studied ends in 2018, but many data are available only up to 2017.

Data were taken mainly from the International Monetary Fund (IMF), the World Bank, and the Organisation for Economic Cooperation and Development (OECD), but some information, for example, on inflation target levels, was collected directly from central banks' websites (Table 4.12 in Appendix 4). The indices used to analyse IT central banks' institutional set-ups were constructed based on a unique data set that was the outcome of the review conducted in this study that collected publicly available information taken either from central banks' websites or from legal acts on central banks.

In principle, no adjustments were introduced to the series included in the analysis. In particular, since annual data are used, no seasonal adjustment was needed.

The baseline empirical model is a panel regression of the following form:

$$y_{i,t} = \alpha_i + \beta X_{i,t-k} + \varepsilon_{i,t},$$

where $i = 1,...,N$ corresponds to individual countries included in the analysis; $t = 1,...,T$—to a time dimension of the panel; and k—to the number of lags included in the model; y is the dependent variable, which is related either to inflation (level, volatility, or deviation from the target) in a given economy (i) for a given year (t) or to GDP growth (level, volatility, or the output gap estimates) in a given economy (i) for a given year (t); X is a matrix of explanatory variables that are likely to affect the dependent variable, also taking into account possible lags (k). Importantly, no autoregression terms are included in the model. The error term is ε and α and β are vectors of parameters to be estimated.

The dependent variables are used as three-year averages[14] of series related to inflation or output. This follows from the desire to ensure the comparability of the obtained results with the previous studies, which used multi-year averages to investigate the importance of institutional set-ups. Furthermore, a three-year period can be seen as corresponding to a medium-term horizon, when the impact of unexpected shocks affecting inflation and output should largely fade away, and the monetary policy transmission mechanism should be allowed to work through the economy.[15] Therefore, three-year averages should not be too strongly affected by one-off transitory events.

The majority of explanatory variables are lagged in order to mitigate problems related to potential endogeneity issues, and to acknowledge the existence of transmission lags. Thus, in particular, series featuring trade openness or financial depth are lagged. Likewise, data describing the cyclical position of an economy, such as inflation or output growth, are included as lagged variables. Indices related to central banks' institutional set-ups are also lagged.

The only variables that should, predominantly, reflect unexpected and, to a great extent, exogenous shocks that almost immediately affect price dynamics and should not be a source of a major endogeneity problem, are contemporaneous (non-lagged). This concerns, most of all, oil prices and exchange rate developments. What is also important with respect to oil prices is that they may affect economies differently—depending on whether a country is a net oil importer or a net oil exporter. For that reason whenever oil prices are included in a set of explanatory variables they are accompanied by an additional series being a product of oil prices and a dummy corresponding to a country being a net oil exporter. This should allow for taking into account the structurally diverse impact of changes in oil prices on various economies.

Considering the results of Hausman tests, in which most specifications indicated that random effects estimators are biased, fixed-effects models are used. Importantly, a fixed-effects estimation excludes variables that are constant for a given country, which means that the approach cannot be employed to investigate the direct impact of the Independent_IT index on policy outcomes.[16] At the same time, because the degree of central banks' independence also impacts other aspects of monetary authorities' institutional set-ups, independence is indirectly captured. This follows from recognising that higher independence most likely translates into higher accountability and transparency requirements that are analysed in great detail, as all other indices characterising central banks' institutional set-ups are included in the regressions.

The analysis begins with specifying models describing a variable of interest related to policy outcomes with the help of various series potentially affecting the dependent variable. When deciding what data to include as repressors—apart from economic reasoning suggesting relationships between certain variables, which is the starting point for the analysis—of primary importance is the statistical significance of the estimated coefficients and their intuitive sign. Also checked is whether the explanatory variables are not too strongly correlated with each other, which could bias the results, or are non-stationary (Table 4.14 in Appendix 4). Moreover, preference is given for series that have broad country and time coverage (Table 4.13 in Appendix 4). This means that whenever certain series are available from different sources, covering various countries, the baseline specification uses variables with most observations and other data are used for robustness checks.[17]

The aim of this step is to select one model for each of the dependent variables that is robust with respect to the full sample estimation and to sub-sample estimations, i.e. separately for advanced economies and for emerging market economies. The values of the estimated coefficients may not be the same for the sub-sample estimations, since there may be good reasons to expect some stronger or weaker links between variables in advanced and emerging market economies. However, what is looked at is the significance of the estimated coefficients.

This stage of the analysis should provide a set-up under which—homogeneously across different sub-samples—the significance of the proposed indices related to central banks' institutional arrangements can be verified.

Thus, the baseline specifications are supplemented first with the Mature_ IT index, then sequentially the Informed_IT index, the Explicatory_IT index, the Transparent_IT index, the Accountable_IT index, and finally the Fully_fledged_IT index to check whether the indices are helpful in explaining the variability of the dependent variables. Verification is based on the statistical significance of the estimated coefficients.

Regarding the estimation method, fixed-effects regression models with Driscoll and Kraay standard errors are employed. They produce robust standard errors for panel regressions with cross-sectional dependence.

All the sub-samples used in the study are quite sizeable. The full sample estimations are based on approximately 500 observations (for 37 countries[18]), while the sub-sample estimations for advanced and emerging market economies use approximately 250 data points[19] (for 14 and 24 countries, respectively[20]).

In order to gain more confidence in the proper specification of the baseline models, a number of richer models are estimated. They include additional explanatory variables that were suggested as control variables in some previous research (Table 4.12 in Appendix 4). The results seem to confirm the choice of the baseline specifications.

4.4.2 Dependent variables used to investigate inflation outcomes

The dependent variables related to meeting the primary objective of IT central banks, namely, maintaining price stability, are defined in various ways. To allow for comparison with the existing literature, the three-year average level and the three-year variance of inflation in a given country for a given year are studied. However, in addition, the three-year average deviation of inflation from the inflation target in a given country for a year is investigated.

When speaking about the deviation of inflation from the inflation target, more specifically a percentage point difference between an average annual inflation rate and the midpoint of the inflation target set in a given country for a given year is analysed.[21] For countries using point targets with tolerance bands, or point targets without tolerance bands[22]—a point target is considered, while for countries using band targets with midpoints, or band targets without midpoints—a midpoint of the band is taken into account.

A selection of explanatory variables includes a macroeconomic series capturing the structural and cyclical characteristics of the analysed economies, together with common global factors, as control variables, and the proposed indices of institutional set-ups, since they are also likely to affect inflation developments. Structural indicators are understood as features of an economy that are not of a short-term nature and change only very gradually (such as the level of GDP per capita, an ongoing disinflation process, the degree of trade openness, financial depth). Variables related to the current economic conditions of a given country reflect short-term developments (such as the inflation level and volatility, economic activity measures, fiscal indicators). In turn, global factors are thought of as depicting phenomena that impact simultaneously most, if not all, countries (such as global inflation, world oil prices, output gap in major economies).

4.4.3 Dependent variables used to investigate output stabilisation

Similarly to the case of inflation outcomes, the dependent variables related to stabilising output are defined in several ways. The starting point used to verify the conclusions from the existing literature takes into account the three-year average level and the three-year variance of GDP growth in a given country for a given year. Next, the three-year average output gap estimates are considered, defined as a percentage point deviation of actual GDP from potential GDP expressed in the percentage of potential GDP in a given country for a given year.

Output gap estimates are computed by applying the Hodrick–Prescott filter on annual GDP data for a given economy, because the IMF and the OECD estimates of output gaps are available only for a small selection of the analysed countries, and cover mainly advanced economies.[23] It should, however, be noted that a comparison of output gap estimates from these different sources shows that they are very close to each other, with a correlation at around 0.9. At the same time, since the output gap is an unobservable variable, whose estimates are subject to uncertainty, the results obtained from investigating policy outcomes based on assessing developments in output gap estimates should be treated with caution.

As in the case of models used to explain inflation outcomes, also regressions analysing output stabilisation take account of structural, cyclical, and global factors, as control variables, as well as the proposed indices of central banks' institutional set-ups. The list of potentially important explanatory variables is, to a great extent, analogous to that discussed with respect to inflation outcomes.

4.5 Models used to analyse policy outcomes and robustness checks

As already noted, the proposed indices of IT central banks' institutional set-ups are added on top of selected models that are specified to explain the variability of the dependent variables related to policy outcomes. This allows for verifying whether institutional arrangements matter for inflation and output developments also when a number of control variables are included in the regressions.

4.5.1 Significance of institutional set-ups for inflation outcomes

When investigating inflation outcomes, it should not be too controversial to start with simply looking at the inflation levels. Intuitively, lower inflation supports maintaining price stability, making it more desired than high inflation. In fact, in advanced economies the most typical inflation out-turns (measured as three-year averages) are between 0% and 2%, but quite frequently inflation between 2% and 4% is also seen. In emerging market economies, inflation is often above 4%, sometimes between 2% and 4%, but rarely between 0% and 2% (Charts 4.1 and 4.2). In both groups of economies there are only a few observations where inflation is negative, and even in these cases rather mildly negative price dynamics is reported (of between –2% and 0%). The lack of persistent deflationary episodes that would result in strongly negative price dynamics means that it can be claimed that the

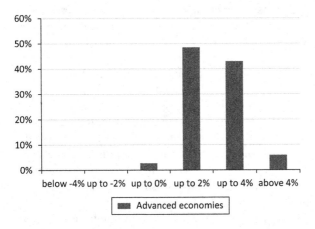

Chart 4.1 Distribution of three-year averages of inflation levels—IT advanced economies.

Source: Own compilation based on inflation data (sources indicated in Table 4.12).

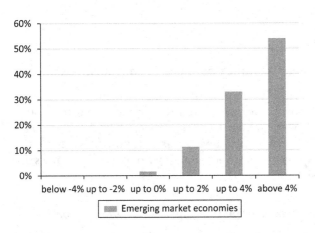

Chart 4.2 Distribution of three-year averages of inflation levels—IT emerging market economies.

lower the inflation level, the better the assessment of central bank's ability to provide price stability.[24] Given such a distribution of inflation outcomes, the models used to explain their variability can be regarded as helpful in identifying what factors support the delivery of price stability.

Analysing the three-year averages of annual inflation rates shows that the following variables are most useful in modelling their changes: a dummy indicating periods of the ongoing disinflation process (predominantly a few initial years of pursuing an inflation targeting framework in some emerging market economies); a dummy indicating 2008 (while three-year averages are used, the dummy indicates all periods that include 2008 in an average); lagged average annual inflation; a lagged output gap; a contemporaneous three-year average exchange rate (its increase denotes depreciation); and a lagged degree of trade openness (Table 4.3). The coefficients have the expected signs and the listed variables are able to explain 70%–80% of the variability of the inflation levels.

Adding lagged indices related to institutional arrangements to the specified baseline models shows that all aspects of central banks' set-ups negatively affect inflation levels in emerging market economies, with several of the estimated coefficients being significantly lower than zero also for advanced economy inflation targeters (this is the case for coefficients linked to the Explicatory_IT index and Transparent_IT index for advanced economies). This would confirm that—especially in emerging market economies, but partly also in advanced economies—higher standards related to the investigated institutional set-ups contribute to lower inflation, and thus to providing price stability. The values of the estimated coefficients are visibly higher for emerging market economy inflation targeters than for advanced economy inflation targeters, which should not be surprising, since inflation levels are much higher and more dispersed in emerging market economies.

While inflation levels are crucial for assessing inflation outcomes, inflation volatility is also of great importance. The more stable inflation is, the more predictable are future prices. Therefore, in the next step, inflation variance is analysed as a dependent variable. Volatility proved, however, much more difficult to model.

After trying many specifications, it turned out that a dummy indicating 2008, lagged average annual inflation, and the contemporaneous three-year volatility of the exchange rate serve to best explain a three-year variance of inflation rates (Table 4.4).[25] The interpretation of the estimated coefficients is in line with intuition and overall the models are explaining around 30%–50% of the variability of the dependent variable.

Regarding inflation volatility, lagged institutional arrangements do seem to matter—this time predominantly for advanced economies, for which they lower inflation volatility. In turn, for emerging market economies, a relevant relationship could be established only in the case of the Informed_IT index, as the rest of the coefficients estimated in that sub-sample are not statistically significant.

Since the study is restricted to inflation targeters only, a natural reference point for assessing policy outcomes with respect to inflation for these economies is the inflation target. Thus, the final step is to analyse deviations of inflation from the targets. Interestingly, for advanced economies, there are more cases of negative deviations compared to positive ones (measured as three-year averages). In turn, emerging market economies report predominantly positive deviations, but the discrepancy between negative and positive deviations is not huge (Charts 4.3 and 4.4). Another point to make is that in both sub-samples there are relatively few larger deviations, with the majority of observations falling between –2 and 2 percentage points,

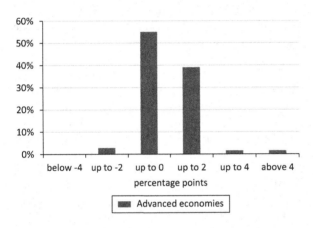

Chart 4.3 Distribution of three-year averages of inflation deviation from target—IT advanced economies.

Source: Own compilation based on inflation data and inflation targets (sources indicated in Table 4.12).

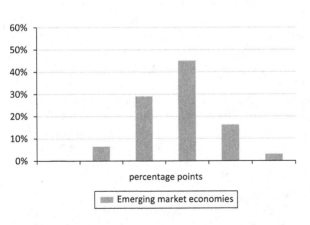

Chart 4.4 Distribution of three-year averages of inflation deviation from target—IT emerging market economies.

270

Table 4.3 Estimation results of models related to inflation levels

	All IT countries	IT advanced economies	IT emerging economies	All IT countries	IT advanced economies	IT emerging economies	All IT countries	IT advanced economies	IT emerging economies	All IT countries	IT advanced economies	IT emerging economies
	Baseline specification			Adding Mature_IT			Adding Informed_IT			Adding Explicatory_IT		
Disinflation	3.93 ***	7.35 ***	1.51 .	3.57 ***	7.05 ***	1.43 *	3.93 ***	7.37 ***	1.39	3.97 ***	7.40 ***	1.53 *
	(3.3)	(6.2)	(1.6)	(3.2)	(6)	(1.9)	(3.2)	(6.1)	(1.4)	(3.2)	(6.1)	(1.8)
Dummy_2008	1.07 ***	0.88 ***	1.40 ***	0.96 ***	0.89 ***	1.13 ***	1.05 ***	0.86 ***	1.35 ***	1.00 ***	0.85 ***	1.21 ***
	(9.6)	(7.5)	(7.4)	(9.1)	(7.2)	(8.3)	(10.1)	(7.5)	(7.6)	(10.6)	(7.4)	(8.3)
CPI_avg_lag_3	0.14 **	0.14 *	0.10 *	0.08 **	0.12 **	0.04	0.14 **	0.14 *	0.08 .	0.13 **	0.13 *	0.06
	(2.7)	(2)	(1.9)	(2.1)	(2.2)	(1)	(2.7)	(1.9)	(1.6)	(2.6)	(1.8)	(1.4)
Output_gap_hp_lag_3	0.16 ***	0.14 ***	0.19 ***	0.18 ***	0.14 ***	0.20 ***	0.17 ***	0.14 ***	0.19 ***	0.17 ***	0.14 ***	0.21 ***
	(4.3)	(3.9)	(4.1)	(4.3)	(3.9)	(4.2)	(4.1)	(3.5)	(4)	(4.1)	(3.8)	(4.1)
FX_scaled_avg_3y	1.21 ***	0.90 .	2.20 ***	0.89 **	0.69	2.06 ***	1.13 ***	0.82 *	2.15 ***	1.07 ***	0.70	2.23 ***
	(3.3)	(1.6)	(3.6)	(2.1)	(1.3)	(4.6)	(3.4)	(1.7)	(4)	(3.1)	(1.4)	(4.9)
Trade_openness_lag_3	-0.03 ***	-0.03 ***	-0.03 **	-0.01	-0.02 **	-0.01	-0.02 ***	-0.03 ***	-0.02 .	-0.02 **	-0.02 ***	-0.01
	(-4.1)	(-4)	(-2.4)	(-0.7)	(-2.7)	(-0.5)	(-3.5)	(-4.1)	(-1.6)	(-2.3)	(-3.5)	(-0.6)
Mature_IT_lag_3				-0.40 ***	-0.15	-0.47 ***						
				(-3.8)	(-1.2)	(-5.2)						
Informed_IT_lag_3							-0.09	-0.04	-0.29 **			
							(-1.2)	(-0.5)	(-2.8)			
Explicatory_IT_lag_3										-0.35 **	-0.19	-0.90 ***
										(-2.4)	(-1.7)	(-3)
No. of observations	509	243	266	509	243	266	509	243	266	509	243	266
N (no. of countries)	37	14	24	37	14	24	37	14	24	37	14	24
T (min)	4	4	4	4	4	4	4	4	4	4	4	4
T (max)	26	26	17	26	26	17	26	26	17	26	26	17
R-squared	0.79	0.79	0.76	0.81	0.79	0.79	0.79	0.79	0.77	0.80	0.79	0.78
Adjusted R-squared	0.77	0.77	0.74	0.79	0.77	0.76	0.77	0.77	0.74	0.78	0.77	0.75

(Continued)

271

Table 4.3 (Continued) Estimation results of models related to inflation levels

	All IT countries	IT advanced economies	IT emerging economies	All IT countries	IT advanced economies	IT emerging economies	All IT countries	IT advanced economies	IT emerging economies	All IT countries	IT advanced economies	IT emerging economies
	Baseline specification			Adding Transparent_IT			Adding Accountable_IT			Adding Fully-fledged_IT		
Disinflation	3.93 *** (3.3)	7.35 *** (6.2)	1.51 . (1.6)	3.98 *** (3.3)	7.36 *** (6.2)	1.69 * (2.1)	3.96 *** (3.3)	7.33 *** (6.3)	1.62 . (1.8)	3.89 *** (3.2)	7.31 *** (6.2)	1.49 * (1.8)
Dummy_2008	1.07 *** (9.6)	0.88 *** (7.5)	1.40 *** (7.4)	1.00 *** (10.8)	0.85 *** (7.7)	1.21 *** (8.8)	1.03 *** (10.8)	0.86 *** (7.7)	1.31 *** (8.8)	0.97 *** (10.2)	0.85 *** (7.8)	1.16 *** (9.1)
CPI_avg_lag_3	0.14 ** (2.7)	0.14 * (2)	0.10 * (1.9)	0.12 ** (2.6)	0.13 * (1.8)	0.05 (1.3)	0.13 ** (2.7)	0.14 * (1.9)	0.07 . (1.6)	0.11 ** (2.4)	0.13 * (1.8)	0.04 (1)
Output_gap_hp_lag_3	0.16 *** (4.3)	0.14 *** (3.9)	0.19 *** (4.1)	0.17 *** (4.1)	0.14 *** (3.8)	0.21 *** (4)	0.17 *** (4.1)	0.14 *** (3.7)	0.20 *** (4)	0.18 *** (4.1)	0.14 *** (3.7)	0.21 *** (4.1)
FX_scaled_avg_3y	1.21 *** (3.3)	0.90 . (1.6)	2.20 *** (3.6)	1.08 *** (3)	0.68 (1.4)	2.34 *** (4.8)	1.07 *** (3.1)	0.74 . (1.5)	2.09 *** (3.7)	0.95 ** (2.6)	0.66 (1.4)	2.15 *** (5)
Trade_openness_lag_3	-0.03 *** (-4.1)	-0.03 *** (-4)	-0.03 ** (-2.4)	-0.02 ** (-2.2)	-0.02 *** (-3.5)	-0.01 (-0.5)	-0.02 *** (-3)	-0.02 *** (-4.1)	-0.02 (-1.1)	-0.01 (-1.6)	-0.02 *** (-3.3)	0.00 (-0.3)
Transparent_IT_lag_3				-0.21 ** (-2.5)	-0.10 (-1.6)	-0.51 ** (-2.9)						
Accountable_IT_lag_3							-0.42 * (-1.8)	-0.18 (-0.9)	-0.86 ** (-2.2)			
Fully-fledged_IT_lag_3										-0.50 ** (-2.7)	-0.20 (-1.4)	-1.01 *** (-4)
No. of observations	509	243	266	509	243	266	509	243	266	509	243	266
N (no. of countries)	37	14	24	37	14	24	37	14	24	37	14	24
T (min)	4	4	4	4	4	4	4	4	4	4	4	4
T (max)	26	26	17	26	26	17	26	26	17	26	26	17
R-squared	0.79	0.79	0.76	0.80	0.79	0.78	0.79	0.75	0.77	0.80	0.79	0.78
Adjusted R-squared	0.77	0.77	0.74	0.78	0.77	0.75	0.78	0.77	0.74	0.78	0.77	0.75

Source: Own compilation based on the constructed indices and macroeconomic variables (sources indicated in Table 4.12).
Notes: Significance codes: *** 0.01; ** 0.05; * 0.1; ` 0.15.

Table 4.4 Estimation results of models related to inflation volatility

	Baseline specification			Adding Mature_IT			Adding Informed_IT			Adding Explicatory_IT		
	All IT countries	IT advanced economies	IT emerging economies	All IT countries	IT advanced economies	IT emerging economies	All IT countries	IT advanced economies	IT emerging economies	All IT countries	IT advanced economies	IT emerging economies
Dummy_2008	2.55 ***	1.51 ***	3.28 ***	2.56 ***	1.70 ***	3.23 ***	2.55 ***	1.51 ***	3.27 ***	2.55 ***	1.54 ***	3.29 ***
	(5.8)	(3.1)	(5.6)	(6.1)	(3.5)	(5.7)	(6)	(3.1)	(5.9)	(5.9)	(3.3)	(5.5)
CPI_avg_lag_3	0.48 ***	0.26 *	0.60 ***	0.43 ***	0.13	0.58 ***	0.46 ***	0.25 *	0.56 ***	0.47 ***	0.24 *	0.61 ***
	(4.7)	(1.9)	(5.6)	(3.4)	(0.8)	(4.5)	(4.3)	(1.8)	(4.9)	(4.4)	(1.8)	(5.1)
FX_scaled_var_3y	102.1 ***	112.8 *	136.7 ***	97.4 **	108.5 *	133.7 .	99.9 **	112.1 *	134.0 .	100.2 **	107.6 *	136.9 .
	(2.8)	(2)	(1.7)	(2.6)	(1.9)	(1.7)	(2.7)	(2)	(1.7)	(2.7)	(1.9)	(1.7)
Mature_IT_lag_3				-0.28 **	-0.55 ***	-0.17						
				(-2.3)	(-3)	(-0.8)						
Informed_IT_lag_3							-0.31 ***	-0.20 *	-0.59 **			
							(-3)	(-1.9)	(-2.1)			
Explicatory_IT_lag_3										-0.21	-0.40 **	0.14
										(-0.9)	(-2.7)	(0.3)
No. of observations	511	242	269	511	242	269	511	242	269	511	242	269
N (no. of countries)	37	14	24	37	14	24	37	14	24	37	14	24
T (min)	4	4	4	4	4	4	4	4	4	4	4	4
T (max)	25	25	17	25	25	17	25	25	17	25	25	17
R-squared	0.42	0.50	0.35	0.42	0.53	0.35	0.42	0.51	0.36	0.42	0.51	0.35
Adjusted R-squared	0.37	0.47	0.28	0.37	0.50	0.28	0.37	0.47	0.29	0.37	0.47	0.28

(Continued)

Table 4.4 (Continued) Estimation results of models related to inflation volatility

	Baseline specification			Adding Transparent_IT			Adding Accountable_IT			Adding Fully_fledged_IT		
	All IT countries	IT advanced economies	IT emerging economies	All IT countries	IT advanced economies	IT emerging economies	All IT countries	IT advanced economies	IT emerging economies	All IT countries	IT advanced economies	IT emerging economies
Dummy_2008	2.55 ***	1.51 ***	3.28 ***	2.55 ***	1.54 ***	3.31 ***	2.55 ***	1.56 ***	3.28 ***	2.55 ***	1.57 ***	3.25 ***
	(5.8)	(3.1)	(5.6)	(5.8)	(3.2)	(5.4)	(5.9)	(3.2)	(5.6)	(6)	(3.3)	(5.7)
CPI_avg_lag_3	0.48 ***	0.26 *	0.60 ***	0.47 ***	0.23 .	0.62 ***	0.47 ***	0.24 *	0.61 ***	0.45 ***	0.21 .	0.59 ***
	(4.7)	(1.9)	(5.6)	(4.3)	(1.7)	(5.1)	(4.4)	(1.8)	(5)	(4)	(1.5)	(4.7)
FX_scaled_var_3y	102.1 ***	112.8 *	136.7 ***	100.9 ***	107.0 *	136.2 .	100.6 *	108.0 *	136.7 .	98.71 **	107.5 *	135.8 .
	(2.8)	(2)	(1.7)	(2.8)	(1.9)	(1.6)	(2.8)	(1.9)	(1.7)	(2.7)	(1.9)	(1.7)
Transparent_IT_lag_3				-0.09	-0.25 **	0.19						
				(-0.6)	(-2.7)	(0.8)						
Accountable_IT_lag_3							-0.46	-0.72 ***	0.11			
							(-1)	(-3.2)	(0.1)			
Fully_fledged_IT_lag_3										-0.41 *	-0.58 ***	-0.25
										(-1.8)	(-3.3)	(-0.6)
No. of observations	511	242	269	511	242	269	511	242	269	511	242	269
N (no. of countries)	37	14	24	37	14	24	37	14	24	37	14	24
T (min)	4	4	4	4	4	4	4	4	4	4	4	4
T (max)	25	25	17	25	25	17	25	25	17	25	25	17
R-squared	0.42	0.50	0.35	0.42	0.51	0.35	0.42	0.51	0.35	0.42	0.52	0.35
Adjusted R-squared	0.37	0.47	0.28	0.37	0.47	0.28	0.37	0.47	0.28	0.37	0.48	0.28

Source: Own compilation based on the constructed indices and macroeconomic variables (sources indicated in Table 4.12).
Notes: Significance codes: *** 0.01; ** 0.05; * 0.1; ˙ 0.15.

Table 4.5 Estimation results of models related to inflation deviations from the target

	Baseline specification			Adding Mature_IT			Adding Informed_IT			Adding Explicatory_IT		
	All IT countries	IT advanced economies	IT emerging economies	All IT countries	IT advanced economies	IT emerging economies	All IT countries	IT advanced economies	IT emerging economies	All IT countries	IT advanced economies	IT emerging economies
Dummy_2008	0.85 *** (5.8)	0.79 *** (5)	0.985 *** (4.8)	0.823 *** (6)	0.82 *** (4.6)	0.866 *** (4.7)	0.84 *** (5.8)	0.774 *** (5.1)	0.97 *** (4.9)	0.809 *** (5.9)	0.781 *** (5.2)	0.876 *** (4.8)
Output_gap_hp_lag_3	0.17 *** (4.3)	0.12 *** (2.9)	0.20 *** (3.8)	0.17 *** (4.3)	0.13 *** (3.1)	0.20 *** (3.7)	0.17 *** (4.3)	0.13 *** (3)	0.20 * (3.8)	0.17 *** (4.2)	0.13 *** (3.1)	0.21 *** (3.6)
Trade_openness_lag_3	-0.02 *** (-3.6)	-0.03 *** (-3.1)	-0.03 ** (-2.3)	-0.01 . (-1.7)	-0.02 ** (-2.6)	-0.02 (-1.1)	-0.02 *** (-3.1)	-0.02 *** (-2.9)	-0.02 * (-1.8)	-0.02 ** (-2.1)	-0.02 ** (-2.6)	-0.02 (-1)
Mature_IT_lag_3				-0.17 . (-1.6)	-0.12 (-0.7)	-0.21 *** (-3.6)						
Informed_IT_lag_3							-0.11 * (-1.8)	-0.09 (-1.1)	-0.10 (-1.2)			
Explicatory_IT_lag_3										-0.3 ** (-2.2)	-0.22 * (-1.8)	-0.47 * (-1.8)
No. of observations	505	240	265	505	240	265	505	240	265	505	240	265
N (no. of countries)	37	14	24	37	14	24	37	14	24	37	14	24
T (min)	4	4	4	4	4	4	4	4	4	4	4	4
T (max)	25	25	17	25	25	17	25	25	17	25	25	17
R-squared	0.55	0.56	0.52	0.55	0.56	0.53	0.55	0.56	0.52	0.55	0.57	0.53
Adjusted R-squared	0.51	0.53	0.47	0.52	0.53	0.48	0.51	0.53	0.46	0.51	0.53	0.47

(Continued)

275

Table 4.5 (Continued) Estimation results of models related to inflation deviations from the target

	Baseline specification			Adding Transparent_IT			Adding Accountable_IT			Adding Fully_fledged_IT		
	All IT countries	IT advanced economies	IT emerging economies	All IT countries	IT advanced economies	IT emerging economies	All IT countries	IT advanced economies	IT emerging economies	All IT countries	IT advanced economies	IT emerging economies
Dummy_2008	0.85 ***	0.79 ***	0.985 ***	0.81 ***	0.783 ***	0.88 ***	0.84 ***	0.79 ***	0.94 ***	0.81 ***	0.79 ***	0.87 ***
	(5.8)	(5)	(4.8)	(6.1)	(5.3)	(4.9)	(6.2)	(5.3)	(5.2)	(6)	(5.3)	(4.9)
Output_gap_hp_lag_3	0.17 ***	0.12 ***	0.20 ***	0.18 ***	0.13 ***	0.21 ***	0.17 ***	0.13 ***	0.20 ***	0.18 ***	0.13 ***	0.20 ***
	(4.3)	(2.9)	(3.8)	(4.1)	(3.1)	(3.6)	(4.2)	(3)	(3.7)	(4.2)	(3.1)	(3.7)
Trade_openness_lag_3	-0.02 ***	-0.03 ***	-0.03 **	-0.02 **	-0.02 **	-0.02	-0.02 **	-0.02 ***	-0.02	-0.01 *	-0.02 **	-0.01
	(-3.6)	(-3.1)	(-2.3)	(-2.1)	(-2.7)	(-0.9)	(-2.7)	(-3)	(-1.4)	(-1.7)	(-2.6)	(-0.9)
Transparent_IT_lag_3				-0.16 *	-0.11 .	-0.25 .						
				(-1.9)	(-1.5)	(-1.5)						
Accountable_IT_lag_3							-0.37 .	-0.27	-0.41			
							(-1.5)	(-1.1)	(-1)			
Fully_fledged_IT_lag_3										-0.33 *	-0.23	-0.45 *
										(-1.9)	(-1.3)	(-2)
No. of observations	505	240	265	505	240	265	505	240	265	505	240	265
N (no. of countries)	37	14	24	37	14	24	37	14	24	37	14	24
T (min)	4	4	4	4	4	4	4	4	4	4	4	4
T (max)	25	25	17	25	25	17	25	25	17	25	25	17
R-squared	0.55	0.56	0.52	0.55	0.57	0.53	0.55	0.56	0.52	0.55	0.57	0.53
Adjusted R-squared	0.51	0.53	0.47	0.51	0.53	0.47	0.51	0.53	0.47	0.52	0.53	0.47

Source: Own compilation based on the constructed indices and macroeconomic variables (sources indicated in Table 4.12).
Notes: Significance codes: *** 0.01; ** 0.05; * 0.1; '.' 0.15.

Table 4.6 Estimation results of models related to inflation deviations from the target controlling for the sign of deviation

	Baseline specification			Adding Mature_IT			Adding Informed_IT			Adding Explicatory_IT		
	All IT countries	IT advanced economies	IT emerging economies	All IT countries	IT advanced economies	IT emerging economies	All IT countries	IT advanced economies	IT emerging economies	All IT countries	IT advanced economies	IT emerging economies
Dummy_2008	0.85 *** (5.8)	0.79 *** (5)	0.98 *** (4.8)	0.83 *** (6.1)	0.82 *** (5)	0.86 *** (4.5)	0.84 *** (6)	0.77 *** (5.6)	0.97 *** (4.8)	0.81 *** (6)	0.78 *** (5.7)	0.87 *** (4.6)
Output_gap_hp_lag_3	0.17 *** (4.3)	0.12 *** (2.9)	0.20 *** (3.8)	0.17 *** (4.1)	0.12 ** (2.7)	0.20 *** (3.5)	0.17 *** (4.1)	0.12 ** (2.7)	0.20 *** (3.6)	0.17 *** (4.1)	0.12 ** (2.7)	0.21 *** (3.6)
Trade_openness_lag_3	-0.02 *** (-3.6)	-0.03 *** (-3.1)	-0.03 ** (-2.3)	-0.01 . (-1.7)	-0.02 *** (-3)	-0.02 (-1.1)	-0.02 *** (-3.1)	-0.02 *** (-3)	-0.02 * (-1.8)	-0.02 ** (-2.1)	-0.02 ** (-2.6)	-0.02 (-1)
Mature_IT_lag_3				-0.17 . (-1.6)	-0.10 (-0.6)	-0.22 *** (-3.1)						
Mature_IT_lag_3 x Dummy_neg_deviation				-0.01 (-0.8)	-0.03 . (-1.7)	0.00 (0.2)						
Informed_IT_lag_3							-0.10 . (-1.6)	-0.08 (-1)	-0.10 (-1.1)			
Informed_IT_lag_3 x Dummy_neg_deviation							-0.02 (-1)	-0.04 * (-2)	-0.01 (-0.2)			
Explicatory_IT_lag_3										-0.3 ** (-2.1)	-0.19 . (-1.6)	-0.48 * (-1.8)
Explicatory_IT_lag_3 x Dummy_neg_deviation										-0.02 (-0.8)	-0.04 * (-1.8)	0.01 (0.2)
No. of observations	505	240	265	431	212	219	431	212	219	431	212	219
N (no. of countries)	37	14	24	37	14	24	37	14	24	37	14	24
T (min)	4	4	4	2	2	2	2	2	2	2	2	2
T (max)	25	25	17	22	22	15	22	22	15	22	22	15
R-squared	0.55	0.56	0.52	0.56	0.57	0.53	0.55	0.57	0.52	0.55	0.57	0.53
Adjusted R-squared	0.51	0.53	0.47	0.52	0.54	0.47	0.51	0.53	0.46	0.51	0.54	0.47

(Continued)

277

Table 4.6 (Continued) Estimation results of models related to inflation deviations from the target controlling for the sign of deviation

	Baseline specification			Adding Transparent_IT			Adding Accountable_IT			Adding Fully_fledged_IT		
	All IT countries	IT advanced economies	IT emerging economies	All IT countries	IT advanced economies	IT emerging economies	All IT countries	IT advanced economies	IT emerging economies	All IT countries	IT advanced economies	IT emerging economies
Dummy_2008	0.85 *** (5.8)	0.79 *** (5)	0.98 *** (4.8)	0.81 *** (6.2)	0.78 *** (5.7)	0.88 *** (4.8)	0.84 *** (6.4)	0.79 *** (5.9)	0.94 *** (5)	0.81 *** (6.1)	0.79 *** (5.8)	0.87 *** (4.7)
Output_gap_hp_lag_3	0.17 *** (4.3)	0.12 *** (2.9)	0.20 *** (3.8)	0.17 *** (4)	0.12 ** (2.7)	0.20 *** (3.5)	0.17 *** (4)	0.12 ** (2.6)	0.20 *** (3.6)	0.17 *** (4)	0.12 ** (2.7)	0.20 *** (3.5)
Trade_openness_lag_3	-0.02 *** (-3.6)	-0.03 *** (-3.1)	-0.03 ** (-2.3)	-0.02 ** (-2.1)	-0.02 ** (-2.8)	-0.02 (-0.9)	-0.02 ** (-2.7)	-0.02 *** (-3.1)	-0.02 (-1.3)	-0.01 (-1.7)	-0.02 ** (-2.8)	-0.01 (-0.9)
Transparent_IT_lag_3				-0.15 . (-1.7)	-0.09 (-1.2)	-0.25 (-1.5)						
Transparent_IT_lag_3 x Dummy_neg_deviation				-0.01 (-0.7)	-0.03 (-1.5)	0.00 (-0.1)						
Accountable_IT_lag_3							-0.36 . (-1.5)	-0.24 (-1)	-0.42 (-1)			
Accountable_IT_lag_3 x Dummy_neg_deviation							-0.02 (-1)	-0.04 * (-2)	0.01 (0.2)			
Fully_fledged_IT_lag_3										-0.33 * (-1.8)	-0.21 (-1.2)	-0.45 * (-1.9)
Fully_fledged_IT_lag_3 x Dummy_neg_deviation										-0.01 (-0.7)	-0.03 * (-1.8)	0.01 (0.2)
No. of observations	505	240	265	431	212	219	431	212	219	431	212	219
N (no. of countries)	37	14	24	37	14	24	37	14	24	37	14	24
T (min)	4	4	4	2	2	2	2	2	2	2	2	2
T (max)	25	25	17	22	22	15	22	22	15	22	22	15
R-squared	0.55	0.56	0.52	0.55	0.57	0.53	0.55	0.57	0.52	0.56	0.57	0.53
Adjusted R-squared	0.51	0.53	0.47	0.51	0.54	0.47	0.51	0.54	0.46	0.52	0.54	0.47

Source: Own compilation based on the constructed indices and macroeconomic variables (sources indicated in Table 4.12).
Notes: Significance codes: *** 0.01; ** 0.05; * 0.1; . 0.15.

whereas advanced economies score somewhat higher in their ability to stay close to the target.[26] Again, the absence of big negative deviations allows for applying a simplified reasoning that the lower the deviation, the better in terms of meeting the inflation target.[27]

Considering three-year averages of inflation deviation from the target, their changes can be explained with a dummy indicating 2008, a lagged output gap, and a lagged degree of trade openness (Table 4.5). The signs of the estimated coefficients are in line with expectations and around 50%–60% of the variability of the dependent variable is explained.

Extending the models with lagged indices related to central banks' institutional set-ups shows that in many of the analysed sub-samples institutional arrangements are reducing the deviations of inflation from the targets (some exceptions are related to coefficients linked to the Informed_IT index and the Accountable_IT index that for both sub-samples proved insignificantly negative, and additionally also to coefficients linked to the Mature_IT index and the Fully_fledged_IT index for advanced economies). Similarly to the case of models analysing inflation levels, this would suggest that more favourable institutional set-ups support maintaining price stability. In turn, the differences in the values of the estimated coefficients for advanced and emerging market economies are often less substantial, since inflation deviations from the target are much more comparable in terms of their values and dispersion in the two groups of countries than was the case for inflation outturns.

In order to control for the sign of deviations, models supplemented with the lagged product of indices used to analyse institutional set-ups and a dummy indicating the negative deviation of inflation from the target are also estimated (Table 4.6). The aim of this step is to check whether in periods of negative deviation better institutional arrangements are helpful in raising inflation. This does not seem to be the case, as in most specifications the impact of institutional set-ups on inflation deviation remains unchanged, i.e. it is either negative or not statistically different than zero.

4.5.2 Significance of institutional set-ups for output stabilisation

Following a similar approach as in the case of modelling inflation outcomes, the analysis of output stabilisation begins with investigating factors affecting GDP growth. A comparison between advanced and emerging market economies shows that—in line with expectations—the dynamics of economic activity are much more muted in the first group of countries, when the most typical GDP growth outturns (measured as three-year averages) are between 2% and 4% (Charts 4.5 and 4.6). In emerging market economies, in almost half of the observations, GDP growth was higher than 4%. Again, negative outturns are rare, and if they occur they are mostly between –2% and 0%.

However, as opposed to inflation for which such levels can be regarded as mildly negative, GDP growth of, for example, –2%, especially when it refers to a three-year average, cannot be described as only slightly negative, and is clearly highly unwelcomed.

When looking at three-year averages of GDP growth, they are quite well explained by lagged GDP growth, a lagged output gap, lagged oil prices that are included together with a variable indicating countries being a net oil exporter, and a lagged exchange rate (Table 4.7). The signs of the estimated coefficients are in line with expectations and the selected variables are explaining around 80% of the variability of the dependent variable.

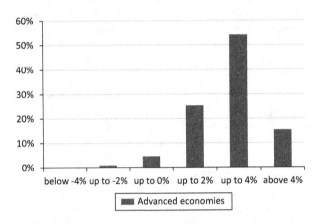

Chart 4.5 Distribution of three-year averages of GDP growth—IT advanced economies.

Source: Own compilation based on GDP data (sources indicated in Table 4.12).

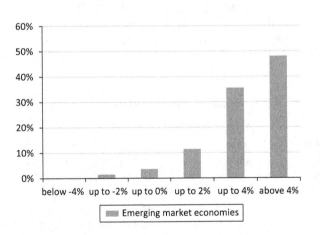

Chart 4.6 Distribution of three-year averages of GDP growth—IT emerging market economies.

280

Analysing the impact of central banks' institutional set-ups shows that not many statistically relevant links can be found between lagged indices related to institutional arrangements and GDP growth. The vast majority of the coefficients are insignificantly different from zero, with the exception of coefficients linked to most institutional indices for emerging market economies that proved negative. For advanced economies, this could be interpreted as a positive finding, since it suggests that institutional arrangements are not curbing GDP growth, whereas for emerging market economies—while more favourable institutional set-ups are mitigating inflation—they are also exerting some dampening impact on GDP growth.

Moving to GDP growth variance seems natural when investigating output stabilisation. The less volatile the GDP growth, the more stable are economic conditions. Similarly to the case of modelling variables related to inflation, GDP growth variance turned out to be more difficult to model than GDP growth.

The variables that were evaluated as most useful in describing three-year variances of GDP growth are the lagged output gap and the lagged output gap in advanced economies that is used as a proxy for the global output gap (Table 4.8).[28] The interpretation of the estimated coefficients is consistent with intuition, and together these two regressors are able to explain close to 50% of the variability of the dependent variable.

Considering GDP growth variance, central banks' lagged institutional arrangements seem irrelevant in most specifications for both advanced and emerging market economies (the only exceptions are coefficients related to the Informed_IT index, the Explicatory_IT index, and the Fully_fledged_IT index for emerging market economies that proved positive, but the latter two only at a 15% significance level). This would signal that institutional arrangements do not visibly affect GDP growth volatility.

When referring to the notion of stabilising output, what is really meant is keeping the output at the highest sustainable level. Neither high but volatile, nor stable but low GDP growth is welcomed. Instead, maintaining a low output gap should be desirable, since it implies that the economy is working close to its potential level that is not posing a risk of an abrupt adjustment. Therefore, the final step is to investigate what factors are affecting output gaps (measured as three-year averages).[29] In fact, the distributions of output gap estimates across advanced and emerging market economies look very much alike (Charts 4.7 and 4.8). The most often reported values are, respectively, between –2% and 0%, as well as between 0% and 2% of potential GDP in both groups of countries.

As already noted, the output gap is an unobservable variable that is difficult to estimate. For that reason, the results obtained during that step of the analysis should be treated with caution. Keeping that in mind, three-year averages of output gaps proved to be best described by lagged GDP growth, lagged oil prices that are again included together with a variable

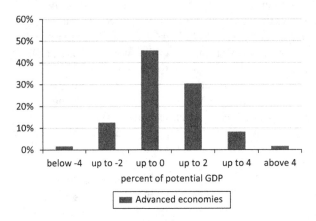

Chart 4.7 Distribution of three-year averages of output gap estimates—IT advanced economies.

Source: Own compilation based on output gap estimates based on the Hodrick–Prescott filter (sources indicated in Table 4.12).

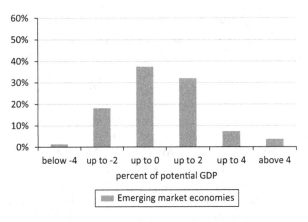

Chart 4.8 Distribution of three-year averages of output gap estimates—IT emerging market economies.

indicating net oil exporters, a lagged exchange rate, lagged global inflation, and lagged ratio of government debt to GDP (Table 4.9). While the estimated coefficients have the expected signs, only around 30%–40% of the variability of the dependent variable can be explained with the specified models.

Looking at lagged indices related to central banks' institutional set-ups, it is clear that there are somewhat more cases when their impact on the dependent variable is relevant. More precisely, in advanced economies one of the institutional arrangements (the Mature_IT index) seems to matter, with its coefficient being statistically positive, while in

Table 4.7 Estimation results of models related to GDP growth

	Baseline specification			Adding Mature_IT			Adding Informed_IT			Adding Explicatory_IT		
	All IT countries	IT advanced economies	IT emerging economies	All IT countries	IT advanced economies	IT emerging economies	All IT countries	IT advanced economies	IT emerging economies	All IT countries	IT advanced economies	IT emerging economies
GDP_growth_lag_3	0.17 *** (5.1)	0.15 *** (4.6)	0.17 *** (3.6)	0.16 *** (4.9)	0.15 *** (4.6)	0.17 *** (3.5)	0.16 *** (5.3)	0.16 *** (4.5)	0.17 *** (3.6)	0.16 *** (4.8)	0.16 *** (4.6)	0.16 *** (3.3)
Output_gap_hp_lag_3	-0.47 *** (-13.2)	-0.47 *** (-11.8)	-0.50 *** (-13.8)	-0.48 *** (-13)	-0.46 *** (-11.9)	-0.52 *** (-12.6)	-0.47 *** (-13.2)	-0.47 *** (-12)	-0.50 *** (-13)	-0.47 *** (-13.2)	-0.47 *** (-11.8)	-0.51 *** (-15)
Oil_prices_avg_lag_3	-0.02 *** (-5)	-0.02 *** (-5.2)	-0.02 *** (-3.9)	-0.01 *** (-4.2)	-0.02 *** (-3.2)	-0.01 * (-2.1)	-0.02 *** (-4.9)	-0.02 *** (-4.9)	-0.02 *** (-3.5)	-0.02 *** (-4.3)	-0.02 *** (-4.1)	-0.01 ** (-2.3)
Oil_prices_avg_lag_3 x Dummy_oil_exporter	0.01 *** (4)	0.00 (-0.3)	0.02 *** (5.1)	0.01 *** (3.3)	0.00 (-0.3)	0.02 *** (3.8)	0.01 *** (3.9)	0.00 (-0.8)	0.02 *** (5.1)	0.01 *** (4)	0.00 (-0.3)	0.02 *** (4.7)
FX_scaled_lag_3	-1.09 ** (-2.7)	-0.93 ** (-2.5)	-2.75 *** (-4.1)	-1.03 ** (-2.8)	-0.84 * (-1.8)	-3.20 *** (-4.7)	-1.13 ** (-2.8)	-1.05 ** (-2.6)	-2.75 *** (-4.1)	-1.07 ** (-2.6)	-1.01 ** (-2.4)	-2.98 *** (-4.7)
Mature_IT_lag_3				-0.09 (-1.3)	-0.04 (-0.4)	-0.24 ** (-2.2)						
Informed_IT_lag_3							0.06 (1)	0.10 (1)	0.04 (0.5)			
Explicatory_IT_lag_3										-0.06 (-0.5)	0.09 (0.5)	-0.50 ** (-2.9)
No. of observations	472	229	243	472	229	243	472	229	243	472	229	243
N (no. of countries)	37	14	24	37	14	24	37	14	24	37	14	24
T (min)	3	3	3	3	3	3	3	3	3	3	3	3
T (max)	25	25	16	25	25	16	25	25	16	25	25	16
R-squared	0.83	0.82	0.82	0.83	0.82	0.83	0.83	0.82	0.82	0.83	0.82	0.83
Adjusted R-squared	0.81	0.81	0.80	0.82	0.81	0.80	0.81	0.81	0.80	0.81	0.81	0.80

(Continued)

Table 4.7 Continue Estimation results of models related to GDP growth

	Baseline specification			Adding Transparent_IT			Adding Accountable_IT			Adding Fully_fledged_IT		
	All IT countries	IT advanced economies	IT emerging economies	All IT countries	IT advanced economies	IT emerging economies	All IT countries	IT advanced economies	IT emerging economies	All IT countries	IT advanced economies	IT emerging economies
GDP_growth_lag_3	0.17 ***	0.15 ***	0.17 ***	0.16 ***	0.16 ***	0.16 ***	0.16 ***	0.16 ***	0.17 ***	0.16 ***	0.16 ***	0.17 ***
	(5.1)	(4.6)	(3.6)	(4.9)	(4.6)	(3.3)	(5)	(4.5)	(3.4)	(4.9)	(4.5)	(3.3)
Output_gap_hp_lag_3	-0.47 ***	-0.47 ***	-0.50 ***	-0.47 ***	-0.47 ***	-0.51 ***	-0.47 ***	-0.47 ***	-0.51 ***	-0.47 ***	-0.47 ***	-0.51 ***
	(-13.2)	(-11.8)	(-13.8)	(-13.2)	(-11.9)	(-14.9)	(-13.2)	(-11.6)	(-14.1)	(-13.1)	(-11.8)	(-13.5)
Oil_prices_avg_lag_3	-0.02 ***	-0.02 ***	-0.02 ***	-0.02 ***	-0.02 ***	-0.01 **	-0.02 ***	-0.02 ***	-0.02 **	-0.02 ***	-0.02 ***	-0.01 *
	(-5)	(-5.2)	(-3.9)	(-4.1)	(-3.7)	(-2.2)	(-4)	(-3.9)	(-2.8)	(-3.7)	(-3.2)	(-2)
Oil_prices_avg_lag_3 x Dummy_oil_exporter	0.01 ***	0.00	0.02 ***	0.01 ***	0.00	0.02 ***	0.01 ***	0.00	0.02 ***	0.01 ***	0.00	0.02 ***
	(4)		(5.1)	(3.9)	(0.1)	(4.9)	(4)	(-0.2)	(4.7)	(3.8)	(-0.1)	(4.5)
FX_scaled_lag_3	-1.09 **	-0.93 **	-2.75 ***	-1.07 **	-1.01 **	-3.02 ***	-1.08 **	-0.99 **	-2.97 ***	-1.07 **	-1.07 **	-3.05 ***
	(-2.7)	(-2.5)	(-4.1)	(-2.6)	(-2.5)	(-5)	(-2.5)	(-2.4)	(-4.9)	(-2.6)	(-2.2)	(-4.8)
Transparent_IT_lag_3				-0.03	0.07	-0.31 ***						
				(-0.4)	(0.6)	(-3.6)						
Accountable_IT_lag_3							-0.04	0.15	-0.51 **			
							(-0.2)	(0.5)	(-2.8)			
Fully_fledged_IT_lag_3										-0.06	0.14	-0.48 **
										(-0.4)	(0.5)	(-2.6)
No. of observations	472	229	243	472	229	243	472	229	243	472	229	243
N (no. of countries)	37	14	24	37	14	24	37	14	24	37	14	24
T (min)	3	3	3	3	3	3	3	3	3	3	3	3
T (max)	25	25	16	25	25	16	25	25	16	25	25	16
R-squared	0.83	0.82	0.82	0.83	0.82	0.83	0.83	0.82	0.83	0.83	0.82	0.83
Adjusted R-squared	0.81	0.81	0.80	0.81	0.81	0.81	0.81	0.81	0.80	0.81	0.81	0.80

Source: Own compilation based on the constructed indices and macroeconomic variables (sources indicated in Table 4.12).
Notes: Significance codes: *** 0.01; ** 0.05; * 0.1; ' 0.15.

Table 4.8 Estimation results of models related to GDP growth volatility

	Baseline specification			Adding Mature_IT			Adding Informed_IT			Adding Explicatory_IT		
	All IT countries	IT advanced economies	IT emerging economies	All IT countries	IT advanced economies	IT emerging economies	All IT countries	IT advanced economies	IT emerging economies	All IT countries	IT advanced economies	IT emerging economies
Output_gap_hp_lag_3	0.90 *** (5)	0.81 *** (4.3)	0.97 *** (4.3)	0.90 *** (5.1)	0.82 *** (4.6)	0.98 *** (4.5)	0.89 *** (5.1)	0.80 *** (4.4)	0.97 *** (4.3)	0.89 *** (5.2)	0.81 *** (4.3)	0.94 *** (4.5)
Advanced_economies_output_gap_lag_3	1.10 ** (2.3)	0.82 ** (2.5)	1.48 ** (2.3)	1.11 ** (2.3)	0.77 * (2.1)	1.60 ** (2.4)	1.14 ** (2.4)	0.84 ** (2.6)	1.53 ** (2.4)	1.15 ** (2.5)	0.82 ** (2.6)	1.63 ** (2.5)
Mature_IT_lag_3				0.05 (0.2)	-0.50 (-1.1)	0.59 (1.5)						
Informed_IT_lag_3							0.34 (1)	0.10 (0.2)	0.68 ** (2.6)			
Explicatory_IT_lag_3										0.53 (0.9)	-0.02 (0)	1.76 . (1.7)
No. of observations	415	231	184	415	231	184	415	231	184	415	231	184
N (no. of countries)	28	14	15	28	14	15	28	14	15	28	14	15
T (min)	3	3	4	3	3	4	3	3	4	3	3	4
T (max)	25	25	17	25	25	17	25	25	17	25	25	17
R-squared	0.47	0.46	0.48	0.47	0.47	0.48	0.47	0.46	0.48	0.47	0.46	0.48
Adjusted R-squared	0.43	0.43	0.43	0.43	0.43	0.43	0.43	0.42	0.43	0.43	0.42	0.43

(Continued)

285

Table 4.8 (Continued) Estimation results of models related to GDP growth volatility

	Baseline specification			Adding Transparent_IT			Adding Accountable_IT			Adding Fully_fledged_IT		
	All IT countries	IT advanced economies	IT emerging economies	All IT countries	IT advanced economies	IT emerging economies	All IT countries	IT advanced economies	IT emerging economies	All IT countries	IT advanced economies	IT emerging economies
Output_gap_hp_lag_3	0.90 ***	0.81 ***	0.97 ***	0.90 ***	0.82 ***	0.95 ***	0.90 ***	0.80 ***	0.97 ***	0.89 ***	0.82 ***	0.96 ***
	(5)	(4.3)	(4.3)	(5.2)	(4.3)	(4.5)	(5.1)	(4.3)	(4.4)	(5.2)	(4.5)	(4.5)
Advanced_economies_output_gap_lag_3	1.10 **	0.82 **	1.48 **	1.12 **	0.80 **	1.56 **	1.12 **	0.84 **	1.51 **	1.14 **	0.80 **	1.60 **
	(2.3)	(2.5)	(2.3)	(2.4)	(2.4)	(2.4)	(2.4)	(2.6)	(2.3)	(2.4)	(2.4)	(2.4)
Transparent_IT_lag_3				0.08	−0.11	0.49						
				(0.3)	(−0.4)	(0.8)						
Accountable_IT_lag_3							0.45	0.18	1.02			
							(0.5)	(0.2)	(0.8)			
Fully_fledged_IT_lag_3										0.34	−0.24	1.26 .
										(0.6)	(−0.4)	(1.5)
No. of observations	415	231	184	415	231	184	415	231	184	415	231	184
N (no. of countries)	28	14	15	28	14	15	28	14	15	28	14	15
T (min)	3	3	4	3	3	4	3	3	4	3	3	4
T (max)	25	25	17	25	25	17	25	25	17	25	25	17
R-squared	0.47	0.46	0.48	0.47	0.46	0.48	0.47	0.46	0.48	0.47	0.47	0.48
Adjusted R-squared	0.43	0.43	0.43	0.43	0.42	0.42	0.43	0.42	0.42	0.43	0.43	0.43

Source: Own compilation based on the constructed indices and macroeconomic variables (sources indicated in Table 4.12).
Notes: Significance codes: *** 0.01; ** 0.05; * 0.1; ˙ 0.15.

Table 4.9 Estimation results of models related to output gap

	All IT countries	IT advanced economies	IT emerging economies	All IT countries	IT advanced economies	IT emerging economies	All IT countries	IT advanced economies	IT emerging economies	All IT countries	IT advanced economies	IT emerging economies
	Baseline specification			Adding Mature_IT			Adding Informed_IT			Adding Explicatory_IT		
GDP_growth_lag_3	0.31 ***	0.33 ***	0.32 ***	0.31 ***	0.32 ***	0.32 ***	0.31 ***	0.33 ***	0.32 ***	0.31 ***	0.33 ***	0.31 ***
	(4.3)	(4.4)	(5.1)	(4.3)	(4.5)	(5.5)	(4.4)	(4.4)	(5.1)	(4.3)	(4.3)	(5.4)
Oil_prices_avg_lag_3	-0.01 .	-0.01 *	-0.01 *	-0.02 **	-0.02 **	0.00	-0.02	-0.01 **	-0.01 .	-0.01	-0.01 **	0.00
	(-1.7)	(-2)	(-1.8)	(-2.3)	(-3.1)	(-0.5)	(-1.9)	(-2.1)	(-1.6)	(-1.6)	(-2.1)	(-0.6)
Oil_prices_avg_lag_3 x Dummy_oil_exporter	0.01 ***	-0.01	0.03 ***	0.01 ***	0.00	0.02 ***	0.012 ***	-0.01	0.027 ***	0.011 ***	-0.01	0.03 ***
	(3.2)	(-1.2)	(6.3)	(3.1)	(-0.9)	(4.3)	(3.3)	(-1.2)	(6.2)	(3.1)	(-1.1)	(5.6)
FX_scaled_lag_3	-2.17 **	-1.3 *	-5.04 ***	-2.16 **	-1.83 *	-5.86 ***	-2.23 ***	-1.33 *	-5.04 ***	-2.13 **	-1.32 *	-5.22 ***
	(-2.6)	(-1.8)	(-3.2)	(-2.6)	(-2)	(-3.1)	(-2.7)	(-1.9)	(-3.2)	(-2.6)	(-1.7)	(-3.1)
CPI_world_avg_lag_3	-0.07 ***	-0.07 ***	-0.73 ***	-0.06 **	-0.04 **	-0.94 ***	-0.06 **	-0.06 ***	-0.74 ***	-0.07 ***	-0.06 ***	-0.89 ***
	(-3.3)	(-4.3)	(-3.9)	(-2.5)	(-2.3)	(-4.8)	(-2.7)	(-3.2)	(-3.8)	(-2.9)	(-3.4)	(-4.8)
Debt_to_GDP_lag_3	-0.04 ***	-0.04 ***	-0.07 ***	-0.04 ***	-0.04 ***	-0.04 **	-0.04 ***	-0.04 ***	-0.07 ***	-0.04 ***	-0.04 ***	-0.06 ***
	(-3.8)	(-3.2)	(-4.3)	(-3.8)	(-3.5)	(-2.6)	(-3.9)	(-3.2)	(-4.2)	(-3.7)	(-3.2)	(-3.9)
Mature_IT_lag_3				0.08	0.66 **	-0.50 **						
				(0.4)	(2.5)	(-2.8)						
Informed_IT_lag_3							0.095	0.025	-0.04			
							(1.2)	(0.2)	(-0.3)			
Explicatory_IT_lag_3										-0.09	0.019	-0.99 ***
										(-0.6)	(0.1)	(-4.5)
No. of observations	500	235	265	500	235	265	500	235	265	500	235	265
N (no. of countries)	37	14	24	37	14	24	37	14	24	37	14	24
T (min)	4	4	4	4	4	4	4	4	4	4	4	4
T (max)	26	26	17	26	26	17	26	26	17	26	26	17
R-squared	0.37	0.46	0.42	0.37	0.50	0.45	0.37	0.46	0.42	0.37	0.46	0.44
Adjusted R-squared	0.31	0.42	0.35	0.31	0.45	0.38	0.31	0.41	0.35	0.31	0.41	0.37

(Continued)

287

Table 4.9 (Continued) Estimation results of models related to output gap (cont.)

	Baseline specification			Adding Transparent_IT			Adding Accountable_IT			Adding Fully-fledged_IT		
	All IT countries	IT advanced economies	IT emerging economies	All IT countries	IT advanced economies	IT emerging economies	All IT countries	IT advanced economies	IT emerging economies	All IT countries	IT advanced economies	IT emerging economies
GDP_growth_lag_3	0.31 *** (4.3)	0.33 *** (4.4)	0.32 *** (5.1)	0.31 *** (4.3)	0.33 *** (4.3)	0.31 *** (5.4)	0.31 *** (4.3)	0.33 *** (4.3)	0.32 *** (5.1)	0.31 *** (4.4)	0.33 *** (4.4)	0.32 *** (5.4)
Oil_prices_avg_lag_3	-0.01 . (-1.7)	-0.01 * (-2)	-0.01 * (-1.8)	-0.01 . (-1.7)	-0.01 ** (-2.2)	-0.01 (-0.7)	-0.01 . (-1.6)	-0.01 * (-1.5)	-0.01 (-1.4)	-0.01 * (-2)	-0.02 ** (-2.5)	0.00 (-0.4)
Oil_prices_avg_lag_3 x Dummy_oil_exporter	0.01 *** (3.2)	-0.01 (-1.2)	0.03 *** (6.3)	0.01 *** (3.2)	-0.01 (-0.9)	0.03 *** (6.2)	0.01 *** (3.2)	-0.01 (-1.1)	0.03 *** (6.2)	0.01 *** (3.2)	-0.01 (-1)	0.03 *** (5.4)
FX_scaled_lag_3	-2.17 ** (-2.6)	-1.30 * (-1.8)	-5.04 *** (-3.2)	-2.18 ** (-2.6)	-1.38 * (-1.9)	-5.34 *** (-3.2)	-2.15 ** (-2.5)	-1.27 * (-1.8)	-5.35 *** (-3.5)	-2.20 *** (-2.7)	-1.50 * (-2)	-5.51 *** (-3.2)
CPI_world_avg_lag_3	-0.07 *** (-3.3)	-0.07 *** (-4.3)	-0.73 *** (-3.9)	-0.07 *** (-2.9)	-0.06 *** (-3.5)	-0.88 *** (-4.9)	-0.07 *** (-3.2)	-0.07 *** (-3.8)	-0.80 *** (-4.4)	-0.06 *** (-2.5)	-0.06 *** (-2.9)	-0.93 *** (-5)
Debt_to_GDP_lag_3	-0.04 *** (-3.8)	-0.04 *** (-3.2)	-0.07 *** (-4.3)	-0.04 *** (-3.8)	-0.04 *** (-3.2)	-0.05 *** (-3.5)	-0.04 *** (-3.7)	-0.04 *** (-3.2)	-0.06 *** (-4)	-0.04 *** (-3.9)	-0.04 *** (-3.3)	-0.05 *** (-3.3)
Transparent_IT_lag_3				0.00 (0)	0.07 (0.6)	-0.51 *** (-4)						
Accountable_IT_lag_3							-0.08 (-0.5)	-0.05 (-0.2)	-0.83 ** (-2.3)			
Fully_fledged_IT_lag_3										0.08 (0.3)	0.26 (1)	-0.99 *** (-3.5)
No. of observations	500	235	265	500	235	265	500	235	265	500	235	265
N (no. of countries)	37	14	24	37	14	24	37	14	24	37	14	24
T (min)	4	4	4	4	4	4	4	4	4	4	4	4
T (max)	26	26	17	26	26	17	26	26	17	26	26	17
R-squared	0.37	0.46	0.42	0.37	0.47	0.44	0.37	0.46	0.43	0.37	0.47	0.44
Adjusted R-squared	0.31	0.42	0.35	0.31	0.42	0.37	0.31	0.41	0.36	0.31	0.42	0.37

Source: Own compilation based on the constructed indices and macroeconomic variables (sources indicated in Table 4.12).
Notes: Significance codes: *** 0.01; ** 0.05; * 0.1; '.' 0.15.

Table 4.10 Estimation results of models related to output gap controlling for the sign of the output gap

	All IT countries	IT advanced economies	IT emerging economies	All IT countries	IT advanced economies	IT emerging economies	All IT countries	IT advanced economies	IT emerging economies	All IT countries	IT advanced economies	IT emerging economies
	Baseline specification			Adding Mature_IT			Adding Informed_IT			Adding Explicatory_IT		
GDP_growth_lag_3	0.31 ***	0.33 ***	0.32 ***	0.30 ***	0.32 ***	0.31 ***	0.29 ***	0.33 ***	0.30 ***	0.30 ***	0.33 ***	0.30 ***
	(4.3)	(4.4)	(5.1)	(4.6)	(4.6)	(5.5)	(4.7)	(4.5)	(5.4)	(4.7)	(4.4)	(5.7)
Oil_prices_avg_lag_3	-0.01 .	-0.01 *	-0.01	-0.02 **	-0.02 ***	-0.01	-0.02 *	-0.01 **	-0.02 *	-0.01 *	-0.01 **	-0.01
	(-1.7)	(-2)	(-1.8)	(-2.5)	(-3.1)	(-1.3)	(-2)	(-2.1)	(-2)	(-1.8)	(-2.1)	(-1.3)
Oil_prices_avg_lag_3 x Dummy_oil_exporter	0.01 ***	-0.01	0.03 ***	0.01 ***	0.00	0.02 ***	0.01 **	-0.01	0.02 ***	0.01 **	-0.01	0.02
	(3.2)	(-1.2)	(6.3)	(2.9)	(-1)	(4)	(2.8)	(-1.2)	(5.9)	(2.8)	(-1.1)	(5.2)
FX_scaled_lag_3	-2.17 **	-1.30 *	-5.04 ***	-2.24 ***	-1.82 **	-5.92 ***	-2.27 ***	-1.33 *	-5.08 ***	-2.15 **	-1.32 *	-5.27 ***
	(-2.6)	(-1.8)	(-3.2)	(-2.7)	(-2)	(-3.5)	(-2.8)	(-1.8)	(-3.7)	(-2.7)	(-1.7)	(-3.6)
CPI_world_avg_lag_3	-0.07 ***	-0.07 ***	-0.73 ***	-0.06 **	-0.04 **	-0.92 ***	-0.06 **	-0.06 ***	-0.72 ***	-0.07 **	-0.06 ***	-0.87 ***
	(-3.3)	(-4.3)	(-3.9)	(-2.4)	(-2.4)	(-4.5)	(-2.6)	(-3.2)	(-3.3)	(-2.7)	(-3.4)	(-4.3)
Debt_to_GDP_lag_3	-0.04 ***	-0.04 ***	-0.07 ***	-0.04 ***	-0.04 ***	-0.04 *	-0.04 ***	-0.04 ***	-0.06 ***	-0.04 ***	-0.04 ***	-0.05 ***
	(-3.8)	(-3.2)	(-4.3)	(-3.9)	(-3.8)	(-2.3)	(-4)	(-3.5)	(-3.7)	(-4)	(-3.5)	(-3.4)
Mature_IT_lag_3				0.10	0.65 **	-0.38 **						
				(0.5)	(2.5)	(-2.2)						
Mature_IT_lag_3 x Dummy_neg_gap				-0.06 *	0.01	-0.13 ***						
				(-1.9)	(0.3)	(-3.2)						
Informed_IT_lag_3							0.16 **	0.02	0.13			
							(2.1)	(0.2)	(0.8)			
Informed_IT_lag_3 x Dummy_neg_gap							-0.08 **	0.00	-0.14 **			
							(-2.2)	(0.2)	(-3)			
Explicatory_IT_lag_3										-0.01	0.02	-0.77 ***
										(0)	(0.1)	(-4)
Explicatory_IT_lag_3 x Dummy_neg_gap										-0.10 *	0.00	-0.18 **
										(-2.1)	(0)	(-2.9)
No. of observations	500	235	265	435	217	218	435	217	218	435	217	218
N (no. of countries)	37	14	24	37	14	24	37	14	24	37	14	24
T (min)	4	4	4	2	2	2	2	2	2	2	2	2
T (max)	26	26	17	24	24	15	24	24	15	24	24	15
R-squared	0.37	0.46	0.42	0.38	0.50	0.47	0.39	0.46	0.46	0.39	0.46	0.47
Adjusted R-squared	0.31	0.42	0.35	0.32	0.45	0.40	0.33	0.41	0.39	0.33	0.41	0.40

(Continued)

289

Table 4.10 (Continued) Estimation results of models related to output gap controlling for the sign of the output gap (cont.)

	Baseline specification			Adding Transparent_IT			Adding Accountable_IT			Adding Fully-fledged_IT		
	All IT countries	IT advanced economies	IT emerging economies	All IT countries	IT advanced economies	IT emerging economies	All IT countries	IT advanced economies	IT emerging economies	All IT countries	IT advanced economies	IT emerging economies
GDP_growth_lag_3	0.31 ***	0.33 ***	0.32 ***	0.30 ***	0.33 ***	0.30 ***	0.30 ***	0.33 ***	0.30 ***	0.30 ***	0.33 ***	0.31 ***
	(4.3)	(4.4)	(5.1)	(4.7)	(4.5)	(5.8)	(4.7)	(4.5)	(5.4)	(4.7)	(4.6)	(5.6)
Oil_prices_avg_lag_3	-0.01 .	-0.01 *	-0.01 *	-0.02 *	-0.01 **	-0.01	-0.02 .	-0.01 *	-0.02 *	-0.02 **	-0.02 **	-0.01
	(-1.7)	(-2)	(-1.8)	(-1.8)	(-2.2)	(-1.4)	(-1.7)	(-1.9)	(-1.8)	(-2.1)	(-2.5)	(-1.2)
Oil_prices_avg_lag_3 x Dummy_oil exporter	0.01 ***	-0.01	0.03 ***	0.01 **	-0.01	0.02 ***	0.01 ***	-0.01	0.03 ***	0.01 ***	-0.01	0.02 ***
	(3.2)	(-1.2)	(6.3)	(2.8)	(-0.9)	(5.9)	(2.8)	(-1.1)	(5.9)	(2.9)	(-1)	(4.9)
FX_scaled_lag_3	-2.17 **	-1.30 *	-5.04 ***	-2.22 **	-1.38 .	-5.36 ***	-2.18 **	-1.27 *	-5.36 ***	-2.23 **	-1.50 *	-5.51 ***
	(-2.6)	(-1.8)	(-3.2)	(-2.8)	(-1.9)	(-3.8)	(-2.6)	(-1.7)	(-3.9)	(-2.8)	(-2)	(-3.7)
CPI_world_avg_lag_3	-0.07 ***	-0.07 ***	-0.73 ***	-0.06 **	-0.06 ***	-0.87 ***	-0.06 **	-0.07 ***	-0.78 ***	-0.06 **	-0.06 ***	-0.91 ***
	(-3.3)	(-4.3)	(-3.9)	(-2.8)	(-3.5)	(-4.3)	(-2.9)	(-3.9)	(-3.9)	(-2.4)	(-2.9)	(-4.5)
Debt_to_GDP_lag_3	-0.04 ***	-0.04 ***	-0.07 ***	-0.04 ***	-0.04 ***	-0.05 ***	-0.04 ***	-0.04 ***	-0.05 ***	-0.04 ***	-0.04 ***	-0.04 **
	(-3.8)	(-3.2)	(-4.3)	(-4)	(-3.5)	(-3.1)	(-4)	(-3.4)	(-3.3)	(-4.1)	(-3.6)	(-2.8)
Transparent_IT_lag_3				0.07	0.07	-0.38 ***						
				(0.8)	(0.5)	(-3.2)						
Transparent_IT_lag_3 x Dummy_neg_gap				-0.08 **	0.00	-0.16 ***						
				(-2.2)	(-0.1)	(-3.2)						
Accountable_IT_lag_3							0.05	-0.05	-0.58			
							(0.3)	(-0.2)	(-1.4)			
Accountable_IT_lag_3 x Dummy_neg_gap							-0.06 *	0.00	-0.12 **			
							(-2)	(0)	(-2.6)			
Fully_fledged_IT_lag_3										0.15	0.27	-0.76 **
										(0.7)	(1)	(-2.6)
Fully_fledged_IT_lag_3 x Dummy_neg_gap										-0.08 **	0.00	-0.15 ***
										(-2.2)	(0)	(-3.1)
No. of observations	500	235	265	435	217	218	435	217	218	435	217	218
N (no. of countries)	37	14	24	37	14	24	37	14	24	37	14	24
T (min)	4	4	4	2	2	2	2	2	2	2	2	2
T (max)	26	26	17	24	24	15	24	24	15	24	24	15
R-squared	0.37	0.46	0.42	0.39	0.47	0.48	0.38	0.46	0.46	0.39	0.47	0.47
Adjusted R-squared	0.31	0.42	0.35	0.33	0.41	0.41	0.32	0.41	0.38	0.33	0.42	0.40

Source: Own compilation based on the constructed indices and macroeconomic variables (sources indicated in Table 4.12).
Notes: Significance codes: *** 0.01; ** 0.05; * 0.1; `.` 0.15.

emerging market economies almost all of the coefficients are statistically negative (the only exception is a coefficient related to the Informed_IT index that proved insignificant). This could suggest that in advanced economies institutional set-ups do not have any material effect on output gaps, whereas in emerging market economies such a link could be established and is negative.

To allow for controlling whether the relationship between institutional arrangements and output gaps changes depending on the sign of the output gap, models supplemented with the product of the indices used to analyse institutional set-ups and a dummy indicating a negative output gap are estimated (Table 4.10). This extension results in more coefficients related to institutional set-ups turning significantly negative, but the general conclusions remain unchanged, indicating that the sign of the output gap does not matter for the investigated links.

4.5.3 Robustness checks

As already mentioned, several robustness checks were conducted. Some of them are reported in detail (Tables 4.15–4.20 in Appendix 4), and some are only briefly discussed when analysing the results.

The first group of robustness checks included considering various formulations of the dependent variables. One approach adopted in this respect applied to all dependent variables, since it related to using multi-year averages of data. Another modification was relevant only for models describing inflation deviations from the target and output gap changes, since in these two cases alternative measures of deviations from the target and alternative estimates of output gaps were used (alternative estimates of output gaps were also employed in models where they were needed as explicatory variables).

Regarding multi-year averages, there are no indisputable reasons behind choosing a three-year period instead of longer or shorter periods. As noted above, three years seems a natural choice given the most typical interpretation of a medium term. However, judging by the horizon of central banks' forecasts, which for some monetary authorities is two rather than three years, it may be reasonable to look also at two-year averages of the analysed data or even at annual observations. Thus, the baseline specifications were also estimated with the dependent variables computed as two-year averages and substituted simply with annual data, which did not invalidate the main results. Longer multi-year averages were not tested, since it would excessively restrict the number of observations.

Moving to the deviations of inflation from the inflation target, setting continuous targets has clearly been a dominant practice in inflation targeting economies. This spoke in favour of using a difference between an average annual inflation rate and the inflation target for a given year as the dependent variable in models describing inflation deviations from the target. However, some countries were, or still are, using end-year targets. To account for that, for observations when an end-year target was valid, the dependent variable was computed as a difference between the end-year annual inflation rate and the end-year inflation target. Since this only applied to a small fraction of observations, such a change did not affect the estimation results.

Considering output gap estimates, which for many of the analysed economies are not easily available, estimates computed by applying the Hodrick–Prescott filter on annual GDP data were used in the specifications of models describing output gap changes and in models where output gaps were used as explicatory variables. The two major advantages of such an approach are, first, that it allowed for calculating output gap estimates for all inflation targeting economies, and second, that this procedure could be applied in a uniform way for all countries. This method, although very simple, should provide a reasonable proxy for output gaps. As noted before, this is corroborated by the fact that, for countries for which the IMF or the OECD estimates of output gaps were available, they proved to be very close to those computed with the help of the Hodrick–Prescott filter. This was also true for estimates derived by applying the Hodrick–Prescott filter on quarterly GDP data, which was also done to confirm the reliability of the results. Using alternative estimates of output gaps taken from the IMF or the OECD significantly restricted the sample, while leaving the estimation results largely unaffected.

The second group of robustness checks encompassed testing the significance of additional explanatory variables in order to avoid disregarding important regressors. Predominantly, variables suggested in the existing literature as control variables were investigated in that stage, and—similarly as in the baseline specifications—included data capturing the structural and cyclical features of the analysed economies, together with global factors. Examples of such variables comprise indicators of overall economic development (GDP per capita), financial depth (money-to-GDP ratio and credit-to-GDP ratio), fiscal position (debt-to-GDP ratio and deficit-to-GDP ratio), external competitiveness (exchange rate, terms-of-trade), and external conditions (oil prices, OECD inflation, output gap in advanced economies). The estimation results for models based on broader sets of explanatory variables are reported in Tables 4.15–4.20 in Appendix 4. They allow for concluding that the main models should not suffer from the omitted variable problem.

Finally, the third group of checks verifying the stability of the results was considered using various sub-samples. Following that procedure, sub-samples restricted to the "old" or the "medium-aged" inflation targeters were applied. On the one hand, it enabled estimating models based on observations derived by setting a simple rule dividing the whole sample into sub-samples, and, on the other hand, it kept the size of the sub-samples reasonably large.[30] Again, it turned out that the sub-samples' results are no grounds to question the main findings.

After considering all the proposed modifications, including a number of alternative specifications noted above, it seems that the results are robust. Thus, they can be used to formulate some policy conclusions.

4.6 Overall assessment of the results and policy conclusions

After analysing the impact of the individual indices of monetary authorities' institutional arrangements on variables associated with inflation and output developments, some general conclusions can be drawn on the importance of institutional set-ups under an inflation targeting framework.

4.6.1 Summarising the estimation results

In order to get an overview of the results, it seems useful to look at a table summarising the signs and the significance of the estimated coefficients related to IT central banks' institutional set-ups in models specified to describe inflation and output developments (Table 4.11). Considering both the full sample estimation results and the sub-samples estimation results allows for identifying differences between advanced economy inflation tar-geters and emerging market economy inflation targeters.

Without going into a detailed analysis of specific aspects of IT central banks' arrangements, the most straightforward finding can be formulated by indicating that, overall, institutional set-ups matter much more for infla-tion developments than for output developments.

In particular, many specifications suggest that the better the institu-tional set-ups, the lower inflation is, the lower its variance, and the lower its deviation from the target. The basis for such conclusions is some-times stronger for advanced economy inflation targeters and sometimes for emerging market economy inflation targeters. However, the direction of the effect is broadly the same—better institutional set-ups in many instances can be associated with easier fulfilment of central banks' obliga-tions to ensure price stability.

In turn, there are much weaker indications that would suggest a link between institutional set-ups and GDP growth, its variance, and output gap developments. At the same time, this finding is more valid for advanced economy inflation targeters compared to emerging market economy infla-tion targeters. For the latter group of countries, several specifications show significant relationships signalling that the better the institutional set-ups, the lower the GDP growth and the lower the output gap, with some

Table 4.11 Overview of the estimation results

		Mature _IT (lag 3)		Independent_IT (lag 3)		Informed _IT (lag 3)	
		Advanced economies	Emerging market economies	Advanced economies	Emerging market economies	Advanced economies	Emerging market economies
Inflation—three-year average	All inflation targeters	Neg.coeff.1-5%		N.A.			
	Sub-samples		Neg.coeff.1 -5%	N.A.			Neg.coeff.1 -5%
Inflation variance—three-year variance	All inflation targeters	Neg.coeff.1-5%		N.A.		Neg.coeff.1-5%	
	Sub-samples	Neg.coeff.1-5%		N.A.		Neg.coeff.10 -15%	Neg.coeff.1 -5%
Inflation deviation from target—three-year average	All inflation targeters	Neg.coeff.10-15%		N.A.		Neg.coeff.10-15%	
	Sub-samples		Neg.coeff.1 -5%	N.A.			
GDP growth—three-year average	All inflation targeters			N.A.			
	Sub-samples		Neg.coeff.1 -5%	N.A.			
GDP growth variance—three-year variance	All inflation targeters			N.A.			
	Sub-samples			N.A.			Pos.coeff.1 -5%
Output gap—three-year average	All inflation targeters			N.A.			
	Sub-samples	Pos.coeff.1-5%	Neg.coeff.1 -5%	N.A.			

Description of coding used:
Neg.coeff.1-5%—negative coefficient significant at 1% or 5% significance level
Neg.coeff.10-15%—negative coefficient significant at 10% or 15% significance level
Blank—coefficient not statistically significant

Source: Own compilation based on estimation results.
Notes: Rows related to all inflation targeters denote relationships indicated by the models based on observations for all countries for all years (i.e. for each country, a period from the adoption of an IT strategy until 2018). In turn, rows related to sub-samples denote relationships indicated by the models based on observations divided into sub-samples of advanced and emerging market economies.

evidence—although not strong—also for increased GDP growth volatility. This could suggest that for emerging market economies—while more favourable institutional set-ups are mitigating inflation—they are also exerting some dampening impact on economic activity. As already noted, conclusions referring to models describing output gap developments should be regarded as preliminary, given the simplified way of estimating output gaps used in the study.

The most general conclusion would probably be that central banks' institutional arrangements should be regarded as important for inflation targeters, since they do impact their ability to provide price stability. Moreover, the fact that the analysed institutional arrangements proved to significantly affect inflation developments, confirms that these arrangements do differ noticeably between inflation targeting central banks.

DIFFERENCES IN INSTITUTIONAL SET-UPS OF IT CENTRAL BANKS

Explicatory_IT (lag 3)		Transparent_IT (lag 3)		Accountable_IT (lag 3)		Fully_fledged_IT (lag 3)	
Advanced economies	Emerging market economies	Advanced economies	Emerging market economies	Advanced economies	Emerging market economies	Advanced economies	Emerging market economies
Neg.coeff.1-5%		Neg.coeff.1-5%		Neg.coeff.10-15%		Neg.coeff.1-5%	
Neg.coeff.10 -15%	Neg.coeff.1 -5%	Neg.coeff.10 -15%	Neg.coeff.1 -5%		Neg.coeff.1 -5%		Neg.coeff.1 -5%
							Neg.coeff.10-15%
Neg.coeff.1 -5%		Neg.coeff.1 -5%		Neg.coeff.1 -5%		Neg.coeff.1 -5%	
	Neg.coeff.1-5%		Neg.coeff.10-15%		Neg.coeff.10-15%		Neg.coeff.10-15%
Neg.coeff.10 -15%	Neg.coeff.10 -15%	Neg.coeff.10 -15%	Neg.coeff.10 -15%				Neg.coeff.10 -15%
	Neg.coeff.1 -5%		Neg.coeff.1 -5%		Neg.coeff.1 -5%		Neg.coeff.1 -5%
	Pos.coeff.10 -15%						Pos.coeff.10 -15%
	Neg.coeff.1 -5%		Neg.coeff.1 -5%		Neg.coeff.1 -5%		Neg.coeff.1 -5%

Pos.coeff.10-15%—positive coefficient significant at 10% or 15% significance level

Pos.coeff.1-5%—positive coefficient significant at 1% or 5% significance level

4.6.2 Important features of the conducted analysis

The above results can be seen as confirming some of the previous findings that suggested the positive contribution of enhancing central banks' institutional arrangements to maintaining price stability, without major negative side effects in terms of limiting output or increasing its volatility, especially in advanced economies.

There are, however, some crucial differences between the previous studies and this analysis. First, the time and the country coverage of this work are significantly larger than those of most other research. Second, the number and the details of investigated aspects of institutional set-ups are extensive compared to many previous works. Third, most of the reviewed literature was based on a cross-section approach that could lead to conclusions valid only for a given period, while this analysis builds on panel regressions that provide more general findings. Fourth, some of the earlier research disregarded even basic control variables, which could artificially increase the significance of institutional set-ups, while this analysis investigates a broad set of potential regressors in order to avoid this charge. The relevance of the included control variables is clearly seen when one compares relationships between institutional arrangements and policy outcomes based on simple correlation coefficients with those based on panel regression coefficients. In many instances, these are not the same, which implies that ignoring control variables results in omitting important information. Fifth, all of the previous works covered economies following various monetary policy strategies, making it hard to disentangle the effects stemming from the different effectiveness of monetary policy regimes versus the effects stemming from different central banks' institutional set-ups applied under the same monetary policy regime, while this analysis focuses on inflation targeters only, which eliminates this problem. Thus, the conclusions delivered with the help of the adopted approach seem more robust.

4.7 Concluding remarks

The aim of Chapter 4 was to answer the main question asked in the study, namely, whether there are major differences in IT central banks' institutional arrangements, and—if yes—whether these differences have a significant impact on the ability of monetary policy to meet its goals.

In order to investigate the issue econometrically, a panel data approach was adopted, since—as shown when verifying the stylised facts—a cross-section analysis could not account for many of the potentially important factors. An encompassing sample of 37 inflation targeting economies, together with a broad set of detailed indices related to IT central banks' institutional set-ups, were considered. When summarising the results, it should also be emphasised that the conclusions drawn from the research are based on models controlling for a number of macroeconomic variables, which should limit the risk of detecting spurious relationships. Moreover, various robustness checks have been conducted in order to establish the most relevant and stable links between the analysed phenomena. Finally, what additionally distinguishes this study from the existing literature is the fact that it includes inflation targeters only, i.e. economies that conduct monetary policy within the same general framework, but following somewhat different institutional arrangements. This allowed for identifying the effects of central banks' institutional set-ups on policy outcomes, without blurring them with a possible impact stemming from the different effectiveness of various monetary policy regimes.

The answer to the main question is based on the importance of the proposed indices related to IT central banks' institutional set-ups for inflation and output developments.[31] In particular, inflation levels, its variance, and inflation deviations from the target were considered when analysing inflation outcomes, while for investigating output outturns for GDP growth, its variance, and output gap estimates were studied.

The conducted research seems to provide solid arguments supporting the hypothesis that the better the institutional set-ups of a given monetary authority pursuing an inflation targeting regime, the greater its policy effectiveness, understood predominantly as delivering low and stable inflation and meeting the inflation target. At the same time, regarding dampening GDP growth, making it more volatile and curbing output gaps, much weaker indications were found, especially for advanced economies. Indirectly, the fact that statistically significant relationships were found between inflation outcomes and institutional arrangements proves that IT central banks' set-ups are not homogeneous across inflation targeters, which is also an important finding.

Notes

1 An extensive overview of empirical studies of central banks' independence can be found, for example, in Eijffinger and de Haan (1996, pp. 63–69) and Laurens, Arnone, and Segalotto (2009, pp. 81–89).
2 The direction of causality in those studies was, however, difficult to judge. Thus, equally likely, the results could be interpreted as showing high turnover rates of central banks' governors in countries with high inflation levels, because the governments of these countries could be more eager to change the governors, as a consequence of central banks' ineffectiveness in combating inflation.
3 Other research topics related to central banks' independence included investigating the link between monetary policy autonomy and central bank credit to the public sector (Cukierman, 1992; de Haan and Sturm, 1992), budget deficit level and variance (Pollard, 1993), growth of output per worker (De Long and Summers, 1992), private investment and productivity growth (Cukierman et al., 1993), as well as disinflation costs (de Hann et al., 1993; Gärtner, 1997).
4 Examples of studies focusing on individual central banks include Ehrmann and Fratzscher (2007) who analysed the US Federal Reserve from early 1994 until mid-2004 and found that more frequent and coherent communication, understood as speaking with one voice, can make policy more predictable, especially amidst large market uncertainty. Similarly, Gerlach-Kristen (2004) investigated the Bank of England's practices related to revealing voting records over the period 1997–2002 and concluded that the publication of voting records also helped to make monetary policy more predictable.
5 Additional areas of research included analysing some more narrowly specified mechanism through which monetary authorities' transparency could affect the economy. Several papers investigated the relationship between central banks' communication and the ability of financial markets to anticipate monetary policy decisions (Lange et al., 2003; Nautz and Schmidt, 2008; Swanson, 2006), and the degree to which transparency can influence financial market expecta-

tions including private forecasts (Romer and Romer, 2000; Ehrmann et al., 2012; Hansen and McMahon, 2016; Lustenberger and Rossi, 2017).

6 An overview of many studies can be found in Blinder et al. (2008) and Balima et al. (2017).

7 In the area of transparency this view was supported, for example, by Crowe (2006) who showed that inflation targeting enhanced transparency.

8 If, for example, exchange rate targeting were a structurally less effective monetary policy framework than inflation targeting, there would be a risk that the links established between central banks' institutional set-ups and policy outcomes, based on a sample including both exchange rate targeters and inflation targeters, would, in fact, reflect the impact of the different effectiveness of monetary policy regimes and not of their institutional arrangements.

9 An additional consequence of analysing inflation targeters only is that under such a set-up monetary policy decisions can be explicitly taken into account, since under an IT framework all central banks treat interest rates as their main policy instrument. Thus, it seems natural to include policy interest rates as a potentially significant regressor in the analysis. At the same time, as already discussed, interest rate policy can, at times, be supplemented with other measures, which can also be considered in the study. However, extending the models with monetary policy variables did not improve the results.

10 The year 2017 is chosen as the end point, since this is the last year for which data for all the countries were available when the analysis was conducted (i.e. 14 IT advanced economies and 28 IT emerging market economies).

11 The size of sub-samples depends on the number of inflation targeters in any given year. Therefore, while sub-samples were selected in such a way as to make them of a similar size, to the extent possible, the number of inflation targeters included in the sub-samples is not the same. For 2008—11 advanced and 16 emerging market economies are taken into account, for 2011, respectively—12 and 19, for 2014—14 and 23, and for 2017—14 and 26.

12 In particular, de Bondt and Vermeulen (2018) show that for G7 economies—that form a much more homogeneous group of countries compared to a sample of all inflation targeters—a business cycle can be as short as around six years for the United States, and as long as around 14 years for Canada and the United Kingdom, with the duration of a business cycle for the rest of the G7 countries being close to seven to eight years.

13 The following economies were therefore not included in the empirical analysis: Argentina, India, Kazakhstan, Russia, and Ukraine.

14 Strictly speaking, in the case of variances these are three-year variances, and not three-year averages of annual variances.

15 The proposed models were also estimated with the dependent variables being annual observations or two-year averages, and the results proved relatively robust.

16 Since the Independent_IT index is a constant for a given economy, the impact of independence on policy outcomes—under the fixed-effects approach—should be captured by the estimated fixed effects. However, looking at correlations of the Independent_IT index with the estimated fixed effects, no statistically significant link could be found. Possibly the estimated fixed effects are also affected by other structural differences between the analysed economies.

17 This is the case for output gap estimates, which are reported by the IMF and the OECD, but only for a relatively small selection of countries. For that reason, these series are used for robustness checks, while the baseline specification is based on estimates of output gaps computed by applying the Hodrick–Prescott

filter on annual GDP data that could be calculated for all IT economies. The Hodrick–Prescott filter is also applied on quarterly GDP data to provide another series used for robustness checks.

18 For some specifications, the country (or the time) coverage may be limited, if data on the included variables are not available for all economies (years).

19 The very similar number of observations in sub-samples for advanced and emerging market economies follows from the fact that while there are fewer IT advanced economies compared to IT emerging market economies, they adopted an inflation targeting framework earlier and thus have been pursuing this strategy for longer.

20 One country—the Czech Republic—is included in both sub-samples, since in 2009 it was reclassified from emerging market economies to advanced economies. Thus, until 2009 the Czech Republic is treated as an emerging market economy, and since 2009 as an advanced economy.

21 In order to conduct some robustness checks, another formulation of the deviation of inflation from the inflation target is used, where for the cases when in a given country for a given year an end-year target was set, a percentage point difference between an end-year annual inflation rate and a midpoint of the end-year inflation target is calculated. The estimation results are, however, unaffected by such a change.

22 Targets specified as "below x%" are included in that category as well.

23 For robustness checks, estimates based on applying the Hodrick–Prescott filter on quarterly GDP data, as well as the IMF and the OECD estimates of output gaps for selected economies are used. The estimation results—after noticing that the IMF and the OECD estimates of output gaps are available mainly for advanced economies—are, however, mostly unaffected by such a change.

24 If strongly negative price dynamics were reported, that claim would not be valid, since strongly negative price dynamics are equally unwelcomed as strongly positive inflation outturns.

25 Only in the case of Australia and New Zealand were quarterly annual inflation rates used to compute inflation variance, since no monthly inflation rates are published for these two countries.

26 When annual deviations of inflation levels from the targets are considered (instead of three-year averages that are chosen as a dependent variable due to reasons indicated above), and the most typical width of tolerance bands are applied to account for the fact that central banks are not able to fully control inflation developments, overall inflation targeters are at the target (±1 percentage point) in 48% of observations. In advanced economies, meeting the inflation target is more frequent than in emerging market economies, with 58% of observations hitting the target (±1 percentage point) in the first group of countries, and 39% in the latter group. This can be regarded as the most straightforward indication of meeting or missing the target.

27 Since big negative and big positive deviations from the target are equally unwelcomed, an attempt to analyse the absolute deviations of inflation from the inflation target in a given country for a given year was undertaken. However, specifying a model that would in a reasonably good way explain the absolute deviations proved very difficult. Apparently, the direction of links between variables is crucial and when the signs of changes of the dependent variable and of some regressors are disregarded, a lot of information is lost, making the task of explaining the absolute deviations highly problematic. Thus, the results are not reported.

28 The IMF is reporting output gap estimates for advanced economies, but not for the world as a single aggregate. Due to the lack of a better proxy for the global output gap, the output gap for that group of economies is used.

29 Additionally, following the same reasoning as used when analysing meeting the inflation targets that treated both positive and negative deviations as undesirable, the absolute output gap estimates in a given country for a given year were investigated. However, similarly as in the case of models employed to explain the absolute deviations of inflation from the targets, specifying a model that would reasonably well explain the absolute output gap estimates proved too difficult. Thus, the results are not reported.

30 For that reason, a sub-sample restricted only to the "new" inflation targeters was not used. It would result in a too limited number of observations.

31 Due to limitations related to using the fixed-effects estimation method, the Independent_IT index could not be included directly in the analysis, although since it forms a part of the Fully_fledged_IT index it was indirectly taken into account.

References

Alesina, A., Summers, L. (1993), "Central Bank Independence and Macroeconomic Performance: Some Comparative Evidence", *Journal of Money, Credit, and Banking*, 25(2), pp. 151–162. https://dx.doi.org/10.2307/2077833

Bade, R., Parkin, M. (1988), *Central Bank Laws and Monetary Policy*, Department of Economics, University of Western Ontario, Canada.

Balima, H. P., Kilama, E. G., Tapsoba, R. (2017), "Settling the Inflation Targeting Debate: Lights from a Meta-Regression Analysis", *IMF Working Paper, No. 213*. www.imf.org/en/Publications/WP/Issues/2017/09/29/Settling-the-Inflation-Targeting-Debate-Lights-from-a-Meta-Regression-Analysis-45253

Blinder, A. S., Ehrmann, M., Fratzscher, M., de Haan, J., Jansen, D.-J. (2008), "Central Bank Communication and Monetary Policy: A Survey of Theory and Evidence", *NBER Working Paper, No. 13932*, pp. 1–74. http://dx.doi.org/10.3386/w13932

Brumm, H. J. (2002), "Inflation and Central Bank Independence Revisited", *Economics Letters*, 77(2), pp. 205–209. http://dx.doi.org/10.1016/s0165-1765(02)00132-5

Brzoza-Brzezina, M. (2011), *Polska polityka pieniężna. Badania teoretyczne I empiryczne*, C.H. Beck.

Campillo, M., Miron, J. (1996), "Why Does Inflation Differ Across Countries?", *NBER Working Paper, No. 5540*, pp. 1–38. http://dx.doi.org/10.3386/w5540

Cecchetti, S. G., Krause, S. (2002), "Central Bank Structure, Policy Efficiency, and Macroeconomic Performance: Exploring Empirical Relationships", *The Federal Reserve Bank of St. Louis Review*, 84(4), pp. 47–60. http://dx.doi.org/10.20955/r.84.47-60

Crowe, Ch. (2006), "Testing the Transparency Benefits of Inflation Targeting: Evidence from Private Sector Forecasts", *IMF Working Paper No. 06/289*. www.imf.org/external/pubs/ft/wp/2006/wp06289.pdf

Crowe, Ch., Mead, E. (2008), "Central Bank Independence and Transparency: Evolution and Effectiveness", *IMF Working Paper, No. 119*, pp. 1–28. https://dx.doi.org/10.5089/9781451869798.001

Cukierman, A. (1992), *Central Bank Strategy, Credibility, and Independence: Theory and Evidence*, MIT Press.

Cukierman, A., Kalaitzidakis, P., Summers, L. H., Webb, S. B. (1993), "Central Bank Independence, Growth, Investment, and Real Rates", *Carnegie-Rochester Conference Series on Public Policy*, 39, pp. 95–140. http://dx.doi.org/10.1016/01 67-2231(93)90005-h

Cukierman, A., Webb, S. B., Neyapti, B. (1992), "Measuring the Independence of Central Banks and Its Effect on Policy Outcomes", *The World Bank Economic Review*, 6(3), pp. 353–398. https://dx.doi.org/10.1093/wber/6.3.353

de Bondt, G., Vermeulen, Ph. (2018), "Business Cycle Duration Dependence and Foreign Recessions", *ECB Working Paper, No. 2205*. www.ecb.europa.eu/pub/pdf/scpwps/ecb.wp2205.en.pdf

de Hann, J., Knot, K., Sturm, J.-E. (1993), "On the Reduction of Disinflation Costs: Fixed Exchange Rates or Central Bank Independence?", *Banca Nazionale del Lavoro Quarterly Review*, 187, pp. 429–443. https://ojs.uniroma1.it/index.php/PSLQuarterlyReview/article/view/10630/10514

de Haan, J., Sturm, J.-E. (1992), "The Case for Central Bank Independence", *Banca Nazionale del Lavoro Quarterly Review*, 182, pp. 305–327. https://ojs.uniroma1.it/index.php/PSLQuarterlyReview/article/view/10634/10518

De Long, J. B., Summers, L. H. (1992), "Macroeconomic Policy and Long-Run Growth", *Federal Reserve Bank of Kansas City Economic Review*, Q IV, pp. 5–29. www.kansascityfed.org/PUBLICAT/ECONREV/EconRevArchive/1992/4Q92long.pdf

Demertzis, M., Hughes Hallett, A. (2007), "Central Bank Transparency in Theory and Practice", *Journal of Macroeconomics*, 29(4), pp. 760–789. http://dx.doi.org/10.1016/j.jmacro.2005.06.002

Dincer, N. N., Eichengreen, B. (2007), "Central Bank Transparency: Where, Why, and with What Effects?", *NBER Working Paper, No. 13003*, pp. 1–51. http://www.nber.org/papers/w13003

Dincer, N. N., Eichengreen, B. (2013), "Central Bank Transparency and Independence: Updates and New Measures", *Bank of Korea Working Paper, No. 21*, pp. 1–56. http://dx.doi.org/10.2139/ssrn.2579544

Ehrmann, M., Eijffinger, S., Fratzscher, M. (2012), "The Role of Central Bank Transparency for Guiding Private Sector Forecasts", *The Scandinavian Journal of Economics*, 3(114), pp. 1018–1052. https://dx.doi.org/10.1111/j.1467-9442.2012.01706.x

Ehrmann, M., Fratzscher, M. (2007), "Social Value of Public Information—Testing the Limits to Transparency", *ECB Working Paper, No. 821*. www.ecb.europa.eu/pub/pdf/scpwps/ecbwp821.pdf

Eijffinger, S., de Haan, J. (1996), "The Political Economy of Central-Bank Independence", *Special Papers in International Economics*, 19, pp. 1–92.

Fry, M., Julius, D., Mahadeva, L., Roger, S., Sterne, G. (2000), "Key Issues in the Choice of Monetary Policy Framework", in: L. Mahadeva, G. Sterne (eds.), *Monetary Policy Frameworks in a Global Context*, Routledge Press, pp. 1–216.

Fuhrer, J. C. (1997), "Central Bank Independence and Inflation Targeting: Monetary Policy Paradigms for the Next Millennium?", *New England Economic Review*, 1-2, pp. 19–36. www.bostonfed.org/publications/new-england-economic-review

/1997-issues/issue-january-february-1997/central-bank-independence-and-inflat
ion-targeting-monetary-policy-paradigms-for-the-next-millennium.aspx

Gärtner, M. (1997), "Time-Consistent Monetary Policy under Output Persistence",
Public Choice, 92(3–4), pp. 429–437. http://journals.kluweronline.com/issn/00
48-5829/contents

Gerlach-Kristen, P. (2004), "Is the MPC's Voting Record Informative About Future
UK Monetary Policy?", *Scandinavian Journal of Economics*, 106(2), pp. 299–
313. https://dx.doi.org/10.1111/j.0347-0520.2004.00359.x

Grilli, V., Masciandaro, D., Tabellini, G., Malinvaud, E., Pagano, M. (1991),
"Political and Monetary Institutions and Public Financial Policies in the Industrial
Countries", *Economic Policy*, 6(13), pp. 342–392. https://dx.doi.org/10.2307
/1344630

Hansen, S., McMahon, M. (2016), "Shocking Language: Understanding the
Macroeconomic Effects of Central Bank Communication", *Journal of
International Economics*, 99, pp. S114–S133. http://dx.doi.org/10.1016/j.jinteco
.2015.12.008

Lange, J., Sack, B., Whitesell, W. (2003), "Anticipations of Monetary Policy in
Financial Markets", *Journal of Money, Credit and Banking*, 35(6), pp. 889–909.
https://dx.doi.org/10.1353/mcb.2003.0044

Laurens, B. J., Arnone, M., Segalotto, J.-F. (2009), *Central Bank Independence,
Accountability, and Transparency. A Global Perspective*, Palgrave Macmillan.

Lustenberger, T., Rossi, E. (2017), "Does Central Bank Transparency and
Communication Affect Financial and Macroeconomic Forecasts?", *SNB Working
Paper, No. 12*, pp. 1–58. www.snb.ch/n/mmr/reference/working_paper_2017_12
/source/working_paper_2017_12.n.pdf

Nautz, D., Schmidt, S. (2008), "Monetary Policy Implementation and the Federal
Funds Rate", *SSRN Electronic Journal*, 33(7), pp. 1274–1284. http://dx.doi.org
/10.2139/ssrn.1121746

Oatley, T. (1999), "Central Bank Independence and Inflation: Corporatism,
Partisanship, and Alternative Indices of Central Bank Independence", *Public
Choice*, 98(3/4), pp. 399–413.

Pollard, P. S. (1993), "Central Bank Independence and Economic Performance",
Federal Reserve Bank of St. Louis Review, 75(4), pp. 21–36.

Posen, A. S. (1993), "Why Central Bank Independence Does Not Cause Low
Inflation: There Is No Institutional Fix for Politics", in: R. O'Brien (ed.), *Finance
and the International Economy*, Oxford University Press, pp. 40–65.

Posso, A., Tawadros, G. B. (2013), "Does Greater Central Bank Independence Really
Lead to Lower Inflation? Evidence from Panel Data", *Economic Modelling*, 33,
pp. 244–247. http://dx.doi.org/10.1016/j.econmod.2013.04.005

Romer, Ch. D., Romer, D. H. (2000), "Federal Reserve Information and the
Behavior of Interest Rates", *American Economic Review*, 90(3), pp. 429–457.
https://dx.doi.org/10.1257/aer.90.3.429

Stasavage, D. (2003), "Transparency, Democratic Accountability, and the Economic
Consequences of Monetary Institutions", *American Journal of Political Science*,
47(3), pp. 389–402. https://dx.doi.org/10.2307/3186104

Sterne, G., Stasavage, D., Chortareas, G. (2002), "Does It Pay to Be Transparent? International Evidence From Central Bank Forecasts", *The Federal Reserve Bank of St. Louis Review*, 84(4), pp. 99–118. http://dx.doi.org/10.20955/r.84.99-118

Sturm, J.-E., de Haan, J. (2001), "Inflation in Developing Countries: Does Central Bank Independence Matter?", *CESifo Working Paper, No. 511*, pp. 1–17. www.cesifo-group.de/DocDL/cesifo_wp511.pdf

Swanson, E. T. (2006), "Have Increases in Federal Reserve Transparency Improved Private Sector Interest Rate Forecasts?", *Journal of Money, Credit and Banking*, 38(3), pp. 791–819. https://dx.doi.org/10.1353/mcb.2006.0046

Walsh, C. E. (2008), "Central Bank Independence", in: S. N. Durlauf, L. E. Blume (eds.), *The New Palgrave Dictionary of Economics*, 2nd Edition, Vol. 1, Palgrave Macmillan, pp. 728–731.

Weber, Ch. S. (2018), "Central Bank Transparency and Inflation (Volatility)—New Evidence", *International Economics and Economic Policy*, 15(1), pp. 21–67. https://dx.doi.org/10.1007/s10368-016-0365-z

Appendix 4: Data sources and additional estimation results

Table 4.12 List of variables with sources

Variable name	Description	Source
Inflation and deviation from the target		
CPI_avg	Average annual inflation rate	IMF—WEO
CPI_var	Variance of monthly annual inflation rates	Own compilation based on IMF—IFS
CPI_deviation_target_simple	Deviation of an average annual inflation rate from the target mid-point	Own compilation based on IMF—WEO
CPI_deviation_target_strict	Deviation of an average annual inflation rate from the target mid-point for continuous targets and deviation of an end-of-year annual inflation rate from the target mid-point for end-of-year targets	Own compilation based on IMF—WEO
Growth and deviation from potential GDP		
GDP_growth	Annual GDP growth	World Bank—WDI
GDP_sa_var	Variance of quarterly annual GDP growth rates, seasonally adjusted	Own compilation based on IMF—IFS and OECD—QNA
Output_gap_hp	Output gap in percent of potential GDP (based on using a HP filter of annual data)	Own compilation based on IMF—WEO
Output_gap_IMF	Output gap in percent of potential GDP	IMF—WEO
Output_gap_OECD	Output gap in percent of potential GDP	OECD—Economic Outlook
Output_gap_WB_annual_hp	Output gap in percent of potential GDP (based on using a HP filter of annual data)	Own compilation based on World Bank—GEM
Output_gap_WB_quartery_hp	Output gap in percent of potential GDP (based on using a HP filter of quarterly data)	Own compilation based on World Bank—GEM
Global and country-specific factors		
CPI_avg_world	Average annual inflation rate	IMF—WEO
Oil_prices_avg	Average spot price of oil	IMF—WEO
Oil_prices_var	Variance of monthly spot price of oil	IMF—WEO
Dummy_oil_exporters	1 for net oil net exporter; 0—otherwise	CIA—after Wikipedia
Advanced_economies_output_gap	Output gap in percent of potential GDP for advanced economies	IMF—WEO

Variable	Description	Source
Trade_openness	Exports and imports of goods and services as a percentage of GDP	Own compilation based on World Bank—WDI
FX_scaled_avg	Average of official exchange rate against USD scaled for 2018=1 (for the United States data on exchange rates against the euro)	World Bank—WDI
FX_scaled_var	Variance of monthly averages of official exchange rate against USD scaled for 2018=1 (for the United States data on exchange rates against the euro)	World Bank—WDI
Terms-of-trade	Terms of trade ratio	World Bank—Exported from datamarket.com
Debt_to_GDP	General government gross debt as a percentage of potential GDP	IMF—WEO
Deficit_to_GDP	General government structural balance as a percentage of potential GDP	IMF—WEO
Money_to_GDP	Broad money as a percentage of GDP	World Bank—WDI
Credit_to_GDP	Domestic credit to private sector as a percentage of GDP	World Bank—WDI
GDP_per_capita_PPP	GDP per capita in PPP (current international $)	World Bank—WDI
Other variables		
Disinflation	1 for disinflation periods; 0—otherwise	
Dummy_2008	1 for 2008 (or for period averages including 2008); 0—otherwise	
Dummy_neg_deviation	1 for periods with negative inflation deviation from the target; 0—otherwise	
Dummy_neg_gap	1 for periods with negative output gap; 0—otherwise	Based on Output_gap_hp
Indices related to central banks' institutional set-ups		
Mature_IT	Index related to an institutional set-up	Own compilation
Independent_IT	Index related to an institutional set-up	Own compilation
Informed_IT	Index related to an institutional set-up	Own compilation
Explicatory_IT	Index related to an institutional set-up	Own compilation
Transparent_IT	Index related to an institutional set-up	Own compilation
Accountable_IT	Index related to an institutional set-up	Own compilation
Fully_fledged_IT	Index related to an institutional set-up	Own compilation

Source: Own compilation.

Notes: IFS—International Financial Statistics, GEM—Global Economic Monitor, WDI—World Development Indicators, WGI—Worldwide Governance Indicators, NAS—National Accounts Statistics, QNA—Quarterly National Accounts, WEO—World Economic Outlook. General remark—subscripts _1y, _2y, _3y used when reporting estimation results denote averages within one-, two-, and three-year periods or—for variances—variance within one-, two-, and three-year periods, respectively.

305

Table 4.13 List of variables with country and time coverage

Variable name	Country coverage	Time coverage	Type of variable	Main usage	Remarks
Inflation and deviation from the target					
CPI_avg	42 countries	All years	Dependent and explanatory	Main regressions	Policy outcome
CPI_var	42 countries	All years	Dependent	Main regressions	Policy outcome
CPI_deviation_ target_simple	42 countries	All years	Dependent	Main regressions	Policy outcome
CPI_deviation_ target_strict	42 countries	All years	Dependent	Robustness check	Policy outcome
Growth and deviation from potential GDP					
GDP_growth	42 countries	Until 2017	Dependent and explanatory	Main regressions	Policy outcome
GDP_sa_var	31 countries	Some gaps	Dependent	Main regressions	Policy outcome
Output_gap_hp	42 countries	All years	Dependent and explanatory	Main regressions	Policy outcome
Output_gap_IMF	10 countries	All years	Dependent and explanatory	Robustness check	Policy outcome
Output_gap_ OECD	18 countries	All years	Dependent and explanatory	Robustness check	Policy outcome
Output_gap_WB_annual_hp	37 countries	Until 2017	Dependent and explanatory	Robustness check	Policy outcome
Output_gap_WB_quartery_hp	36 countries	Until 2017	Dependent and explanatory	Robustness check	Policy outcome
Global and country-specific factors					
CPI_avg_world	Not applicable	All years	Explanatory	Main regressions	
Oil_prices_avg	Not applicable	All years	Explanatory	Main regressions	
Oil_prices_var	Not applicable	All years	Explanatory	Main regressions	

Dummy_oil_exporters	42 countries	All years	Explanatory	Main regressions	
Advanced_economies_output_gap	Not applicable	All years	Explanatory	Main regressions	
Trade_openness	42 countries	Until 2017	Explanatory	Main regressions	
FX_scaled_avg	42 countries	All years	Explanatory	Main regressions	
FX_scaled_var	42 countries	All years	Explanatory	Main regressions	
Terms-of-trade	41 countries	Until 2015	Explanatory	Main regressions	
Debt_to_GDP	42 countries	Some gaps	Explanatory	Robustness check	
Deficit_to_GDP	37 countries	Some gaps	Explanatory	Robustness check	
Money_to_GDP	41 countries	Some gaps	Explanatory	Robustness check	
Credit_to_GDP	41 countries	Some gaps	Explanatory	Robustness check	
GDP_per_capita_PPP	42 countries	Until 2017	Explanatory	Robustness check	
Other variables					
Disinflation	42 countries	All years	Explanatory	Main regressions	
Dummy_2008	Not applicable	Not applicable	Explanatory	Main regressions	
Dummy_neg_deviation	42 countries	All years	Explanatory	Main regressions	
Dummy_neg_gap	42 countries	All years	Explanatory	Main regressions	
Indices related to central banks' institutional set-ups					
Mature_IT	42 countries	All years	Explanatory	Main regressions	Institutional set-up
Independent_IT	42 countries	All years	Explanatory	Main regressions	Institutional set-up
Informed_IT	42 countries	All years	Explanatory	Main regressions	Institutional set-up
Explicatory_IT	42 countries	All years	Explanatory	Main regressions	Institutional set-up
Transparent_IT	42 countries	All years	Explanatory	Main regressions	Institutional set-up
Accountable_IT	42 countries	All years	Explanatory	Main regressions	Institutional set-up
Fully_fledged_IT	42 countries	All years	Explanatory	Main regressions	Institutional set-up

Source: Own compilation.

307

Table 4.14 Unit root test for variables

Variable name	Fisher-type unit-root test based on Phillips–Perron tests			
	N (no. of countries)	T (average)	Test statistic: Inverse chi-squared	df	p-value
Inflation and deviation from the target					
CPI_avg_3y	37	14.8	128.39	74	0.00
CPI_var_3y	37	14.9	340.20	74	0.00
CPI_deviation_target_simple_3y	37	14.7	82.26	74	0.24
CPI_deviation_target_strict_3y	37	14.7	78.53	74	0.34
Ablotute_CPI_deviation_target_simple_3y	37	14.7	113.10	74	0.00
Ablotute_CPI_deviation_target_strict_3y	37	14.7	108.34	74	0.01
Growth and deviation from potential GDP					
GDP_growth_3y	37	13.8	91.66	74	0.08
GDP_sa_var_3y	28	15.7	61.18	56	0.30
Output_gap_hp_3y	37	14.8	173.55	74	0.00
Output_gap_IMF_3y	10	18.4	93.37	20	0.00
Output_gap_OECD_3y	18	18.3	47.33	36	0.10
Output_gap_WB_annual_hp_3y	32	14.6	122.87	64	0.00
Output_gap_WB_quartery_hp_3y	31	14.9	177.13	62	0.00
Global and country-specific factors					
CPI_avg_world	37	16.8	379.79	74	0.00
Oil_prices_avg_3y	37	16.8	31.50	74	1.00
Oil_prices_var_3y	37	16.8	120.71	74	0.00
Dummy_oil_exporters					
Advanced_economies_output_gap	37	16.8	34.54	74	1.00

Trade_openness	37	15.7	83.78	74	0.20
FX_scaled_avg_3y	37	16.8	29.03	74	1.00
FX_scaled_var_3y	37	16.5	183.26	74	0.00
Terms-of-trade	36	14.0	250.22	72	0.00
Terms-of-trade_OECD	22	18.7	31.56	44	0.92
Terms-of-trade_monthly_WB	23	18.1	105.48	46	0.00
Debt_to_GDP	37	16.6	60.83	74	0.86
Deficit_to_GDP	32	17.3	185.87	64	0.00
Money_to_GDP	36	15.3	56.83	72	0.90
Credit_to_GDP	36	15.5	129.20	72	0.00
GDP_per_capita_PPP	37	15.8	8.74	74	1.00
Other variables					
Disinflation					
Dummy_2008					
Dummy_neg_deviation					
Dummy_neg_gap					
Indices related to central banks' institutional set-ups					
Mature_IT	37	16.8	52.24	74	0.97
Independent_IT	37	16.8	121.70	74	0.00
Informed_IT	37	16.8	62.89	74	0.82
Explicatory_IT	37	16.8	106.07	74	0.01
Transparent_IT	37	16.8	90.61	74	0.09
Accountable_IT	37	16.8	107.83	74	0.01
Fully_fledged_IT					

Source: Own compilation.

309

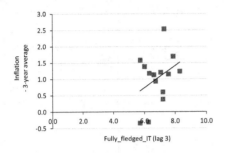 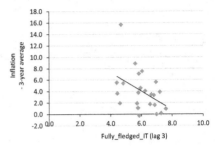

Chart 4.9 Fully_fledged_IT index and inflation— IT advanced economies (2017).

Chart 4.10 Fully_fledged_IT index and inflation—IT emerging market economies (2017).

Notes: Lines show fitted linear regressions. Source: Own compilation based on the constructed indices and macroeconomic variables (sources indicated in Table 4.12).

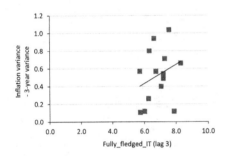 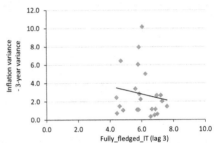

Chart 4.11 Fully_fledged_IT index and inflation variance—IT advanced economies (2017).

Chart 4.12 Fully_fledged_IT index and inflation variance—IT emerging market economies (2017).

Notes: Inflation variance denotes the variance of monthly annual inflation rates (quarterly annual inflation rates, if monthly data are not available). Lines show fitted linear regressions. Source: Own compilation based on the constructed indices and macroeconomic variables (sources indicated in Table 4.12).

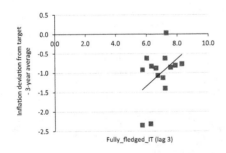 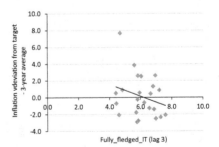

Chart 4.13 Fully_fledged_IT index and inflation deviation from target—IT advanced economies (2017).

Chart 4.14 Fully_fledged_IT index and inflation deviation from target—IT emerging market economies (2017).

Notes: Inflation deviation from target denotes deviation of an average annual inflation rate from the target midpoint. Lines show fitted linear regressions. Source: Own compilation based on the constructed indices and macroeconomic variables (sources indicated in Table 4.12).

310

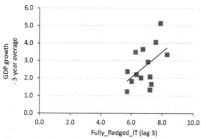

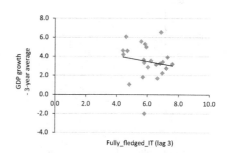

Chart 4.15 Fully_fledged_IT index and GDP growth—IT advanced economies (2017).

Chart 4.16 Fully_fledged_IT index and GDP growth—IT emerging market economies (2017).

Notes: Lines show fitted linear regressions. Source: Own compilation based on the constructed indices and macroeconomic variables (sources indicated in Table 4.12).

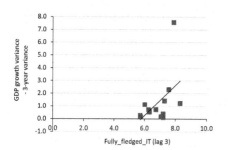

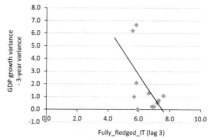

Chart 4.17 Fully_fledged_IT index and GDP growth variance—IT advanced economies (2017).

Chart 4.18 Fully_fledged_IT index and GDP growth variance—IT emerging market economies (2017).

Notes: GDP growth variance denotes variance of quarterly annual GDP growth rates, seasonally adjusted. Lines show fitted linear regressions. Source: Own compilation based on the constructed indices and macroeconomic variables (sources indicated in Table 4.12).

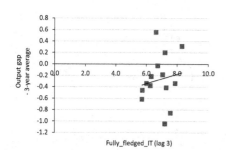

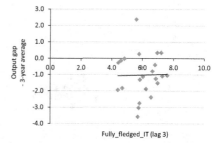

Chart 4.19 Fully_fledged_IT index and output gap—IT advanced economies (2017).

Chart 4.20 Fully_fledged_IT index and output gap—IT emerging market economies (2017).

Notes: Output gap denotes output gap in percentage of potential GDP, estimated using the Hodrick–Prescott filter on annual IMF data. Lines show fitted linear regressions. Source: Own compilation based on the constructed indices and macroeconomic variables (sources indicated in Table 4.12).

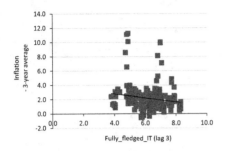

Chart 4.21 Fully_fledged_IT index and inflation—IT advanced economies (full sample).

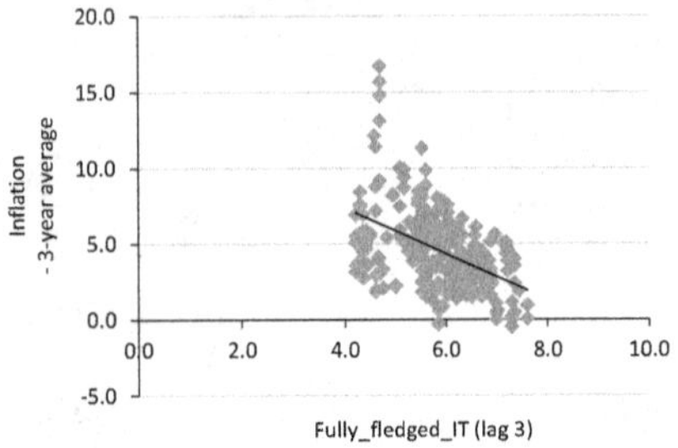

Chart 4.22 Fully_fledged_IT index and inflation—IT emerging market economies (full sample).

Notes: See notes to the previous charts. Source: Own compilation based on the constructed indices and macroeconomic variables (sources indicated in Table 4.12).

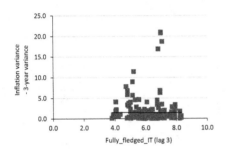
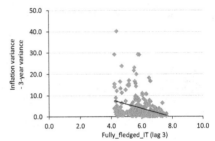

Chart 4.23 Fully_fledged_IT index and inflation variance—IT advanced economies (full sample).

Chart 4.24 Fully_fledged_IT index and inflation variance—IT emerging market economies (full sample).

Notes: See notes to previous charts. Source: Own compilation based on the constructed indices and macroeconomic variables (sources indicated in Table 4.12).

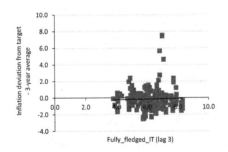
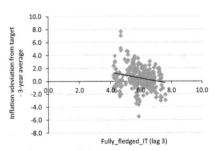

Chart 4.25 Fully_fledged_IT index and inflation deviation from target—IT advanced economies (full sample).

Chart 4.26 Fully_fledged_IT index and inflation deviation from target—IT emerging market economies (full sample).

Notes: See notes to previous charts. Source: Own compilation based on the constructed indices and macroeconomic variables (sources indicated in Table 4.12).

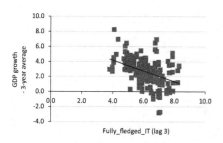

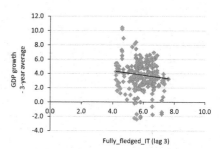

Chart 4.27 Fully_fledged_IT index and GDP growth—IT advanced economies (full sample).

Chart 4.28 Fully_fledged_IT index and GDP growth—IT emerging market economies (full sample).

Notes: See notes to previous charts. Source: Own compilation based on the constructed indices and macroeconomic variables (sources indicated in Table 4.12).

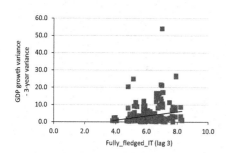

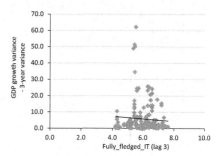

Chart 4.29 Fully_fledged_IT index and GDP growth variance—IT advanced economies (full sample).

Chart 4.30 Fully_fledged_IT index and GDP growth variance—IT emerging market economies (full sample).

Notes: See notes to previous charts. Source: Own compilation based on the constructed indices and macroeconomic variables (sources indicated in Table 4.12).

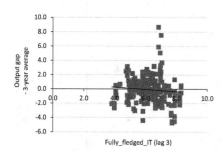

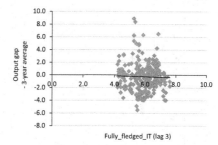

Chart 4.31 Fully_fledged_IT index and output gap—IT advanced economies (full sample).

Chart 4.32 Fully_fledged_IT index and output gap—IT emerging market economies (full sample).

Notes: See notes to previous charts. Source: Own compilation based on the constructed indices and macroeconomic variables (sources indicated in Table 4.12).

Table 4.15 Robustness check of models related to inflation levels

	Baseline specification			Adding oil prices			Adding global inflation			Adding global output gap		
	All IT countries	IT advanced economies	IT emerging economies	All IT countries	IT advanced economies	IT emerging economies	All IT countries	IT advanced economies	IT emerging economies	All IT countries	IT advanced economies	IT emerging economies
Disinflation	3.93 ***	7.35 ***	1.51 .	3.92 ***	7.70 ***	1.27 **	3.60 ***	7.07 ***	1.59 .	3.96 ***	7.39 ***	1.57 .
	(3.3)	(6.2)	(1.6)	(3.2)	(5.8)	(2.7)	(3.3)	(6.2)	(1.6)	(3.4)	(6.2)	(1.6)
Dummy_2008	1.07 ***	0.88 ***	1.40 ***	1.07 ***	0.83 ***	1.51 ***	1.08 ***	0.87 ***	1.38 ***	1.43 ***	1.05 ***	1.72 ***
	(9.6)	(7.5)	(7.4)	(9)	(6.1)	(6.8)	(9.2)	(7.7)	(6.3)	(6.4)	(6.7)	(4.3)
CPI_avg_lag_3	0.14 **	0.14 *	0.10 *	0.14 **	0.13 .	0.07	0.13 **	0.13 *	0.11 **	0.16 ***	0.14 *	0.11 **
	(2.7)	(2)	(1.9)	(2.5)	(1.7)	(1.5)	(2.6)	(1.9)	(2.7)	(3.4)	(1.9)	(2.6)
Output_gap_hp_lag_3	0.16 ***	0.14 ***	0.19 ***	0.17 ***	0.14 ***	0.19 ***	0.17 ***	0.15 ***	0.19 ***	0.18 ***	0.16 ***	0.19 ***
	(4.3)	(3.9)	(4.1)	(4.3)	(3.9)	(4.4)	(4.4)	(3.8)	(4.7)	(5.7)	(4.7)	(4.5)
FX_scaled_avg_3y	1.21 ***	0.90 .	2.20 ***	1.20 *	1.39 *	3.19 ***	1.20 ***	0.83	2.09 ***	1.59 ***	1.16 *	2.45 ***
	(3.3)	(1.6)	(3.6)	(1.8)	(2)	(3.2)	(3.1)	(1.4)	(3.2)	(4)	(2)	(3.7)
Trade_openness_lag_3	-0.03 ***	-0.03 ***	-0.03 **	-0.03 ***	-0.03 ***	-0.04 **	-0.03 ***	-0.03 ***	-0.03 **	-0.03 ***	-0.03 ***	-0.03 **
	(-4.1)	(-4)	(-2.4)	(-3.1)	(-4.7)	(-2.3)	(-3.6)	(-3.5)	(-2.4)	(-4.5)	(-4.2)	(-2.5)
Oil_prices_avg_3y				0.00	0.01	0.02 *						
				(0.6)	(1.3)	(1.8)						
Oil_prices_avg_3y x Dummy_oil_exporter				-0.02 ***	-0.01	-0.04 ***						
				(-3.1)	(-1.4)	(-10.5)						
CPI_world_avg_lag_3							0.04 ***	0.01 .	-0.08			
							(3.1)	(1.5)	(-0.5)			
Advanced_economies_output_gap_lag_3										-0.13 .	-0.08	-0.11
										(-1.5)	(-1)	(-0.8)
No. of observations	509	243	266	509	243	266	509	243	266	509	243	266
N (no. of countries)	37	14	24	37	14	24	37	14	24	37	14	24
T (min)	4	4	4	4	4	4	4	4	4	4	4	4
T (max)	26	26	17	26	26	17	26	26	17	26	26	17
R-squared	0.79	0.79	0.76	0.80	0.79	0.79	0.80	0.79	0.76	0.80	0.79	0.77
Adjusted R-squared	0.77	0.77	0.74	0.78	0.77	0.76	0.78	0.77	0.73	0.78	0.77	0.74

Table 4.15 (Continued)

	All IT countries	IT advanced economies	IT emerging economies	All IT countries	IT advanced economies	IT emerging economies	All IT countries	IT advanced economies	IT emerging economies	All IT countries	IT advanced economies	IT emerging economies
	Baseline specification			Adding terms-of-trade			Adding fiscal debt			Adding fiscal deficit		
Disinflation	3.93 ***	7.35 ***	1.51 .	3.92 ***	7.34 ***	1.47 .	1.42	omitted	1.40	0.93	omitted	0.92
	(3.3)	(6.2)	(1.6)	(3.2)	(6.4)	(1.7)	(1.2)		(1.1)	(0.9)		(0.8)
Dummy_2008	1.07 ***	0.88 ***	1.40 ***	1.08 ***	0.88 ***	1.40 ***	1.12 ***	0.87 ***	1.39 ***	1.16 ***	0.85 ***	1.44 ***
	(9.6)	(7.5)	(7.4)	(10.1)	(7.5)	(7.9)	(7.9)	(6.2)	(7.9)	(8)	(5.4)	(8.8)
CPI_avg_lag_3	0.14 **	0.14 *	0.10 *	0.14 **	0.14 *	0.08 .	0.09 *	0.07	0.10 *	0.11 **	0.08 .	0.12 **
	(2.7)	(2)	(1.9)	(2.6)	(2)	(1.6)	(2)	(1.3)	(2.1)	(2.4)	(1.5)	(2.7)
Output_gap_hp_lag_3	0.16 ***	0.14 ***	0.19 ***	0.16 ***	0.14 ***	0.20 ***	0.17 ***	0.12 ***	0.21 ***	0.15 ***	0.15 ***	0.13 ***
	(4.3)	(3.9)	(4.1)	(4)	(3.9)	(3.5)	(5)	(5)	(4.1)	(5)	(6.1)	(3.2)
FX_scaled_avg_3y	1.21 ***	0.90 .	2.20 ***	1.31 ***	0.88 .	2.52 ***	1.58 ***	1.43 ***	1.78 ***	1.17 **	1.04 *	1.35 *
	(3.3)	(1.6)	(3.6)	(3.8)	(1.6)	(4.4)	(3.6)	(2.8)	(2.6)	(2.2)	(2.1)	(1.8)
Trade_openness_lag_3	-0.03 ***	-0.03 ***	-0.03 **	-0.02 ***	-0.03 ***	-0.02 *	-0.03 ***	-0.02 ***	-0.04 **	-0.03 ***	-0.03 ***	-0.03 **
	(-4.1)	(-4)	(-2.4)	(-4.3)	(-4)	(-2.1)	(-3.4)	(-3.4)	(-2.6)	(-4.4)	(-3.5)	(-2.2)
Terms_of_trade_lag_3				-0.48 .	-0.04	-1.18 **						
				(-1.5)	(-0.2)	(-2.4)						
Debt_to_GDP_lag_3							0.00	-0.01 *	0.02			
							(-0.7)	(-2)	(1.2)			
Deficit_to_GDP_lag_3										-0.03	0.02	-0.11 *
										(-0.8)	(0.5)	(-2.1)
No. of observations	509	243	266	502	243	259	500	235	265	459	230	229
N (no. of countries)	37	14	24	36	14	23	37	14	24	32	14	19
T (min)	4	4	4	4	4	4	4	4	4	4	4	4
T (max)	26	26	17	26	26	17	26	26	17	25	25	17
R-squared	0.79	0.79	0.76	0.80	0.79	0.78	0.81	0.70	0.76	0.77	0.70	0.69
Adjusted R-squared	0.77	0.77	0.74	0.78	0.77	0.75	0.79	0.67	0.73	0.75	0.67	0.65

315

Table 4.15 (Continued)

	Baseline specification			Adding money			Adding credit			Adding economic development		
	All IT countries	IT advanced economies	IT emerging economies	All IT countries	IT advanced economies	IT emerging economies	All IT countries	IT advanced economies	IT emerging economies	All IT countries	IT advanced economies	IT emerging economies
Disinflation	3.93 ***	7.35 ***	1.51 .	3.90 ***	7.30 ***	1.00	3.92 ***	7.25 ***	1.30 .	3.87 ***	7.30 ***	1.38 *
	(3.3)	(6.2)	(1.6)	(3.2)	(6.1)	(1.1)	(3.3)	(6.2)	(1.6)	(3.2)	(6.3)	(1.8)
Dummy_2008	1.07 ***	0.88 ***	1.40 ***	1.09 ***	0.93 ***	1.29 ***	1.08 ***	0.89 ***	1.30 ***	0.99 ***	0.85 ***	1.00 ***
	(9.6)	(7.5)	(7.4)	(10.7)	(8)	(7)	(10.8)	(7.7)	(7.2)	(10.7)	(7.6)	(6.9)
CPI_avg_lag_3	0.14 **	0.14 *	0.10 *	0.14 ***	0.15 **	0.07	0.15 ***	0.15 **	0.08	0.13 *	0.13 *	0.04
	(2.7)	(2)	(1.9)	(2.9)	(2.1)	(1.5)	(2.9)	(2.2)	(1.5)	(2.7)	(1.9)	(0.9)
Output_gap_hp_lag_3	0.16 ***	0.14 ***	0.19 ***	0.17 ***	0.14 ***	0.19 ***	0.17 ***	0.14 ***	0.21 ***	0.17 ***	0.14 ***	0.23 ***
	(4.3)	(3.9)	(4.1)	(4.2)	(3.5)	(3.7)	(4.1)	(4.1)	(3.8)	(4.2)	(3.8)	(4)
FX_scaled_avg_3y	1.21 ***	0.90 .	2.20 ***	1.21 ***	0.91 .	2.60 ***	1.28 ***	1.04 *	2.64 ***	0.92 **	0.63	2.50 ***
	(3.3)	(1.6)	(3.6)	(3.2)	(1.7)	(4.1)	(3.7)	(1.8)	(4.3)	(2.5)	(1.2)	(4.9)
Trade_openness_lag_3	-0.03 ***	-0.03 ***	-0.03 **	-0.02 ***	-0.03 ***	-0.03 *	-0.03 ***	-0.03 ***	-0.03 **	-0.02 **	-0.02 ***	-0.01
	(-4.1)	(-4)	(-2.4)	(-3.1)	(-3.3)	(-2)	(-4)	(-4.5)	(-2.2)	(-2.7)	(-3.7)	(-0.4)
Money_to_GDP_lag_3				0.00	0.00	-0.04 **						
				(-0.9)	(0.3)	(-2.5)						
Credit_to_GDP_lag_3							0.00	0.00	-0.02 *			
							(0.1)	(0.7)	(-2)			
GDP_per_capita_PPP_lag_3										0.00 **	0.00	0.00 ***
										(-2.4)	(-1.2)	(-4.3)
No. of observations	509	243	266	482	216	266	488	236	252	509	243	266
N (no. of countries)	37	14	24	36	13	24	36	14	23	37	14	24
T (min)	4	4	4	4	4	4	4	4	4	4	4	4
T (max)	26	26	17	24	24	17	25	25	17	26	26	17
R-squared	0.79	0.79	0.76	0.79	0.80	0.78	0.79	0.80	0.77	0.80	0.79	0.78
Adjusted R-squared	0.77	0.77	0.74	0.77	0.78	0.75	0.77	0.78	0.74	0.78	0.77	0.76

Source: Own compilation based on the constructed indices and macroeconomic variables (sources indicated in Table 4.12).
Notes: Significance codes: *** 0.01; ** 0.05; * 0.1; ' 0.15.

Table 4.16 Robustness check of models related to inflation volatility

	All IT countries	IT advanced economies	IT emerging economies	All IT countries	IT advanced economies	IT emerging economies	All IT countries	IT advanced economies	IT emerging economies	All IT countries	IT advanced economies	IT emerging economies
	Baseline specification			Adding oil price volatility			Adding terms-of-trade			Adding trade openness		
Dummy_2008	2.55 ***	1.51 ***	3.28 ***	3.46 ***	1.981 ***	4.86 ***	2.546 ***	1.49 ***	3.29 ***	2.578 ***	1.51 ***	3.34 ***
	(5.8)	(3.1)	(5.6)	(10.7)	(5.1)	(11.1)	(5.7)	(3.1)	(5.6)	(5.8)	(3.3)	(5.6)
CPI_avg_lag_3	0.48 ***	0.26 *	0.60 ***	0.45 ***	0.25 *	0.59 ***	0.45 ***	0.26 *	0.56 ***	0.47 ***	0.24 *	0.60 ***
	(4.7)	(1.9)	(5.6)	(4.2)	(1.8)	(5.2)	(4.4)	(2)	(5.3)	(4.6)	(1.7)	(5.4)
FX_scaled_var_3y	102.1 ***	112.8 *	136.7 ***	122.8 ***	115.8 *	217.9 ***	103.3 ***	113.3 *	138.3 .	100.8 **	110.9 *	139.6 *
	(2.8)	(2)	(1.7)	(3.7)	(2)	(3.1)	(2.9)	(2)	(1.7)	(2.8)	(2)	(1.8)
Oil_prices_var_3y				0.00 ***	0.00 **	0.00 ***						
				(-6.1)	(-2.1)	(-5)						
Oil_prices_var_3y x Dummy_oil_exporter				0.00 *	0.00 ***	0.00						
				(-1.9)	(-3.1)	(-1)						
Terms_of_trade_lag_3							0.38	0.54	0.55			
							(0.3)	(0.6)	(0.3)			
Trade_openness_lag_3										-0.01	-0.03 **	-0.02
										(-0.9)	(-2.7)	(-0.7)
No. of observations	511	242	269	511	242	269	504	242	262	511	242	269
N (no. of countries)	37	14	24	37	14	24	36	14	23	37	14	24
T (min)	4	4	4	4	4	4	4	4	4	4	4	4
T (max)	25	25	17	25	25	17	25	25	17	25	25	17
R-squared	0.42	0.50	0.35	0.43	0.51	0.38	0.41	0.50	0.34	0.42	0.51	0.35
Adjusted R-squared	0.37	0.47	0.28	0.38	0.47	0.31	0.36	0.46	0.27	0.37	0.48	0.28

Table 4.16 (Continued)

	Baseline specification			Adding GDP variance			Adding economic development		
	All IT countries	IT advanced economies	IT emerging economies	All IT countries	IT advanced economies	IT emerging economies	All IT countries	IT advanced economies	IT emerging economies
Dummy_2008	2.55 ***	1.51 ***	3.28 ***	1.70 ***	0.52 *	2.67 ***	2.55 ***	1.52 ***	3.26 ***
	(5.8)	(3.1)	(5.6)	(4.9)	(1.8)	(4.5)	(5.8)	(3.1)	(5.3)
CPI_avg_lag_3	0.48 ***	0.26 *	0.60 ***	0.36 ***	0.22 .	0.43 ***	0.48 ***	0.25 *	0.60 ***
	(4.7)	(1.9)	(5.6)	(5.7)	(1.6)	(5.2)	(4.5)	(1.8)	(5.3)
FX_scaled_var_3y	102.1 ***	112.8 *	136.7 ***	134.8 ***	72.50 *	211.6 **	101.5 **	111.4 *	136.8 .
	(2.8)	(2)	(1.7)	(3.7)	(1.8)	(2.8)	(2.7)	(1.9)	(1.7)
GDP_sa_var_3y				0.02	0.19 ***	-0.04 *			
				(1)	(5.1)	(-1.9)			
GDP_per_capita_PPP_lag_3							0.00	0.00	0.00
							(-0.3)	(-0.6)	(-0.1)
No. of observations	511	242	269	414	230	184	511	242	269
N (no. of countries)	37	14	24	28	14	15	37	14	24
T (min)	4	4	4	3	3	4	4	4	4
T (max)	25	25	17	24	24	17	25	25	17
R-squared	0.42	0.50	0.35	0.41	0.58	0.31	0.42	0.50	0.35
Adjusted R-squared	0.37	0.47	0.28	0.36	0.55	0.23	0.37	0.46	0.28

Source: Own compilation based on the constructed indices and macroeconomic variables (sources indicated in Table 4.12).
Notes: Significance codes: *** 0.01; ** 0.05; * 0.1; ' 0.15.

318

Table 4.17 Robustness check of models related to inflation deviations from the target

	Baseline specification			Adding disinflation dummy			Adding domestic inflation			Adding exchange rate		
	All IT countries	IT advanced economies	IT emerging economies	All IT countries	IT advanced economies	IT emerging economies	All IT countries	IT advanced economies	IT emerging economies	All IT countries	IT advanced economies	IT emerging economies
Dummy_2008	0.85 ***	0.79 ***	0.98 ***	0.86 ***	0.80 ***	0.99 ***	0.86 ***	0.86 ***	0.98 ***	0.96 ***	0.85 ***	1.23 ***
	(5.8)	(5)	(4.8)	(5.7)	(5.1)	(4.8)	(6.4)	(5.6)	(5)	(6.4)	(5.4)	(5.6)
Output_gap_hp_lag_3	0.17 ***	0.12 ***	0.20 ***	0.18 ***	0.13 ***	0.20 ***	0.16 ***	0.10 **	0.19 ***	0.17 ***	0.12 ***	0.20 ***
	(4.3)	(2.9)	(3.8)	(4.5)	(3.6)	(4)	(4.4)	(2.4)	(4)	(4.4)	(2.9)	(4.2)
Trade_openness_lag_3	-0.02 ***	-0.03 ***	-0.03 **	-0.02 ***	-0.02 ***	-0.03 **	-0.02 ***	-0.02 ***	-0.03 **	-0.02 ***	-0.03 ***	-0.03 **
	(-3.6)	(-3.1)	(-2.3)	(-3.4)	(-2.9)	(-2.2)	(-3.4)	(-3.1)	(-2.2)	(-3.4)	(-3.2)	(-2.3)
Disinflation				1.06 *	1.99 ***	0.32						
				(1.9)	(3.1)	(0.4)						
CPI_avg_lag_3							0.04	0.10 .	0.02			
							(0.9)	(1.6)	(0.3)			
FX_scaled_avg_3y										1.10 **	0.75	2.04 ***
										(2.7)	(1.4)	(4)
No. of observations	505	240	265	505	240	265	505	240	265	505	240	265
N (no. of countries)	37	14	24	37	14	24	37	14	24	37	14	24
T (min)	4	4	4	4	4	4	4	4	4	4	4	4
T (max)	25	25	17	25	25	17	25	25	17	25	25	17
R-squared	0.55	0.56	0.52	0.55	0.59	0.52	0.55	0.58	0.52	0.55	0.56	0.54
Adjusted R-squared	0.51	0.53	0.47	0.51	0.56	0.46	0.51	0.54	0.46	0.52	0.53	0.49

Table 4.17 (Continued)

	All IT countries	IT advanced economies	IT emerging economies	All IT countries	IT advanced economies	IT emerging economies	All IT countries	IT advanced economies	IT emerging economies	All IT countries	IT advanced economies	IT emerging economies
	Baseline specification			Adding oil prices			Adding global inflation			Adding global output gap		
Dummy_2008	0.85 ***	0.79 ***	0.98 ***	0.86 ***	0.77 ***	1.00 ***	0.87 ***	0.80 ***	0.97 ***	1.04 ***	0.80 ***	1.27 ***
	(5.8)	(5)	(4.8)	(5.3)	(4)	(4.9)	(5.8)	(5.6)	(4.1)	(5)	(4.8)	(3.9)
Output_gap_hp_lag_3	0.17 ***	0.12 ***	0.20 ***	0.17 ***	0.12 ***	0.21 ***	0.18 ***	0.15 ***	0.21 ***	0.18 ***	0.13 **	0.20 ***
	(4.3)	(2.9)	(3.8)	(4.4)	(2.9)	(4)	(4.4)	(4.1)	(4.5)	(4.9)	(2.8)	(4.2)
Trade_openness_lag_3	-0.02 ***	-0.03 ***	-0.03 **	-0.03 ***	-0.03 ***	-0.03 **	-0.02 ***	-0.02 **	-0.03 **	-0.02 ***	-0.03 ***	-0.03 **
	(-3.6)	(-3.1)	(-2.3)	(-3.5)	(-4.5)	(-2.3)	(-3.4)	(-2.7)	(-2.3)	(-3.7)	(-3.1)	(-2.5)
Oil_prices_avg_3y				0.00	0.00	0.01 *						
				(1.1)	(0.6)	(1.9)						
Oil_prices_avg_3y x Dummy_oil_exporter				-0.02 ***	-0.01 *	-0.03 ***						
				(-5.2)	(-2)	(-8.4)						
CPI_world_avg_lag_3							0.03 **	0.03 ***	-0.18			
							(2.5)	(3.2)	(-1.4)			
Advanced_economies_output_gap_lag_3										-0.08	-0.01	-0.10
										(-0.9)	(-0.1)	(-0.9)
No. of observations	505	240	265	505	240	265	505	240	265	505	240	265
N (no. of countries)	37	14	24	37	14	24	37	14	24	37	14	24
T (min)	4	4	4	4	4	4	4	4	4	4	4	4
T (max)	25	25	17	25	25	17	25	25	17	25	25	17
R-squared	0.55	0.56	0.52	0.57	0.57	0.56	0.56	0.59	0.53	0.55	0.56	0.52
Adjusted R-squared	0.51	0.53	0.47	0.53	0.53	0.50	0.52	0.56	0.47	0.51	0.52	0.47

Table 4.17 (Continued)

	All IT countries	IT advanced economies	IT emerging economies	All IT countries	IT advanced economies	IT emerging economies	All IT countries	IT advanced economies	IT emerging economies	All IT countries	IT advanced economies	IT emerging economies
	Baseline specification			Adding terms-of-trade			Adding fiscal debt			Adding fiscal deficit		
Dummy_2008	0.85 *** (5.8)	0.79 *** (5)	0.98 *** (4.8)	0.86 *** (5.9)	0.80 *** (5.1)	0.99 *** (4.9)	0.88 *** (6.1)	0.74 *** (4.7)	1.08 *** (5.7)	0.95 *** (6.2)	0.71 *** (4.1)	1.16 *** (6.9)
Output_gap_hp_lag_3	0.17 *** (4.3)	0.12 *** (2.9)	0.20 *** (3.8)	0.17 *** (4.1)	0.13 *** (3.1)	0.18 *** (3.5)	0.20 *** (5.2)	0.15 *** (5.6)	0.25 *** (4.5)	0.16 *** (4.7)	0.17 *** (6.6)	0.14 *** (3.2)
Trade_openness_lag_3	-0.02 *** (-3.6)	-0.03 *** (-3.1)	-0.03 ** (-2.3)	-0.02 *** (-3.4)	-0.03 *** (-3.3)	-0.02 * (-2.1)	-0.03 *** (-4.1)	-0.02 *** (-3.4)	-0.04 *** (-3.2)	-0.02 *** (-3.9)	-0.02 *** (-3.2)	-0.02 ** (-2.2)
Terms_of_trade_lag_3				-0.22 (-0.7)	-0.89 . (-1.6)	0.11 (0.3)						
Debt_to_GDP_lag_3							0.01 ** (2.8)	-0.00 (-0.1)	0.05 *** (4.1)			
Deficit_to_GDP_lag_3										-0.04 (-1)	0.01 (0.2)	-0.10 ** (-2.6)
No. of observations	505	240	265	498	240	258	496	232	264	456	228	228
N (no. of countries)	37	14	24	36	14	23	37	14	24	32	14	19
T (min)	4	4	4	4	4	4	4	4	4	4	4	4
T (max)	25	25	17	25	25	17	25	25	17	24	24	17
R-squared	0.55	0.56	0.52	0.55	0.56	0.53	0.56	0.60	0.54	0.59	0.62	0.55
Adjusted R-squared	0.51	0.53	0.47	0.52	0.53	0.47	0.53	0.57	0.49	0.56	0.59	0.50

Table 4.17 (Continued)

	Baseline specification			Adding money			Adding credit			Adding economic development		
	All IT countries	IT advanced economies	IT emerging economies	All IT countries	IT advanced economies	IT emerging economies	All IT countries	IT advanced economies	IT emerging economies	All IT countries	IT advanced economies	IT emerging economies
Dummy_2008	0.85 ***	0.79 ***	0.98 ***	0.87 ***	0.83 ***	0.88 ***	0.83 ***	0.77 ***	0.92 ***	0.80 ***	0.78 ***	0.76 ***
	(5.8)	(5)	(4.8)	(6)	(5.2)	(4.4)	(5.9)	(5.3)	(4.5)	(5.8)	(5.1)	(4)
Output_gap_hp_lag_3	0.17 ***	0.12 ***	0.20 ***	0.17 ***	0.12 **	0.20 ***	0.18 ***	0.14 ***	0.20 ***	0.18 ***	0.13 ***	0.21 ***
	(4.3)	(2.9)	(3.8)	(4.2)	(2.6)	(3.5)	(4.4)	(3.8)	(3.6)	(4.3)	(3.2)	(3.6)
Trade_openness_lag_3	-0.02 ***	-0.03 ***	-0.03 **	-0.02 ***	-0.03 ***	-0.02 *	-0.02 ***	-0.03 ***	-0.03 **	-0.02 **	-0.02 **	-0.01
	(-3.6)	(-3.1)	(-2.3)	(-2.8)	(-2.7)	(-2)	(-3.3)	(-2.9)	(-2.2)	(-2.1)	(-2.4)	(-0.9)
Money_to_GDP_lag_3				-0.00	0.00	-0.03 **						
				(-0.7)	(0.2)	(-2.7)						
Credit_to_GDP_lag_3							-0.00	-0.00	-0.01			
							(-1.1)	(-0.4)	(-1.2)			
GDP_per_capita_PPP_lag_3										-0.00 **	-0.00 *	-0.00 **
										(-2.4)	(-2)	(-2.9)
No. of observations	505	240	265	478	213	265	485	234	251	505	240	265
N (no. of countries)	37	14	24	36	13	24	36	14	23	37	14	24
T (min)	4	4	4	4	4	4	4	4	4	4	4	4
T (max)	25	25	17	24	24	17	24	24	17	25	25	17
R-squared	0.55	0.56	0.52	0.55	0.57	0.53	0.55	0.57	0.51	0.56	0.57	0.53
Adjusted R-squared	0.51	0.53	0.47	0.51	0.53	0.48	0.51	0.54	0.45	0.52	0.54	0.48

Source: Own compilation based on the constructed indices and macroeconomic variables (sources indicated in Table 4.12).
Notes: Significance codes: *** 0.01; ** 0.05; * 0.1; · 0.15.

Table 4.18 Robustness check of models related to GDP growth

	Baseline specification			Adding global inflation			Adding global output gap			Adding terms-of-trade		
	All IT countries	IT advanced economies	IT emerging economies	All IT countries	IT advanced economies	IT emerging economies	All IT countries	IT advanced economies	IT emerging economies	All IT countries	IT advanced economies	IT emerging economies
GDP_growth_lag_3	0.17 ***	0.15 ***	0.17 ***	0.17 ***	0.17 ***	0.17 ***	0.17 ***	0.14 ***	0.19 ***	0.17 ***	0.16 ***	0.17 ***
	(5.1)	(4.6)	(3.6)	(5.2)	(5.1)	(3.6)	(4.7)	(4.1)	(3.8)	(5.1)	(4.7)	(3.6)
Output_gap_hp_lag_3	-0.47 ***	-0.47 ***	-0.50 ***	-0.48 ***	-0.50 ***	-0.49 ***	-0.47 ***	-0.50 ***	-0.48 ***	-0.48 ***	-0.47 ***	-0.50 ***
	(-13.2)	(-11.8)	(-13.8)	(-13)	(-12.3)	(-12.2)	(-14.7)	(-18.8)	(-12.7)	(-13.9)	(-12)	(-15.2)
Oil_prices_avg_lag_3	-0.02 ***	-0.02 ***	-0.02 ***	-0.02 ***	-0.02 ***	-0.02 ***	-0.02 ***	-0.02 ***	-0.02 ***	-0.02 ***	-0.02 ***	-0.02 ***
	(-5)	(-5.2)	(-3.9)	(-5.2)	(-6.2)	(-4)	(-5.2)	(-4.9)	(-4.7)	(-5)	(-5.2)	(-3.8)
Oil_prices_avg_lag_3 x Dummy_oil_exporter	0.01 ***	0.00	0.02 ***	0.01 ***	0.00	0.02 ***	0.01 ***	0.00	0.02 ***	0.01 ***	0.00	0.02 ***
	(4)	(-0.3)	(5.1)	(4.1)	(-0.8)	(5.4)	(4)	(-0.3)	(5.1)	(3.2)	(-0.7)	(4.7)
FX_scaled_lag_3	-1.09 **	-0.93 **	-2.75 ***	-1.27 ***	-1.26 ***	-2.81 ***	-1.07 **	-1.08 **	-2.82 ***	-1.01 **	-0.87 **	-2.65 ***
	(-2.7)	(-2.5)	(-4.1)	(-3)	(-3.1)	(-4.4)	(-2.6)	(-2.7)	(-4.7)	(-2.5)	(-2.5)	(-3.4)
CPI_world_avg_lag_3				-0.02 **	-0.03 ***	-0.06						
				(-2.5)	(-3.4)	(-0.4)						
Advanced_economies_output_gap_lag_3							-0.03	0.10	-0.11 **			
							(-0.6)	(1.3)	(-2.2)			
Terms_of_trade_lag_3										0.58	0.39	0.25
										(1.1)	(1.2)	(0.3)
No. of observations	472	229	243	472	229	243	472	229	243	466	229	237
N (no. of countries)	37	14	24	37	14	24	37	14	24	36	14	23
T (min)	3	3	3	3	3	3	3	3	3	3	3	3
T (max)	25	25	16	25	25	16	25	25	16	25	25	16
R-squared	0.83	0.82	0.82	0.83	0.84	0.82	0.83	0.83	0.83	0.83	0.82	0.81
Adjusted R-squared	0.81	0.81	0.80	0.82	0.82	0.80	0.81	0.81	0.80	0.81	0.81	0.79

323

Table 4.18 (Continued)

	Baseline specification			Adding trade openness			Adding fiscal debt			Adding fiscal deficit		
	All IT countries	IT advanced economies	IT emerging economies	All IT countries	IT advanced economies	IT emerging economies	All IT countries	IT advanced economies	IT emerging economies	All IT countries	IT advanced economies	IT emerging economies
GDP_growth_lag_3	0.17 ***	0.15 ***	0.17 ***	0.17 ***	0.16 ***	0.17 ***	0.16 ***	0.16 ***	0.16 ***	0.17 ***	0.13 ***	0.19 ***
	(5.1)	(4.6)	(3.6)	(5.2)	(4.5)	(3.8)	(5.1)	(5.6)	(3.8)	(5)	(4.7)	(4.1)
Output_gap_hp_lag_3	-0.47 ***	-0.47 ***	-0.50 ***	-0.48 ***	-0.47 ***	-0.50 ***	-0.51 ***	-0.52 ***	-0.54 ***	-0.48 ***	-0.50 ***	-0.50 ***
	(-13.2)	(-11.8)	(-13.8)	(-13.1)	(-11.5)	(-14.5)	(-14.8)	(-12.4)	(-19.2)	(-11.9)	(-13)	(-11.1)
Oil_prices_avg_lag_3	-0.02 ***	-0.02 ***	-0.02 ***	-0.01 ***	-0.02 ***	-0.02 ***	-0.01 ***	-0.01 ***	-0.02 ***	-0.02 ***	-0.02 ***	-0.02 ***
	(-5)	(-5.2)	(-3.9)	(-6.1)	(-4.5)	(-3)	(-4.4)	(-4.3)	(-3.5)	(-4.8)	(-5.5)	(-4.4)
Oil_prices_avg_lag_3 x Dummy_oil_exporter	0.01 ***	0.00	0.02 ***	0.01 **	0.00	0.02 ***	0.01 ***	0.00 .	0.02 ***	0.01 ***	0.00	0.02 ***
	(4)	(-0.3)	(5.1)	(2.7)	(-0.6)	(4.7)	(3)	(-1.7)	(4.6)	(3.8)	(-1.1)	(4.6)
FX_scaled_lag_3	-1.09 **	-0.93 **	-2.75 ***	-1.01 ***	-0.83 **	-2.70 ***	-0.66 **	-0.36	-1.94 ***	-0.96 **	-0.90 *	-2.80 ***
	(-2.7)	(-2.5)	(-4.1)	(-2.9)	(-2.7)	(-4.4)	(-2.2)	(-1.1)	(-3.4)	(-2.3)	(-2.1)	(-4.5)
Trade_openness_lag_3				-0.01	-0.01	-0.01 **						
				(-1.5)	(-0.7)	(-2.2)						
Debt_to_GDP_lag_3							-0.03 ***	-0.02 ***	-0.05 ***			
							(-4.3)	(-3.6)	(-4.7)			
Deficit_to_GDP_lag_3										0.07 ***	0.12 ***	0.02
										(3.3)	(4.3)	(0.7)
No. of observations	472	229	243	466	229	237	472	229	243	427	216	211
N (no. of countries)	37	14	24	36	14	23	37	14	24	32	14	19
T (min)	3	3	3	3	3	3	3	3	3	3	3	3
T (max)	25	25	16	25	25	16	25	25	16	24	24	16
R-squared	0.83	0.82	0.82	0.83	0.83	0.83	0.85	0.84	0.84	0.83	0.84	0.82
Adjusted R-squared	0.81	0.81	0.80	0.82	0.82	0.80	0.83	0.82	0.82	0.82	0.82	0.80

Table 4.18 (Continued)

	Baseline specification			Adding money			Adding credit			Adding economic development		
	All IT countries	IT advanced economies	IT emerging economies	All IT countries	IT advanced economies	IT emerging economies	All IT countries	IT advanced economies	IT emerging economies	All IT countries	IT advanced economies	IT emerging economies
GDP_growth_lag_3	0.17 ***	0.15 ***	0.17 ***	0.16 ***	0.14 ***	0.16 ***	0.17 ***	0.15 ***	0.17 ***	0.16 ***	0.16 ***	0.16 ***
	(5.1)	(4.6)	(3.6)	(4.4)	(3.9)	(3.5)	(5.1)	(4.8)	(3.8)	(4.6)	(4.6)	(3.5)
Output_gap_hp_lag_3	-0.47 ***	-0.47 ***	-0.50 ***	-0.48 ***	-0.46 ***	-0.50 ***	-0.48 ***	-0.47 ***	-0.50 ***	-0.47 ***	-0.47 ***	-0.50 ***
	(-13.2)	(-11.8)	(-13.8)	(-14)	(-12.3)	(-13.5)	(-12.9)	(-12.3)	(-13.7)	(-13.1)	(-11.8)	(-13.1)
Oil_prices_avg_lag_3	-0.02 ***	-0.02 ***	-0.02 ***	-0.01 ***	-0.01 ***	-0.02 ***	-0.02 ***	-0.02 ***	-0.02 ***	-0.01 ***	-0.02 **	-0.01 **
	(-5)	(-5.2)	(-3.9)	(-3.8)	(-3.4)	(-3.8)	(-5.4)	(-5)	(-3.9)	(-2.6)	(-2.8)	(-2.2)
Oil_prices_avg_lag_3 x Dummy_oil_exporter	0.01 ***	0.00	0.02 ***	0.01 ***	0.00 .	0.02 ***	0.01 ***	0.00	0.02 ***	0.01 ***	0.00	0.02 ***
	(4)	(-0.3)	(5.1)	(3.7)	(-1.6)	(9.1)	(4.1)	(-0.4)	(4.7)	(4)	(-0.8)	(4.2)
FX_scaled_lag_3	-1.09 **	-0.93 **	-2.75 ***	-1.24 **	-1.08 **	-2.65 ***	-1.07 **	-1.12 **	-2.93 ***	-1.14 **	-0.92 **	-2.77 ***
	(-2.7)	(-2.5)	(-4.1)	(-2.6)	(-2.2)	(-3.8)	(-2.5)	(-2.4)	(-4.9)	(-2.8)	(-2.5)	(-4.1)
Money_to_GDP_lag_3				-0.01	-0.01	-0.02						
				(-1.3)	(-0.9)	(-1.4)						
Credit_to_GDP_lag_3							0.00	-0.01	0.01 **			
							(-0.1)	(-1.1)	(2.3)			
GDP_per_capita_PPP_lag_3										0.00	0.00	0.00
										(-0.7)	(0.6)	(-1)
No. of observations	472	229	243	447	204	243	453	222	231	472	229	243
N (no. of countries)	37	14	24	36	13	24	36	14	23	37	14	24
T (min)	3	3	3	3	3	3	3	3	3	3	3	3
T (max)	25	25	16	23	23	16	24	24	16	25	25	16
R-squared	0.83	0.82	0.82	0.83	0.82	0.83	0.83	0.82	0.82	0.83	0.82	0.82
Adjusted R-squared	0.81	0.81	0.80	0.81	0.80	0.80	0.81	0.81	0.80	0.81	0.81	0.80

Source: Own compilation based on the constructed indices and macroeconomic variables (sources indicated in Table 4.12).
Notes: Significance codes: *** 0.01; ** 0.05; * 0.1; ˙ 0.15.

325

Table 4.19 Robustness check of models related to GDP growth volatility

	Baseline specification			Adding exchange rate volatility			Adding oil price volatility			Adding terms-of-trade		
	All IT countries	IT advanced economies	IT emerging economies	All IT countries	IT advanced economies	IT emerging economies	All IT countries	IT advanced economies	IT emerging economies	All IT countries	IT advanced economies	IT emerging economies
Output_gap_hp_lag_3	0.90 *** (5)	0.81 *** (4.3)	0.97 *** (4.3)	0.90 *** (5.3)	0.76 *** (4.7)	1.02 *** (5)	0.85 *** (5.3)	0.78 *** (4)	0.93 *** (4.5)	0.89 *** (5.1)	0.80 *** (4.4)	0.92 *** (4.1)
Advanced_economies_ output_gap_lag_3	1.10 ** (2.3)	0.82 ** (2.5)	1.48 ** (2.3)	1.08 ** (2.4)	0.47 . (1.7)	1.49 ** (2.7)	1.04 ** (2.1)	0.75 ** (2.3)	1.43 * (2.1)	1.11 ** (2.2)	0.83 ** (2.5)	1.55 * (2)
FX_scaled_var_3y				7.41 (0.1)	190.5 (1.4)	−208.1 * (−1.9)						
Oil_prices_var_3y							0.00 (1.3)	0.00 . (1.6)	0.00 (0.6)			
Oil_prices_var_3y x Dummy_oil_exporter							0.00 (−1.4)	−0.01 . (−1.7)	0.00 (0.2)			
Terms-of-trade_lag_3										0.94 (0.6)	0.54 (0.3)	2.50 (0.7)
No. of observations	415	231	184	414	230	184	415	231	184	408	231	177
N (no. of countries)	28	14	15	28	14	15	28	14	15	27	14	14
T (min)	3	3	4	3	3	4	3	3	4	3	3	4
T (max)	25	25	17	24	24	17	25	25	17	25	25	17
R-squared	0.47	0.46	0.48	0.47	0.51	0.49	0.48	0.49	0.48	0.47	0.46	0.48
Adjusted R-squared	0.43	0.43	0.43	0.43	0.47	0.44	0.44	0.45	0.42	0.43	0.42	0.42

Table 4.19 (Continued)

	Baseline specification			Adding trade openness			Adding CPI variance			Adding economic development		
	All IT countries	IT advanced economies	IT emerging economies	All IT countries	IT advanced economies	IT emerging economies	All IT countries	IT advanced economies	IT emerging economies	All IT countries	IT advanced economies	IT emerging economies
Output_gap_hp_lag_3	0.90 ***	0.81 ***	0.97 ***	0.91 ***	0.79 ***	0.98 ***	0.89 ***	0.22 .	0.98 ***	0.91 ***	0.79 ***	1.04 ***
	(5)	(4.3)	(4.3)	(5.1)	(4.3)	(4.4)	(5)	(1.6)	(4.4)	(5.2)	(4.3)	(4.6)
Advanced_economies_ output_gap_lag_3	1.10 **	0.82 **	1.48 **	1.10 **	0.82 **	1.46 **	1.07 **	0.89 **	1.62 **	1.09 **	0.85 **	1.24 **
	(2.3)	(2.5)	(2.3)	(2.3)	(2.5)	(2.2)	(2.2)	(2.6)	(2.3)	(2.3)	(2.6)	(2.1)
Trade_openness_lag_3				0.02	-0.03	0.03						
				(0.8)	(-0.9)	(0.7)						
CPI_var_3y							0.05	0.92 ***	-0.19 .			
							(0.5)	(3.4)	(-1.5)			
GDP_per_capita_PPP_lag_3										0.00	0.00	0.00
										(-0.1)	(0.2)	(-0.9)
No. of observations	415	231	184	415	231	184	415	231	184	415	231	184
N (no. of countries)	28	14	15	28	14	15	28	14	15	28	14	15
T (min)	3	3	4	3	3	4	3	3	4	3	3	4
T (max)	25	25	17	25	25	17	25	25	17	25	25	17
R-squared	0.47	0.46	0.48	0.47	0.47	0.48	0.47	0.55	0.48	0.47	0.46	0.48
Adjusted R-squared	0.43	0.43	0.43	0.43	0.43	0.42	0.43	0.52	0.43	0.43	0.42	0.43

Source: Own compilation based on the constructed indices and macroeconomic variables (sources indicated in Table 4.12).
Notes: Significance codes: *** 0.01; ** 0.05; * 0.1; '.' 0.15.

Table 4.20 Robustness check of models related to output gap

	Baseline specification			Adding domestic output gap			Adding global output gap			Adding terms-of-trade		
	All IT countries	IT advanced economies	IT emerging economies	All IT countries	IT advanced economies	IT emerging economies	All IT countries	IT advanced economies	IT emerging economies	All IT countries	IT advanced economies	IT emerging economies
GDP_growth_lag_3	0.31 *** (4.3)	0.33 *** (4.4)	0.32 *** (5.1)	0.29 *** (4.4)	0.32 *** (4.2)	0.29 *** (5.1)	0.35 *** (6.1)	0.32 *** (4.4)	0.34 *** (5.8)	0.31 *** (4.3)	0.32 *** (4.3)	0.31 *** (4.8)
Oil_prices_avg_lag_3	-0.01 . (-1.7)	-0.01 * (-2)	-0.01 * (-1.8)	-0.01 * (-1.8)	-0.01 * (-2)	-0.02 * (-2)	-0.02 ** (-2.1)	-0.01 * (-2)	-0.02 ** (-2.8)	-0.01 * (-1.8)	-0.01 * (-2)	-0.02 ** (-2.3)
Oil_prices_avg_lag_3 x Dummy_oil_exporter	0.01 *** (3.2)	-0.01 (-1.2)	0.03 *** (6.3)	0.01 *** (3.1)	-0.01 (-1.1)	0.02 *** (6)	0.01 ** (2.8)	-0.01 (-1.1)	0.03 *** (6.3)	0.01 * (1.9)	-0.01 (-1)	0.02 *** (4.3)
FX_scaled_lag_3	-2.17 ** (-2.6)	-1.30 * (-1.8)	-5.04 *** (-3.2)	-2.06 ** (-2.5)	-1.30 * (-1.8)	-4.94 *** (-3.6)	-2.16 ** (-2.5)	-1.33 * (-1.8)	-5.04 *** (-3)	-1.95 ** (-2.4)	-1.43 * (-1.8)	-4.80 *** (-3.1)
CPI_world_avg_lag_3	-0.07 *** (-3.3)	-0.07 *** (-4.3)	-0.73 *** (-3.9)	-0.06 *** (-2.9)	-0.07 *** (-4.2)	-0.73 *** (-3.7)	-0.07 *** (-4)	-0.06 *** (-4.2)	-0.62 *** (-2.9)	-0.06 *** (-3.1)	-0.07 *** (-4.2)	-0.64 *** (-3.1)
Debt_to_GDP_lag_3	-0.04 *** (-3.8)	-0.04 *** (-3.2)	-0.07 *** (-4.3)	-0.04 *** (-3.8)	-0.04 *** (-3.1)	-0.05 *** (-3.6)	-0.05 *** (-4.8)	-0.04 *** (-3.4)	-0.06 *** (-4.1)	-0.04 *** (-3.4)	-0.04 *** (-3.2)	-0.06 *** (-4)
Output_gap_hp_lag_3				0.09 (1.2)	0.00 (0)	0.14 ** (2.3)						
Advanced_economies_output_gap_lag_3							-0.17 . (-1.5)	0.03 (0.3)	-0.14 (-1.2)			
Terms_of_trade_lag_3										1.77 ** (2.5)	-0.65 (-1)	2.23 * (1.8)
No. of observations	500	235	265	500	235	265	500	235	265	500	235	265
N (no. of countries)	37	14	24	37	14	24	37	14	24	37	14	24
T (min)	4	4	4	4	4	4	4	4	4	4	4	4
T (max)	26	26	17	26	26	17	26	26	17	26	26	17
R-squared	0.37	0.46	0.42	0.38	0.46	0.45	0.38	0.47	0.43	0.37	0.47	0.42
Adjusted R-squared	0.31	0.42	0.35	0.32	0.41	0.37	0.32	0.42	0.35	0.31	0.42	0.35

Table 4.20 (Continued)

	Baseline specification			Adding trade openness			Adding fiscal deficit			Adding money		
	All IT countries	IT advanced economies	IT emerging economies	All IT countries	IT advanced economies	IT emerging economies	All IT countries	IT advanced economies	IT emerging economies	All IT countries	IT advanced economies	IT emerging economies
GDP_growth_lag_3	0.31 *** (4.3)	0.33 *** (4.4)	0.32 *** (5.1)	0.30 *** (4.3)	0.33 *** (4.2)	0.30 *** (5.4)	0.34 *** (4.4)	0.28 *** (3.9)	0.38 *** (5.2)	0.31 *** (4.3)	0.34 *** (4.5)	0.31 *** (5.3)
Oil_prices_avg_lag_3	-0.01 . (-1.7)	-0.01 * (-2)	-0.01 * (-1.8)	-0.02 ** (-2.1)	-0.01 ** (-2.1)	-0.02 ** (-2.2)	-0.01 * (-1.8)	-0.01 ** (-2.1)	-0.02 ** (-2.3)	-0.02 * (-1.8)	-0.02 ** (-2.1)	-0.01 (-1.6)
Oil_prices_avg_lag_3 x Dummy_oil_exporter	0.01 *** (3.2)	-0.01 (-1.2)	0.03 *** (6.3)	0.01 *** (3.9)	-0.01 (-1.1)	0.03 *** (5.4)	0.01 ** (2.5)	-0.01 * (-1.9)	0.03 *** (4.8)	0.01 ** (2.8)	-0.01 ** (-2.2)	0.03 *** (7.2)
FX_scaled_lag_3	-2.17 ** (-2.6)	-1.30 * (-1.8)	-5.04 *** (-3.2)	-2.26 ** (-2.6)	-1.30 * (-1.8)	-4.95 *** (-3.4)	-2.45 *** (-2.9)	-1.68 ** (-2.2)	-5.88 *** (-4)	-2.61 *** (-2.7)	-1.49 . (-1.6)	-4.88 *** (-3)
CPI_world_avg_lag_3	-0.07 *** (-3.3)	-0.07 *** (-4.3)	-0.73 *** (-3.9)	-0.06 *** (-3.2)	-0.07 *** (-4.2)	-0.74 *** (-3.9)	-0.09 *** (-4.3)	-0.07 *** (-4.2)	-0.70 *** (-4.1)	-0.06 ** (-2.7)	-0.05 *** (-3.2)	-0.79 *** (-5.8)
Debt_to_GDP_lag_3	-0.04 *** (-3.8)	-0.04 *** (-3.2)	-0.07 *** (-4.3)	-0.05 *** (-3.9)	-0.04 *** (-3.2)	-0.09 *** (-4.4)	-0.05 *** (-4.6)	-0.03 *** (-3)	-0.08 *** (-5.3)	-0.04 *** (-3.7)	-0.04 *** (-3.7)	-0.06 *** (-3.8)
Trade_openness_lag_3				0.02 . (1.6)	0.00 (0)	0.04 ** (2.5)						
Deficit_to_GDP_lag_3							-0.01 (-0.4)	0.13 *** (4.1)	-0.07 (-1.1)			
Money_to_GDP_lag_3										0.00 (0.7)	0.01 * (1.7)	-0.03 (-1.2)
No. of observations	500	235	265	500	235	265	459	230	229	482	216	266
N (no. of countries)	37	14	24	37	14	24	32	14	19	36	13	24
T (min)	4	4	4	4	4	4	4	4	4	4	4	4
T (max)	26	26	17	26	26	17	25	25	17	24	24	17
R-squared	0.37	0.46	0.42	0.37	0.46	0.44	0.39	0.50	0.46	0.37	0.48	0.43
Adjusted R-squared	0.31	0.42	0.35	0.32	0.41	0.37	0.33	0.45	0.39	0.31	0.42	0.36

Table 4.20 (Continued)

	Baseline specification			Adding credit			Adding economic development		
	All IT countries	IT advanced economies	IT emerging economies	All IT countries	IT advanced economies	IT emerging economies	All IT countries	IT advanced economies	IT emerging economies
GDP_growth_lag_3	0.31 *** (4.3)	0.33 *** (4.4)	0.32 *** (5.1)	0.31 *** (4.5)	0.31 *** (4.3)	0.31 *** (4.6)	0.31 *** (4.4)	0.33 *** (4.4)	0.32 *** (5.2)
Oil_prices_avg_lag_3	-0.01 . (-1.7)	-0.01 * (-2)	-0.01 * (-1.8)	-0.02 ** (-2.2)	-0.01 ** (-2.2)	-0.02 ** (-2.6)	-0.01 (-1.8)	-0.02 ** (-2.5)	-0.01 (-1.1)
Oil_prices_avg_lag_3 x Dummy_oil_exporter	0.01 *** (3.2)	-0.01 (-1.2)	0.03 *** (6.3)	0.01 ** (2.8)	-0.01 * (-1.9)	0.03 *** (6)	0.01 *** (3.2)	-0.01 (-1.4)	0.03 *** (5.2)
FX_scaled_lag_3	-2.17 ** (-2.6)	-1.30 * (-1.8)	-5.04 *** (-3.2)	-2.23 ** (-2.8)	-1.50 * (-2)	-5.14 *** (-3.4)	-2.21 ** (-2.5)	-1.26 . (-1.7)	-4.96 *** (-3)
CPI_world_avg_lag_3	-0.07 *** (-3.3)	-0.07 *** (-4.3)	-0.73 *** (-3.9)	-0.09 *** (-4.7)	-0.09 *** (-5.9)	-0.65 *** (-3.2)	-0.07 ** (-2.6)	-0.06 *** (-3.1)	-0.82 *** (-3.5)
Debt_to_GDP_lag_3	-0.04 *** (-3.8)	-0.04 *** (-3.2)	-0.07 *** (-4.3)	-0.04 *** (-4)	-0.04 *** (-3.5)	-0.06 *** (-4.1)	-0.04 *** (-3.9)	-0.04 *** (-3.3)	-0.06 *** (-3.9)
Credit_to_GDP_lag_3				0.01 (1.3)	0.00 (-0.6)	0.01 (1)			
GDP_per_capita_PPP_lag_3							0.00 (-0.5)	0.00 (0.6)	0.00 (-0.9)
No. of observations	500	235	265	488	236	252	500	235	265
N (no. of countries)	37	14	24	36	14	23	37	14	24
T (min)	4	4	4	4	4	4	4	4	4
T (max)	26	26	17	25	25	17	26	26	17
R-squared	0.37	0.46	0.42	0.38	0.48	0.42	0.37	0.47	0.42
Adjusted R-squared	0.31	0.42	0.35	0.32	0.43	0.35	0.31	0.42	0.35

Source: Own compilation based on the constructed indices and macroeconomic variables (sources indicated in Table 4.12).
Notes: Significance codes: *** 0.01; ** 0.05; * 0.1; ' 0.15.

CONCLUSIONS

Final remarks on inflation targeting

Over the last three decades, an inflation targeting (IT) framework clearly became very popular; however, while the 1990s and the early 2000s were the years of its unquestionable successes, the global financial crisis of 2008 marked a point at which sentiments towards IT started to change.

Inflation targeting still enjoys strong support, but some economists doubt whether it will remain the dominant strategy, especially given the fact that it was proposed as a way to lower inflation, whereas currently many monetary authorities are much more concerned with excessively low price growth. Moreover, the crisis has shown that price stability, to which inflation targeting has effectively contributed, is not a sufficient condition to maintain the overall macroeconomic stability of an economy, including financial stability. Additionally, in the aftermath of the recent global and European crises, several IT central banks were confronted with the problem of providing sufficient monetary policy accommodation due to the zero lower bound (ZLB) constraint. Thus, the role of financial stability in monetary policy considerations and the issue of extending the scope of monetary policy measures have become widely discussed topics.

Whereas, before the crises, the mainstream view was that pursuing monetary policy aimed at ensuring price stability while limiting output volatility would also result in maintaining financial stability, and that the only instrument needed to achieve that was interest rates, the global financial crisis and the European sovereign crisis proved these beliefs wrong. Therefore, the current disputes mainly concern incorporating financial stability issues into central banks' mandates, and finding effective ways to cope with the ZLB problem. The discussions on these topics have yet to conclude, but the solutions already applied by several monetary authorities indicate that there is quite a wide consensus around two ideas. First, that there is a need to develop macroprudential frameworks involving central banks, with possibly some dose of "leaning against the wind" of their monetary policies against growing imbalances, in order to safeguard financial stability. Second—with

331

respect to the ZLB—that the array of available non-standard monetary policy tools should be broadened with monetary authorities ready to reach for them again in case of a severe downturn. Clear evidence of the latter point is central banks' reaction to the Covid-19 pandemic that took the form of massive recourse to non-standard measures visible across the world.

While incorporating the outcomes of the ongoing discussions may result in a further evolution of an inflation targeting framework, it may also lead to developing an alternative monetary policy regime. Deciding at which point a change already means a new strategy is difficult, in particular when it comes to analysing inflation targeting, since this framework has been continuously modified, and—over the years—flexibility has started to be its major strength. Moreover, while certain features have been assessed as essential for IT, inflation targeting has no precise definition, and even its constituting elements are formulated in rather general terms. This follows from the fact that—although IT principles were based on ideas developed within monetary economics—inflation targeting was first adopted as a pragmatic approach to monetary policy without deep theoretical foundations. As a consequence, an IT regime has many shades, as evidenced by the variety of its institutional set-ups.

However, when looking at some of the proposals to reformulate the conduct of monetary policy, especially those related to promoting alternative targeting rules, a turning point—beyond which it will no longer be possible to speak of an IT strategy, but of a new regime—may be approaching. For now, however, inflation targeting is still the dominant framework for big and medium-sized economies, with no obvious candidates to replace it. Thus, while the critique should not be disregarded, the outlook for inflation targeting continues to be quite favourable.

Interestingly, New Zealand—the pioneer of IT—in early 2019 changed the central bank's mandate by substituting a single objective with a dual mandate that encompasses both price stability and supporting maximum sustainable employment. Despite this modification, the Reserve Bank of New Zealand emphasises that it continues to apply a flexible inflation targeting framework, and that adding the objective directly related to employment is only reinforcing the flexibility of its monetary policy regime. Likewise, the recent announcement of average inflation targeting by the US Federal Reserve is not questioning the foundations of inflation targeting and is to be flexibly applied.

Indeed, it seems that inflation targeting is a highly flexible approach to monetary policy and allows for a reasonable balance between rules and discretion. Probably the best way to describe its essence is to call it—after Ben S. Bernanke and Frederic S. Mishkin—constrained discretion, which is likely to be one of the reasons why this framework has been so compelling to many central banks. The past three decades have clearly shown that—due to such characteristics—inflation targeting has been effective in delivering low and stable inflation without destabilising output. And despite the recent critique, even in the wake of crises, IT turned out to be quite helpful in combating their consequences.

The fact that some beneficial effects of using an IT regime have been much more visible in emerging market economies may indirectly imply that institutional arrangements do matter. Inflation targeting requires meeting high accountability and transparency standards accompanying the considerable independence of central banks, which in the case of less developed countries willing to become inflation targeters may translate into a necessity to significantly enhance their institutional set-ups. The effort of developed economies in that respect, which generally—independently of the monetary policy strategy used—can be expected to act under better institutional arrangements, might be less visible when switching to inflation targeting. Therefore, the adoption of an IT framework by an emerging market economy may simply mean investing heavily in improving its central bank's institutional set-ups, which, indeed, seems to pay off.

For these reasons, investigating how the key elements of the strategy have been implemented in practice by various inflation targeters, and, in particular, whether the institutional features have evolved over time, seemed justified. This allowed for drawing conclusions on the importance of central banks' institutional set-ups for policy outcomes, since the research was aimed at answering the question of whether there are significant differences in IT central banks' institutional arrangements, and—if yes—whether they influence the ability of monetary authorities to meet their policy goals. Considering the already large number of countries following an inflation targeting framework and their importance in the world economy, understanding which factors affect the ability of central banks to deliver price stability and stabilise output was considered valuable.

For the advocates of inflation targeting, this may be seen as a way to identify the sources of strength of inflation targeting, while for the opponents of inflation targeting, this may be viewed as a way to indicate which elements of IT institutional set-ups should be kept even if the need to replace this strategy with another regime will, indeed, result in a change. Therefore, the findings of the study may be relevant for different audiences, but especially for central banks already pursuing an IT strategy, or those preparing to adopt it.

Comparison with existing literature

An important feature of this study is that it concerns only economies following the same monetary policy strategy, namely, inflation targeters. The significant advantage of such an approach was that comparing IT central banks' ability to deliver monetary policy goals was, indeed, focusing on the role of IT institutional set-ups, i.e. answering the main question asked in this work. The potential disadvantage of limiting the sample to inflation targeters that, almost by definition, have a lot in common, in particular with respect to applying high accountability and transparency standards, was that not much heterogeneity between them would be visible, and thus it would not be possible to establish a robust link between institutional set-ups and policy outcomes. This, however, turned out not to be the case, which allowed for drawing valuable conclusions. Moreover, including 42 economies in the review that have started to follow an inflation targeting strategy over the last 30 years resulted in around 640 annual observations to be investigated, which formed a rich data set to analyse. While the quantitative analysis encompassed a slightly smaller number of countries, with 37 inflation targeters included in the modelling parts, the full sample used to estimate regressions was also sizeable with around 500 observations.

The conducted review of IT monetary authorities enabled detecting differences between the applied institutional arrangements, but—in contrast to many other reviews—it also indicated the evolution of institutional set-ups over time. This helped to notice that, in some instances, the changes resulted in developing a dominant practice, while in other dimensions visible differences still persist. Importantly, unlike other studies, this study encompassed both advanced and emerging market economy inflation targeters, which makes it one of the broadest overviews in existence.

Regarding the results obtained from the quantitative analysis, there are also apparent differences between previous research and this work that should be mentioned. First, the time and country coverage of the study, as well as the number and details of the investigated aspects of institutional set-ups, was significantly larger than in most other research. Second, contrary to most of the existing literature that was based on a cross-section approach, this work built on panel regressions that should provide more general findings, valid not only for a specific point in time. As shown when referring to the stylised facts, selecting a year for a cross-section analysis may considerably affect the results. Third, as opposed to some of the reviewed papers that did not include even basic control variables, which could artificially raise the significance of institutional arrangements, this study investigated a very rich set of potential regressors in order to make the conclusions more solid. The need to include control variables became apparent when one compared relationships between institutional arrangements and policy outcomes based on simple correlation coefficients with those based on panel regression coefficients. The fact that, in many cases, these were not the same signalled that ignoring control variables would mean disregarding important information that may strongly influence the findings. Fourth, all of the previous research analysed economies following various monetary policy regimes, making it difficult to disentangle the effects stemming from the different effectiveness of monetary policy strategies and those stemming from central banks' institutional set-ups. In turn, as already mentioned, this analysis focused on inflation targeters only, which eliminated this issue. At the same time, given the already relatively broad data set, restricting the sample to inflation targeters was not problematic. Overall, all of these factors should make the findings delivered with the help of the adopted approach more robust.

Evaluating the research hypothesis

Regarding the research hypothesis, based on the analysis carried out, it can be concluded that, indeed, the quality of the institutional set-ups of monetary authorities pursuing an inflation targeting regime materially affects monetary policy effectiveness. The empirical research indicated that the better the institutional arrangements governing a given IT central bank, the higher its policy effectiveness, understood primarily as delivering low and stable inflation and meeting the inflation target. The finding that institutional set-ups have a material impact on monetary policy outcomes with respect to inflation developments indirectly confirmed that differences in institutional arrangements applied by IT central banks are significant. Some, although much weaker, evidence was provided to establish a link between the institutional set-ups and output developments, but this was the case only for emerging market economies where better institutional arrangements seemed to translate into somewhat lower gross domestic product (GDP) growth and output gaps, with even less strong indication for increased GDP growth volatility.

Moreover, considering the individual steps undertaken in order to draw the final conclusions, there are several other relevant findings to report.

First, the detailed review of central banks' institutional arrangements indicated that the crucial IT features are implemented in various ways, translating into different institutional set-ups. In particular, the comparison between advanced and emerging market economies showed that, while in many instances there is hardly any difference to be noted, in some aspects, the approach to IT of advanced economies differs significantly from that of emerging market economies. Key similarities include, to a great extent, formulating the central banks' mandate, choosing the exchange rate regime, selecting the targeted measure of inflation, indicating the target horizon, deciding on the size and composition of decision-making bodies, safeguarding personal independence, and designing the main features of the accountability mechanism, including the use of certain communication tools such as inflation projections. Some, but no major, differences can be seen in the case of the frequency of decision-making meetings, the organisation of decision-making processes, guaranteeing financial independence, holding regular press conferences, and publishing minutes or open letters. In turn, the most visible divergences relate to such features as target type and level, releasing voting records, the involvement of government representatives in decision-making, the ownership of forecasts, and publishing projections of variables other than inflation.

Second, the comparison of IT central banks' implementation of the key features of the strategy proved that, in almost all respects, institutional arrangements used in IT advanced economies are superior—judged by the existing research or recognised practice—to those used by IT emerging market economies. This is valid for many dimensions related to accountability and transparency. However, this does not hold for the measure of central banks' independence, which may signal that emerging market economies acknowledged the importance of central banks' independence when drafting legal acts (what needs to be kept in mind is that the index measures only formal independence, which may not always correspond to the actual monetary authorities' autonomy). At the same time, the values of the proposed indices for some emerging market economies are already very similar to those for advanced economies. In fact, looking at advanced and emerging market economies within the distinguished "age" groups of inflation targeters indicated that countries which adopted an IT regime more or less at the same time, and thus have a similarly long experience with pursuing inflation targeting, are applying quite similar institutional arrangements, irrespective of whether they are classified as advanced or emerging market economies.

Third, the analysis of the evolution of IT central banks' institutional setups showed that they have been visibly improving over time for the vast majority of inflation targeters. This means that the solutions favoured in the literature or preferred in practice have become more widespread among the analysed monetary authorities. This supports the claim that pursuing an IT regime enhances the institutional arrangements governing central banks.

Additionally, the review of experiences with pursuing an IT strategy and the discussions summarising the main lessons learnt from the recent crises suggest that the crises have influenced IT central banks' approach to financial stability issues and broadened the use of non-standard monetary policy instruments. Importantly, the attitude of IT central banks to financial stability does not differ significantly between advanced and emerging market economies, while the scope of employing unorthodox measures—at least, until the Covid-19 pandemic, which is already beyond the scope of the study—was much more frequent in the first group of countries. The latter observation follows from the fact that these were predominantly advanced economies that faced the problem of an effective lower bound for the nominal interest rates. At the same time, the recent global and European crises did not seem to disturb the tendencies to a general improvement in central banks' institutional arrangements related to accountability and transparency, since these have not changed in recent years, compared to a more distant past. The crises have, however, initiated debates on the possible redesigning of monetary policy frameworks in order to cope with new

336

challenges, such as secular stagnation or the flattening of the Phillips curve. However, as of yet, only preliminary conclusions have been reached.

Conveying the main messages

The range of topics included in the study was broad, which is reflected in its length. To make it easier to follow—whenever possible—the reviewed issues were illustrated with charts and recapitulated in tables. This was also done to present the key findings of the empirical research, which were summarised visually in tables. As a result, the number of charts and tables is rather big, but it should considerably facilitate comprehending the main points raised in the analysis and increase the readability of the work. For the same reason, some information needed to fully understand a given section of the study was repeatedly recalled—even though it was discussed in some earlier parts. The motivation behind such a practice was that it eliminated the need to search for relevant details in different chapters. This unavoidably resulted in some minor repetitions, although their extent was minimised.

Areas for further research

A number of areas can be identified as requiring further research. They would, however, necessitate significant additional studies.

First of all, the approach adopted in this work did not allow for verifying whether the index directly linked to central banks' independence matters for policy outcomes. The reason was that the index referring to that aspect of monetary authorities' institutional set-up was based on analysing the currently applicable laws, and thus it was treated as a constant for each inflation targeter. In turn, the use of the fixed effects estimation method excluded constants as potential regressors in the specified models. The best way to investigate the importance of monetary authorities' autonomy would be to collect detailed information on how the degree of independence granted to central banks changed over time within the analysed economies. With respect to legal autonomy, this could be done by reviewing the evolution of legal acts governing the investigated central banks, to the extent that these are available. In order to recognise the fact that legal independence may not fully correspond to actual independence, some adjustments based, for example, on including the indices provided by the World Bank on the rule of law, the strength of legal rights, or undue influence and corruption, could be used. Since, in the past, independence was often found to influence policy effectiveness, analysing that issue would be warranted. At the same time, what should be stressed is that indirectly the degree of central banks' independence was captured in the study, since it also impacts on other aspects of monetary authorities' institutional set-ups—most likely translating into higher accountability and transparency requirements that were analysed in great detail.

Moreover, considering the fact that institutional arrangements governing central banks were found to vary visibly between inflation targeters, it would be useful to try to identify the reasons behind these differences in the institutional set-ups. Indicators related to the level of economic development may potentially be important in such an analysis, but factors related to political preferences may also significantly influence the choice of the arrangements regulating central banks' set-ups (though the two sets of variables may be correlated).

Finally, two issues that were only partially covered in this study, but deserve much more attention, are the role of financial stability considerations in monetary policy conducted under an IT regime and the inclusion of non-standard measures in an inflation targeting framework. Regarding financial stability, its relationship with monetary policy depends, to a significant extent, on the institutional solutions adopted in a given country that regulate the links between the two areas. Investigating how financial stability issues affect the formulation of monetary policy seems valid. With respect to unorthodox instruments, an interesting question to ask is whether unconventional measures should be considered an integral part of an IT strategy as its extension, or whether they should still be treated as exceptional tools that may be required only in very specific circumstances.

Given the already very broad set of information collected for the purpose of this study, the indicated topics were assessed to be beyond the scope of the presented analysis.

Supplement: Indices of central banks' institutional set-ups in inflation targeting economies

Table S1 Indices of central banks' institutional set-ups in the analysed inflation targeting economies

Country	Year	Mature _IT	Independent _IT	Informed _IT	Explicatory _IT	Transparent _IT	Accountable _IT	Fully_fledged _IT	Streched _IT
Albania	2009	7.5	7.2	6.5	4.3	4.3	6.5	6.0	2.5
	2010	7.5	7.2	6.5	4.3	4.3	6.5	6.0	3.0
	2011	7.5	7.2	6.5	4.3	4.3	6.5	6.0	3.0
	2012	7.5	7.2	6.5	4.3	4.3	6.5	6.0	3.0
	2013	7.5	7.2	6.5	4.3	4.3	6.5	6.0	3.0
	2014	8.0	7.2	7.5	4.8	5.0	7.0	6.6	5.0
	2015	8.0	7.2	8.0	5.2	5.0	7.0	6.7	5.0
	2016	8.0	7.2	8.0	5.2	5.0	7.0	6.7	5.0
	2017	8.0	7.2	8.0	5.2	5.0	7.0	6.7	5.0
	2018	8.0	7.2	8.0	5.2	5.0	7.0	6.7	5.0
Argentina	2016	1.5	5.0	4.0	3.7	3.5	4.5	3.7	3.0
	2017	2.5	5.0	4.0	3.7	3.5	4.5	3.9	3.0
	2018	2.5	5.0	4.0	3.7	3.5	4.5	3.9	3.0
Armenia	2006	6.0	6.2	6.2	3.3	5.3	6.5	5.6	2.5
	2007	5.0	6.2	6.2	3.3	5.3	6.5	5.4	2.5
	2008	5.0	6.2	6.2	3.3	5.3	6.5	5.4	2.5
	2009	5.0	6.2	6.2	3.3	5.3	6.5	5.4	2.5
	2010	5.5	6.2	6.2	3.3	5.3	6.5	5.5	3.0
	2011	6.0	6.2	6.8	3.3	5.3	6.5	5.6	3.0
	2012	6.5	6.2	6.8	3.3	5.3	6.5	5.8	3.0
	2013	5.5	6.2	6.8	3.3	5.3	6.5	5.6	3.0
	2014	5.5	6.2	6.8	3.3	5.3	6.5	5.6	3.0
	2015	6.5	6.2	6.8	3.3	5.3	6.5	5.8	3.0
	2016	7.0	6.2	6.8	3.3	5.3	6.5	5.9	3.0
	2017	7.0	6.2	6.8	3.3	5.3	6.5	5.9	3.0

(Continued)

Table S1 (Continued) Indices of central banks' institutional set-ups in the analysed inflation targeting economies

Country	Year	Mature _IT	Independent _IT	Informed _IT	Explicatory _IT	Transparent _IT	Accountable _IT	Fully_fledged _IT	Streched _IT
Australia	2018	7.0	6.2	6.8	3.3	5.3	6.5	5.9	3.0
	1993	5.8	3.3	4.0	3.7	3.0	4.5	4.1	0.5
	1994	5.8	3.3	4.0	3.7	3.0	4.5	4.1	0.5
	1995	5.8	3.3	4.0	3.7	3.0	4.5	4.1	0.5
	1996	5.8	3.3	4.0	3.7	3.0	4.5	4.1	0.5
	1997	5.8	3.3	6.5	4.3	4.0	5.5	4.9	0.5
	1998	6.3	3.3	6.5	4.3	4.0	5.5	5.0	0.5
	1999	6.3	3.3	6.5	4.3	4.0	5.5	5.0	0.5
	2000	6.3	3.3	6.5	4.3	4.0	5.5	5.0	2.5
	2001	6.3	3.3	6.5	4.3	4.0	5.5	5.0	2.5
	2002	6.3	3.3	6.5	4.3	4.0	5.5	5.0	2.5
	2003	6.8	3.3	6.5	4.3	4.0	5.5	5.1	2.5
	2004	7.0	3.3	6.5	4.3	4.0	5.5	5.1	2.5
	2005	7.0	3.3	6.5	4.3	4.0	5.5	5.1	2.5
	2006	7.0	3.3	6.5	4.3	5.3	5.5	5.3	2.5
	2007	7.5	3.3	6.8	4.3	5.8	6.0	5.6	3.5
	2008	7.5	3.3	6.8	4.3	5.8	6.0	5.6	2.5
	2009	7.5	3.3	6.8	4.3	5.8	6.0	5.6	2.5
	2010	7.5	3.3	6.8	4.3	5.8	6.0	5.6	2.5
	2011	7.5	3.3	6.8	4.3	5.8	6.0	5.6	2.5
	2012	7.5	3.3	7.5	4.3	5.8	6.0	5.7	2.5
	2013	7.5	3.3	7.5	4.3	5.8	6.0	5.7	2.5
	2014	7.5	3.3	7.5	4.3	5.8	6.0	5.7	2.5
	2015	7.5	3.3	7.5	4.3	5.8	6.0	5.7	2.5
	2016	7.5	3.3	7.5	4.3	5.8	6.0	5.7	2.5
	2017	7.5	3.3	7.8	4.3	5.8	6.0	5.8	2.5
	2018	7.5	3.3	7.8	4.3	5.8	6.0	5.8	2.5
Brazil	1999	3.5	3.0	6.5	4.3	6.7	6.5	5.1	1.0

Year								
2000	3.5	3.0	6.5	4.3	6.7	6.5	5.1	1.0
2001	4.0	3.0	6.5	4.3	6.7	6.5	5.2	1.0
2002	4.0	3.0	6.5	4.3	6.7	6.5	5.2	3.0
2003	3.5	3.0	6.5	4.3	6.7	6.5	5.1	3.0
2004	4.5	3.0	6.5	4.3	6.7	6.5	5.2	3.0
2005	4.5	3.0	6.5	4.3	6.7	6.5	5.2	3.0
2006	4.5	3.0	7.3	4.7	6.7	6.5	5.4	3.0
2007	4.5	3.0	7.3	4.7	6.7	6.5	5.4	3.0
2008	4.5	3.0	7.3	4.7	6.7	6.5	5.4	3.0
2009	5.5	3.0	7.3	4.7	6.7	6.5	5.6	3.0
2010	5.5	3.0	7.3	4.7	6.7	6.5	5.6	3.0
2011	5.5	3.0	7.3	5.0	6.7	6.5	5.6	3.0
2012	5.5	3.0	7.3	5.0	7.7	6.5	5.8	3.0
2013	5.5	3.0	7.3	5.0	7.7	6.5	5.8	3.0
2014	5.5	3.0	7.3	5.0	7.7	6.5	5.8	3.0
2015	5.5	3.0	7.0	5.5	7.7	6.5	5.9	3.0
2016	5.0	3.0	7.3	5.5	8.2	6.5	5.9	3.0
2017	5.0	3.0	7.3	5.5	8.2	6.5	5.9	3.0
2018	5.0	3.0	7.3	5.5	8.2	6.5	5.9	3.0
1991	5.5	4.2	2.7	2.5	4.5	4.5	4.0	1.0
1992	5.5	4.2	2.7	2.5	4.5	4.5	4.0	1.0
1993	5.0	4.2	2.7	2.5	4.5	4.5	3.9	1.0
1994	5.0	4.2	6.1	3.7	5.5	4.8	4.9	1.0
1995	5.0	4.2	6.1	3.7	5.5	4.8	4.9	1.0
1996	6.5	4.2	6.1	3.7	6.0	4.8	5.2	1.0
1997	6.5	4.2	6.1	3.7	6.0	4.8	5.2	1.0
1998	6.5	4.2	6.1	3.7	6.0	4.8	5.2	1.0
1999	7.0	4.2	6.1	3.7	6.0	4.8	5.3	1.0
2000	7.0	4.2	6.6	3.7	6.7	5.5	5.5	1.0
2001	7.5	4.2	6.6	4.7	6.7	5.5	5.9	1.0
2002	7.5	4.2	6.6	4.7	6.7	5.5	5.9	3.0

Canada

(Continued)

341

Table S1 (Continued) Indices of central banks' institutional set-ups in the analysed inflation targeting economies

Country	Year	Mature _IT	Independent _IT	Informed _IT	Explicatory _IT	Transparent _IT	Accountable _IT	Fully_fledged _IT	Streched _IT
	2003	7.5	4.2	6.6	4.7	6.7	5.5	5.9	3.0
	2004	7.5	4.2	6.6	4.7	6.7	5.5	5.9	3.0
	2005	7.5	4.2	6.6	4.7	6.7	5.5	5.9	3.0
	2006	7.5	4.2	7.0	4.7	6.7	5.5	5.9	3.0
	2007	7.5	4.2	7.0	4.7	6.7	5.5	5.9	3.0
	2008	7.5	4.2	7.0	4.7	6.7	5.5	5.9	3.0
	2009	7.5	4.2	7.6	4.7	6.7	5.5	6.0	5.0
	2010	7.5	4.2	7.6	4.7	6.7	5.5	6.0	5.0
	2011	7.5	4.2	7.6	4.7	6.7	5.5	6.0	3.0
	2012	7.5	4.2	7.6	4.7	6.7	5.5	6.0	3.0
	2013	7.5	4.2	7.6	4.7	6.7	5.5	6.0	3.0
	2014	7.5	4.2	7.6	4.7	6.7	5.5	6.0	3.0
	2015	7.5	4.2	7.6	4.7	6.7	5.5	6.0	3.0
	2016	7.5	4.2	7.6	4.7	6.7	5.5	6.0	3.0
	2017	7.5	4.2	7.3	4.7	6.7	5.5	6.0	3.0
	2018	7.5	4.2	7.3	4.7	6.7	5.5	6.0	3.0
Chile	1999	7.5	4.7	2.0	4.2	4.7	5.5	4.7	0.5
	2000	7.5	4.7	7.3	5.7	6.3	6.0	6.2	0.5
	2001	7.5	4.7	7.3	5.7	6.3	6.0	6.2	0.5
	2002	7.5	4.7	7.3	5.7	6.3	6.0	6.2	0.5
	2003	7.5	4.7	7.3	5.7	6.3	6.0	6.3	2.5
	2004	8.0	4.7	7.3	5.7	6.3	6.0	6.6	2.5
	2005	8.0	4.7	7.3	6.2	7.3	6.0	6.6	2.5
	2006	8.0	4.7	7.3	6.2	7.3	6.0	6.5	2.5
	2007	7.5	4.7	7.3	6.2	7.3	6.0	6.5	2.5
	2008	7.5	4.7	7.3	6.2	7.3	6.0	6.6	2.5
	2009	8.0	4.7	7.3	6.2	7.3	6.0	6.7	2.5
	2010	8.5	4.7	7.3	6.2	7.3	6.0		2.5

2011	8.5	4.7	7.3	6.2	7.3	6.0	6.7	2.5
2012	8.5	4.7	7.3	6.2	7.3	6.0	6.7	2.5
2013	8.5	4.7	7.3	6.2	7.3	6.0	6.7	2.5
2014	8.5	4.7	7.3	6.2	7.3	6.0	6.7	2.5
2015	8.5	4.7	7.3	6.2	7.3	6.0	6.7	2.5
2016	8.5	4.7	7.3	6.2	7.3	6.0	6.7	2.5
2017	8.5	4.7	7.3	7.2	9.0	6.0	7.1	2.5
2018	8.5	4.7	7.3	7.5	9.3	6.0	7.2	2.5
Colombia								
1999	6.0	5.5	6.7	4.8	5.7	7.0	5.9	0.5
2000	6.0	5.5	6.7	4.8	5.7	7.0	5.9	0.5
2001	6.0	5.5	7.3	4.8	5.7	7.0	6.1	0.5
2002	6.0	5.5	7.3	4.8	5.7	7.0	6.1	2.5
2003	6.0	5.5	7.7	4.8	5.7	7.0	6.1	2.5
2004	6.5	5.5	7.7	4.8	5.7	7.0	6.2	2.5
2005	6.5	5.5	7.7	4.8	5.7	7.0	6.2	2.5
2006	6.5	5.5	7.7	4.8	5.7	7.0	6.2	2.5
2007	7.0	5.5	7.7	5.3	7.3	7.5	6.7	2.5
2008	7.0	5.5	7.7	5.3	7.3	7.5	6.7	2.5
2009	7.0	5.5	7.7	5.3	7.3	7.5	6.7	2.5
2010	7.0	5.5	7.7	5.3	7.3	7.5	6.7	2.5
2011	8.0	5.5	7.7	5.3	7.3	7.5	6.9	2.5
2012	8.0	5.5	7.7	5.3	7.3	7.5	6.9	2.5
2013	8.0	5.5	7.7	5.3	7.3	7.5	6.9	2.5
2014	8.5	5.5	7.7	5.3	7.3	7.5	7.0	2.5
2015	8.5	5.5	7.7	5.8	7.8	7.5	7.1	2.5
2016	8.5	5.5	7.7	6.2	8.2	7.5	7.2	2.5
2017	8.5	5.5	7.7	6.2	8.2	7.5	7.2	2.5
2018	8.5	5.5	7.7	6.5	8.2	7.5	7.3	2.5

(Continued)

Table S1 (*Continued*) Indices of central banks' institutional set-ups in the analysed inflation targeting economies

Country	Year	Mature _IT	Independent _IT	Informed _IT	Explicatory _IT	Transparent _IT	Accountable _IT	Fully_fledged _IT	Streched _IT
Czech Rep.	1998	2.5	6.7	6.2	5.7	7.7	8.0	6.1	1.0
	1999	2.5	6.7	6.2	5.7	7.7	8.0	6.1	1.0
	2000	2.5	6.7	6.2	5.7	7.7	8.0	6.1	1.0
	2001	4.0	6.7	6.5	5.7	7.7	8.0	6.4	1.0
	2002	5.7	6.7	6.5	5.7	7.7	8.0	6.7	1.0
	2003	6.2	6.7	6.5	5.7	7.7	8.0	6.8	2.5
	2004	6.2	6.7	6.5	5.7	7.7	8.0	6.8	2.5
	2005	6.7	6.7	6.5	5.7	7.7	8.0	6.9	2.5
	2006	7.2	6.7	6.5	5.7	7.7	8.0	6.9	2.5
	2007	7.2	6.7	6.5	5.7	7.7	8.0	6.9	2.5
	2008	7.7	6.7	8.0	6.3	8.3	8.0	7.5	2.5
	2009	8.2	6.7	8.0	6.3	8.3	8.0	7.6	2.5
	2010	7.7	6.7	8.0	6.3	8.3	8.0	7.5	2.5
	2011	7.7	6.7	8.0	6.8	8.8	8.0	7.7	2.5
	2012	7.7	6.7	8.0	6.8	8.8	8.0	7.7	2.5
	2013	7.7	6.7	8.0	6.8	8.8	8.0	7.7	4.5
	2014	7.2	6.7	8.0	6.8	8.8	8.0	7.6	4.5
	2015	7.2	6.7	8.0	6.8	8.8	8.0	7.6	4.5
	2016	7.2	6.7	8.0	6.8	8.8	8.0	7.6	4.5
	2017	8.2	6.7	8.0	6.8	8.8	8.0	7.7	4.5
	2018	8.2	6.7	8.0	6.8	8.8	8.0	7.7	4.5
Dominican Rep.	2012	4.0	5.3	6.2	3.0	2.8	6.3	4.6	0.5
	2013	4.0	5.3	6.2	3.0	2.8	6.3	4.6	0.5
	2014	4.0	5.3	6.2	3.0	2.8	6.3	4.6	0.5
	2015	4.5	5.3	6.2	3.0	2.8	6.3	4.7	0.5
	2016	4.5	5.3	6.2	3.0	2.8	6.3	4.7	0.5
	2017	5.0	5.3	6.2	3.0	2.8	6.3	4.8	0.5
	2018	5.0	5.3	6.2	3.0	2.8	6.3	4.8	0.5

Euro area								
1999	8.5	7.7	2.7	3.7	5.5	5.0	5.5	0.5
2000	8.5	7.7	6.1	5.0	6.8	5.8	6.7	0.5
2001	8.5	7.7	6.1	5.0	6.8	5.8	6.7	0.5
2002	8.5	7.7	6.1	5.0	6.8	5.8	6.7	0.5
2003	9.0	7.7	6.1	5.0	6.8	5.8	6.7	0.5
2004	9.0	7.7	6.1	5.0	7.5	6.5	7.0	2.5
2005	9.0	7.7	6.1	5.0	7.5	6.5	7.0	2.5
2006	9.0	7.7	6.1	5.0	7.5	6.5	7.0	2.5
2007	9.0	7.7	6.1	5.0	7.5	6.5	7.0	2.5
2008	9.5	7.7	6.1	5.0	7.5	6.5	7.0	2.5
2009	9.5	7.7	6.1	5.0	7.5	6.5	7.0	2.5
2010	9.5	7.7	6.1	5.0	7.5	6.5	7.0	2.5
2011	9.5	7.7	6.1	5.0	7.5	6.5	7.0	2.5
2012	9.5	7.7	6.1	5.0	7.5	6.5	7.0	2.5
2013	9.5	7.7	7.2	5.0	7.5	6.5	7.2	4.5
2014	9.5	7.7	7.2	5.0	7.5	6.5	7.2	7.5
2015	9.5	7.7	7.7	5.3	9.2	7.0	7.7	7.5
2016	9.5	7.7	7.7	5.3	9.2	7.0	7.7	6.5
2017	9.5	7.7	7.7	5.3	9.2	7.0	7.7	6.5
2018	9.5	7.7	7.7	5.3	9.2	7.0	7.7	6.5
Georgia								
2009	4.0	6.5	5.5	5.7	6.5	6.5	5.8	2.5
2010	4.5	6.5	5.5	5.7	6.5	6.5	5.9	2.5
2011	4.5	6.5	5.5	5.7	6.5	6.5	5.9	2.5
2012	3.5	6.5	5.5	5.7	6.5	6.5	5.7	2.5
2013	4.5	6.5	7.0	6.0	6.5	6.5	6.2	2.5
2014	5.0	6.5	7.0	6.0	6.5	6.5	6.2	2.5
2015	5.5	6.5	7.0	6.0	6.5	6.5	6.3	2.5
2016	5.5	6.5	8.3	6.5	7.2	6.5	6.7	2.5
2017	6.0	6.5	8.3	6.5	7.2	6.5	6.8	2.5
2018	6.5	6.5	8.3	6.5	7.2	6.5	6.9	2.5
Ghana								
2007	3.5	4.0	5.3	4.8	6.5	3.3	4.6	0.0

(*Continued*)

345

Table S1 (*Continued*) Indices of central banks' institutional set-ups in the analysed inflation targeting economies

Country	Year	Mature _IT	Independent _IT	Informed _IT	Explicatory _IT	Transparent _IT	Accountable _IT	Fully_fledged _IT	Streched _IT
	2008	3.5	4.0	6.0	4.8	6.5	3.3	4.7	0.0
	2009	3.0	4.0	6.0	4.8	6.5	3.3	4.6	0.0
	2010	3.0	4.0	6.0	4.8	6.5	3.3	4.6	0.0
	2011	3.0	4.0	6.0	4.8	6.5	3.3	4.6	0.0
	2012	3.5	4.0	6.0	4.8	6.5	3.3	4.7	0.0
	2013	3.5	4.0	6.0	4.8	6.5	3.3	4.7	0.0
	2014	3.5	4.0	6.0	4.8	6.5	3.3	4.7	0.0
	2015	3.5	4.0	6.0	4.8	6.5	3.3	4.7	0.0
	2016	3.5	4.0	6.0	4.8	6.5	3.3	4.7	0.0
	2017	4.0	4.0	6.0	4.8	6.5	3.3	4.8	0.0
	2018	4.0	4.0	6.0	4.8	6.5	3.3	4.8	0.0
Guatemala	2005	4.0	5.3	5.2	4.0	3.8	6.3	4.8	0.5
	2006	5.0	5.3	5.8	4.5	5.5	6.8	5.5	0.5
	2007	4.0	5.3	5.8	4.5	5.5	6.8	5.3	0.5
	2008	3.5	5.3	5.8	4.5	5.5	6.8	5.2	0.5
	2009	3.5	5.3	5.8	4.5	5.5	6.8	5.2	0.5
	2010	4.0	5.3	5.8	4.5	5.5	6.8	5.3	0.5
	2011	3.0	5.3	6.5	4.5	5.5	6.8	5.2	0.5
	2012	4.0	5.3	6.5	4.5	5.8	7.2	5.5	0.5
	2013	4.5	5.3	6.5	4.5	5.8	7.2	5.6	0.5
	2014	4.5	5.3	6.5	4.5	5.8	7.2	5.6	0.5
	2015	6.0	5.3	6.5	4.5	5.8	7.2	5.9	0.5
	2016	6.0	5.3	6.5	4.5	5.8	7.2	5.9	0.5
	2017	6.0	5.3	6.5	4.5	5.8	7.2	5.9	0.5
	2018	6.0	5.3	6.5	4.5	5.8	7.2	5.9	0.5
Hungary	2001	2.5	6.5	5.8	3.7	4.7	6.5	4.9	3.0
	2002	3.0	6.5	5.8	3.7	4.7	6.5	5.0	4.0
	2003	3.5	6.5	5.8	3.7	4.7	6.5	5.1	4.0

Year								
2004	3.5	6.5	5.8	3.7	4.7	6.5	5.1	4.0
2005	3.5	6.5	5.8	4.5	7.0	7.0	5.7	4.0
2006	4.0	6.5	7.2	5.5	8.0	7.5	6.4	4.0
2007	7.5	6.5	7.2	5.5	8.0	7.5	7.0	4.0
2008	7.5	6.5	7.2	5.5	8.0	7.5	7.0	5.0
2009	7.5	6.5	7.2	5.5	8.0	7.5	7.0	3.0
2010	8.0	6.5	7.2	5.5	8.0	7.5	7.1	5.0
2011	8.5	6.5	7.2	5.5	8.0	7.5	7.2	5.0
2012	8.5	6.5	7.2	5.5	8.0	7.5	7.2	5.0
2013	8.5	6.5	7.2	5.5	9.0	7.5	7.4	6.0
2014	8.5	6.5	7.2	5.5	9.0	7.5	7.4	6.0
2015	7.5	6.5	7.2	5.5	9.0	7.5	7.2	7.0
2016	7.5	6.5	7.2	5.5	9.0	7.5	7.2	7.0
2017	7.5	7.0	7.2	5.5	9.0	7.5	7.2	7.0
2018	7.5	7.0	7.2	5.5	9.0	7.5	7.2	8.0

Iceland

Year								
2001	6.0	7.0	8.0	5.3	5.7	8.0	6.7	8.0
2002	6.0	7.0	8.0	5.3	5.7	8.0	6.7	3.0
2003	6.0	7.0	8.0	5.3	5.7	8.0	6.7	3.0
2004	6.5	7.0	8.0	5.3	5.7	8.0	6.7	3.0
2005	6.5	7.0	8.0	5.3	5.7	8.0	6.7	3.0
2006	7.5	7.0	8.0	5.3	5.7	8.0	6.9	3.0
2007	7.5	7.0	8.0	5.3	5.7	8.0	6.9	3.0
2008	8.0	7.0	8.0	5.3	5.7	8.0	7.0	3.0
2009	8.0	7.0	8.5	6.5	7.3	8.5	7.6	4.0
2010	8.0	7.0	8.5	6.5	7.3	8.5	7.6	4.0
2011	9.0	7.0	8.5	6.5	7.3	8.5	7.8	4.5
2012	9.0	7.0	8.5	6.5	7.3	8.5	7.8	4.5
2013	9.0	7.0	8.5	6.5	7.3	8.5	7.8	4.5
2014	9.0	7.0	8.5	6.5	7.3	8.5	7.8	4.5
2015	9.0	7.0	8.5	6.5	7.3	8.5	7.8	4.5
2016	9.0	7.0	8.5	6.5	7.3	8.5	7.8	4.5

(Continued)

347

Table S1 (*Continued*) Indices of central banks' institutional set-ups in the analysed inflation targeting economies

Country	Year	Mature _IT	Independent _IT	Informed _IT	Explicatory _IT	Transparent _IT	Accountable _IT	Fully_fledged _IT	Streched _IT
India	2017	9.0	7.0	8.5	6.5	7.3	8.5	7.8	4.5
	2018	9.0	7.0	8.5	6.5	7.3	8.5	7.8	4.5
	2015	7.0	4.0	6.7	4.7	4.8	4.8	5.3	3.0
	2016	5.5	4.0	6.7	6.7	8.5	5.3	6.1	3.0
	2017	5.5	4.0	6.7	6.7	8.8	5.3	6.2	3.0
	2018	5.5	4.0	6.7	6.7	8.8	5.3	6.2	3.0
Indonesia	2005	4.5	6.7	3.1	4.3	6.0	9.0	5.6	3.0
	2006	4.5	6.7	3.1	4.3	6.0	9.0	5.6	3.0
	2007	4.5	6.7	3.1	4.3	6.0	9.0	5.6	3.0
	2008	5.0	6.7	3.1	4.3	6.0	9.0	5.7	3.0
	2009	5.0	6.7	3.1	4.8	6.5	9.0	5.9	3.0
	2010	4.5	6.7	3.1	4.8	6.5	9.0	5.8	3.0
	2011	5.5	6.7	3.1	4.8	6.5	9.0	5.9	3.0
	2012	4.5	6.7	3.1	4.8	6.5	9.0	5.8	3.0
	2013	5.5	6.7	3.1	4.8	6.5	9.0	5.9	3.0
	2014	5.5	6.7	3.1	4.8	6.5	9.0	5.9	3.0
	2015	6.5	6.7	3.1	4.8	6.5	9.0	6.1	3.0
	2016	6.5	6.7	3.1	4.8	6.5	9.0	6.1	3.0
	2017	6.5	6.7	3.1	4.8	6.5	9.0	6.1	3.0
	2018	6.5	6.7	3.1	4.8	6.5	9.0	6.1	3.0
Israel	1992	3.5	7.0	4.5	3.8	4.0	6.0	4.8	2.0
	1993	4.0	7.0	4.5	3.8	4.0	6.0	4.9	2.0
	1994	4.0	7.0	4.5	3.8	4.0	6.0	4.9	2.0
	1995	3.0	7.0	4.5	3.8	4.0	6.0	4.7	2.0
	1996	3.5	7.0	4.5	3.8	4.0	6.0	4.8	2.0
	1997	3.5	7.0	4.5	3.8	4.0	6.0	4.8	2.0
	1998	3.5	7.0	4.5	3.8	4.0	6.0	4.8	2.0
	1999	5.5	7.0	4.5	3.8	4.0	6.0	5.1	2.0

	Year								
	2000	5.5	7.0	4.5	3.8	4.0	6.0	5.1	2.0
	2001	6.0	7.0	4.5	3.8	4.0	6.0	5.2	2.0
	2002	6.5	7.0	4.5	3.8	4.0	6.0	5.3	2.0
	2003	7.0	7.0	4.5	3.8	4.0	6.0	5.4	3.5
	2004	8.0	7.0	4.5	3.8	4.0	6.0	5.5	3.5
	2005	8.0	7.0	4.5	3.8	4.0	6.0	5.5	3.5
	2006	8.5	7.0	4.5	4.3	5.7	6.5	6.1	3.5
	2007	8.5	7.0	4.5	4.3	5.7	6.5	6.1	3.5
	2008	8.5	7.0	4.5	4.3	5.7	6.5	6.1	4.5
	2009	8.5	7.0	4.5	4.3	5.7	6.5	6.1	5.5
	2010	8.5	7.0	4.5	4.3	5.7	6.5	6.2	4.5
	2011	8.5	7.0	5.2	4.3	5.7	6.5	6.3	4.5
	2012	8.5	7.0	5.7	4.3	5.7	6.5	6.3	3.5
	2013	8.5	7.0	5.7	4.3	5.7	6.5	6.3	4.5
	2014	8.5	7.0	5.7	4.8	6.3	6.0	6.5	5.0
	2015	8.5	7.0	6.7	4.8	6.3	6.0	6.5	6.0
	2016	8.5	7.0	6.7	5.7	7.3	6.0	6.9	6.0
	2017	8.5	7.0	7.2	5.7	7.3	6.0	6.9	6.0
	2018	8.5	7.0	7.2	6.7	9.0	6.8	7.2	6.0
Japan	2012	8.5	5.2	7.2	6.7	9.0	6.8	7.2	6.0
	2013	8.5	5.2	7.2	6.7	9.0	6.8	7.2	6.0
	2014	8.5	5.2	7.2	6.7	9.0	6.8	7.2	6.0
	2015	8.5	5.2	7.3	8.0	9.7	7.5	7.7	6.0
	2016	8.5	5.2	7.3	8.0	9.7	7.5	7.8	6.0
	2017	9.0	5.2	7.3	8.0	9.7	7.5	7.8	6.0
	2018	9.0	5.2	7.3	8.0	9.7	7.5	7.8	6.0
Kazakhstan	2015	6.0	4.3	4.7	4.2	3.8	4.8	4.6	2.5
	2016	5.0	4.3	5.0	4.2	3.8	4.8	4.5	2.5
	2017	5.0	4.3	5.0	4.2	3.8	4.8	4.5	2.5
	2018	5.0	4.3	5.0	4.2	3.8	4.8	4.5	2.5
Korea	1998	3.5	5.3	3.0	2.7	3.0	7.0	4.1	1.0

(Continued)

Table S1 (Continued) Indices of central banks' institutional set-ups in the analysed inflation targeting economies

Country	Year	Mature _IT	Independent _IT	Informed _IT	Explicatory _IT	Transparent _IT	Accountable _IT	Fully_fledged _IT	Streched _IT
	1999	5.0	5.3	3.0	2.7	3.0	7.0	4.3	1.0
	2000	4.3	5.3	3.0	2.7	3.0	7.0	4.2	1.0
	2001	4.3	5.3	5.8	3.3	3.3	7.3	4.9	1.0
	2002	4.3	5.3	6.2	3.3	3.3	7.3	5.0	1.0
	2003	4.8	5.3	6.2	3.3	3.3	7.3	5.0	3.0
	2004	5.3	5.3	6.2	3.3	3.3	7.3	5.1	3.0
	2005	5.3	5.3	6.5	3.3	3.3	7.3	5.2	3.0
	2006	5.3	5.3	6.5	3.3	3.3	7.3	5.2	3.0
	2007	6.0	5.3	6.5	3.3	3.3	7.3	5.3	3.0
	2008	6.5	5.3	6.5	3.3	3.3	7.3	5.4	3.0
	2009	6.5	5.3	6.5	3.3	3.3	7.3	5.4	3.0
	2010	6.5	5.3	6.5	3.8	5.0	7.8	5.8	3.0
	2011	7.5	5.3	6.5	3.8	5.0	7.8	6.0	3.0
	2012	7.5	5.3	7.5	4.8	6.0	8.3	6.6	5.0
	2013	7.5	5.3	7.5	4.8	6.0	8.3	6.6	5.0
	2014	7.5	5.3	7.5	5.8	8.0	8.3	7.1	5.0
	2015	7.5	5.3	7.5	5.8	8.0	8.3	7.1	5.0
	2016	8.0	5.3	7.5	5.8	8.7	9.0	7.4	5.0
	2017	8.0	5.3	8.0	6.2	8.7	9.0	7.5	5.0
	2018	8.0	5.3	8.0	6.2	8.7	9.0	7.5	5.0
Mexico	2001	8.0	6.7	3.0	4.2	3.2	6.5	5.2	0.5
	2002	8.0	6.7	5.8	4.8	4.2	7.5	6.2	0.5
	2003	8.0	6.7	5.8	4.8	4.7	8.0	6.3	0.5
	2004	8.0	6.7	5.8	4.8	4.7	8.0	6.3	0.5
	2005	8.0	6.7	5.8	4.8	4.7	8.0	6.3	0.5
	2006	8.5	6.7	5.8	4.8	4.7	8.0	6.4	0.5
	2007	8.5	6.7	5.8	4.8	4.7	8.0	6.4	2.0
	2008	8.5	6.7	5.8	4.8	4.7	8.0	6.4	2.0

Country	Year								
	2009	8.5	6.7	5.8	4.8	4.7	8.0	6.4	2.0
	2010	8.5	6.7	6.5	4.8	4.7	8.0	6.5	2.0
	2011	9.0	6.7	7.0	5.7	6.3	8.5	7.2	2.0
	2012	9.0	6.7	7.0	5.7	6.3	8.5	7.2	2.0
	2013	9.0	6.7	7.0	5.7	6.0	8.0	7.0	2.0
	2014	9.0	6.7	7.0	5.7	6.0	8.0	7.0	2.0
	2015	9.0	6.7	7.0	5.7	6.0	8.0	7.0	2.0
	2016	9.0	6.7	7.0	5.7	6.0	8.0	7.0	2.0
	2017	9.0	6.7	7.0	5.7	6.0	8.0	7.0	2.0
	2018	9.0	6.7	7.0	5.7	6.0	8.0	7.0	2.0
Moldova	2010	6.5	7.2	5.8	3.8	3.5	7.5	5.7	2.5
	2011	6.5	7.2	5.2	3.8	3.5	7.5	5.6	2.5
	2012	6.5	7.2	5.2	3.8	3.5	7.5	5.6	2.5
	2013	6.0	7.2	5.2	4.5	5.5	8.0	6.0	2.5
	2014	6.0	7.2	5.2	4.5	5.5	8.0	6.0	2.5
	2015	6.5	7.2	5.2	4.5	5.5	8.0	6.1	2.5
	2016	7.0	7.2	5.2	4.5	5.5	8.0	6.2	2.5
	2017	7.0	7.2	6.2	5.5	6.5	8.5	6.8	2.5
	2018	7.0	7.2	6.2	5.8	6.5	8.5	6.9	2.5
New Zealand	1990	6.5	4.5	5.3	5.2	5.5	8.0	5.8	0.5
	1991	6.5	4.5	5.3	5.2	5.5	8.0	5.8	0.5
	1992	6.5	4.5	5.3	5.2	5.5	8.0	5.8	0.5
	1993	7.0	4.5	5.3	5.2	5.5	8.0	5.9	0.5
	1994	7.0	4.5	5.3	5.2	5.5	8.0	5.9	0.5
	1995	7.5	4.5	5.3	5.2	5.5	8.0	6.0	0.5
	1996	7.0	4.5	5.3	5.2	5.5	8.0	5.9	0.5
Philippines	2002	5.7	6.8	7.5	4.3	6.0	7.0	6.2	3.0
	2003	5.7	6.8	8.2	4.3	6.0	7.0	6.3	3.0
	2004	5.2	6.8	8.2	4.3	6.0	7.0	6.2	3.0
	2005	5.2	6.8	8.2	4.3	6.0	7.0	6.2	3.0
	2006	5.2	6.8	8.2	4.3	6.0.0	7.0	6.2	3.0

(Continued)

Table S1 (*Continued*) Indices of central banks' institutional set-ups in the analysed inflation targeting economies

Country	Year	Mature _IT	Independent _IT	Informed _IT	Explicatory _IT	Transparent _IT	Accountable _IT	Fully_fledged _IT	Streched _IT
	2007	5.7	6.8	8.2	4.3	6.0	7.0	6.3	3.0
	2008	6.2	6.8	8.2	4.3	6.0	7.0	6.4	3.0
	2009	6.2	6.8	8.2	4.3	6.0	7.0	6.4	3.0
	2010	5.7	6.8	8.2	4.3	6.0	7.0	6.3	3.0
	2011	6.2	6.8	8.2	4.3	6.0	7.0	6.4	3.0
	2012	7.7	6.8	8.7	4.7	6.0	7.0	6.8	3.0
	2013	7.7	6.8	8.7	4.7	6.0	7.0	6.8	3.0
	2014	8.2	6.8	8.7	4.7	6.0	7.0	6.9	3.0
	2015	8.2	6.8	8.7	4.7	6.0	7.0	6.9	3.0
	2016	8.2	6.8	8.7	4.7	6.0	7.0	6.9	3.0
	2017	8.2	6.8	8.7	4.7	6.0	7.0	6.9	3.0
	2018	8.2	6.8	8.7	4.7	6.0	7.0	6.9	3.0
Poland	1999	4.0	7.5	3.0	2.7	3.0	6.0	4.4	1.5
	2000	4.0	7.5	3.0	2.7	3.0	6.0	4.4	3.0
	2001	4.0	7.5	3.0	3.7	4.3	6.0	4.7	3.0
	2002	5.5	7.5	3.0	3.7	4.3	6.0	5.0	3.0
	2003	5.5	7.5	3.0	3.7	4.3	6.0	5.0	3.0
	2004	7.0	7.5	6.5	4.0	5.3	7.0	6.2	3.5
	2005	7.0	7.5	6.5	4.0	5.3	7.0	6.2	3.5
	2006	7.0	7.5	6.5	4.0	5.3	7.0	6.2	3.5
	2007	7.5	7.5	6.5	4.5	7.0	7.5	6.7	3.5
	2008	7.5	7.5	6.5	4.5	6.6	7.2	6.6	3.5
	2009	8.0	7.5	6.5	4.5	6.6	7.2	6.7	3.5
	2010	8.0	7.5	6.5	4.5	6.6	7.2	6.7	3.5
	2011	8.0	7.5	6.5	4.5	6.6	7.2	6.7	3.5
	2012	8.0	7.5	7.5	5.5	7.6	7.7	7.3	5.5
	2013	8.0	7.5	7.5	5.5	7.6	7.7	7.3	5.5
	2014	8.0	7.5	7.5	5.5	7.6	7.7	7.3	3.5

	Year								
Romania	2015	8.0	7.5	7.5	5.5	7.6	7.7	7.3	3.5
	2016	8.0	7.5	7.5	5.5	7.6	7.7	7.3	3.5
	2017	8.0	7.5	7.5	5.5	7.6	7.7	7.3	3.5
	2018	8.0	7.5	7.5	5.5	7.6	7.7	7.3	0.5
	2005	4.2	7.2	6.7	4.3	4.3	5.0	5.3	2.5
	2006	4.7	7.2	6.7	4.3	4.3	5.0	5.4	2.5
	2007	5.2	7.2	6.7	4.3	4.3	5.0	5.4	2.5
	2008	5.2	7.2	6.7	4.3	4.3	5.0	5.4	2.5
	2009	5.2	7.2	6.7	4.3	4.3	5.0	5.4	2.5
	2010	5.7	7.2	6.7	4.3	4.3	5.0	5.5	2.5
	2011	6.2	7.2	6.7	4.3	4.3	5.0	5.6	2.5
	2012	6.2	7.2	6.7	4.3	4.3	5.0	5.6	2.5
	2013	7.7	7.2	6.7	4.3	4.3	5.0	5.9	2.5
	2014	7.7	7.2	6.7	4.3	4.3	5.0	5.9	2.5
	2015	8.2	7.2	7.7	5.3	5.3	5.5	6.5	2.5
	2016	8.7	7.2	7.7	5.8	7.0	6.0	7.0	3.5
	2017	8.7	7.2	7.7	5.8	7.0	6.0	7.0	2.5
	2018	8.7	7.2	7.7	5.8	7.0	6.0	7.0	2.5
Russia	2015	6.0	6.3	6.3	3.2	4.7	6.5	5.5	5.0
	2016	6.0	6.3	6.3	3.2	4.7	6.5	5.5	5.0
	2017	6.0	6.3	6.3	3.2	4.7	6.5	5.5	5.0
	2018	7.0	6.3	6.3	3.2	4.7	6.5	5.7	5.0
Serbia	2009	3.5	6.2	5.2	3.3	3.5	6.5	4.9	5.0
	2010	4.5	6.2	5.5	3.3	3.5	8.0	5.2	3.5
	2011	5.0	6.2	6.5	3.8	3.8	8.0	5.5	3.5
	2012	5.5	6.2	6.5	3.8	3.8	8.0	5.5	3.5
	2013	5.5	6.2	6.5	3.8	3.8	8.0	5.6	3.5
	2014	6.0	6.2	6.5	3.8	3.8	8.0	5.6	3.5
	2015	6.5	6.2	6.5	3.8	3.8	8.0	5.7	3.5
	2016	6.5	6.2	6.5	3.8	3.8	8.0	5.8	3.5
	2017	6.5	6.2	6.5	3.8	3.8	8.0	5.8	3.5

(Continued)

Table S1 (Continued) Indices of central banks' institutional set-ups in the analysed inflation targeting economies

Country	Year	Mature _IT	Independent _IT	Informed _IT	Explicatory _IT	Transparent _IT	Accountable _IT	Fully_fledged _IT	Streched _IT
South Africa	2018	6.5	6.2	6.5	3.8	3.8	8.0	5.8	3.5
	2000	4.8	2.5	4.8	3.3	4.0	4.8	4.0	1.0
	2001	4.8	2.5	4.8	3.3	4.0	4.8	4.0	1.0
	2002	4.8	2.5	4.8	3.3	4.0	4.8	4.0	1.0
	2003	4.8	2.5	4.8	3.3	4.0	4.8	4.0	1.0
	2004	4.8	2.5	4.8	3.3	4.0	4.8	4.0	3.0
	2005	5.3	2.5	4.8	3.3	4.0	4.8	4.1	3.0
	2006	5.3	2.5	4.8	3.3	4.0	4.8	4.1	3.0
	2007	5.3	2.5	4.8	3.3	4.0	4.8	4.1	3.0
	2008	5.3	2.5	4.8	3.3	4.0	4.8	4.1	3.0
	2009	5.5	2.5	4.8	3.3	4.0	4.8	4.2	3.0
	2010	6.0	2.5	5.1	3.0	4.0	4.8	4.2	3.0
	2011	6.0	2.5	5.1	3.0	4.0	4.8	4.2	3.0
	2012	6.5	2.5	5.1	3.0	4.0	4.8	4.3	3.0
	2013	6.5	2.5	5.1	3.0	4.0	4.8	4.3	3.0
	2014	6.5	2.5	5.5	3.7	5.0	4.8	4.7	3.0
	2015	6.5	2.5	5.5	4.2	6.0	4.8	4.9	3.0
	2016	6.5	2.5	5.5	4.2	6.0	4.8	4.9	3.0
	2017	6.5	2.5	5.5	4.2	6.0	4.8	4.9	3.0
	2018	6.5	2.5	5.5	4.2	6.0	4.8	4.9	3.0
Sweden	1995	8.0	6.5	5.8	4.7	4.3	6.5	6.0	0.5
	1996	8.0	6.5	5.8	4.7	4.3	6.5	6.0	0.5
	1997	8.0	6.5	5.8	4.7	4.3	6.5	6.0	2.5
	1998	8.0	6.5	5.8	4.7	4.3	6.5	6.0	2.5
	1999	8.0	6.5	5.8	5.2	6.0	6.5	6.3	2.5
	2000	8.5	6.5	5.8	5.2	6.0	6.5	6.4	2.5
	2001	8.5	6.5	5.8	5.2	6.0	6.5	6.4	3.5
	2002	8.5	6.5	5.8	5.2	6.0	6.5	6.4	2.5

2003	8.5	6.5	5.8	6.2	7.3	6.5	6.8	2.5
2004	8.5	6.5	5.8	6.2	7.3	6.5	6.8	2.5
2005	9.0	6.5	5.8	6.2	7.3	6.5	6.9	2.5
2006	9.0	6.5	5.8	6.2	7.3	6.5	6.9	2.5
2007	9.0	6.5	8.0	7.2	8.3	7.5	7.7	3.5
2008	9.0	6.5	8.0	7.2	8.3	7.5	7.7	3.5
2009	9.0	6.5	8.0	7.3	10.0	7.5	8.1	4.5
2010	9.0	6.5	8.0	7.3	10.0	7.5	8.1	3.5
2011	9.0	6.5	8.0	7.3	10.0	7.5	8.1	3.5
2012	9.0	6.5	8.0	7.3	10.0	7.5	8.1	3.5
2013	9.5	6.5	8.0	7.3	10.0	7.5	8.1	3.5
2014	9.5	6.5	8.0	7.3	10.0	7.5	8.1	3.5
2015	9.5	6.5	8.0	7.3	10.0	7.5	8.1	5.5
2016	9.5	6.5	8.0	7.3	10.0	7.5	8.1	5.5
2017	7.8	6.5	8.0	7.3	10.0	7.5	7.9	5.5
2018	7.8	6.5	8.0	7.3	10.0	7.5	7.9	5.5
Switzerland								
2000	8.0	7.0	5.7	3.0	4.7	6.0	5.7	0.5
2001	8.0	7.0	5.7	3.0	4.7	6.0	5.7	0.5
2002	8.0	7.0	5.7	3.0	4.7	6.0	5.7	0.5
2003	8.0	7.0	5.7	3.0	4.7	6.0	5.7	2.0
2004	8.0	7.0	5.7	3.0	4.7	6.0	5.7	2.0
2005	8.5	7.0	5.7	3.0	4.7	6.0	5.8	2.0
2006	8.5	7.0	5.7	3.0	4.7	6.0	5.8	2.0
2007	8.5	7.0	5.7	3.0	4.7	6.0	5.8	2.0
2008	8.5	7.0	5.7	3.0	4.7	6.0	5.8	2.0
2009	8.5	7.0	5.7	3.0	4.7	6.0	5.8	4.0
2010	9.0	7.0	5.7	3.0	4.7	6.0	5.9	4.0
2011	8.5	7.0	5.7	3.0	4.7	6.0	5.8	4.0
2012	8.5	7.0	5.7	3.0	4.7	6.0	5.8	4.0
2013	8.0	7.0	5.7	3.0	4.7	6.0	5.7	4.0
2014	8.0	7.0	5.7	3.0	4.7	6.0	5.7	5.0

(Continued)

Table S1 (*Continued*) Indices of central banks' institutional set-ups in the analysed inflation targeting economies

Country	Year	Mature _IT	Independent _IT	Informed _IT	Explicatory _IT	Transparent _IT	Accountable _IT	Fully_fledged _IT	Streched _IT
	2015	9.0	7.0	5.7	3.0	4.7	6.0	5.9	5.0
	2016	9.0	7.0	5.7	3.0	4.7	6.0	5.9	4.0
	2017	9.0	7.0	5.7	3.0	4.7	6.0	5.9	4.0
	2018	9.0	7.0	5.7	3.0	4.7	6.0	5.9	4.0
Thailand	2000	4.8	5.0	9.3	5.5	4.7	8.0	6.2	1.0
	2001	4.8	5.0	9.3	5.5	4.7	8.0	6.2	1.0
	2002	4.8	5.0	9.3	5.5	4.7	8.0	6.2	1.0
	2003	4.8	5.0	9.3	5.5	4.7	8.0	6.2	1.0
	2004	4.8	5.0	9.3	5.5	4.7	8.0	6.2	1.0
	2005	5.3	5.0	9.3	5.5	4.7	8.0	6.3	1.0
	2006	5.3	5.0	9.3	5.5	4.7	8.0	6.3	1.0
	2007	5.3	5.0	9.3	5.5	4.7	8.0	6.3	1.0
	2008	5.3	5.0	9.3	5.5	4.7	8.0	6.3	1.0
	2009	4.8	5.0	9.3	6.0	5.2	8.0	6.4	1.0
	2010	5.3	5.0	9.3	6.0	5.2	8.0	6.5	1.0
	2011	5.3	5.0	9.3	6.5	6.8	8.5	6.9	1.0
	2012	5.8	5.0	9.3	6.5	6.8	8.5	7.0	1.0
	2013	5.8	5.0	9.3	6.5	6.8	8.5	7.0	2.5
	2014	5.8	5.0	9.3	6.5	6.8	8.5	7.0	2.5
	2015	6.0	5.0	9.3	6.5	6.8	8.5	7.0	2.5
	2016	6.0	5.0	9.3	6.5	6.8	8.5	7.0	2.5
	2017	6.0	5.0	9.3	6.5	6.8	8.5	7.0	2.5
	2018	6.0	5.0	9.3	6.5	6.8	8.5	7.0	2.5
Turkey	2006	4.0	6.2	6.3	2.8	6.0	7.5	5.5	3.5
	2007	4.0	6.2	6.3	2.8	6.0	7.5	5.5	3.5
	2008	4.0	6.2	6.7	2.8	6.0	7.5	5.5	3.5
	2009	3.5	6.2	6.7	2.8	6.0	7.5	5.4	4.5
	2010	3.5	6.2	6.7	2.8	6.0	7.5	5.4	5.5

	Year								
	2011	4.0	6.2	6.7	2.8	6.0	7.5	5.5	5.5
	2012	4.0	6.2	6.7	2.8	6.0	7.5	5.5	5.5
	2013	4.0	6.2	6.7	2.8	6.0	7.5	5.5	5.5
	2014	4.5	6.2	6.7	2.8	6.0	7.5	5.6	5.5
	2015	4.0	6.2	6.7	2.8	6.0	7.5	5.5	5.5
	2016	4.5	6.2	6.7	2.8	6.0	7.5	5.6	5.5
	2017	4.5	6.2	7.2	3.2	6.0	7.5	5.7	5.5
	2018	4.5	6.2	7.2	3.2	6.0	7.5	5.7	5.5
Uganda	2011	6.3	3.8	5.3	3.3	3.0	4.3	4.4	3.0
	2012	6.3	3.8	5.3	3.3	3.0	4.3	4.4	3.0
	2013	6.3	3.8	5.7	3.3	3.0	4.3	4.4	3.0
	2014	6.3	3.8	5.7	3.3	3.0	4.3	4.4	3.0
	2015	6.3	3.8	5.7	3.3	3.0	4.3	4.4	3.0
	2016	6.8	3.8	5.7	3.0	3.0	4.3	4.4	3.0
	2017	6.8	3.8	5.7	3.0	3.0	4.3	4.4	3.0
	2018	6.8	3.8	5.7	3.0	3.0	4.3	4.4	3.0
Ukraine	2017	3.5	7.5	8.3	5.3	5.5	7.0	6.2	3.5
	2018	3.5	7.5	8.3	5.3	5.5	7.0	6.2	3.5
United Kingdom	1992	4.3	3.2	2.5	2.7	2.2	7.5	3.7	1.0
	1993	4.3	3.2	5.3	3.7	3.2	8.5	4.7	1.0
	1994	4.3	3.2	5.7	3.7	3.2	8.5	4.7	1.0
	1995	4.8	3.2	5.7	3.7	3.2	8.5	4.8	1.0
	1996	4.8	3.2	6.3	3.7	3.2	8.5	4.9	3.0
	1997	5.3	3.2	6.3	5.2	6.1	8.5	5.8	3.0
	1998	5.8	3.2	6.3	5.2	6.1	8.5	5.9	3.0
	1999	5.8	3.2	6.3	5.2	6.1	8.5	5.9	3.0
	2000	5.8	3.2	6.3	5.2	6.1	8.5	5.9	3.0
	2001	5.8	3.2	7.3	5.7	6.8	9.0	6.3	3.0
	2002	6.3	3.2	7.3	5.7	6.8	9.0	6.4	3.0
	2003	6.5	3.2	7.3	5.7	6.8	9.0	6.4	3.0
	2004	6.5	3.2	7.7	5.7	6.8	9.0	6.5	3.0

(Continued)

Table S1 (Continued) Indices of central banks' institutional set-ups in the analysed inflation targeting economies

Country	Year	Mature_IT	Independent_IT	Informed_IT	Explicatory_IT	Transparent_IT	Accountable_IT	Fully_fledged_IT	Stretched_IT
	2005	6.5	3.2	7.7	5.7	6.8	9.0	6.5	3.0
	2006	7.0	3.2	7.7	5.7	6.8	9.0	6.5	3.0
	2007	7.0	3.2	7.7	5.7	6.8	9.0	6.5	3.0
	2008	7.0	3.2	7.7	5.7	6.8	9.0	6.5	3.0
	2009	7.0	3.2	7.7	5.7	6.8	9.0	6.5	5.0
	2010	7.0	3.2	7.7	5.7	6.8	9.0	6.5	5.0
	2011	7.0	3.2	7.7	5.7	6.8	9.0	6.5	5.0
	2012	7.0	3.2	7.7	5.7	6.8	9.0	6.5	5.0
	2013	7.0	3.2	7.7	5.7	6.8	9.0	6.5	7.0
	2014	7.0	3.2	7.7	5.7	6.8	9.0	6.5	7.0
	2015	7.0	3.2	7.7	5.7	8.0	8.5	6.7	6.0
	2016	7.0	3.2	7.7	5.7	8.0	8.5	6.7	6.0
	2017	7.0	3.2	8.2	6.0	8.0	8.5	6.8	6.0
	2018	7.0	3.2	8.2	6.0	8.0	8.5	6.8	6.0
United States	2012	7.0	4.0	8.0	6.5	8.8	5.5	6.6	4.0
	2013	7.0	4.0	8.0	6.5	8.8	5.5	6.6	4.0
	2014	7.0	4.0	8.0	6.5	8.8	5.5	6.6	3.0
	2015	7.0	4.0	8.0	6.5	8.8	5.5	6.6	1.0
	2016	7.0	4.0	8.0	6.5	8.8	5.5	6.6	1.0
	2017	7.5	4.0	8.0	6.5	8.8	5.5	6.7	1.0
	2018	7.5	4.0	8.0	6.5	8.8	5.5	6.7	1.0

Source: Own compilation based on information from central banks' websites.

358

INDEX

accountability of central banks: *de facto* 188; *de jure* 188; *ex ante* 188; *ex post* 188; impact of 5, 252–255; importance of 33–34, 53, 64, 67, 188–189, 191; information 188; measures of 194, 196–198; on objectives 188; procedural 188; standards of 149–155

Accountable_IT index 197; comparison of 212, 216, 219, 224–226; construction of 207–208

adaptive expectations 19

annual reports 148, 150–152, 205–206, 208

asset purchases *see* quantitative easing

autonomy of central banks *see* independence of central banks

average inflation targeting 63–65, 332

Balassa, B. 49

Balassa-Samuelson effect 49, 132

band target *see* inflation target, types of

band target with midpoint *see* inflation target, types of

Barro, R. J. 21, 33, 187

Bernanke, B. S. 30

Blinder, A. S. 32, 54, 190

Bretton Woods system 35

cacophony 54, 205

Calvo pricing model 23–24

Calvo staggered pricing *see* Calvo pricing model

cash-in-advance constraint 22

Christiano, L. 24

clean-up after approach 56–58; *see also* financial stability

collegial decision-making bodies *see* committees

committees 52, 141–142; collegial 51, 54, 142, 146–147; individualistic 51, 54; *see also* decision-making bodies

communication of central banks *see* transparency of central banks

consensus 52, 146–148, 202

constraint discretion 30, 53, 67, 332

continuous target *see* inflation target, horizon of

control variables 252–254, 266–267, 294, 296, 334; *see also* explanatory variables

credibility of central banks 4, 32–34, 53–54, 61, 67, 188, 190–191, 197, 207

credit easing 59–60, 160–166, 228

cross-section set-up 256–261

decision-making bodies 142–144, 335; *see also* committees; members of decision-making bodies; single policymaker

decision-making meetings: frequency of 144–146, 204

decision-making process 139, 141–142, 146–147

deflationary spiral 49

democratic control of central banks *see* accountability of central banks

dependent variables 264, 266–267, 291–292

discretionary strategies 37, 40; historical background of 40–43

disinflation 110, 122–123, 132, 135, 171n52, 172n77, 266, 269

dynamic-inconsistency problem *see* time-inconsistency problem
dynamic stochastic general equilibrium model (DSGE) 24, 70n22

eclectic strategies 37, 40; historical background of 40–43
economic activity objective 104–105
economic independence of central banks *see* instrument independence of central banks
effective lower bound (ELB) *see* zero lower bound (ZLB)
effectiveness of monetary policy 4, 54–57, 253, 334–335
end-year target *see* inflation target, horizon of
escape clauses 48, 129, 198–199
European sovereign crisis 57, 60
exchange rate commitment 59–60, 109, 160–166, 228
exchange rate regime 106–110, 199, 335; *de facto* 107–108; *de jure* 107–109
exchange rate targeting: characteristics of 37–38; historical background of 40–44; as monetary policy rule 31
explanatory variables 264, 266–267, 291–292
Explicatory_IT index 196; comparison of 212, 215, 217, 224, 226; construction of 203–205

fear of floating 45, 106
financial stability 26–27, 57–58, 61–62, 65–67, 156–158, 227–228, 331, 336; reports on 157–159, 228–231
financial stability objective 104–105
fiscal dominance 61
forecast 51, 53, 136–140, 201–204, 209–211, 335; horizon of 137, 202, 209; ownership of 139, 141, 202, 204, 209; preparation of 136–137; variables 138–140, 202, 209, 336
forward guidance 59–60, 160–166; open-ended 60, 160; state-contingent 60, 160; time-contingent 60, 160, 228
forward guidance: calendar-based *see* forward guidance, time-contingent
forward guidance: conditional *see* forward guidance, state-contingent
Friedman, M. 18–19, 29

Friedman rule 36, 49, 187
full voting records *see* voting records
Fully_fledged_IT index 197; comparison of 212, 217–220, 225–227; construction of 207, 209–211

global financial crisis 25–26, 57, 60
goal independence of central banks 46, 110, 186, 192, 198–200
Gordon, D. B. 21, 33, 187
government representative 110–113, 142, 200–201, 335–336
Great Depression 16, 18, 35
Great Moderation 25–26, 55, 57, 70n25
Greenspan, A. 57

Hansen, A. H. 17, 25
Hicks, J. R. 17
Hume, D. 16
hyperinflation 35

incentive contracts 34, 187; *see also* Rogoff conservative central banker
independence of central banks: actual 192–193, 251, 336; evolution of 4; formal 192–193, 201, 336; impact of 250–252, 254; importance of 34, 53, 61, 67, 186–188, 191; measures of 192–193, 196–198
Independent_IT index 196; comparison of 212, 214–215, 223, 226; construction of 198, 200–201
inflation: core 47, 122, 128–132; headline 39, 47, 122, 128–130, 198–199; optimal level of 48–50
inflation reports 53, 148, 150–152, 202, 205–206, 208
inflation target: aspects of 46–51; changes of 119–124, 198–199; horizon of 47, 119, 123, 131–132, 172n77, 198–199, 209, 292, 335; level of 48–50, 119, 121–124, 132–135, 198–199, 209, 335; types of 47, 119–122, 124–128, 170–171n48, 198–199, 266, 335
inflation targeters 7–8; "medium-aged" 221, 222–227, 292–293; "new" 221–222, 223–227; "old" 220, 222–227, 292–293

inflation targeting: characteristics of 1, 3, 39, 44–45, 67, 332; effectiveness of 54–57; flexible 48, 53, 58, 65, 67–68, 132, 263; historical background of 40–44; as monetary policy rule 30; strict 48, 67

inflationary bias 33–34, 46, 187–188, 190, 251

Informed_IT index 196; comparison of 212, 215–216, 223–224, 226; construction of 201–203

institutional arrangements see institutional set-ups

institutional rules see institutional set-ups

institutional set-ups of central banks: definition of 3, 32–34; impact of 267–291; importance of 56, 186–191, 196, 333–334; measures of 196–211

instrument independence of central banks 46, 110, 119, 186–187, 192, 200–201; financial 73n64, 118–119, 187, 201, 335; functional 73n64, 110–113, 187, 198; institutional 73n64, 110–113, 187, 201; personal 73n64, 113–118, 187, 198, 335

interest rate projections 138–140, 172–173n95

intermediate targets 28, 38, 40, 51

IS-LM model 17, 68n5

Keynes, J. M. 16, 19, 69n9

Keynesianism 16–17, 69n9

k-percent rule 29

Kydland, F. 21–22, 33, 187

leaning against the wind approach 56–58, 67, 331; see also financial stability

liquidity trap 17

Lucas, R. E. 20

Lucas critique 20, 69n12

macroprudential policies 27, 58, 62, 66–67, 105–106, 157–158, 175n152, 227, 229, 331

majority vote 52, 146–148, 201–204

mandates of central banks 104–105, 110, 189, 198–200, 209–211, 332, 335; see also monetary policy objectives

Mature_IT index 196; comparison of 212–214, 222–223, 226, 234n10; construction of 198–199

McCallum rule 71–72n38

measurement bias 49

members of decision-making bodies: external 142–143, 201–202; internal 142–143; see also decision-making bodies

menu costs 23

microeconomic foundations see microfoundations

microfoundations 20, 22–24

minutes 54, 148, 150–153, 189, 195, 205–206, 208, 335

Mishkin, F. S. 30, 57

missing disinflation 26

missing inflation 26

monetarism 18–19

monetary financing 61, 118–119, 187

monetary policy aims see monetary policy objectives

monetary policy framework see monetary policy strategy

monetary policy goals see monetary policy objectives

monetary policy instruments: conventional 28, 49, 60–61, 71n32, 71n34, 158–160, 228, 231; unconventional 57–63, 67–68, 109, 158–167, 227–229, 232, 332, 336

monetary policy instruments: non-standard see monetary policy instruments, unconventional

monetary policy instruments: standard see monetary policy instruments, conventional

monetary policy instruments: unorthodox see monetary policy instruments, unconventional

monetary policy measures see monetary policy instruments

monetary policy objectives 45; multiple 104–105, 189, 199–200; single 105, 199–200, 332; see also mandates of central banks

monetary policy regime see monetary policy strategy

monetary policy rules 28–31, 64; instrument 29, 35;

intermediate-target 29–31, 35; targeting 29–30, 63
monetary policy strategies: definition of 28, 34; evolution of 40–44; historical background of 35–37
monetary policy targets *see* monetary policy objectives
monetary policy tools *see* monetary policy instruments
monetary targeting: characteristics of 38–39; historical background of 36, 40–43; importance of 34; as monetary policy rule 30
money-in-the-utility function concept 22
Muth, J. F. 20

natural interest rate 16, 25–26, 68n3
natural unemployment rate 19–20
negative interest rates 59, 160–166, 228
neoclassical synthesis 17–18
new classical school 20–21
new Keynesian economics 22–23
new neoclassical synthesis 23–25
nominal anchor 27, 31–32, 36–40, 46, 67
nominal gross domestic product (GDP) targeting 58, 63, 71n37; importance of 35; as monetary policy rule 30
nominal rigidities 23, 69n16
non-accelerating inflation rate of unemployment (NAIRU) *see* natural rate of unemployment

oil price shocks 18, 35
open letters 53, 149, 155–156, 207–208, 335
openness of central banks *see* transparency of central banks

panel set-up 261–266
parliamentary hearings *see* reporting to parliament
Phelps, E. S. 19
Phillips, A. W. 17
Phillips curve 17; flattening of 25–26, 68, 337; hybrid 24; long-run 19; new Keynesian 24; short-run 19
point target *see* inflation target, types of
point target with tolerance bands *see* inflation target, types of

political independence of central banks *see* goal independence of central banks
Prescott, E. 21–22, 33, 187
press conferences 53, 149–152, 202–206, 208, 335
press releases 53, 148, 150–153, 205–206, 208
price-level targeting 58, 63, 71n37, 72n39; importance of 35; as monetary policy rule 30; temporary 63
price stability objective 104–105
projection *see* forecast
prudential frameworks *see* macroprudential policies

quantitative easing 59–60, 160–166, 228
quantity theory of money 16, 18, 68n2

ratio of votes *see* voting records
rational expectations 20–23, 36
real business cycle school 21–22
reappointment 115–117, 187, 198, 200
recommendations 139, 141, 147, 202–203
reporting to parliament 53, 153–155, 207–208
reputation of central banks *see* credibility of central banks
Ricardo, D. 16
Rogoff, K. 33, 64
Rogoff conservative central banker 33, 186–187; *see also* incentive contracts

Samuelson, P. A. 17, 49
Sargent, T. J. 20
Schwartz, A. J. 18
secular stagnation 25–26, 68, 70n26, 336
Sims. Ch. 22
single policymaker 52, 142, 146; *see also* decision-making bodies
Solow, R. M. 17
speeches 53, 203, 205
stagflation 18, 69n8
Steuart, J. 16
Stretched_IT index 227; comparison of 228–232; construction of 228
Summers, L. 25
Svensson, L. E. O. 28

Taylor contracts *see* Taylor pricing model
Taylor pricing model 23–24
Taylor principle 24
Taylor rule 24, 29
term of office 113–117, 187, 193, 198, 200
time-inconsistency problem 21, 27, 32–33, 36
Tinbergen rule 58
tolerance bands: asymmetric 125; symmetric 126; width of 121–128, 199
transparency of central banks: economic 189; impact of 6, 252–255; importance of 33–34, 53, 64, 67, 189–191; measures of 194–195, 196–198; operational 189–190; policy 189, 207; political 189, 198, 203; procedural 189, 203; standards of 149–155
Transparent_IT index 196; comparison of 212, 215–216, 218, 224, 226; construction of 205–207

voting records 54, 147–150, 189, 195, 204–207, 209, 297n4, 335
voting rights 111–113, 200

Wallace, N. 20
Walsh, C. E. 33–34, 64
Wicksell K., 16, 68n3

zero lower bound (ZLB) 25–26, 39, 48–50, 57–59, 62–66, 70n27, 161, 167–168, 227, 331–332, 336

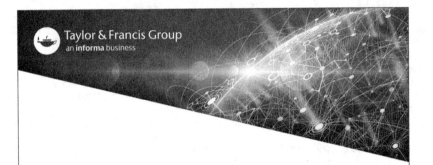

Printed in the United States
by Baker & Taylor Publisher Services